MIGRATION AND WELFARE IN THE NEW EUROPE

Social protection and the challenges of integration

Edited by Emma Carmel, Alfio Cerami and Theodoros Papadopoulos

First published in Great Britain in 2012 by

The Policy Press
University of Bristol
Fourth Floor
Beacon House
Queen's Road
Bristol BS8 1QU
UK

t: +44 (0)117 331 4054
f: +44 (0)117 331 4093
tpp-info@bristol.ac.uk
www.policypress.co.uk

North American office:
The Policy Press
c/o International Specialized Books Services (ISBS)
920 NE 58th Avenue, Suite 300
Portland, OR 97213-3786, USA
t: +1 503 287 3093
f: +1 503 280 8832
e-mail info@isbs.com

British Library Cataloguing in Publicaton Data
A catalogue record for this book is available from the British Library.

Library of Congress Cataloging-in-Publication Data
A catalog record for this book has been requested.

ISBN 978 1 84742 643 7 paperback

Cover design by The Policy Press
Front cover: image kindly supplied by Flavio Takemoto
Printed and bound in Great Britain by Hobbs, Southampton
The Policy Press uses environmentally responsible print partners

This book is dedicated to all those migrants who lost their lives trying to reach Europe

Contents

List of tables and figures   vii

List of abbreviations   ix

Notes on contributors   x

Acknowledgements   xiv

one   Governing migration and welfare: institutions and emotions in the production of differential integration   1
Emma Carmel and Alfio Cerami

Part I: Theoretical background

two   Immigration and the variety of migrant integration regimes in the European Union   23
Theodoros Papadopoulos

three   European Union migration governance: utility, security and integration   49
Emma Carmel

four   Human rights and the politics of migration in the European Union   67
Alfio Cerami

five   Labour migration and labour market integration: causes and challenges   85
Bent Greve

Part II: Migration and social protection policies in the EU: country studies

six   Towards a security-oriented migration policy model? Evidence from the Italian case   105
Tiziana Caponio and Paolo R. Graziano

seven   Differential inclusion in Germany's conservative welfare state: policy legacies and structural constraints   121
Lutz C. Kaiser and Regine Paul

eight   Welfare or work: migrants' selective integration in Finland   143
Saara Koikkalainen, Timo Tammilehto, Olli Kangas, Marja Katisko, Seppo Koskinen and Asko Suikkanen

nine   Migration in Hungary: historical legacies and differential integration   159
Ioana Rusu

ten   Wilful negligence: migration policy, migrants' work and the absence of social protection in the UK   177
Mick Wilkinson and Gary Craig

Part III: Social and migration policy nexus: critical issues

eleven   Local immigrant communities, welfare and culture: an integration/segregation dilemma   197
Siniša Zrinščak

twelve   Contentious opportunities: comparing metropolitan policymaking   213
          for immigrants in France and Italy
          Manlio Cinalli and Alessandra El Hariri

thirteen   A categorical immigration policy: welfare, integration and the   227
          production of inequality
          John Gal and Jennifer Oser

fourteen   Conclusions: what future for migration?   245
          Emma Carmel, Alfio Cerami and Theodoros Papadopoulos

Index   259

List of tables and figures

Tables

2.1   Foreign-born residents as % of total population in 18 EU member states,   27
        1985–2005 and projections for 2010 and 2030

2.2a   Three largest groups of foreign citizens residing in EU member states   30
        by citizenship, 2008

2.2b   Three largest groups of asylum applicants in EU member states   31
        by citizenship, 2009

2.3   Aggregated estimates of irregular migrant populations in the EU27   33
        reported in 2008

2.4   Sectoral distribution of foreign-born workers (15- to 64-year-olds), 2007   35

2.5   Characteristics of migrant integration regimes and immigration   40
        experience in 23 EU member states

2.6   Migrant Integration Policy Index (MIPEX): individual component   47
        indicators

7.1   Population in Germany with and without a migration background, 2005   130

7.2   Employment and unemployment rate of German- and foreign-born   131
        population in Germany (15- to 64-year-olds, 2004)

7.3   Literacy point differences (reading skills) between second-generation   135
        migrant pupils and non-migration background pupils (15-year-olds)

12.1   Population and administrative structures of Paris and Lyon, Rome   218
        and Milan

12.2   Left-right cleavages across the national and the urban level in Paris,   219
        Lyon, Rome and Milan

12.3   Metropolitan policymaking on immigrant integration in Paris,   221
        Rome, Lyon and Milan

13.1   Take-up of old age benefits among elderly men, 2004   235

Figures

2.1   The embeddedness of a national migrant integration regime in the EU   38

5.1   Variations in migration and labour market intersection by characteristics   87

7.1   Net migration in Germany, 1954–2007   124

7.2   Poverty rates of the immigrant and the German population, 2005   132

7.3   Educational and occupational attainment of the immigrant and the   134
        German population, 2005

9.1   Hungary's net migration rate, 1955–2007 (per 1,000 inhabitants)   163

9.2   Migration inflows and outflows in Hungary, 1989–99   164

9.3   Migration inflows and outflows in Hungary, 2000–07   165

13.1   Migrants in selected countries, 2000   229

13.2   Immigration to Israel, 1948–2004   230

13.3   The impact of taxes and transfers in Israel, 2001–07   235

13.4   Post-transfers and taxes poverty in Israel by categorical status   236

List of abbreviations

A8	Accession 8 (countries)
CEEC	Central and Eastern European country
Comecon	Council for Mutual Economic Assistance
EEA	European Economic Area
EFTA	European Free Trade Association
ESPAnet	Network for European Social Policy Analysis
EU	European Union
EUFRA	European Union Fundamental Rights Agency
EUMC	European Union Monitoring Centre on Racism and Xenophobia
EU27	the 27 member states of the European Union
GDP	gross domestic product
GLA	Gangmasters Licensing Authority
HMO	homes in multiple occupation
ILO	International Labour Organization
IOM	International Organization for Migration
MIPEX	Migrant Integration Policy Index
MRN	Migrants' Rights Network
NGO	non-governmental organisation
OECD	Organisation for Economic Co-operation and Development
OMC	open method of coordination
POS	political opportunities structure
RRAA	Race Relations Amendment Act
SAWS	Seasonal Agricultural Workers Scheme
TCN	third-country national
TFEU	Treaty on the Functioning of the European Union
UN	United Nations
WAVE	Welfare and Values in Europe (project)
WRS	Worker Registration Scheme

Notes on contributors

Tiziana Caponio is Researcher at the Department of Political Studies of the University of Turin, Italy and Research Affiliate at FIERI (Forum for International and European Research on Immigration). Her research interests are in the policymaking of migration policy, with a special focus on local policy, as well as on immigrants' and second generations' integration processes. Among her recent publications is: *The local dimension of migration policy and policy-making* (edited with Maren Borkert, 2010, Amsterdam University Press, 2010).

Emma Carmel is Lecturer in Social Policy at the University of Bath, UK. Her research is in the field of critical governance studies, with a particular focus on social and public policy governance and the political sociology of the European Union. She has published work on social security and migration policies in the UK and the European Union, and on state–third sector relations. She was, from 2003-08, editor and then co-editor of the *Journal of European Social Policy*.

Alfio Cerami is Research Associate at the Centre d'études européennes at Sciences Po, Paris, France. His research concentrates on how political, economic and social transformations influence the process of democratisation and of consolidation of democratic institutions in transition and developing countries. His most recent publications include *Post-communist welfare pathways. Theorizing social policy transformations in Central and Eastern Europe* (together with P. Vanhuysse, 2009, Palgrave Macmillan), *Promoting human security: Ethical, normative and educational frameworks in Western Europe* (together with P. Burgess et al, 2007, UNESCO) and *Social policy in Central and Eastern Europe. The emergence of a new European welfare regime* (2006, LIT Verlag).

Manlio Cinalli is Associate Research Professor at Sciences Po, Paris, France. His research focuses on comparative political behaviour, the politics of ethnic relations and integration, networks and multi-level public policies. He has published more than 20 articles in scholarly journals and volumes and is currently Research Director of the French projects for YOUNEX and EURISLAM (EU Framework Seven Programme).

Gary Craig is Emeritus Professor of Social Justice and Associate Fellow of the Wilberforce Institute for the Study of Slavery and Emancipation at the University of Hull, UK, where he has led the team researching modern slavery. He is also Visiting Professor at Durham University, UK. He has recently published *Social justice and public policy* (edited with others, 2008, The Policy Press) and *Community capacity building* (with others, 2010, OECD) and has collated a 2010 *Reader on child slavery* (The Policy Press).

Alessandra El Hariri obtained her Master's research degree at the LUISS University of Rome, Italy and is Research Officer at CEVIPOF, Sciences Po, Paris, France. Her studies focus on questions of immigration, integration and ethnicity. She is currently working on the contentious politics of asylum, in particular the perception of asylum seekers vis-à-vis European institutions and European Union public policies.

John Gal is Associate Professor at the Baerwald School of Social Work and Social Welfare at the Hebrew University of Jerusalem, Israel. He chairs ESPAnet Israel and heads the social welfare studies team at the Taub Center for Social Policy Studies in Israel. His fields of interest include social policy in Israel and in a comparative perspective, and he has recently been working on issues of immigration and welfare. Recent books include a study on income maintenance in Israel, a study of the history of unemployment policy in Israel and a book on policy practice in social work together with Idit Weiss-Gal.

Paolo R. Graziano is Assistant Professor at the Department of Institutional Analysis and Public Management, Bocconi University, Milano, Italy. He has produced both authored books and edited volumes and contributed to several edited volumes as well as publishing in major international journals. His research interests are in the politics of welfare state reform, Europeanisation, employment policy, social policy and European Union policies.

Bent Greve is Professor in Welfare State Analysis at the University of Roskilde in Denmark. He has published extensively on welfare policy, tax expenditures, public sector expenditure and financing and labour market policy and development. He is regional and special issues editor of *Social Policy & Administration: An International Journal of Policy and Research*. Recent publications include *Occupational welfare. Winners and losers* (Edward Elgar, 2007), a special Issue on 'Choice' (*Social Policy & Administration*, vol 6, 2009) and in 2010 an edited book *Happiness and social policy in Europe* (Edward Elgar).

Lutz C. Kaiser is Professor of Economics and Social Sciences at the North Rhine-Westphalia University of Applied Sciences Cologne, Germany, Research Fellow at the Institute for the Study of Labor (IZA Bonn) and Research Affiliate at the German Institute for Economic Research (DIW-Berlin). His research interests include regional and local policy, migration and integration, diversity, human and social capital, work and family life balance, job satisfaction, social policy evaluation, applied microeconomics and micro panel data development. He is a member of the editorial board of the *Eurasian Economic Review* and he has written reports for the German labour and family ministries.

Olli Kangas is Research Professor and Head of the Research Department at the Social Security Institution of Finland. His research interests have revolved around comparative studies of social institutions, their causes and consequences in terms of politics, income distribution, inequality and poverty.

Marja Katisko is Researcher and PhD candidate at the Department of Social Policy at the Faculty of Social Sciences, University of Helsinki, Finland. Her research focuses on immigrants' work experiences in Finland.

Saara Koikkalainen is Researcher and PhD candidate at the Department of Social Studies at the University of Lapland, Finland. Her research focuses on skilled mobility from Finland to Europe and vice versa, and she has published work on the experiences of Finns working abroad.

Seppo Koskinen is Professor in Labour Law and Social Security Law at the University of Lapland, Finland. His research interests are employment law, anti-discrimination and equality law, particularly in relation to immigration and temporary agency work, and protection of privacy in the working life.

Jennifer Oser is a PhD candidate in The Federmann School of Public Policy and Government at The Hebrew University of Jerusalem, Israel. In addition to immigration and social policy, her research interests include democratic participation and participatory inequality, the political environment of public policymaking and comparative research of the welfare state and policy agenda setting.

Theodoros Papadopoulos is Lecturer in Social Policy at the University of Bath, UK, and Visiting Professor at the School of Governance, University of Maastricht, the Netherlands. His research interests are in the governance of social security, comparative labour market and employment policies in Europe and social and family policies in Greece.

Regine Paul is a PhD candidate in European Social Policy, University of Bath, UK. Her research scrutinises labour migration policy in the European Union and member states, concentrating on Germany, France and the UK. She is interested in the mechanisms and logics of border drawing and the institutional meanings of 'migration management' in welfare states, market capitalisms and labour markets. Her work more broadly concerns critical analyses of state–market relations with regard to governance and public policy.

Ioana Rusu is PhD candidate in Political Science, Centre d'études européennes, Sciences-Po, Paris, France. Her research interests include European migration policies, labour migration, and high-skilled immigration policies in advanced industrial countries.

Asko Suikkanen is Professor of Sociology at the University of Lapland, Finland. His research interests have, over the years, included societal change, working life risks, the functioning of social security systems, and questions of labour market, education and social innovations. Many of his publications are evaluation oriented, assessing the structural changes of society.

Timo Tammilehto is Researcher and PhD candidate at the University of Lapland, Finland. His research interests are in the field of employment law, social security and working time. A recent publication includes: *The Finnish social security system and work-related immigration* (with S. Koskinen, in Finnish, 2010, Forum: Edilex/ Edita Publishing Ltd).

Mick Wilkinson is Lecturer in Race and Social Justice and Senior Researcher at the Contemporary Slavery Research Centre, Wilberforce Institute, University of Hull, UK. Among his most recent publications are: *An evaluation of the Gangmasters Licensing Authority* (2009, Oxfam) and *Migrant workers in the Humber sub-region* (2008, Hull City Council).

Siniša Zrinščak is Professor of Social Policy and Head of the Department of Social Work at the University of Zagreb, Croatia. His main scientific interests include comparative and European social policy, religious and social policy changes in post-communism and civil society development.

Acknowledgements

This volume is the result of several years of discussions, meetings and reflections on the future of European migration policies, as well as on the future of migration more broadly. It is impossible to do justice to all those scholars, researchers, civil society and human rights activists, members of non-governmental organisations, journalists as well as civil servants of international institutions, who, in one way or another, have contributed to enlarge our knowledge on the urgent problem of ensuring social inclusion and integration for migrants. Our first thanks therefore go to all those who made us aware of the urgent need to write such a volume. The editors would like to thank the participants of the stream 'Migration and social protection in the enlarged European Union' held during the ESPAnet (The Network for European Social Policy Analysis) annual conference at the Finnish Centre for Pensions in Helsinki (Finland) from 18-20 September 2008 for lively debate and valuable comments. The editors would also like to thank the authors of this volume for having decided to participate, as well as for their patience for our requests for revisions. Alfio Cerami would like to thank Renaud Dehousse, Director of the Centre d'études européennes of Sciences Po for providing an excellent research environment and for constant support during the writing of this volume. Emma Carmel thanks Regine Paul for her always insightful and stimulating company through European migration studies; Emma and Theodoros Papadopoulos also thank Phoebe and Nicholas, whose rightly unwavering disregard for grown-up concerns has offered a necessary respite from co-editing. A special thank-you goes to Emily Watt and The Policy Press for having believed in this project and for their tolerance in our not always timely delivery. A special thanks goes also to the three anonymous referees for the extremely valuable and thoughtful comments and critiques. Without the help of all the above, this volume would simply not have been possible. It goes without saying that whatever faults remain are entirely the editors' responsibility.

ONE

Governing migration and welfare: institutions and emotions in the production of differential integration

Emma Carmel and Alfio Cerami

We called for workers, and human beings came.
(Max Frisch, Swiss writer)

Introduction

This book takes as its central empirical theme the *interaction* of migration, migration policies and social protection in Europe. It argues that migration and social policy governance in the European Union (EU) results in differentiated but co-existing modes of integration and segregation, inclusion and exclusion for migrants,[1] with considerable variation between and within member states of the EU. These variations are produced and regulated by the interaction of social protection, welfare and migration policies, labour market structures, migration histories and available opportunities for social, political and cultural integration across the institutional architecture at local, national and EU levels.

There are therefore three elements to the empirical analysis presented in this book: the variation in policy combinations which interact in different settings and contexts; the existence of different institutional levels with different legal and policymaking roles, across which policy interactions are played out; and, finally, the consequent variation in modes of differential inclusion open for different migrant groups. These three elements are each given varying emphasis in the contributions to the book, depending on their case or their analytical focus. It is the way in which these elements are combined across the contributions in sum which form the book's empirical and analytical terrain: *the interaction of social and migration policies in specific political, economic and social contexts, which affects migrants' welfare, well-being and inclusion.* This chapter sketches the overall treatment of these three elements that form the empirical scope of the book (variation of policy combinations; variation in institutional architecture and politics; variation in resulting integration and inclusion). Having established the book's empirical scope, we go on in this chapter to provide some more critical reflections on how we can interpret and explain the emergence of policy variation in complex and contentious policy fields, such as migration and migrant integration. For this, we turn particularly to the emerging US literature on the role of emotions in policymaking, much of which has developed, not accidentally, in relation to US immigration policy. Finally, we outline the individual contributions that make up this volume.

Empirical scope: policies, institutions and differential integration

Policy interaction in migration governance

The first element that defines the empirical and analytical scope of the book is the question of interacting policies in particular settings. The book is about migration and welfare, but it is important to specify that we take a rather broad view of what constitutes welfare – and indeed, what constitutes social protection. Our primary concern is with the broader settings of welfare provision rather than, for example, specific 'integration policies', such as language classes or housing allowances. The book presents several national case studies as well as cross-national comparisons of particular settings to explore how patterns of migrants' welfare in the broadest sense – their integration, and/or segregation and exclusion – are shaped by the combinations of policies interacting in different labour markets and against the background of different migration histories.

The focus on interacting policies and settings means that among the national cases we address, different combinations of policies and settings will be significant. The specific focus depends on those policy combinations and interactions that most sharply define or throw into relief the ways in which migrants' inclusion and integration are shaped in particular countries or cases. As a result, the chapters do not confine themselves to analysing the classic welfare and social protection policies, but range quite widely, examining the interactions of education policies (Kaiser and Paul, Chapter Seven); labour market structure, employment regulation and law (Papadopoulos, Chapter Two; Caponio and Graziano, Chapter Six; Kaiser and Paul, Chapter Seven; Koikkalainen et al, Chapter Eight; Wilkinson and Craig, Chapter Ten); human rights (Cerami, Chapter Four); social protection and integration policies, including those specifically directed at migrants and those which apply more generally (Papadopoulos, Chapter Two; Koikkalainen et al, Chapter Eight; Rusu, Chapter Nine; Gal and Oser, Chapter Thirteen); political participation locally and nationally (Kaiser and Paul, Chapter Seven; Zrinščak, Chapter Eleven; Cinalli and El Hariri, Chapter Twelve); and labour migration policies more generally (Papadopoulos, Chapter Two; Carmel, Chapter Three).

Considerable attention is also given in the chapters to the importance of informal aspects of the governance of migrant integration and how this is combined with more formal legal positions. This means that when we discuss the interaction of policies, we also interpret 'policy' broadly, in the tradition of organisational sociology, concerned with 'non-decisions' (Bachrach and Baratz, 1963), as well as with more recent institutionalist work recognising the importance of norms and organisational rules (March and Olsen, 1989) and discourses in determining what counts as 'policy' and how policy gets made (Schmidt, 2006, 2008; see also Campbell and Pedersen, 2001; Hay, 2006). So contributions draw our attention to the significance of: informal norms in policy implementation generally (Caponio and Graziano, Chapter Six); informal structural or personal discrimination in employment practice (Koikkalainen et al, Chapter Eight; Wilkinson and Craig, Chapter Ten); informal labour markets in structuring differential – not always disadvantageous – inclusion for migrants (Caponio and Graziano, Chapter Six; Rusu, Chapter Nine; Zrinščak, Chapter Eleven); and informal, intra-community strategies for integration (Zrinščak, Chapter Eleven). As such, the contributors engage with the actions of actors in the polity, in politics and in policy, across the local, national and EU levels, as well as, in some cases, with the actions of non-state actors, such as non-governmental organisations (NGOs) and local migrant communities.

Institutions and scale in migration governance

The second element determining the empirical scope of the book is therefore the question of scale. The book is concerned with the 'new' EU of 27 member states that came into being in 2007. It is still important to recognise the impact on individual member states and on the union as a whole of the two accessions of 2004 and 2007, whose implications for EU policymaking, and for social, employment, economic and migration policymaking are only now becoming embedded in the Union's architecture, programmes and goals (see Carmel, Chapter Three). This is especially the case for migration policy, where the process of accession came at some cost to the countries acceding in 2004 and 2007, with changes to their own external and foreign policies (Rusu, Chapter Nine) and limits to their rights of free movement within the Union. Indeed these changes are only now normalising in the case of 2004 accessions, and have some way to go in the case of Romania and Bulgaria. For this reason, and to draw attention to the multiple scales on which the interactions of policies affecting migrants take place, the adjective 'new' is still applied to our analysis of the Union.

The multiple scales on which migration policy is made includes of course, that of the EU and national states, where a burgeoning literature seeks to address the mutual effects and processes of EU and national policymaking (Morris, 2002; Lavenex and Ucarer, 2002; Schierup et al, 2006; Baldaccini et al, 2007; Menz, 2009). As argued by Theodoros Papadopoulos (see Chapter Two, this volume), and illustrated in several of the other contributions, there are clearly significant and profound differences in the pathways to, and possibilities for, migrant integration which are produced by the logics of interacting policies and political economies at national level. These make each case unique, and, unlike in other policy areas, make cross-national classification systems of similarity and difference difficult to sustain (for an example, see Koopmans, 2010).

However, as pointed out in the contributions from Emma Carmel (Chapter Three, on the EU) and Alfio Cerami (Chapter Four, on human rights), there are also additional framing and discursive effects as well as legal and political commitments for EU members. That all our case studies are members of the Union is significant, and in the field of immigration (border control, visa, residence regulation) and of integration (welfare provision, social and economic rights for migrants, labour market structure as well as more general social protection provision), the role of the Union is important.

These commitments attempt to assert limits on the variability of migration/ social policy governance, and inscribe new ways of doing migration and integration policies, providing new reference points for what is 'good' or 'effective', 'legitimate' or 'appropriate' policy, politics and practice. This inscription in its most positive light can be seen as part of the new experimental governance of the Union, finding pathways to coherent EU policymaking (Sabel and Zeitlin, 2010), but it can also be experienced as an imposition, ignored and contested (Lendvai and Stubbs, 2004; Schimmelfennig and Sedelmeier, 2004; Falkner et al, 2005). In all cases, however, such commitments beyond the national state remain an important feature of the impact of the institutional architecture and strategic possibilities of the EU (for a review, see, for instance, Schmidt, 2006; Graziano and Vink, 2007; Dehousse, 2010). In member states, they shape what is available as a political and policy resource to define and challenge the limits of policymaking in a particular field – in our case, migration and social policies.

Attention has been given to the factors that may hinder or foster policy formulation and innovation both at national and EU level, such as historical legacies and existing institutional structures (Pierson, 1996); the actions of actors situated in supranational bureaucracies and polities (Haas, 1968); nationally-driven negotiations and procedures of institutionalisation (Moravcsik, 1998); or the complex bargaining activities placed at the most disparate levels of the decision-making process (local, regional, national and supranational) (Hooghe and Marks, 2001). Only more recently has a sociological approach on European integration emerged (see Saurugger, 2008; Guiraudon and Favell, 2010). Here, attention has shifted from analysing institutional arrangements and practices to the social construction of institutions, to processes of interiorisation and the creation of social and institutional norms seen as crucial factors in the process of institutional and policy change, and this is the perspective drawn on to assess the role of the EU and international norm-building in this volume (Carmel, Chapter Three; Cerami, Chapter Four).

Any evaluation of the 'European' level of policymaking, and its relationship to national policy, should, however, also be viewed in the light of the significance of sub-national policymaking. It is clear that attention to *local* policymaking and local integration strategies, and their place in national contexts, can reveal much about the variety and particularity of migrants' integration experience (Caponio and Borkert, 2010; Wilkinson and Craig, Chapter Ten; Zrinščak, Chapter Eleven; Cinalli and El Hariri, Chapter Twelve). Attention to local policymaking and its variety enables us to interrogate more closely the national logics of integration implied in particular sets of policies (see Koopmans, 2010), while still acknowledging the important structuring role of local and national polity and politics.

The emphasis on the multiple levels of the polity on which policy is made also marks out the book as one which, contra to the strong transnationalism argument (Schiller et al, 1995; Portes, 1997; Faist, 2000), contends that states – or multi-level polities – remain vital to understanding the differential inclusion or integration of migrants in Europe. The strong transnationalism argument offers many insights into the ways in which specific migrants in specific countries maintain daily lives, social relationships, family, businesses and political activities across national borders in an era of increased migration. These arguments can and should challenge our view of 'Fortress Europe', making a significant contribution to understanding its very partial efficacy, if not its intention, and they can be combined with analyses of the significance of the structures and relations of national and international states (see Itzigsohn, 2000). They also draw attention to the importance of the *sociology of globalisation* (Martin et al, 2006; Martell, 2010) in shaping migrants' 'integration' in countries of destination, indicating that we need to reconsider questions of 'integration' in a context where 'belonging' may not be regarded as an exclusive property of one territorial state or another.

Nonetheless, the contributions to this book demonstrate that migrants' putative transnational lives and experiences do not render state borders absent or irrelevant. Rather they demonstrate that the possibilities of living transnational lives remain not determined, but certainly shaped and regulated, by the contentious politics of migration and social policy governance across all levels of policymaking in the Union. The analyses presented here in sum make a case for attending to the significant effects of local and national polities with the political economy and policymaking in the EU, which affects emigration from countries of origin, terms and conditions of arrival, stay, residence, employment opportunities, social rights and political participation (Hansen, 2009).

As a result of the multiple scales of analysis, the contributions in this volume show that what we see in Europe is not merely the well-acknowledged 'securitisation' of migration policies, the attempted construction of a 'Fortress Europe' legitimised by discourses of terrorism and security threats, which can draw on racist and xenophobic attitudes and discourses (Huysmans, 2006; Geddes, 2008; see Cerami, Chapter Four). We also find evidence of the 'managed migration' agenda, which reached its ascendancy in the EU in the mid-2000s, and which results in highly selective and variable gatekeeping of labour migrants in and outside the EU's labour markets (Favell and Hansen, 2002; van Houtum and Pijpers, 2007; Menz, 2009). We find evidence to support the contention that welfare states structure migrants' rights in unexpected ways (Sainsbury, 2006), and that the logics of 'integration' produced jointly by welfare states and labour market participation involve questioning expectations about which societies and welfare states are 'good' at integration or inclusion (Koopmans, 2010).

Institutions and policies in the production of differential integration

This brings us to the third element of the book's empirical analysis: the issue of variation in differential inclusion. Here we are concerned with assessing the results of the interaction of the policy combinations across multi-level polity – the first two elements of our empirical analysis. What are the results for migrants' integration and welfare of this varied interaction that we can observe across a range of cases? We discuss the comparative results of the empirical contributions in more detail in the conclusion to this volume, but it is important to outline here what we mean by differential integration or inclusion. By differential inclusion, we refer to the ways in which different migrant groups are affected by variations in access to the labour market (formal and informal), social benefits and services, education, as well as political and cultural rights and provisions within and between countries. In identifying variations in differential integration, we draw both implicitly and explicitly on work which has explored the variations in rights of migrants to a range of social benefits (Morissens, 2006; Sainsbury, 2006), on Lydia Morris's (2002) concept of civic stratification and on work which more generally emphasises the importance of the changing political economy of migration in the structuring of migrants' integration (see, for example, Schierup et al, 2006, pp 240-6). Morris argued that in order to manage the contradictory forces shaping migration policies, states in Europe were developing highly stratified classification systems to determine migrants' rights. All our case studies provide evidence for these arguments – that migrants' rights are clearly separate from those of prior residents in welfare systems; that among migrants, there are clear distinctions made between legal and policy categories or status of migrant and the rights that attach to these categories; and that these distinctions are jointly shaped by specific conditions in the variably segmented labour markets of Europe's political economy (see also Doomernik and Jandl, 2008; Yeates, 2009).

As Charles Tilly (2004) has argued, the construction of fictitious, even symbolic, social boundaries is not a rare human activity. Social boundaries separate 'us' from a not always well-identified 'them'. Explaining the formation, transformation, activation and suppression of social boundaries becomes, in this context, a crucial undertaking for improved understanding of contemporary migration politics and policies. Social mechanisms of selection, segregation and exclusion of individuals – whether cognitive, environmental or relational (see McAdam et al, 2001; Tilly, 2001) – are not simply individually held. They can also be, and often are, supported, even directly promoted or instigated, for politically or electorally motivated reasons. In consequence, such social boundaries are not merely innocuous survival strategies, but can perform significant social and political roles, including in policymaking, thus having substantial societal impacts on the lives of those included and/or excluded.

However, the contributions also demonstrate three additional features of differential integration of migrants that enable us to develop the idea of stratification in new ways. First, that the civic stratification and the logics which sustain it in any one country, which Morris observed, are not fixed, but can change quite rapidly, and in some cases, have already done so (for example, cases of Germany and UK in the 2000s). Second, that migrants can find themselves moving among categories whose place in the 'stratification' may be worse rather than 'better', and that apparently worse positions in terms of rights (working as an illegally resident migrant) may not always result in worse welfare in every respect (for example, regularisation of residence status can mean that newly legal migrants find it difficult to compete with illegally resident workers for employment in informal labour markets, while still finding it difficult to access employment in the formal labour market (Slavnić, 2007) (although this should not detract from the real and profound vulnerability of the status of illegal residence; see Calavita, 2005).

Third and most significantly, what the contributions to this volume show is that inclusion is not merely differentiated by access to 'social rights' in the welfare system, by logics of stratification, or by changing global political economy, but also by reference to the fact that for different migrant groups, some policy mechanisms for integration/segregation are dominant and/or are combined differently even within the same country. Thus in some cases, employment in the informal or formal labour market dominates the form of integration, but it is how this interacts with variable access to social services or benefits, or discrimination against particular migrant groups, which eventually shapes the pattern of differential inclusion for migrants. An example might be instructive here. Koopmans (2010) argues that the Scandinavian model of migrant integration (his reference is Sweden) is (surprisingly) exclusionary in practice. Yet our Finnish example indicates that there are clear social boundaries which govern access to the labour market, leaving some but by no means all migrants to be integrated via social protection provision (*pace* Koopmans), so that this initial process of differentiation must be recognised. In addition, however, it is also the case that beyond this dominant marker of differentiation, for those in the labour market, integration remains further differentiated by country of origin and sector.

Thus, in the field of *sociology of globalisation*, a coherent theoretical approach able to grasp the different and multi-faceted aspects of welfare restructuring and recalibration (Kuhnle, 2000; Hemerijck, 2010) must involve an exploration of the synergies that exist between migration policies at local, regional, national and transnational level, since these greatly influence the social mobility and social stratification of migrants. This itself has consequently significant implications for the possibilities for 'transnationalism' of migrants' lives, affecting the economics of their migration(s), as well as the possibilities of enhancing their welfare and well-being, through social, familial and cultural contexts.

Politics of policymaking in the contentious migration field: institutional architecture and beyond

The country case studies show that existing institutional structures greatly influence the current migration politics adopted but the case studies make clear that other co-influencing factors must also be taken into account to explain this differential inclusion of particular migrant groups: from the political economy of welfare and labour markets (Finland, the UK, Italy) discussed above; the incapacity of governance mechanisms (the UK and Italy); inadequacy of policy measures (Germany and the UK); and the specific geo-political position and historical inheritances in the field of migration which, in some cases, continue to be central (Hungary and Italy), and in others are receding in importance in the face of alternative pressures (Germany). What they do not tell us is how we can explain the processes of policymaking which result in this complex empirical terrain in general terms while keeping in our sights the specific conditions which attach to policymaking in this highly contentious policy field. Most of the remainder of this chapter is concerned with the significance of the contentiousness of this policy area and the implications of this for the factors we need to account for in our analysis of public policymaking in this field.

In doing so, we draw on an emerging body of work, primarily from the US, which highlights the role of emotions and feelings in explaining policymaking and policy change. Some of this literature was specifically developed to analyse immigration policymaking in the US (for an excellent review, see Brader et al, 2008), while other literature has more recently focused on Western European countries as well (see, for instance, Fetzer, 2000; Sniderman et al, 2004). We argue in this chapter that this perspective on the importance of feelings and emotions (Elster, 1999, 2008, 2009) in policymaking offers to shed some light on how we might start to explain specific policy combinations across institutional scales which produce the patterns of differential inclusion explored by the contributors. We did not set out to write the volume with the role of emotions as a fully-fledged theoretical framework. Its significance has rather emerged inductively from the contributions in the book, and the remainder of this chapter sets out our critical reflections on how we can interpret the role of emotion in policymaking, and how we read this in the remaining contributions to the volume.

So, while it is possible to identify that specific migration policy options are sometimes led by a rational calculus (such as economic defence strategies), we also find processes of concealment (Schierup et al, 2006, chapter 1), the use of alternative policy arenas to disguise policymaking (Guiraudon, 2003), and evidence of contradictory policies and practice. The differentiated inclusion which we observe from the cases in this volume indicate that *rationality* and *emotion* have often gone hand in hand in shaping the possibilities and practice of policymaking for migrant integration. Negative feelings based on false assumptions about the supposedly negative consequences of a more liberal migration policy sustain negative discourses and political formations which then compound the formation of additional negative feelings among the population and the policy community; these then influence further actions. In this context, self-fulfilling prophecies (Merton, 1968), as important social mechanisms in the process of institutional and policy change (Hedström and Swedberg, 1998; Hedström, 2008; Hedström and Bearman, 2009), have played a far from irrelevant role. Importantly, as a recent study on political misperception has shown (Nyhan and Reifler, 2010), once wrong information has been introduced by the media or political parties, all other attempts to correct the initial false or unsubstantiated belief become extremely difficult, which can also lead to a 'backfire effect', reinforcing the initial false and unsubstantiated beliefs. In the following section the role of emotions is briefly sketched. The aim here is to provide a better understanding of the different and complex decision-making processes that lead to the formulation and implementation of specific migration policies with their repercussions on the attitudes and behaviour of citizens and the construction of new social boundaries.

Emotions, beliefs, preferences and opportunities

Despite the attention given by social scientists to institutional mechanisms (for example, self-reinforcing mechanisms, positive feedbacks and so on; see, for instance, Hall and Taylor, 1996; Pierson, 2004; Streeck and Thelen, 2005), surprisingly little consideration has been given in political science to emotions as crucial drivers of institutional and policy change. Yet the contributions in this volume indicate that emotions (Elster, 1999, 2008, 2009) play, by contrast, a central role in institutional and policy change, favouring the formation of specific beliefs (Rydgren, 2009) and preferences (Freese, 2009), which in turn, structure the attitudes of citizens and institutional agents and subsequently, limit the set of opportunities available (Petersen, 2009).

Rational or irrational (see below), emotions can influence the construction of specific *beliefs* about the particular features which determined 'in' and 'out' groups are supposed to possess.[2] Mediated by political discourse which mixes real or perceived 'rational' interests with fear and resentment, the characteristics of the 'in group' are often over-emphasised, while the 'others', the 'foreigners', are seen as holders of different values, or as 'non-members' of the 'in group' space. Self-glorifying attitudes within 'in groups', reminding themselves of their good qualities, are present everywhere in contemporary European societies, with the National Front in France, the Northern League in Italy or the FPÖ in Austria being the most dramatic political examples (for a review, see Eatwell, 1997; Mudde, 2007).

The formation of *preferences* goes, however, beyond a rational calculation of objective material gains and losses, but may also have much to do with the preferences for inter-group homogeneity established on the basis of emotionally driven self-referential beliefs.[3] Thus in the field of migration policy, commonplace references to 'our' culture, 'our' territory, 'our' economy, 'our' rights, 'our' heritage and 'our' nation express the everyday constitution of deeply problematic and exclusionary social boundaries, both national and European, historical and contemporary. These expressions of 'banal nationalism' (Billig, 1990) gain particular emotional and political saliency in the context of (im)migration policymaking, especially at national level, and can significantly affect the process of differential inclusion with the subsequent political and policy choices available (see, for example, the contributions on Italy, Finland, Germany, Hungary, Israel and the UK).

Emotions, beliefs and preferences do not remain confined in an ideational limbo but structure the set of *opportunities* available for policy change and institutional innovation. In our everyday life, by mixing rational and irrational motivations (for example, interest-maximising as well as unjustified anxiety-driven concerns), we assign specific characteristics to the members of the 'out group' which, subsequently, produce an important impact on our attitudes, behaviour and type of policymaking to be implemented. For Jon Elster (2006, 2008, 2009), the distinction between *rational* and *irrational behaviour* is, in fact, a trivial misunderstanding, because, as Raymond Boudon has also emphasised (2003), reason is often subjected to emotions, but emotions often rely on reasoning to crystallise. As argued by Frank (1988), passions often serve our interests in a co-producing and self-sustaining process of interest-maximising preference formation and vice versa.[4] Importantly for our purposes, rational and irrational feelings of obligation, duty and solidarity play a far from irrelevant role in constructing varieties of differential inclusion with associated policies. These may involve a positive perception of cultural and ethnic diversity, thus fostering the inclusion of 'out groups' (Banting and Kymlicka, 2006; van Oorschot, 2008; Mau and Burkhardt, 2009), but may also trigger concerns (Sniderman et al, 2004) as well as anxiety, excessive ethnic identification, resentment and reaction towards 'the foreigners' (Fetzer, 2000; Brader et al, 2008).

Unsurprisingly, racism and xenophobia are again on the increase throughout the European continent. The EU Fundamental Rights Agency (EUFRA) annual report (2009) has re-affirmed, for example, that substantial progress in the respect of human rights still has to be done both at national and EU level, including judicial prosecution for racist crimes. According to the EU independent agency, 'during the period 2000-07, 11 out of the 12 member states which collect sufficient criminal justice data on racist crime experienced a general upward trend in recorded racist crime' (EUFRA, 2009, p 10).[5] Just to quote a few of the most notable examples, in 2007 the following were officially reported: Belgium, 1,289 crimes; Czech Republic, 196 crimes; Denmark, 35 incidents; Germany, 17,607 (unspecified definition); France, 707 reports; Ireland, 224 reports; Austria, 752 complaints; Poland, 238 crimes; Slovakia, 155 crimes; Finland, 698 crimes; Sweden, 2,813 crimes; England and Wales, 61,262 incidents (EUFRA, 2009, Table 1.1, p 25). These are not isolated acts, but found a basis in the attitudes and beliefs of European citizens' (EUFRA, 2009, p 10). As argued in several EUFRA/European Monitoring Centre on Racism and Xenophobia (EUMC) reports (see EUMC, 2005, 2006; EUFRA, 2007, 2008, 2009), racism and prejudice here are key determinants for segregation that can take place in the workplace but more generally in public life, for example in respect of education, health and housing. Anti-semitism and right-wing extremist assaults are also on the increase, and the victims are for the most part migrants and people from minority ethnic groups. Migrants also remain the most discriminated at work, and in various aspects of social life (EUFRA, 2009).

A recent Eurobarometer survey has shown that while, due to the global financial crisis, migration is not at the top of the European citizens' concerns as in previous years, it still comes second place after economic and crime-related indicators (Eurobarometer, 2009a, p 11). However, according to a quarter of respondents, immigration should still be a central issue for future activities of EU institutions in the coming years, supposedly moving towards more restrictive policies (Eurobarometer, 2009b, p 165). As several right-wing political factions in Europe claim, the benefits of the progress that European societies have acquired (and regardless of the benefits obtained during the colonial period) must first be distributed among country nationals and only secondarily to migrants – often conceptualised as temporarily tolerated 'guest' workers. The contributions in this volume make clear the dangers that this type of emotionally driven policymaking and social boundary construction entails.

Structure of the volume

The book is divided into three parts with a summary conclusion. Part I examines the key issues and parameters for the book's subject matter. Part II is dedicated to country case studies, involving five worlds of welfare: Italy, Germany, Finland, Hungary and the UK. Each chapter analyses the relationship between social protection principles and practice and the treatment of migrants in social policy, before selecting examples that illustrate this relationship in practice. Part III discusses in further detail issues of differential integration and segregation from a range of perspectives, focusing more directly on questions of the production and politics of this differential integration and its alternatives. All contributions in this volume highlight a differentiated approach towards the inclusion of EU and non-EU migrants, with relatively, but not exclusively, more extensive inclusion strategies and less negative emotional attitudes for the citizens of EU countries. In addition, this pattern seems to apply with the inclusion of migrant citizens with whom closer historical, ethnic and cultural ties already exist, highlighting the ongoing importance of nationality and ethnicity (which, however, do not always have mutually reinforcing effects). However, other distinctions between migrants – most notably the key terms and conditions under which they are able to enter, reside and are expected to integrate, whether via participation in formal or informal employment, under a variety of conditions, or via social and political organisations and policymaking institutions, or via access to welfare services or benefit – can cut across those between EU and non-EU migrants.

In Chapter Two, Theodoros Papadopoulos explores the complexity of migration and migrants' status in EU member states, with particular emphasis on how labour market conditions and welfare provisions, and their interrelation, can affect migrants' integration via *social integration regimes*. He emphasises the importance of different political economies for understanding the significance of different patterns of migrant labour and thus generates a general empirical context for many of the remaining chapters in the book. He provides some critical reflections on the implications of the economic crisis for migration in Europe, before assessing migrant integration into national labour markets, and other central features of integration regimes.

In Chapter Three Emma Carmel explains how an apparently coherent set of policy concerns and institutional arrangements have been constructed around the theme of migration in the EU. Once dominated by an emphasis on security, EU migration governance has taken on new dimensions since the Treaty of Amsterdam in 1997, now considerably enhanced in the Lisbon Treaty of 2009 and the new (2010) economic and social programme Europe 2020. The long-standing historical distinction between free movement (intra-EU migration) and migration policies in the EU has increasingly been blurred, and EU migration governance is now assembled around the interlinked political, institutional and discursive logics of security, utility and (specific and limited) integration.

Alfio Cerami, in Chapter Four, explores human rights and the politics of migration in the EU. He argues that the 'politics of migration' cannot be simply understood in terms of a 'politics of regulation' as the current leading national and EU discourses seem to emphasise, but it must also be understood in terms of a 'politics of integration' of non-EU citizens and the respect for their basic and inalienable human rights. The chapter calls for the establishment of a new migration politics in the EU based on moral and ethical principles, which fully take account of the changes in the globalised world. In this context, *new EU discourses based on new transnational moral and ethical arguments* that emphasise universal moral respect and egalitarian reciprocity are advocated.

In Chapter Five, Bent Greve discusses push and pull factors related to labour migration, highlighting how they are related to various labour market conditions and requirements (skilled/unskilled/top professionals) in the European context. The chapter emphasises the complexity of decisions to migrate, including decisions to return, as involving a wide range of factors, from familial, cultural and political. It draws attention to the importance of treating migration as both a temporary event and as a process, by exploring the importance and implications of cross-border and short-term mobility on a more global labour market.

Tiziana Caponio and Paolo Graziano in Chapter Six open the second part of the volume by investigating the evolution of migration policies in Italy, focusing on the social protection and integration of immigrants. Part of the Southern European migratory regime, migration can be addressed as a 'quasi-new' phenomenon in Italy, with different governments finding themselves particularly unprepared to tackle this problem, while also reducing existing rights for immigrants. Integration policies are depicted as poorly developed, which, combined with territorially fragmented migratory regimes, tend to reproduce the more general structural weakness of the welfare states in these countries.

Lutz Kaiser and Regine Paul in Chapter Seven evaluate the differential integration of categories of migrant in Germany, emphasising the impact of policy legacies on the pathways of integration, and the different domains through which migrant groups are able to access rights. They argue that even second-generation migrants continue to fare less well in employment and in education than those without a migration background, although differences by nationality of immigrant also persist. Not only are new privileged categories of migrant being identified, but the political and civic rights for long-term resident migrants of all generations remain limited.

Saara Koikkalainen, Timo Tammilehto, Olli Kangas, Marja Katisko, Seppo Koskinen and Asko Suikkanen in Chapter Eight continue the analysis on different 'social Europes' by examining migrants' differential integration in Finland as a member of the so-called Nordic model of welfare (see Kuhnle, 2009). Their chapter highlights the social difficulties of dealing 'emotionally' with the rapid increase in ethnically distinct migrants in the early 1990s. They also note the more subtle and everyday exclusions felt by more privileged migrant workers from EU member states. Criticisms against immigration have been raised, so that non-Western immigrants in particular face a 'double dilemma': if they work they are accused of taking the jobs of Finns, but if they do not, they are accused of taking advantage of the generous welfare system.

Ioana Rusu in Chapter Nine demonstrates that 'Hungary's accession to the EU has had, and continues to have, an effect on its migration policy', involving strengthening border management and prevention of irregular migration and labour movements, harmonisation of visa regimes and establishment of readmission agreements with neighbouring states. However, over 80 per cent of immigrants in Hungary are ethnic Hungarians, and the subject of privileged integration strategies implemented to assimilate them. As Rusu demonstrates, state relationships, historical ties between neighbouring countries and Hungary, and pre-existing interactions between social networks developed by migrants across pre-communist, communist, and post-communist periods help to explain this 'ethnically determined migration' situation.

In Chapter Ten Mick Wilkinson and Gary Craig complete the second part of the book, and explore the situation of migrants in the UK, a country with a longstanding history of immigration, focusing in particular on contemporary migrant workers. Recent policy in the UK has promoted temporary migration on a range of terms depending on labour market sector and migrant skills. In this context, Wilkinson and Craig highlight a significant lack of social protection for migrant workers and the 'wilful negligence' of British governments for both regular and undocumented migrants working especially in low-skill sectors. Their contribution therefore highlights the importance of the interaction of labour market conditions, immigration policies and (the lack of) social protection policies (see Chapter Two) in producing insecurity and exploitation for migrant workers in the UK case.

Opening Part III of the book, Siniša Zrinščak in Chapter Eleven explores local immigrant communities, welfare and culture, discussing the integration/segregation dilemma. He highlights the important role of social networks in the life of immigrants, both for migration as well as for the forms of, and paths to, integration of immigrants in their countries of destination. His contribution is based on the findings of the comparative research project Welfare and Values in Europe (WAVE), and draws attention to the indispensable role of local immigrant social networks (family, ethnic and religious organisations) not only in the more general social orientation of immigrants, but also in articulating and realising their welfare needs. Zrinščak argues that this central role in social integration and orientation should alert us to the importance of cultural elements in promoting the welfare rights and well-being of immigrants. As a result, immigrant social networks must become a crucial element in any analysis of migration and welfare.

Manlio Cinalli and Alessandra El Hariri in Chapter Twelve continue this sectoral analysis in their exploration of the contentious opportunities and metropolitan policymaking for immigrants in France and Italy, focusing on policymaking in Paris, Lyon, Rome and Milan. They emphasise the explanatory role of contextual environments and 'political opportunities', arguing that the inclusion of migrants and immigrant communities must take account of the urban level, as metropolitan politics of social protection and integration strategies are at the core of migrants' day-to-day experiences of integration. These local strategies must be understood within a theoretical framework that has territorial distinctions, different levels of government and variable configurations of power at the core of its analysis.

Finally, in Chapter Thirteen, John Gal and Jennifer Oser discuss the implications of what they call a categorical immigration policy for the poverty of immigrants. The authors argue that many immigrants to Israel fare better than existing, notably Arab, populations on a number of economic and social parameters. The fundamental position of Israel is to accept and even encourage Jewish immigrants, and to support their assimilation by the creation of economically costly, but politically acceptable, policy measures, specifically designed for the category of immigrant. While Gal and Oser note that some immigrant groups fare less well than others – notably Jewish immigrants from Ethiopia – the case of Israel nonetheless demonstrates that immigrant poverty is not immutable. It requires, however, a view of the state and nation at odds with those in most EU countries, even some which historically have had similar regimes of integration for privileged groups, such as Germany (see Chapter Seven), or still do (see Chapter Nine), thus posing questions about the political sustainability of such a strategy, certainly in the current conditions of immigration politics in the EU.

Notes

[1] We refer to 'integration' rather generically as a social process concerned with the full possibility of participation in social, economic and political life. In this context, our usage has much in common with the terminology of social inclusion common in the field of social policy, and we use the terms 'integration' and 'inclusion' interchangeably.

[2] Deciding who is part of the 'in' and 'out' group – that is, included or excluded as potential beneficiaries of societal benefits – is often not simply a matter of rational calculus (X ostracises Y because it is in X's personal rational and direct interest to do so), but also a matter of feelings towards the 'out' group (X ostracises Y because it is the owner of some

characteristics, such as colour of the skin or 'race', that contrast with the characteristics or idealised characteristics of X).

[3] While *homophily*, that is, the preference of human beings to look for similar partners, has been widely explored, especially in sociology and social psychology (for a review, see Feld and Grofman, 2009), very little is still known about whether any clear parallel can be found at societal level. However, there seems some preference for particular kinds of cultural homogeneity in neighbourhoods (see Bruch and Mare, 2009), which might imply potential relevance of homophily for explaining some aspects of migration policymaking.

[4] Emotions and rationality should, therefore, be considered as intertwined (Illouz and Finkelman, 2009), contiguous entities (Damasio, 1994), which depend, and are based on, continuous actions and interactions of actors embedded in a specific culture, including political and institutional cultures (Bandelj, 2009; Berezin, 2009). Examples of this mutual and self-reinforcing relationship have been found not simply in studies on partner selection (Zelizer, 2005; Illouz and Finkelman, 2009), but also on economic action (Becker, 1991; Bourdieu, 2005; Beckert, 2006, 2008) and social interactions (Collins, 2004; Berezin, 2009).

[5] In addition to this, in 2007, in 14 of the EU's 27 member states (the majority) there is either a total absence of any publicly available official criminal justice data on racist crime or simply limited reporting on a few court cases.

References

Bachrach, P. and Baratz, M.S. (1963) 'Decisions and nondecisions: an analytical framework', *The American Political Science Review*, vol 57, no 3, pp 632-42.

Baldaccini, A., Guild, E. and Toner, H. (eds) (2007) *Whose freedom, security and justice? EU immigration and asylum and policy*, Portland, OR: Hart Publishing.

Bandelj, N. (2009) 'Emotions in economic action and interaction', *Theory and Society*, vol 38, no 4, pp 347-66.

Banting, K.G. and Kymlicka, W. (eds) (2006) *Multi-culturalism and the welfare state*, Cambridge: Cambridge University Press.

Becker, G.S. (1991) *A treatise on the family*, Cambridge, MA: Harvard University Press.

Beckert, J. (2006) 'Was tun? Die emotionale Konstruktion von Zuversicht bei Entscheidungen unter Ungewissheit' ['What is to be done? The emotional construction of confidence in decision-making under conditions of uncertainty'], in A. Scherzberg (ed) *Kluges Entscheiden: Disziplinäre Grundlagen und interdisziplinäre Verknüpfungen, [Deciding wisely: Disciplinary basis and interdisciplinary linkages]* Tübingen: Mohr Siebeck, pp 123-41.

Beckert, J. (2008) *Inherited wealth* (translated by Thomas Dunlap), Princeton, NJ: Princeton University Press.

Berezin, M. (2009) 'Exploring emotions and the economy: new contributions from sociological theory', *Theory and Society*, vol 38, no 4, pp 335-46.

Billig, M. (1990) *Banal nationalism*, Cambridge: Cambridge University Press.

Boudon, R. (2003) 'Beyond rational choice theory', *Annual Review of Sociology*, vol 29, no 1, pp 1-21.

Bourdieu, P. (2005) *The social structures of economy* (translated by Chris Turner), Cambridge: Polity Press.

Brader, T., Valentino, N. and Suhay, E. (2008) 'What triggers public opposition to immigration? Anxiety, group cues and immigration threat', *American Journal of Political Science*, vol 52, no 4, pp 959-76.

Bruch, E. and Mare, R. (2009) 'Segregation dynamics', in P. Hedström and P. Bearman, *The Oxford handbook of analytical sociology*, Oxford: Oxford University Press, pp 269-93.

Calavita, K. (2005) *Immigrants at the margins. Law, race and social exclusion in Southern Europe*, Cambridge: Cambridge University Press.

Campbell, J.L. and Pedersen, O.K. (2001) 'Introduction', in J.L. Campbell and O.K. Pedersen (eds) *The rise of neoliberalism and institutional analysis*, Princeton, NJ: Princeton University Press, pp 1-24.

Caponio, T. and Borkert, M. (eds) (2010) *Local dimension of migration policymaking*, IMISCOE reports, Amsterdam: Amsterdam University Press.

Collins, R. (2004) *Interaction ritual chains*, Princeton, NJ: Princeton University Press.

Damasio, A.R. (1994) *Descartes' error: Emotion, reason and the human brain*, New York, NY: Penguin.

Dehousse, R. (ed) (2010) *Politique européenne*, Paris: Presses de Sciences Po.

Doomernik, J. and Jandl, M. (eds) (2008) *Modes of migration regulation and control in Europe*, IMISCOE Reports Series, Amsterdam: Amsterdam University Press.

Eatwell, R. (ed) (1997) *European political cultures*, London: Routledge.

Elster, J. (1999) *Alchemies of the mind*, Cambridge: Cambridge University Press.

Elster, J. (2008) *Reason and rationality*, Princeton: Princeton University Press.

Elster, J. (2009) 'Emotions', in P. Hedström and P. Bearman (eds) *The Oxford handbook of analytical sociology*, Oxford: Oxford University Press, pp 51-71.

EUFRA (European Union Fundamental Rights Agency) (2007) *Annual report*, Vienna: EUFRA.

EUFRA (2008) *Annual report*, Vienna: EUFRA.

EUFRA (2009) *Annual report*, Vienna: EUFRA.

EUMC (European Union Monitoring Centre on Racism and Xenophobia) (2005) *Annual report on the situation regarding racism and xenophobia in the member states of the European Union*, Vienna: EUMC.

EUMC (2006) *Annual report on the situation regarding racism and xenophobia in the member states of the European Union*, Vienna: EUMC.

Eurobarometer (2009a) *Eurobarometer 72. Public opinion in the European Union*, Brussels: European Commission.

Eurobarometer (2009b) *Eurobarometer 71. Public opinion in the European Union*, Brussels: European Commission.

Faist, T. (2000) *The volume and dynamics of international migration and transnational social spaces*, Oxford: Oxford University Press.

Falkner, G., Treib, O., Hartlapp, M. and Leiber, S. (2005) *Complying with Europe: EU harmonisation and soft law in the member states*, Cambridge: Cambridge University Press.

Favell, A. and Hansen, R. (2002) 'Markets against politics: migration, EU enlargement and the idea of Europe', *Journal of Ethnic and Migration Studies*, vol 28, no 4, pp 581-601.

Feld, S. and Grofman, B. (2009) 'Homophily and the focused organization of ties', in P. Hedström and P. Bearman (eds) *The Oxford handbook of analytical sociology*, Oxford: Oxford University Press, pp 521-43.

Fetzer, J. (2000) *Public attitudes toward immigration in the United States, France and Germany*, New York, NY: Cambridge University Press.

Frank, R.H. (1988) *Passions within reason: The strategic role of the emotions*, New York, NY: W.W. Norton & Company.

Freese, J. (2009) 'Preferences', in P. Hedström and P. Bearman (eds) *The Oxford handbook of analytical sociology*, Oxford: Oxford University Press, pp 94-114.

Geddes, A. (2008) *Immigration and European integration. Beyond fortress Europe?* (2nd edn), Manchester and New York: Manchester University Press.

Graziano, P.R. and Vink, M.P. (eds) (2007) *Europeanization: New research agendas*, Basingstoke: Palgrave Macmillan.

Guiraudon, V. (2003) 'The constitution of a European immigration policy domain: a political sociology approach', *Journal of European Public Policy*, vol 10, no 2, pp 263-82.

Guiraudon, V. and Favell, A. (eds) (2010) *The sociology of the European Union*, Basingstoke: Palgrave Macmillan.

Haas, E.B. (1968) *The uniting of Europe: Political, social and economic forces 1950-1957* (2nd edn), Stanford, CA: Stanford University Press.

Hall, P.A. and Taylor, R.C.R. (1996) 'Political science and the three new institutionalisms', *Political Studies*, vol 44, no 5, pp 936-57.

Hansen, R. (2009) 'The poverty of postnationalism: citizenship, immigration, and the new Europe', *Theory and Society*, vol 38, no 1, pp 1-24.

Hay, C. (2006) 'Constructivist institutionalism', in R.A.W. Rhodes, S.A. Binder and B.A. Rockman (eds) *The Oxford handbook of political institutions*, Oxford: Oxford University Press, pp 56-74.

Hedström, P. (2008) 'Studying mechanisms to strengthen causal inferences in quantitative research', in J.M. Box-Steffensmeier, H.E. Brady and D. Collier (eds) *The Oxford handbook of political methodology*, Oxford: Oxford University Press, pp 319-29.

Hedström, P. and Bearman, P. (eds) (2009) *The Oxford handbook of analytical sociology*, Oxford: Oxford University Press.

Hedström, P. and Swedberg, R. (1998) 'Social mechanisms: an introductory essay', in P. Hedström and R. Swedberg, *Social mechanisms: An analytical approach to social theory*, Cambridge: Cambridge University Press, pp 1-31.

Hemerijck, A. (2010) *In search of a new welfare state*, Oxford: Oxford University Press.

Hooghe, L. and Marks, G. (2001) *Multi-level governance and European integration*, Lanham, MD: Rowman and Littlefield.

Huysmans, J. (2006) *The politics of insecurity. Fear, migration and asylum in the EU*, London: Routledge.

Illouz, E. and Finkelman, S. (2009) 'Exploring emotions and the economy: new contributions from sociological theory', *Theory and Society*, vol 38, no 4, pp 401-22.

Itzigsohn, J. (2000) 'Immigration and the boundaries of citizenship: the institutions of immigrants' political transnationalism', *International Migration Review*, vol 34, no 4, pp 1126-54.

Koopmans, R. (2010) 'Trade-offs between equality and difference: immigrant integration, multiculturalism and the welfare state in cross-national perspective', *Journal of Ethnic and Migration Studies*, vol 36, no 1, pp 1-26.

Kuhnle, S. (ed) (2000) *The survival of the European welfare state*, London: Routledge.

Kuhnle, S. (2009) 'The Nordic model: ambiguous, but useful concept', in H. Obinger and E. Rieger (eds) *Wohlfahrtsstaatlichkeit in entwickelten Demokratien: Herausforderungen, Reformen, Perspektiven* [*Welfare stateness in developed democracies: Challenges, reforms, perspectives*], Frankfurt/New York: Campus Verlag, pp 275-94.

Lavenex, S. and Ucarer, E.M. (eds) (2002) *Migration and the externalities of European integration*, Lanham, MD: Lexington Books.

Lendvai, N. and Stubbs, P. (2004) 'Policies as translation. Situating transnational social policies', in S.M. Hodgson and Z. Irving (eds) *Policy reconsidered: Meanings, politics and practices*, Bristol: The Policy Press.

MacAdam, D., Tarrow, S. and Tilly, C. (2001) *Dynamics of contention*, Cambridge: Cambridge University Press.

March, J.G. and Olsen, J.P. (1989) *Rediscovering institutions: The organizational basis of politics*, New York: Free Press.

Martell, L. (2010) *The sociology of globalization*, Cambridge: Polity Press.

Martin, D., Metzger, J.L. and Pierre, P. (2006) 'The sociology of globalization: theoretical and methodological reflections', *International Sociology*, vol 21, no 4, pp 499-521.

Mau, S. and Burkhardt, C. (2009) 'Migration and welfare state solidarity in Western Europe', *Journal of European Social Policy*, vol 19, no 3, pp 213-29.

Menz, G. (2009) *The political economy of managed migration*, Oxford: Oxford University Press.

Merton, R.K. (1968) 'The self-fulfilling prophecy', in R.K. Merton (ed) *Social theory and social structure*, New York, NY: Free Press, pp 475-90.

Moravcsik, A. (1998) *The choice of Europe: Social purpose and state power from Messina to Maastricht*, Ithaca, NY and London: Cornell University Press.

Morissens, A. (2006) 'Immigrants, unemployment and Europe's varying welfare regimes', in C. Parsons and T. Smeeding (eds) *Immigration and the transformation of Europe*, Cambridge: Cambridge University Press, pp 172-99.

Morris, L. (2002) *Managing migration: Civic stratification and migrants' rights*, London: Routledge.

Mudde, C. (2007) *Populist radical parties in Europe*, Cambridge: Cambridge University Press.

Nyhan, B. and Reifler, J. (2010) 'When corrections fail: the persistence of political misperceptions', *Political Behavior*, vol 32, no 2, pp 303-30.

Petersen, T. (2009) 'Opportunities', in P. Hedström and P. Bearman (eds) *The Oxford handbook of analytical sociology*, Oxford: Oxford University Press, pp 115-39.

Pierson, P. (1996) 'The path to European integration: a historical institutionalist analysis', *Comparative Political Studies*, vol 29, no 2, pp 123-63.

Pierson, P. (2004) *Politics in time. History, institutions and social analysis*, Princeton, NJ: Princeton University Press.

Portes, A. (1997) 'Immigration theory for a new century: some problems and opportunities', *International Migration Review*, vol 31, no 4, pp 799-825.

Rydgren, J. (2009) 'Beliefs', in P. Hedström and P. Bearman (eds) *The Oxford handbook of analytical sociology*, Oxford: Oxford University Press, pp 72-93.

Sabel, C. F. and Zeitlin, J. (2010) 'Learning from difference: the new architecture of experimentalist governance in the EU', in C.F. Sabel and J. Zeitlin (eds) *Experimentalist governance in the European Union: Towards a new architecture*, Oxford: Oxford University Press, pp 1-28.

Sainsbury, D. (2006) 'Immigrants' social rights in comparative perspective: welfare regimes, forms in immigration and immigration policy regimes', *Journal of European Social Policy*, vol 16, no 3, pp 229-44.

Saurugger, S. (2008) 'Une sociologie de l'integrátion Européenne?', *Politique Européenne*, vol 25, Spring, pp 5-22.

Schierup, C., Hansen, P. and Castles, S. (2006) *Migration, citizenship, and the European welfare state: A European dilemma*, Oxford: Oxford University Press.

Schiller, N.G., Basch, L. and Blanc, C.S. (1995) 'From immigrant to transmigrant: theorizing transnational migration', *Anthropological Quarterly*, vol 68, no 1, pp 48-63.

Schimmelfennig, F. and Sedelmeier, U. (2004) 'Governance by conditionality: EU rule transfer to the candidate countries of Central and Eastern Europe', *Journal of European Public Policy*, vol 11, no 4, pp 661-79.

Schmidt, V.A. (2006) *Democracy in Europe. The EU and national polities*, Oxford: Oxford University Press.

Schmidt, V.A. (2008) 'Discursive institutionalism: the explanatory power of ideas and discourse', *Annual Review of Political Science*, vol 11, pp 303-26.

Slavnić, Z. (2007) 'Informalisation of the economy and the recommodification of labour', in E. Berggren, B. Likić-Brborić, G. Toksöz and N. Trimikliniotis (eds) *Irregular migration, informal labour and community: A challenge for Europe*, Maastricht: Shaker Publishing.

Sniderman, P., Hagendoorn, L. and Prior, M. (2004) 'Predispositional factors and situational triggers. Exclusionary reactions to immigrant minorities', *American Political Science Review*, vol 98, no 1, pp 35-49.

Streeck, W. and Thelen, K. (2005) 'Introduction: institutional change in advanced political economies', in W. Streeck and K. Thelen (eds) *Beyond continuity. Institutional change in advanced political economies*, Oxford: Oxford University Press, pp 1-39.

Tilly, C (2001) 'Mechanisms in political processes', *Annual Review of Political Science*, vol 4, pp 21-41.

Tilly, C. (2004) 'Social boundary mechanisms', *Philosophy of the Social Sciences*, vol 34, no 2, pp 211-36.

van Houtum, H. and Pijpers, R. (2007) 'The European Union as a gated community: the two-faced border and immigration regime of the EU', *Antipode*, pp 291-309.

van Oorschot, W. (2008) 'Solidarity towards immigrants in European welfare states', *International Journal of Social Welfare*, vol 17, pp 3-14.

Yeates, N. (2009) *Globalising care economies and migrant workers: Explorations in global care chains*, Basingstoke: Palgrave Macmillan.

Zelizer, V.A. (2005) *The purchase of intimacy*, Princeton, NJ: Princeton University Press.

Part I
Theoretical background

Immigration and the variety of migrant integration regimes in the European Union

Theodoros Papadopoulos

Introduction

The purpose of this chapter is twofold. First, to provide an overview of the characteristics and trends of inward migration in the European Union (EU), including preliminary evidence on the impact of the unfolding economic crisis on immigration. Second, to explore the universe of diverse policies that regulate migration and the patterns of differential inclusion in EU member states, by introducing the concept of national migrant integration regimes. The variety of migrant integration regimes in the EU is explored empirically by comparing indicators for integration policies, migrants' employment characteristics and levels of immigration. As such, the chapter also provides a comparative empirical backdrop to the individual case studies and comparisons offered in the second and third parts of the book.

Migration and European social space: a brief historical overview

Migration is not a recent phenomenon in Europe. Much of Europe's history is inexorably linked to migrations, voluntary or forced, which have shaped the continent's social fabric, its historical narratives and national identities, its political economies, labour markets and welfare systems (on the history of migration in Europe, see Castles and Miller, 2009; also Bade, 2003; Moch, 1993, 2007). Major emigrations to the US or the metropolitan centres of Western Europe took place from Ireland, Scandinavia and later from Eastern Europe in the 19th century, and then Southern Europe (especially Italy and Greece) in the early 20th century. These emigrations stemmed from the exigencies of economic depredation as well as political oppression, but there were also migrations both to and from Northern and Western Europe, associated with imperial ambitions and trade. The latter continue to strongly colour immigration policies and patterns in France, the UK, Portugal and Belgium, for example. In Central and South Eastern Europe, processes of nation building in the face of the collapse of the Ottoman and Austro-

Hungarian Empires by the early 20th century involved a rather different set of circumstances than those in most of Western Europe. They were less affected by migration than by the status and political rights that should attach to non-migrant 'national minorities' (for example, Hungarians in Romania), and which today have an effect on migration and migration policies (see Chapter Nine).

It is in the aftermath of the Second World War that the contemporary history of migration in Europe begins. The division between East and West was followed by major population movements – often among the national minorities mentioned above – destined primarily towards Central and Western European countries. In Eastern Europe, from the late 1940s until the collapse of the regimes in 1989/90, population movement in all the 'Warsaw Pact' countries was strictly controlled, although many operated minor contract worker schemes, and educational and work exchange programmes with other communist countries. In Western Europe there were two major developments in the immediate aftermath of the war that had a profound impact on migration up until 1973. First, the enormous pace and intensity of post-war reconstruction, and its demand for labour in a context where women's employment was discouraged; and second, the start – and increasingly rapid pace – of de-colonisation by imperial powers. This trend appeared to slow down towards the beginning of the 1970s, with 1973 as a milestone year. According to Bade (2003, p 231), 'the 1973 "oil-price-shock" was less a trigger than a final chance to stop immigration and [labour] recruitment' in destination countries, as fears of economic stagnation met with rising reservations about the capacity of societies and their welfare states to incorporate the immigrants and their families.

For the next two-and-a-half decades, immigration and especially labour migration remained at relatively low levels in Europe, although it by no means stopped, as rights of settlement for former colonial 'subjects' and for family reunification became established. The situation changed dramatically after 1989/90. The collapse of the Eastern block regimes, the civil wars in the Balkans, intensifying internationalisation of the market economy and the accelerating process of European economic integration had significant – although not uniform – impacts on migration patterns in Europe (Jordan and Düvell, 2003). Many of these are highlighted in our case study chapters in Part II of this volume. During the next two decades the vast majority of European countries experienced substantial rises in inward migration, the trends and characteristics of which we examine in the next section.

Trends and characteristics of migration and immigration in contemporary Europe

A note on the empirical challenges of immigration statistics

Statistical data cannot tell us about the subjective experiences of migrants but they can elucidate the socio-economic context of such experiences and of the policies aiming at regulating migration. Still, attempts to empirically capture these macro-level phenomena are not immune from difficulties. At least two key challenges are encountered by such attempts. One challenge concerns the difficulties in generating data that enables us to access meaningful information about the reality of migration and of migrants' lives in general. The other challenge concerns the difficulties in constructing data that is accurate and meaningfully *comparable* across countries (for an extensive discussion of the poor comparability of migration statistics, see Kupiszewska and Nowok, 2005; Lemaitre, 2005). This chapter adopts an inclusive approach where difficulties with data are highlighted and then integrated in the narrative of the comparative analysis. The latter is organised in subsections, each exploring a number of key questions. Wherever possible, attention is drawn to definitional problems and operationalisation issues so that the reader can gain a balanced perspective of what the data reveal and their limitations.

Migration trends and projections

Two key questions are addressed in this subsection: how many migrants are there living in the EU countries and what have been the immigration trends in recent years? The most commonly used statistical sources for data on migration in Europe are Eurostat and the Organisation for Economic Co-operation and Development (OECD). Both report measurements of systematically recorded legal or 'regular' migration. However, most Eurostat publications and measurements refer to the concept of *foreign citizen*[1] or foreign population while the OECD refers to the concept, and publishes indicators, of *foreign-born population*. The former concept is considerably narrower as it includes only those who retain the nationality of their country of origin, while the latter – the foreign-born population – is broader as it includes all those who ever migrated from their country of birth to the country where they reside. This section explores data from both sources.

According to Eurostat (2009), at the beginning of 2008 there were 30.8 million foreign citizens living in the EU27, representing six per cent of the total EU27 population. In considering how different member states might be concerned about the volume and pattern of foreign citizens' residence (and what policy or regulatory concerns might result), two further questions arise. First, how many of these were citizens of other EU member states; and, second, what patterns might be observed in terms of the distribution of different national citizens across the different member states.

A simple cross-national observation of migration in the EU shows not only a concentration of foreign citizens in a number of core states, but also a divide between countries that have minimal foreign populations and countries with rather substantial numbers. In addition, it also shows that in terms of numbers of migrants, intra-EU migration is much more significant than migration into the EU. In particular, approximately 37 per cent of foreign citizens residing in the EU27 in 2008 were nationals of another EU member state. Around three quarters of all foreign citizens lived in the five most populous countries (Germany, Spain, the UK, France and Italy), while those countries with the largest *proportions* of non-national citizens were among the smaller states – including Luxembourg (43 per cent), Latvia (18 per cent), Estonia (17 per cent), Cyprus (16 per cent) and Ireland (13 per cent). Spain is the only country that could be included in both groups – high numbers and high proportions – of resident foreign citizens (12 per cent). The EU countries where non-nationals were less than one per cent of their population were Romania, Poland, Bulgaria and Slovakia (Eurostat, 2009a).

Bearing this in mind, it is important to make a number of qualifications:

- the category 'foreign citizens' does not necessarily include all migrants, as naturalisations may change this substantially, implying a differential impact on countries with *ius solis* rather than *ius sanguinis* citizenship regulation (see, for example, Eurostat, 2009b);
- not all migrants are foreign citizens;
- migration also includes temporary movements or seasonal mobility;
- statistics based on legal residence cannot account for irregular/undocumented migration; and
- regularisations, which have been used relatively often in Spain, Italy, Greece and Belgium, might affect the relevant numbers from year to year.

Against this background it would be more fruitful to explore statistical data that adopt a broader definition of immigration. Table 2.1 presents statistical data from the OECD covering the period 1985-2005 as well as projections for 2010 and 2030 and own calculations on percentage growth and percentage points increase for the period 1995-2010. Recorded foreign-born population as a percentage of total population is used as a proxy indicator for the level of (regular) in-migration in 18 EU countries. Countries are ranked in descending order according to the percentage growth in recorded foreign-born population for the period 1995-2010.

Most of the 18 EU member states recorded very low levels of foreign-born residents as a percentage of their total population in 1985. During the decade 1995-2005, in all but two countries (Belgium and Poland) the percentage of foreign-born residents increased, with some countries recording exceptional growth. If projections for 2010 are realised, Spain will have seen the percentage of foreign-born residents growing by a remarkable 464 per cent during the period 1995-2010, followed by Italy (185 per cent), Ireland (169 per cent) and Finland (110 per cent), although the latter's will still be comparatively low in terms of the overall share of the population. Greece will have experienced nearly 100 per cent growth during this period while Denmark, Austria, the UK and Sweden will also record high increases. At the other end, France and Belgium record very small growth, 1.9 and 1.1 per cent respectively. If we use 1985 as the base year, growth in the foreign-born populations in many of these countries is even higher. These trends illustrate the point made earlier, namely that, during the last two decades, the vast majority of European countries experienced substantial rises in the size

Table 2.1: Foreign-born residents as % of total population in 18 EU member states, 1985–2005 and projections for 2010 and 2030 (in descending order of % growth)

	1985	1995	2005	2010[a]	2030[a]	1995–2010[a]	
						% growth	% points difference
Spain	1.1	2.5	11.1	14.1	6.2	464.0	11.6
Italy	2.2	2.6	4.3	7.4	5.5	184.6	4.8
Ireland	6.4	7.3	14.1	19.6	9.0	168.5	12.3
Finland	1.0	2.0	3.0	4.2	3.4	110.0	2.2
Greece	3.1	5.1	8.8	10.1	13.0	98.0	5.0
Denmark	3.7	4.8	7.2	8.8	10.0	83.3	4.0
Austria	3.7	8.9	15.1	15.6	15.0	75.3	6.7
Portugal	3.5	5.3	7.3	8.6	11.6	62.3	3.3
UK	6.5	7.3	9.1	10.4	12.4	42.5	3.1
Sweden	7.8	10.3	12.4	14.1	16.6	36.9	3.8
Hungary	3.2	2.8	3.1	3.7	3.4	32.1	0.9
Germany	–	11.1	12.3	13.1	b	18.0	2.0
Netherlands	5.3	9.0	10.1	10.5	11.2	16.7	1.5
Slovakia	–	2.1	2.3	2.4	2.8	14.3	0.3
Luxembourg	28.3	33.4	37.4	35.2	30.6	5.4	1.8
France	10.8	10.5	10.7	10.7	14.9	1.9	0.2
Belgium	9.0	9.0	6.9	9.1	14.9	1.1	0.1
Poland	3.5	2.5	1.8	2.2	b	−12.0	−0.3

Notes: [a] Projected foreign-born population from major source countries.
[b] No projection available.

Sources: Lowell (2009); UN (2009); OECD (2009a); author's own calculations

of their foreign-born populations. This is especially the case in the countries of Southern Europe that, from being traditionally emigration countries, transformed into countries facing net inward migration. Still, projections for 2030 indicate that for some countries these trends are unlikely to continue. The levels of foreign-born population are expected to decline substantially in Spain, Italy and Ireland and to some degree in Luxembourg (for an explanation of the projection methods, see Lowell, 2009). In France, Belgium, Greece and Portugal and, to a lesser degree, in the UK and Sweden, growth is expected to continue, while for the rest of the EU countries immigration is expected to stabilise. However, the 2008-09 economic crisis might change these trajectories. The next subsection provides a preliminary assessment of its impact.

The impact of economic crisis on EU in-migration

It is now well documented that one of the biggest contributors to increased *labour* migration flows to the EU15 was EU enlargement. However, it appears that migration from Central Eastern European countries was mainly of a temporary character. Recent evidence shows that migrant workers from Central Eastern Europe may be returning to their countries of origin (Galgóczi et al, 2009; OECD, 2009a).

The unfolding economic crisis may be one of the explanations. There is some evidence that, at least in the short term, the crisis has negatively affected flows of regulated labour migration to EU member states and especially intra-EU free movement migration. For example, during the period 2007-08, Spain and the UK each experienced a decrease of approximately 25 per cent in inward migration from other EU member states, with the UK recording at least a 40 per cent drop during 2008-09 (OECD, 2010). At the same period decreases in regulated migration from non-EU countries were also recorded but much smaller: six per cent in Spain and five per cent in the UK, although in the case of the UK the following year's drop was more substantial (17 per cent for 2008-09). Similar trends were recorded in Ireland, while the Netherlands has experienced a 'levelling off' in the rate of increase of EU free movement migration (OECD, 2009a, p 33). Moreover, assessments of the impact of the crisis on irregular immigration also point to reductions in numbers, as unemployment is expected to rise across the EU (Frontex, 2009).

However, it is as yet unclear how deep and how extensive this impact will be and how it will interact with various policy initiatives. The interrelated financial and labour market dynamics between sending and receiving countries make assessments of the impact of the crisis rather more complicated. Poland is an interesting example here. It has been argued that a combination of labour shortages in key sectors (for example, construction), the introduction of attractive repatriation policy 'packages' by the Polish government in 2007 and unfavourable developments in exchange rates have resulted in a substantial number of Polish migrants returning home during the period immediately before and during the economic crisis (OECD, 2009a, p 60). Further, measures such as restrictions on family reunification (Italy), limits on the renewal of temporary work permits (Spain, Italy) or the provision of incentives to unemployed migrants to return to their home country (Spain, Czech Republic) may also explain current repatriation trends (OECD, 2009a, pp 40-1).

However, as the economic downturn hits those countries in the EU with the highest numbers of foreign-born residents, the likely reductions in remittances, foreign investment or economic activity (for example, exports) in the countries of origin may heighten and extend the impact of the crisis to these countries as well. In this context, uncertainty over the labour market and the wider economic situation of the country of origin is likely to act as a deterrent factor for repatriation. Remaining in the destination country, where welfare benefits and services or future labour market opportunities are better than in the country of origin, will be the only sensible option for many migrants. In addition, with recent stringent cuts in public sector expenditure and knock-on effects on employment and economic growth in several countries (eg, Greece, Italy, Spain, Ireland, the UK, Latvia, Hungary, Romania), pressures to migrate to other member states might increase, both for intra-EU migrants and also for the migrants currently resident in these states. Against this background, the capacity of welfare systems in destination countries to respond to the dual challenge of reduced economic resources and increasing socio-political and welfare demands will be seriously tested by the economic crisis. Debates and political pressures surrounding the key issues of acceptable levels of inward migration and migrant integration will intensify as EU countries and their political economies enter a period of economic stagnation, accompanied in some cases by severe austerity measures.

Countries of origin: the kaleidoscope of recorded (regular) immigration and asylum seekers

The next key question is where do migrants come from? Table 2.2a provides Eurostat data for the three largest groups of foreign citizens in 24 EU member states in 2008. To facilitate the comparison of the relative significance of these groups, data are presented both as actual numbers and as percentages of the total foreign citizens' populations residing in the destination country. In addition, data are presented according to geographical proximity to facilitate the exploration of similarities and differences in the regional patterns of immigration. Any comparisons should be made with caution as percentages vary substantially between countries; in some, one of the groups may represent the majority of foreign citizens (for example, Latvia, Slovenia, Greece); in others, a large minority (Germany, Luxembourg, Czech Republic); and in others they may represent only relatively more numerous groups among a larger number of similar size groups (for example, France).

Limitations aside, these data record the largest group of regular migrants in EU27 comprising foreign citizens who came from Turkey (7.9 per cent) followed by Morocco (5.6 per cent) and Romania (5.4 per cent). A clear pattern in their geographical distribution is observable; Turkish citizens predominantly reside in Western European countries and Germany, Romanian citizens reside mainly in Italy, Spain and Hungary, and Moroccan citizens in Italy, Spain and France. When the immigration experience in individual countries is examined, the emerging patterns highlight the importance of geographical proximity and cultural and historical links and networks as explanatory factors for both internal and external EU migration. In Sweden, Finland, Latvia and Lithuania some of the largest groups comprise their own citizens while the latter three also record high percentages of Russian citizens (although in Latvia and Lithuania these are national minorities stemming from the Soviet era). In Western European countries, substantial intra-EU migration is observable, but also the importance of cultural and historical links, especially in France. In Belgium and Luxembourg, citizens of other EU member states predominate while the reverse is true for Germany and the Netherlands, both of which record large numbers of foreign citizens originating from Turkey. The combined importance of geographical proximity and cultural and historical links is not only visible in the UK, where the largest groups comprise citizens

Table 2.2a: Three largest groups of foreign citizens residing in EU member states by citizenship, 2008 (absolute numbers and % of total population of foreign citizens resident in the member states, presented according to geographical proximity)

	Citizens of		%	Citizens of		%	Citizens of		%
EU27	Turkey	2,419,000	7.9	Morocco	1,727,000	5.6	Romania	1,677,000	5.4
Latvia	Recognised non-citizens[b]	371,700	89.5	Russia	28,500	6.9	Lithuania	3,400	0.8
Lithuania	Russia	12,800	29.7	Belarus	4,700	10.9	Stateless	4,200	9.7
Finland	Russia	26,200	19.8	Estonia	20,000	15.1	Sweden	8,300	6.3
Sweden	Finland	80,400	15.3	Iraq	40,000	7.6	Denmark	38,400	7.3
Denmark	Turkey	28,800	9.7	Iraq	18,300	6.1	Germany	18,000	6.0
Netherlands	Turkey	93,700	13.6	Morocco	74,900	10.9	Germany	62,400	9.1
Belgium	Italy	169,000	17.4	France	130,600	13.4	Netherlands	123,500	12.7
Luxembourg	Portugal	76,600	37.2	France	26,600	12.9	Italy	19,100	9.3
France[a]	Portugal	492,000	13.6	Algeria	477,500	13.2	Morocco	461,500	12.7
Germany	Turkey	1,830,100	25.2	Italy	570,200	7.9	Poland	413,000	5.7
Poland	Germany	11,800	20.5	Ukraine	6,100	10.6	Russia	3,700	6.4
Czech Republic	Ukraine	103,400	29.7	Slovakia	67,900	19.5	Vietnam	42,300	12.2
Slovakia	Czech Republic	6,000	14.6	Poland	4,000	9.8	Ukraine	3,700	9.2
Hungary	Romania	65,900	37.3	Ukraine	17,300	9.8	Germany	14,400	8.2
Austria	Serbia and Montenegro	132,600	15.9	Germany	119,800	14.3	Turkey	109,200	13.1
Slovenia	Bosnia and Herzegovina	32,500	47.3	Serbia	13,800	20.1	FYROM[c]	7,400	10.9
Romania	Moldova	5,500	21.0	Turkey	2,200	8.4	China	1,900	7.3
Bulgaria	Russia	9,000	36.7	Ukraine	2,200	8.8	Greece	1,600	6.6
Greece	Albania	577,500	63.7	Ukraine	22,300	2.5	Georgia	17,200	1.9
Malta	UK	4,100	26.5	India	900	6.0	Serbia	800	5.1
Italy	Romania	625,300	18.2	Albania	402,000	11.7	Morocco	365,900	10.7
Spain	Romania	734,800	14.0	Morocco	649,800	12.3	Ecuador	423,500	8.0
Portugal	Brazil	70,100	15.7	Cape Verde	64,700	14.5	Ukraine	39,600	8.9
UK	Poland	392,800	9.9	Ireland	347,900	8.8	India	296,500	7.5

Notes: Detailed data for Estonia, Ireland and Cyprus were not available. Data are rounded to the nearest 100.
[a] 2005 data.
[b] According to Eurostat (2009b), 'a recognised non-citizen is a person who is neither a citizen of the reporting country nor of any other country'.
[c] FYROM: Former Yugoslav Republic of Macedonia.

Source: Eurostat (2009b)

Table 2.2b: Three largest groups of asylum applicants in EU member states by citizenship, 2009 (according to geographical proximity)

| | Applicants | | Citizenships of main groups of asylum applicants | | | | | |
	2009	Per million inhabitants[a]	First group	%	Second group	%	Third group	%
EU27	260,730	520	Afghanistan	8	Russia	8	Somalia	7
Estonia	40	30	Afghanistan	25	Georgia	13	Russia	13
Latvia	60	25	Afghanistan	33	Uzbekistan	17	Syria	8
Lithuania	450	135	Russia	54	Georgia	17	Sri Lanka	4
Finland	4,915	925	Somalia	23	Iraq	23	Russia	12
Sweden	24,175	2,610	Somalia	24	Iraq	10	Afghanistan	7
Denmark	3,725	675	Afghanistan	28	Syria	10	Russia	9
Netherlands	16,140	980	Somalia	37	Iraq	13	Afghanistan	9
Belgium	21,645	2,015	Russia	13	Kosovo[b]	12	Afghanistan	9
Luxembourg	480	975	Kosovo[b]	27	Iraq	14	Bosnia and Herzegovina	7
France	47,625	740	Kosovo[b]	10	Sri Lanka	8	Russia	8
Germany	31,810	390	Iraq	22	Afghanistan	11	Kosovo[b]	6
Poland	10,595	280	Russia	54	Georgia	39	Armenia	1
Czech Republic	1,240	120	Ukraine	16	Kazakhstan	15	Mongolia	13
Slovakia	810	150	Pakistan	21	Georgia	12	Moldova	9
Hungary	4,665	465	Kosovo[b]	38	Afghanistan	26	Serbia	11
Austria	15,785	1,890	Russia	23	Afghanistan	14	Kosovo[b]	8
Slovenia	200	100	Bosnia and Herzegovina	20	Kosovo[b]	15	Serbia	10
Romania	965	45	Moldova	15	Pakistan	11	Afghanistan	9
Bulgaria	855	110	Iraq	36	Stateless	15	Afghanistan	7
Greece	15,925	1,415	Pakistan	23	Georgia	14	Bangladesh	11
Cyprus[c]	2,665	(3,345)	India	11	Sri Lanka	9	Occupied Palestinian Territories	9
Malta	2,385	(5,765)	Somalia	60	Nigeria	12	Eritrea	11
Italy	17,470	290	Nigeria	23	Somalia	9	Pakistan	8
Spain	3,005	65	Nigeria	15	Ivory Coast	10	Colombia	8
Portugal	140	15	Eritrea	14	Guinea	14	Mauritania	11
Ireland	2,690	605	Nigeria	21	Pakistan	10	China	7
UK[c]	30,290	490	Zimbabwe	25	Afghanistan	12	Iran	7

Notes: [a] Number of applicants registered during the year relative to population as of 1 January 2009. Population data are provisional for Belgium and the UK. Data are rounded to the nearest 5.
[b] Kosovo under UN Security Council Resolution 1244.
[c] According to Eurostat, the data for Cyprus and the UK would be higher if calculated in the same way as for the other countries in the table.
Source: Eurostat (2010)

from Poland, Ireland and India, but also in Central and Eastern Europe, where many of the largest groups comprise citizens of proximate countries, and especially citizens of the Ukraine. An interesting case here is the Czech Republic, where one of the largest groups comprises Vietnamese citizens (originally sent as contract workers or students in the pre–1989 period). Cultural and other links with Brazil and Cape Verde seem to affect the pattern of inward migration in Portugal, while in Greece, Italy and to some extent Spain, proximity seems to be the key factor. Foreign citizens from Albania are by far the predominant group in Greece and the second largest in Italy, while citizens from Morocco are the second largest group in Spain and the third largest in Italy. Still, Spain also records a large number of citizens from Ecuador.

When the data of asylum seekers are compared (see Table 2.2b), the diversity of national experiences is further amplified. We should note, however, that as with Table 2.2a, numbers and percentages vary substantially and due caution should be made in the interpretation of the findings. Agreements on what counts as a 'safe country', migration networks, historical and geographical links, proximity to conflict zones (for example, Kosovo, ex-Soviet territories, occupied Palestine), political prioritisation of some conflicts over others, appear to be among the key reasons for seeking asylum in a particular country. The three largest groups of asylum seekers in the EU27 comprise applicants from Afghanistan, Russia and Somalia, while the three top countries in absolute numbers of asylum applications are, in descending order, France, Germany and the UK. Still, when the volume of applications is measured against the population, Sweden, Austria and Greece experience the highest numbers of asylum applications per million inhabitants among the large EU countries. The same indicator is very high for Malta and Cyprus but in their case, as countries with fewer than one million inhabitants each, the number provided is for indicative purposes only. In Central and Western European countries, applicants from the Kosovo province form large groups of asylum seekers while applicants from Somalia are well represented in Finland, Sweden, the Netherlands and Malta. While applicants from Afghanistan are fairly evenly distributed across the geographical clusters, applicants from Russia seek asylum mostly in the Northern and North Eastern EU countries and those from Iraq mainly in Western and Northern EU states.

Irregular migration: challenge or feature of national political economies?

The picture of migrant populations would be incomplete without taking into account the extent of irregular (undocumented) migration. Statistics and estimates for irregular migration are notoriously difficult to generate and for many years estimates were either very unreliable or missing for many countries. The creation of the European Database on Irregular Migration was a great step forward in addressing this challenge. Based on data generated and analysed for the purposes of this database (Kovacheva and Vogel, 2009), Table 2.3 presents aggregated estimates of irregular migrant populations for all the EU27. The data provided here are national averages between low and high estimates presented according to geographical proximity. It should be noted that these data are based on national studies and estimations – that is, were not generated using the same methodology – and, although reported in 2008, correspond to different years. They are probably the best estimates currently available but they should be interpreted with considerable caution.

When irregular migrant populations are taken into account, substantial variations emerge between countries. Greece tops the ranking order as the country with the largest estimated number of irregular migrants as a percentage of the population (1.7 per cent). Slightly more than a fifth of the foreign population residing in the country is estimated to be undocumented migrants. Estimates for Cyprus, Malta, Ireland, the UK and Belgium calculate the irregular migrant population at more than one per cent of the population, although as a percentage of foreign population the variation is extensive, from 46.5 per cent in Malta to 10.5 per cent in Ireland. At the other end of the spectrum, estimates for the Nordic countries, Finland, Sweden and Denmark, and for Estonia, Latvia, Lithuania, Romania and Bulgaria, indicate very small numbers of irregular migrants as percentages of the respective total populations. Still, as percentages of the *foreign*

Table 2.3: Aggregated estimates of irregular migrant populations in the EU27 reported in 2008 (presented according to geographical proximity)

	% of population	% of foreign population
Estonia	0.56	3.0
Latvia	0.30	2.0
Lithuania	0.30	25.0
Finland	0.19	8.5
Sweden	0.11	2.0
Denmark	0.06	1.0
Netherlands	0.59	14.0
Belgium	1.03	11.5
Luxembourg	0.59	1.5
France	0.46	8.0
Germany	0.40	4.5
Poland	0.46	(91.0)
Czech Republic	0.56	20.0
Slovakia	0.33	54.5
Hungary	0.30	18.0
Austria	0.44	4.5
Slovenia	0.30	11.5
Romania	0.04	34.5
Bulgaria	0.04	12.5
Greece	1.70	21.5
Cyprus	1.58	10.5
Malta	1.58	46.5
Italy	0.62	13.0
Spain	0.70	7.0
Portugal	0.85	20.5
Ireland	1.05	10.5
UK	1.05	17.5
EU27	0.58	10.0

Note: Each value represents the average between minimum and maximum estimations. Data for Poland's percentage of foreign population is the minimum value as the maximum estimated value exceeded by 3.5 times the total foreign population. Individual estimates correspond to different years.

Source: Author's calculations based on Kovacheva and Vogel (2009)

population, the irregular migrant populations estimated for Slovakia, Hungary, Lithuania, Slovenia, Romania and Bulgaria are considerable, ranging from 11.5 per cent in Slovenia to more than half the foreign population (54.5 per cent) in

Slovakia. The fact that these are among the countries which, overall, record the lowest percentages of foreign-born population, leads us to conclude there are at least two types of countries where irregular migration is high: those countries where inward migration is extensive and irregular migration is a significant part of it, and those countries (mainly Central and Eastern European) where inward migration is very limited but, within it, the percentage of irregular migrants is high.

The centrality of irregular migration in understanding current challenges regarding the integration of migrants in the EU is now well documented (Jordan and Düvell, 2003; Berggren et al, 2007; Jordan, 2007; Düvell, 2009). States' ad hoc efforts to contain the 'market' in illegal cross-border mobility are often ineffective, and this has been a significant factor in the emergence of EU migration governance in terms of joint border control and the development of common policies (Lahav and Guiraudon, 2006; Neske and Doomernik, 2006). Discussing in detail the explanations for the diversity of irregular migration goes beyond the scope of this chapter. However, it is important to emphasise that the levels and type of irregular immigration are also directly connected to the level of each country's shadow economy and, consequently, its political economy and its welfare regime.

Indeed, the dramatic growth of both regular and irregular immigration during the last two decades coincided, and to a large extent is associated, with parallel processes of welfare retrenchment, labour recommodification, de-familisation and the subsequent commodification of care experienced by European societies during the same period (Papadopoulos, 2005; Andall, 2006; Menz, 2006; Likić-Brborić, 2007; Schierup, 2007; Slavnić, 2007, 2010; Standing, 2009). According to Standing (2009), the migration currently experienced is more heterogeneous than in the past. Although there are still 'plenty of settler migrants [...] much of the rise in mobility has been circular or temporary, while more has been illegal, unauthorised, undocumented and "without nationality"' (p 68). Together with the needs generated by an ageing population, the substantial increases in the labour force participation of women observed in many EU countries has also given rise to demand for labour to provide childcare or residential care for older people (Yeates, 2009). This has been especially significant for Southern European countries (Sciortino, 2004; Bettio et al, 2006; Caponio and Graziano, Chapter Six), but is also evident in the recruitment of healthcare staff in the UK, for example.

Further, developed nations responded to shortages of high skills – many created due to chronic under-funding of welfare services, education and health sectors, as well as the growing demands of high technology sectors, and in Central and Eastern Europe, by emigration – by recruiting high skilled professionals from other less developed countries, either in the EU or outside it (on Central and Eastern Europe trends and exceptions, see Menz, 2009, pp 232, 267). In low skill sectors like domestic services, agriculture or construction, demand for migrant workers has increased dramatically – undocumented migrants are extensively used in all, but particularly in domestic services and agriculture, and in fact in many sectors migrant workers are over-represented in the respective labour force. These trends can be seen in Table 2.4, which provides comparative data on the sectoral

Table 2.4: Sectoral distribution of foreign-born workers (15- to 64-year-olds), 2007 selected European countries (%)

	AUT	BEL	CHE	DEU	DNK	ESP	FRA	GBR	GRC	HUN	ITA	LUX	NLD	PRT	SWE
Agriculture and fishing	1.3	1.2	1.0	1.1	a	**4.5**	1.1	0.6	4.8	a	3.4	0.7	1.4	a	0.6
Mining	a	a	a	a	a	0.2	a	0.4	a	a	a	a	a	a	a
Manufacturing non-durable food products	**3.0**	2.2	**1.6**	**3.7**	**3.9**	2.4	2.3	**2.9**	**3.0**	a	**1.9**	0.9	**3.0**	a	**1.4**
Manufacturing non-durable other products	**6.2**	4.8	**5.1**	**6.7**	4.0	3.7	3.8	3.9	**5.3**	**8.9**	**7.3**	2.0	**4.7**	4.9	4.1
Manufacturing durable	11.4	6.6	**11.4**	**19.9**	8.3	5.1	7.6	5.8	6.4	11.7	**13.4**	**4.6**	9.8	5.7	**10.6**
Electricity, gas and water supply	a	0.6	0.4	0.3	a	0.1	0.3	a	a	a	0.7	a	a	a	a
Construction	**10.0**	**8.2**	**8.4**	**6.7**	3.3	**21.0**	**10.1**	5.7	**32.0**	**10.0**	**14.8**	**13.6**	4.8	**15.9**	3.2
Wholesale	15.0	13.9	13.7	12.4	14.0	13.0	12.1	11.8	10.3	**19.9**	10.8	11.5	12.2	14.3	10.7
Hotels and restaurants	12.0	8.0	7.4	**8.4**	7.8	**14.7**	6.9	**8.6**	10.2	3.6	**8.1**	6.1	6.8	8.3	**7.8**
Transport	**6.3**	6.7	4.5	5.4	**7.7**	4.5	6.3	**7.8**	2.4	4.6	4.6	3.9	**6.9**	5.0	**7.0**
Financial intermediation	1.4	2.1	4.6	1.5	1.7	1.0	2.2	**4.9**	a	a	0.7	**12.7**	2.7	1.8	1.1
Real estate, renting and business activities	**11.5**	**13.7**	**12.6**	10.1	**11.6**	7.7	**14.6**	**15.2**	3.8	**8.6**	9.1	**14.3**	**16.1**	9.4	**14.1**
Real estate and renting	**2.1**	**0.9**	1.2	0.8	a	1.1	**1.9**	1.4	a	a	0.7	**0.9**	0.8	**0.9**	1.2
Computer, research and development, other business activities	4.4	**12.8**	9.5	5.2	**10.8**	3.0	7.3	13.9	1.9	7.6	4.8	10.3	10.8	4.7	9.8
Security activities and industrial cleaning	**5.0**	a	**1.9**	**4.1**	a	**3.6**	**5.4**	a	**1.8**	a	**3.6**	3.1	**4.4**	**3.9**	**3.1**
Public administration and extra territorial organisations	3.4	**10.9**	3.1	2.5	3.4	1.2	7.0	5.0	1.3	a	1.5	12.6	6.0	6.5	4.2
Education	3.1	5.6	5.9	4.3	**8.0**	2.0	5.5	7.1	1.5	**8.9**	2.3	2.8	5.4	**6.8**	**11.4**
Health and social work	**9.1**	9.8	**13.6**	10.4	**19.5**	4.1	11.2	**14.4**	2.6	**8.4**	4.9	7.8	**15.2**	**7.3**	**19.3**
Other community services	**5.5**	**4.5**	5.2	**5.7**	4.9	2.7	4.1	4.9	2.1	**5.3**	**5.6**	2.9	4.4	4.9	4.3
Private households	a	**1.2**	**1.6**	**1.0**	a	**12.2**	**4.8**	0.6	**14.0**	a	**11.4**	**3.4**	a	**5.4**	a
Total	100	100	100	100	100	100	100	100	100	100	100	100	100	100	100

Notes: Numbers in bold signify over-representation of migrant workers in the respective labour force. Country abbreviations are: AUT – Austria; BEL – Belgium; CZE – the Czech Republic; DEU – Germany; DNK – Denmark; ESP – Spain; FRA – France; GBR – United Kingdom; GRC – Greece; HUN – Hungary; ITA – Italy; LUX – Luxembourg; NLD – the Netherlands; PRT – Portugal; SWE – Sweden.

a No data available.

Source: OECD (2009)

distribution of employment among foreign-born workers. This suggests that if we are to explain integration and inclusion, we not only need to assess which categories of migrants are integrated via which domains – labour market, welfare system, political inclusion (see also Chapter One, this volume). We also need to evaluate the further differentiation of inclusion produced by the variability of the terms and conditions under which 'integration' in particular domains (in this case, the labour market) is experienced by different migrants (as workers in different labour market sectors, informal/formal, service/industry), with different skills, and facing different conditions (see also Clark and Drinkwater, 2008).

Further, the link between increasing immigration, the increasing 'precariatisation' of labour forces across Europe and the chronic undermining of organised labour in EU members states in its capacity to defend hard-won employment and social rights, should be highlighted here. Aside the various differences between national welfare and employment regimes in the EU, it remains the case that cross-border mobility, temporary or otherwise, directly alters the power dynamics between key social actors associated with post-war political settlements in welfare and labour rights (Schierup, 2007). Unintentionally or not:

> [m]igrants are the light infantry of global capitalism. Unattached to local customs of solidarity and class identity, they weaken the effect of protective regulations and the bargaining power of local groups, particularly when the migration is temporary or illegal. (Standing, 2009, pp 68-9)

Indeed, often, the employers' implicit perspective is that '[m]igrant and immigrant workers are valuable because they are vulnerable' (Bauder, 2006, p 22). Against this background, policies towards the social integration of migrants become crucial elements in the restructuring of power dynamics between labour and capital in the post-industrial societies of Europe. Migrants as social and economic actors, but crucially the policies that govern their mobility and differential integration, become the new elements in the process of the institutional redesign of national political economies in the new Europe (see also Slavnić, 2010).

The integration of migrants: from policies to regimes

The previous section provided an overview of immigration trajectories, discussed how they are likely to be affected by the unfolding economic crisis and compared key aspects of national immigration experiences across the EU. Beyond the general trend of growing inward migration, the kaleidoscope of recorded regular in-migration, asylum seekers and estimated irregular migration revealed a number of strong affinities in terms of regional and historico-cultural patterns, but also important differences in the individual EU member states' experience of migration. Public feeling, attitudes and political discourse are shaped by these diverse experiences that, in turn, have an impact on patterns of differential inclusion, as we can observe in the case studies presented in Part II of the book. Of key importance here is the predominance of EU or non-EU migration, especially in the case of neighbouring countries and countries at the borders of the EU, feelings of apparent or assumed linguistic and cultural affinities between migrants and resident populations and the extent and role of irregular migration in national political economies.

This diverse and complex picture can be understood as both a product of, and a contributor to, European and national immigration policies and politics, illustrating both the extent and complexity of socio-economic transformation underway in European societies and their political economies. At the heart of this transformation lies the process of the social integration of migrants (Morawska, 2001). To explore it, I employ an analytical framework developed in a previous work (Papadopoulos, 2005), where social processes are perceived as power dynamics between social agents unfolding in three dimensions: relational, institutional and discursive.

In the case of the social integration of migrants, the relational dimension involves a multiplicity of practices in the economic, political, cultural and inter-personal domains that, at the micro-level, establish the multiple relationships between the migrant and the destination society (for an exploration of this dimension see Chapter Eleven). Further, these relationships are, to a large degree, *institutionally* regulated by a dense web of policy interactions between interpenetrating levels of governance (local, national, cross-national, supra-national) across different policy domains (rights to resident, citizenship and welfare, employment, health, education etc). At the same time as these institutional arrangements maintain the historically specific form of political economy in which migrants find themselves, migrants are, of course, themselves actors, and their presence and actions may reproduce or alter the character of these arrangements. Finally, through these micro-level practices and institutional regulations, different *discursive* constructions of the '*integrated* migrant' are actualised: some migrants are institutionally 'recognised' as members of society in the country of destination, who can be 'different but equal to us' (multiculturalism) or 'similar and equal to us' (assimilation). Some are granted partial institutional 'recognition', others temporary institutional 'recognition' and still others are excluded entirely.

Embarking from this analytical approach, this chapter focuses on the institutional dimension of social integration processes,[2] as it is articulated at the national level of governance. In particular, the plethora of policies concerning migrants at this governance level are incorporated under the concept of *national migrant integration regime*. Figure 2.1 provides the analytical schema of the embeddedness of a national migrant integration regime, its key elements and their interactions. The main elements taken into account are: social welfare policies, citizenship and immigration policies, and labour market policies and practices shaping the formal/informal employment mix. In turn a national migrant integration regime is embedded in its corresponding national political economy, and is influenced by

Figure 2.1: The embeddedness of a national migrant integration regime in the EU

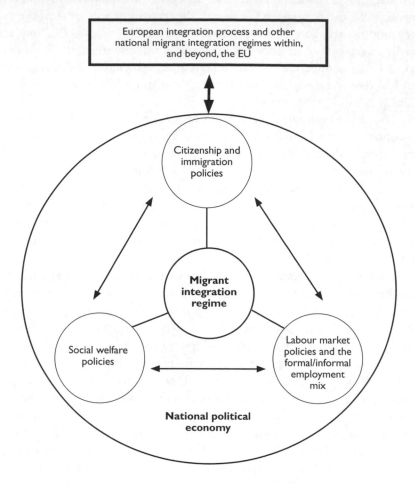

its interaction with other national political economies and migrant integration regimes within, and beyond, the EU as well as its interaction with the EU's politico-economic integration process. Consequently, an emerging EU migrant integration regime can be understood as comprising a variety of national migrant integration regimes and *competing* supra-national modes of governance, the latter being attempts at EU level to govern and steer the variety of national regimes.

In the remainder of this chapter, I bring together selected indicators that will be used as empirical proxies to explore comparatively the various components of national migrant integration regimes in the EU.

Towards a new typology?

Various works have highlighted the inadequacies and limitation of the most influential typologies to date (that is, varieties of capitalism and the variations and revisions of Esping-Andersen's [1990] welfare regime typology) to accommodate the reality of migration, immigration policies and its interactions with welfare, production and employment regimes (Menz, 2006; Sainsbury, 2006; Doomernik and Jandl, 2008). In addition, various attempts have been made to provide alternative typologies. Some, like Sainsbury, tried to accommodate earlier work on immigration *policy* regimes,[3] and offered a typology based on the interaction between welfare regimes and immigration regimes by using ideal-typical case studies (Sainsbury, 2006). Other authors developed typologies on the basis of countries' experience of immigration *flows* more generally (Triandafyllidou and Gropas, 2007), while Düvell has constructed a more sophisticated six-category typology on the basis of the interactions between institutional tolerance towards regular migration, irregular migration and irregular work (Düvell, 2009).

I argue that such typologies, although useful as starting points, can obstruct our attempt to understand and explain what is a very rich diversity of national experiences and political economies, especially as the latter are also interlinked in complementary, if unequal, positions in the emerging social and politico-economic *European* space of EU27. It is one of the conclusions following research for this chapter that when it comes to their individual national migrant integration regimes, each of the EU member states is indeed 'different', reflecting unique combinations of geography and borders, individual regime elements and national immigration experiences, all of which are mediated by EU participation and often in tension with EU economic and policy imperatives. Thus, this chapter will spend its final part reflecting on this rich diversity, by means of indicators, but avoid the understandable temptation to reduce this diversity into a new typology. Still, to avoid lengthy descriptions of each country, the discussion that follows uses, heuristically, a five-fold division of welfare regimes in Europe to reflect on the data, thus also roughly corresponding to the case studies in Part II of the book.

Presented in Table 2.5 are two sets of indicators representing proxies for (a) the national migrant integration regime elements and (b) the immigration experience for each country. The former is captured by the following indicators:

- The 'type of social welfare model' was used as a proxy for the character of the welfare system.
- The MIPEX composite indicator was used as a proxy for citizenship and immigration policies (the individual components of this index and their scores are provided in Table 2.6 in the Appendix to this chapter).
- The labour market access MIPEX index, extent of employment of migrants (% of total), low skilled migrants (% of migrant employment) and irregular migration (% of total population) are used as proxies for labour market characteristics and the formal/informal mix.
- 'Foreign-born' (% of total population) is used as the proxy for the national immigration 'experience'.

With regard to what have traditionally been considered as comprehensive (Nordic) welfare systems we observe substantial differences between their citizenship and immigration policies, with Denmark being the most exclusive. However, the immigration policies of Sweden score the highest in the MIPEX index, making Sweden a unique case that combines a relatively open attitude to migration with very high levels of formal integration, although there are debates about its de facto inclusion when one includes labour market participation (see below). Migration in Finland is comparatively very low but has grown dramatically, and as Koikkalainen et al show in Chapter Eight, the shortcoming here is really having access to the Finnish labour market and being integrated in the welfare

Table 2.5: Characteristics of migrant integration regimes and immigration experience in 23 EU member states

	1. Social welfare model[a]	2. Citizenship and immigration policies composite index	3. Labour market access index	4. Employment of migrants (% of total)	5. Low skilled (% of migrant employment)	6. Irregular migrants (% total population)	7. Foreign-born population (% total population)
Sweden	1	88	100	12.8	25.1	0.11	14.1
Finland	1	67	70	2.8	4.3	0.19	4.2
Denmark	1	44	40	6.6	13.1	0.06	8.8
Netherlands	2	68	70	10.7	24.3	0.59	10.5
Belgium	2	69	75	10.3	16.2	1.03	9.1
Luxembourg	2	55	45	45.4	71.9	0.59	35.2
France	2	55	50	11.2	21.2	0.46	10.7
Germany	2	53	50	12.8	27.5	0.40	13.1
Austria	2	39	45	16.1	36.2	0.44	15.6
UK	3	63	60	11.1	14.4	1.05	10.4
Ireland	3	53	50	14.8	23.0	1.05	19.6
Portugal	4	79	90	8.0	11.8	0.85	8.6
Italy	4	65	85	9.0	23.2	0.62	7.4
Spain	4	61	90	15.9	33.6	0.70	14.1
Greece	4	40	40	8.7	38.4	1.70	10.1
Poland	5	44	25	0.3	0.2	0.46	2.2
Czech Republic	5	48	50	1.9	3.2	0.56	–
Hungary	5	48	40	1.8	1.8	0.30	3.7
Slovenia	5	55	60	–	–	0.30	–
Estonia	6	46	75	–	–	0.56	–
Latvia	6	30	20	–	–	0.30	–
Lithuania	6	45	55	–	–	0.30	4.0
Slovakia	6	40	55	0.6	0.5	0.33	–

Notes: [a] Social welfare systems: 1: comprehensive; 2: conservative/corporatist; 3: liberal; 4: conservative/familistic; 5: post-communist/conservative; 6: post-communist/ rudimentary.
Sources: 1: author's typology based on Fegner (2007); 2 and 3: based on MIPEX indicators (see Appendix, Table 2.6); 4 and 5: OECD (2009a); 6: author's calculations based on Kovacheva and Vogel (2009); 7: projections for 2010 (UN, 2009)

state. For Düvell (2009), these countries are intolerant to regular and irregular migration and intolerant to irregular work, and to some extent this is supported by the data. These results, with the Finnish case study, provide a confirmation of, and a counter-point to, Koopmans' (2010) argument that generous welfare systems, combined with relatively closed labour markets, perform rather badly on integration and well-being of migrants. It seems to confirm the importance of the *combination* of labour market and welfare system, so that good benefits for migrants do not of themselves improve their welfare. However, as Carmel and Cerami argue in Chapter One, what our case studies also show is that different migrant groups, whether deliberately or by default, are integrated through different domains, and under different conditions in the same country, with consequently variable effects for the stratification of their rights and for their welfare.

With regard to what have traditionally been considered as conservative (continental) welfare regimes, the Bismarckian tradition meets a large variety of integration policies, ranging from highly integrative (Belgium) to deeply exclusionary (Austria). The numbers and origins of migrants and the recent experience or high growth in migration can at least partly explain this diversity, but it should be analysed alongside the labour market composition. Luxembourg aside, Austria has the highest percentage of foreign-born in both employment and low-skilled employment among the countries in this group. Low-skilled migrant employment in all the countries is very high, which can partly be explained by population ageing and processes of de-familisation resulting in commodification of care, but perhaps, as our German case suggests, may also require close attention to 'chains' of inclusion and exclusion which are constructed by specific policy interactions (see Chapter Seven). For Düvell (2009), these countries are tolerant of regular migration but intolerant of irregular migration and to irregular work, which appears to be, at least partly, supported by the data.

For those traditionally considered as liberal welfare regimes (Ireland and the UK), the easy access to the labour market indicated by high levels of participation in the labour force is accompanied by high exposure to old and new social risks in the flexible labour market (see Chapter Ten). Ireland's reverse experience from an emigration to immigration country is highlighted by the remarkable growth in immigration and the rather modest integration policies. For Düvell (2009), these countries are tolerant to regular migration, intolerant to irregular migration and tolerant to irregular work – at least until 2004 for the UK – which appears to be supported by the data.

In respect of countries associated with the familistic welfare regime, these are 'quasi' new immigration countries (see Chapter Six), with insecurity as a key characteristic. Goís and Marques (2009) argue for Portugal, although this might be extended to Greece and parts of both Spain and Italy, that the migration system is a result of its semi-peripheral position in the global economy – within, but on the margins of, the core European economy – which affects both immigration and emigration patterns. In all four Southern European countries, migrants clearly and disproportionately work in low-skill sectors, and in all countries, but especially in Spain, irregular migrants as a percentage of the total migrant ('foreign-born') population is relatively high. These are regimes where precariousness, and lack of social protection, is evident for all workers in low-skill sectors – and this is compounded for migrant workers, especially for the undocumented and those working illegally (Lawrence, 2007). Greece, similarly to Austria for the conservative welfare regime group, stands out as especially exclusionary. Of all the countries traditionally characterised by familistic welfare regime, Portugal appears to have a much more coherent set of policies and approach in dealing with migrants and their social and labour market integration, as indicated by the MIPEX index, and it is noticeable that unlike the other countries in this group, Portugal also has the lowest percentage of irregular migration and the lowest percentage increase in inward migration overall, suggesting a more 'managed' migrant integration regime.

Finally, in the case of Central and Eastern European countries, migration is really a new phenomenon as many, although not all, of these countries are countries of emigration. When it comes to integrating new migrants (such as Chinese nationals or nationals coming from neighbouring countries), ethnic tensions, political conflicts and the communist heritage still play a role, so that in the case of Hungary (as described by Rusu in Chapter Nine), the inclusion of ethnic Hungarians is privileged to other forms of inclusion to migrants. It is not clear how far this case can be extrapolated to other countries (see Woolfson, 2007, on Estonia; Menz, 2009, pp 228-32, on Poland). The MIPEX indicator results certainly suggest that many of these countries do not have policies in place for the integration of non-national migrants in the labour market or social protection. Nonetheless the numbers of in-migrants are (unlike in Greece or Austria), as yet, relatively small, which will tend to reduce the social and political pressure for policy change in this respect, however problematic the experience of individual migrants may be.

Conclusion

This chapter presented an overview of key recent and current trends in migration in Europe, exploring the diversity and variety of immigration experience among EU member states, and the impact this has on how we can evaluate the interaction of migration, migration policies and social protection policies across Europe. It was argued that together, the interaction of welfare regime, informal and formal labour markets (and their relationship), and immigration and citizenship regimes combine to form distinct national migrant integration regimes. Rather than construct a specified typology, the chapter used the well-recognised welfare regime categorisation as a starting point for considering the variety of interactions between welfare, political economy and immigration regimes across the EU member states, forming a comparative backdrop to many of the contributions to this book.

More broadly, central to this analysis is the importance of the political economy of welfare and the changing political economy of labour. With increased informalisation of economies, migrants become economically tolerated, indeed necessary, participants in the re-ordering of the political economy of Europe. While specific groups of migrants are considered necessary for sustaining welfare capitalism (especially in relation to ageing populations) and high-skill growth, migrant workers in general also play a role in further undermining the problematic co-existence of the post-war welfare settlement with reliance on post-Fordist and post-industrial economic growth (Slavnić, 2010). Not only does the encouragement of migration for utilitarian purposes sit uneasily with strong anti-immigration currents in policymaking, but it has other possible political and social consequences as well. The decision, on the one hand, to include (some) migrants, to offer policies which permit their social, political and economic integration, or on the other, the decision to tolerate (other) migrants' segregation and/or insist on their exclusion, become decisions which can affect the changing power dynamics in Europe. Migrants are social and economic actors, and the migration, welfare and labour market policies which structure the conditions of possibility for their integration and their recognition as political actors are emerging as very significant significant factors in shaping the institutional redesign of European political economies.

Notes

[1] Eurostat (2009a) defines citizenship as 'the particular legal bond between an individual and his or her State, acquired by birth or naturalisation, whether by declaration, choice, marriage or other means under national legislation. Foreign citizens refer to persons who are not citizens of the country in which they reside. They also include persons of unknown citizenship and stateless persons'.

[2] Here I take a functional view of integration, rather than a normative one. Migrants are 'integrated' into a labour market, in a particular place, which might leave them marginalised or in a 'subordinate' position to other migrants, or to non-migrants, but they are integrated, by playing a specific role in relation to a society or specific form of political economy (Bauder, (2006, p 9).

[3] The notion of immigration policy regime (Faist, 1995), and also the related 'incorporation regime' (Soysal, 1994) refers to policies aiming at regulating immigrants' inclusion in or exclusion from society. According to Sainsbury (2006): 'The immigration regime consists of rules and norms that govern immigrants' possibilities to become a citizen, to acquire residence and work permits, and to participate in economic, cultural and political life'.

References

Andall, J. (2006) 'Migration mobility in European diasporic space', in C. Parsons and T. Smeeding (eds) *Immigration and the transformation of Europe*, Cambridge: Cambridge University Press, pp 274–97.

Bade, K. (2003) *Migration in European history*, Oxford: Wiley-Blackwell.

Bauder, H. (2006) *Labor movement: How migration regulates labor markets*, New York: Oxford University Press.

Berggren, E., Likić-Brborić, B., Toksöz, G. and Trimikliniotis, N. (eds) (2007) *Irregular migration, informal labour and community: A challenge for Europe*, Maastricht: Shaker Publishing.

Bettio, F., Simonazzi, A. and Villa, P. (2006) 'Change in care regimes and female migration: the "care drain" in the Mediterranean', *Journal of European Social Policy*, vol 16, no 3, pp 271-85.

Castles, S. and Miller, M.J. (2009) *The age of migration: International population movements in the modern world* (4th edn), Basingstoke: Palgrave Macmillan.

Clark, K. and Drinkwater, S. (2008) 'The labour-market performance of recent migrants', *Oxford Review of Economic Policy*, vol 24, no 3, pp 495-516.

Doomernik, J. and Jandl, M. (eds) (2008) *Modes of migration regulation and control in Europe*, IMISCOE Reports Series, Amsterdam: Amsterdam University Press.

Düvell, F. (2009) *Pathways into irregularity: The social construction of irregular migration*, Comparative Policy Brief CLANDESTINO Project, Athens: ELIAMEP.

Eurostat (2009a) *Population of foreign citizens in the EU27 in 2008*, News Release 184, Luxembourg: Eurostat.

Eurostat (2009b) *Statistics in focus*, 6/94, Luxembourg: Eurostat.

Faist, T. (1995) 'Boundaries of welfare states: immigrants and social rights on the national and supranational level', in R. Miles and D. Thraenhardt (eds) *Migration and European integration. The dynamics of inclusion and exclusion*, London: Pinter, pp 177-95.

Fenger, H. (2007) 'Welfare regimes in Central and Eastern Europe: incorporating post-communist countries in a welfare regime typology', *Contemporary Issues and Ideas in Social Sciences*, vol 3, no 2, pp 1-30.

Frontex (2009) *The impact of the global economic crisis on illegal migration to the EU*, Risk Analysis Unit, Warsaw, August.

Galgóczi, B., Leschke, J. and Watt, A. (2009) *Intra-EU labour migration: Flows, effects and policy responses*, ETUI Working Paper 2009/03, Brussels: ETUI.

Góis, P. and Marques, J.C. (2009) 'Portugal as a semi-peripheral country in the global migration system', *International Migration*, vol 47, no 3, pp 21-50.

Jordan, B. (2007) 'Migration regimes and irregular migration', in E. Berggren, B. Likić-Brborić, G. Toksöz and N. Trimikliniotis (eds) *Irregular migration, informal labour and community: A challenge for Europe*, Maastricht: Shaker Publishing, pp 40-50.

Jordan, B. and Düvell, F. (2003) *Migration: The boundaries of equality and justice*, Cambridge: Polity Press.

Koopmans, R. (2010) 'Trade-offs between equality and difference: immigrant integration, multiculturalism and the welfare state in cross-national perspective', *Journal of Ethnic and Migration Studies*, vol 36, no 1, pp 1-26.

Kovacheva, V. and Vogel, D. (2009) 'The size of the irregular foreign resident population in the European Union in 2002, 2005 and 2008: aggregated estimates', Annex 3 to Working Paper No 4, HWWI (Hamburg Institute of International Economics), Database on Irregular Migration.

Kupiszewska, D. and Nowok, B. (2005) *Comparability of statistics on international migration flows in the European Union*, Central European Forum For Migration Research, CEFMR Working Paper 7/2005, Warsaw: CEFMR.

Lahav, G. and Guiraudon, V. (2006) 'Actors and venues in immigration control: closing the gap between political demands and policy outcomes', *West European Politics*, vol 29, no 2, pp 201-23.

Lawrence, C.M. (2007) *Blood and oranges: European markets and immigrant labour in rural Greece*, Oxford: Berghahn Books.

Lemaitre, G. (2005) *The comparability of international migration statistics problems and prospects*, Statistics Brief No 9, Paris: OECD.

Likić-Brborić B. (2007) 'Globalisation, EU enlargement and new migratory landscapes: the challenge of the informal economy and contingencies for "decent work"', in E. Berggren, B. Likić-Brborić, G. Toksöz and N. Trimikliniotis (eds) *Irregular migration, informal labour and community: A challenge for Europe*, Maastricht: Shaker Publishing, pp 165-82.

Lowell, B.L. (2009) 'Immigration "pull" factors in OECD countries over the long term', in OECD, *The future of international migration to OECD countries*, Paris: OECD.

Menz, G. (2006) '"Useful Gastarbeiter", burdensome asylum seekers, and the second wave of welfare retrenchment: exploring the nexus between migration and the welfare state', in C. Parsons and T. Smeeding (eds) *Immigration and the transformation of Europe*, Cambridge: Cambridge University Press, pp 393-418.

Menz, G. (2009) *The political economy of managed migration*, Oxford: Oxford University Press.

Moch, L.P. (1993) *Moving Europeans: Migration in Western Europe since 1650*, Bloomington, IN and Indianapolis, IN: Indiana University Press.

Moch, L.P. (2007) 'Connecting migration and world history: demographic patterns, family systems and gender', *International Review of Social History*, vol 52, pp 97-104.

Morawska, E. (2001) 'Structuring migration: the case of Polish income-seeking travellers to the West', *Theory and Society*, vol 30, pp 47-80.

Neske, M. and Doomernik, J. (2006) 'Comparing notes: perspectives on human smuggling in Austria, Germany, Italy and the Netherlands', *International Migration*, vol 44, no 4, pp 39-58.

OECD (Organisation for Economic Co-operation and Development) (2008) *A profile of immigrant populations in the 21st century: Data from OECD countries*, Paris: OECD.

OECD (2009a) *International Migration Outlook: SOPEMI*, Paris: OECD.

OECD (2009b) *The future of international migration to OECD countries*, Paris: OECD.

OECD (2010) 'The economic crisis had its greatest effect on free-movement migration: an interview with Georges Lemaitre', 23 February (www.oecd.org/document/6/0,3343,en_2649_33931_44638406_1_1_1_1,00.html).

Papadopoulos, T. (2005) *The recommodification of European labour: Theoretical and empirical explorations*, ERI Working Paper WP-05-03, Bath: European Research Institute, University of Bath.

Sainsbury, D. (2006) 'Immigrants' social rights in comparative perspective: welfare regimes, forms in immigration and immigration policy regimes', *Journal of European Social Policy*, vol 16, no 3, pp 229-44.

Schierup, C.U. (2007) '"Bloody subcontracting" in the network society: migration and post-Fordist restructuring across the European Union', in E. Berggren, B. Likić-Brborić, G. Toksöz and N. Trimikliniotis (eds) *Irregular migration, informal labour and community: A challenge for Europe*, Maastricht: Shaker Publishing, pp 150-65.

Sciortino, G. (2004) 'Immigration in a Mediterranean welfare state: the Italian experience in comparative perspective', *Journal of Comparative Policy Analysis*, vol 6, no 2, pp 111-29.

Slavnić, Z. (2007) 'Informalisation of the economy and the recommodification of labour', in E. Berggren, B. Likić-Brborić, G. Toksöz and N. Trimikliniotis (eds) *Irregular migration, informal labour and community: A challenge for Europe*, Maastricht: Shaker Publishing.

Slavnić, Z. (2010) 'Political economy of informalization', *European Societies*, vol 12, no 1, pp 3-23.

Soysal, Y.N. (1994) *Limits of citizenship: Migrants and postnational membership in Europe*, Chicago, IL: Chicago University Press.

Standing, G. (2009) *Work after globalization: Building occupational citizenship*, Cheltenham: Edward Elgar.

Triandafyllidou, A. and Gropas, R. (2007) *European immigration: A sourcebook*, Aldershot: Ashgate.

UN (United Nations) (2009) *International migration 2009*, New York, NY: Department of Economic and Social Affairs Population Division, UN.

Woolfson, C. (2007) 'Labour standards and migration in the New Europe: post-communist legacies and perspectives', *European Journal of Industrial Relations*, vol 13, no 2, pp 199-218.

Yeates, N. (2009) *Globalising care economies and migrant workers: Explorations in global care chains*, Basingstoke: Palgrave Macmillan.

Appendix

Table 2.6: Migrant Integration Policy Index (MIPEX): individual component indicators

Anti-discrimination		Access to nationality		Political participation		Long-term residence		Family reunion		Labour market access	
Sweden	94	Sweden	71	Sweden	93	Sweden	76	Sweden	92	Sweden	100
Portugal	87	Belgium	71	Luxembourg	84	Belgium	74	Portugal	84	Spain	90
Hungary	85	Portugal	69	Finland	81	Spain	70	Italy	79	Portugal	90
UK	81	UK	62	Netherlands	80	UK	67	Slovenia	71	Italy	85
Netherlands	81	Ireland	62	Portugal	79	Portugal	67	Lithuania	68	Estonia	75
France	81	France	54	Germany	66	Poland	67	Finland	68	Belgium	75
Slovenia	79	Netherlands	51	Ireland	59	Italy	67	Spain	66	Netherlands	70
Finland	75	Czech Republic	50	Belgium	57	Denmark	66	Poland	66	Finland	70
Belgium	75	Poland	45	Italy	55	Netherlands	65	Malta	66	UK	60
Italy	69	Luxembourg	45	Denmark	52	Malta	65	UK	65	Slovenia	60
Cyprus	60	Finland	44	France	50	Finland	63	Germany	63	Slovakia	55
Ireland	58	Slovenia	41	Spain	46	Slovenia	63	Estonia	63	Lithuania	55
Greece	58	Spain	41	UK	41	Czech Republic	61	Belgium	61	Germany	50
Luxembourg	56	Slovakia	40	Czech Republic	38	Estonia	60	Netherlands	61	Ireland	50
Spain	50	Lithuania	38	Austria	34	Greece	55	Czech Republic	60	France	50
Germany	50	Germany	38	Estonia	30	Austria	53	Luxembourg	58	Czech Republic	50
Lithuania	48	Hungary	36	Hungary	29	Germany	51	Ireland	55	Austria	45
Poland	46	Cyprus	36	Malta	19	Slovakia	51	Hungary	53	Luxembourg	45
Slovakia	44	Italy	33	Cyprus	18	Latvia	50	France	51	Hungary	40
Austria	42	Denmark	33	Slovenia	15	Hungary	50	Latvia	51	Greece	40
Malta	38	Malta	29	Slovakia	14	Luxembourg	50	Greece	50	Denmark	40
Latvia	33	Estonia	26	Poland	14	France	50	Slovakia	48	Cyprus	40
Denmark	33	Latvia	25	Greece	14	Cyprus	50	Denmark	48	Malta	30
Czech Republic	27	Greece	25	Lithuania	12	Lithuania	50	Austria	47	Poland	25
Estonia	23	Austria	22	Latvia	11	Ireland	50	Cyprus	39	Latvia	20
EU25	58.9		43.5		44.3		59.4		57.6		56.4
standard deviation	20.7		14.6		26.3		10.0		15.7		21.0
0.5 SD > mean	69.2		50.8		57.5		64.4		65.4		66.9
0.5 SD < mean	48.6		36.2		31.2		54.4		49.7		45.9

Note: Shaded areas represent scores within ± 0.5 standard deviations from the mean.
Source: MIPEX database, available from www.integrationindex.eu/ and author's own calculations

THREE

European Union migration governance: utility, security and integration

Emma Carmel

Introduction[1]

Policies relating to migration and immigration are always embedded in a range of different policy fields, subject to contrasting strategic interests and discursive framings, and embroiled in the contentious politics of who can or should enter and 'belong' in a state, and under what terms. For the European Union (EU) this complexity is multiplied. It is not a state, and it has uneven, and shared or secondary control over its borders; it has highly variable policy instruments at its disposal and highly variable political legitimacy to intervene in different policy areas (for a recent review, see Wallace et al, 2010). Nonetheless, despite this complexity, this chapter argues that there is an identifiable, and increasingly clearly articulated form of migration governance evident at EU level, which has important roles to play in member states. This chapter traces key elements of the EU's migration governance through the history of the EU's engagement in and production of policies on migration. It argues that migration governance in the EU is made coherent, 'manageable' and authoritative by linking two political and discursive logics – those of utility and security – via a third, social integration.

In particular, the chapter suggests that there is an incomplete and problematic but remarkably little contested set of claims and institutional re-orderings (see also Stone Sweet and Sandholtz, 1998; Börzel, 2010) whose centrality has been cemented with the most recent legal and programmatic changes in the EU of 2009 and 2010. They determine the scope and character of EU migration governance, through the underpinning logic of linking security, utility and social integration. This attempt to construct coherent migration governance in the EU is articulated with the highly politicised arenas at national and local level (see the case study chapters in Part II of this volume), leading to profound effects on differential inclusion and representing a significant impetus to the imbrication of EU migration governance in the Union's member states.

Migration governance in conditions of complexity

This chapter treats the interest and activities of the EU in migration policies as being about the creation of migration governance. As such, this chapter is concerned with analysing the configuration of processes, actors, institutions and outputs in the field of migration in the EU as something more than the sum of its parts – as governance. Treating this configuration – or, as we will see below, 'assemblage' – as governance, rather than as a process of policymaking, involves two analytical advantages. First, it involves examining migration governance *in toto*, thereby treating it as embedded in broader Union institutional architectures and political programmes. At the same time, we can also evaluate the meaning of this governance for what it can tell us more broadly about the differential integration of migrants emerging at national and even local levels (see, for example, Chapters Eleven and Twelve, this volume), and the conditions of possibility for alternatives.

Several aspects of migration policies in the EU have been addressed in a range of major studies, including the parameters of EU migration policies in their economic, juridical, political and social dimensions (see, for example, Bommes and Geddes, 2000; Kostakopoulou, 2001; Schierup et al, 2006; Menz, 2009); the engagement of states in and outside the EU in various combinations (Lavenex, 2001, 2006); the insertion into member state politics (Favell and Hansen, 2002; Boswell, 2009); and its export out of member state politics into quasi-professionalised formal and informal agencies and policymaking authorities (Guiraudon, 2000; Lahav and Guiraudon, 2006). These studies largely, although not entirely, treat each of these as separate aspects of migration policy. This is the case both for policymaking processes, where different aspects of migration policy come under different institutional leads (that is, different directorate-generals, involving different policy actors), and are also subject to different institutional architectures in the EU (for example, legislative procedures such as directives versus deliberative procedures such as the open method of coordination [OMC]). But it is also true of this burgeoning literature on different aspects of migration policy that despite the long-term recognition among many analysts of the links between these aspects at national and EU level (Faist, 1995; Parsons and Smeeding, 2006; Favell, 2008; Baldaccini et al, 2007) there has been little analysis of EU migration governing processes as a whole.[2] These governing processes are produced over time and in concrete spaces through their structured but unstable relationships in a range of changing configurations. It is the overarching, but ambiguous and sometimes contradictory configurations of recent migration governance that this chapter sets out to analyse.

Governance complexity and assembling coherence in migration policies

The question of coherence in a complex and diverse field like migration concerns, first, establishing the limits and terms of reference of policymaking, including geographical scope and extension; and second, generating the strategies, goals and action which jointly mark a complex set of interacting policies and institutions as a particular 'governable terrain' (Carmel and Harlock, 2008). To construct a policy area as governable terrain involves having a policy area recognised as an object to be governed; accumulating the actors with mutually recognised authority to act; articulating the specific policy concerns; and demarcating the policy goals and instruments which are to be contested in relation to it. That is, it requires the notional construction of some political, discursive, institutional, juridical or other degree of coherence, to create a recognisable, 'governable' terrain – in our case, the terrain of migration governance.

This is not to suggest that political action nor indeed governing requires policy or political coherence per se (see McKee, 2009). This is particularly the case in the context of the EU's 'experimentalist governance', characterised by what Sabel and Zeitlin (2010) call 'directly deliberative polyarchy'. For Sabel and Zeitlin, the EU is characterised by rule making among a range of non-hierarchically ordered actors where uncertainty (and lack of coherence) about goals is managed through governance processes which invite and produce recursive deliberation about goals, always leaving the possibility of constructing new articulations of, and solutions to, policy problems (see also also Esmark, 2007; Börzel, 2010).[3] As such, we should not expect, nor even wish for, coherence. In addition, as argued in Chapter One, given the centrality of feeling in constructing conditions of possibility for policy action, and the character of migration governance, any aim to identify the rationally coherent construction of migration governance is likely to be unsuccessful. Particular migration policies may indeed offer gross logics or 'coherent' rationales, for example in labour migration (Menz, 2009), in border control (Neal, 2009), or in development policy or foreign affairs (Lavenex and Uçarer, 2002; Boswell, 2003; Potemkina, 2005). But if, as in this chapter, the aim is to grasp the target, political force and forms of EU migration governance as a whole, there must be some accounting for how the separate and contradictory strands of policymaking in linked fields are brought together, and under what terms.

To explore how this is done, and with what effects, this chapter borrows from Newman and Clarke's (2009) treatment of governance as 'assemblage' to draw attention to the work required to assemble different elements in the process of governing a particular policy field. Policy actors are constantly engaged in the work of assembling the tools, instruments, resources and conceptualisations which define a particular mode of governance in a particular policy field. Processes of assemblage and re-assemblage are inscribed within formal and informal historicised processes and structures; they are therefore inscribed within, and themselves shape, existing power relations. This work of assemblage is especially evident where the policy field is itself relatively new, or being re-formed, in our case, from a security and justice issue securely separated from issues of free movement, to a matter of economic and social policy.

Migration versus free movement: changing boundaries of migration governance

One of the defining features of EU migration governance has been the explicit and determined institutional, legal and discursive separation of policies concerned with the migration of non-EU citizens and those concerned with the migration of EU citizens. The right to free movement of workers has been considered one of the most important rights in the EU and was established in the Treaty of Rome. With the Maastricht Treaty of 1992, this was extended to the free movement of citizens, with additional rights attached to EU citizenship, such as the right to vote in local and national elections (a right not available even for long-term resident third-country nationals [TCNs] in many member states). From the perspective of the Union's founding principles, and core purpose and activities, the difference may seem clear enough. As citizens of the Union, the citizens of member states should have the right of free movement, or the very foundational idea of a single market is violated (Martiniello, 2006, pp 313-15). However, the duality of free movement as being about the creation of the internal market, *and* about citizenship rights, means that policies relating to intra-EU migration of EU citizens have been legitimised by reference to the logics of market creation, but as the rights have extended, they have broader implications for coherence with migration policies and access to differential integration according to their citizenship status (see Morris, 2002, p 27; Carmel and Cerami, Chapter One, this volume). Moreover, while the distinction might appear to hold institutionally, legally and discursively, politically the situation is more contested and ambiguous.

First, the free movement of workers can itself be put in question as a universal right to be applied to all EU citizens. It was denied for two years to citizens of Spain, Portugal and Greece following their accession, and a multitude of restrictions were applied to the free movement of workers from the acceeding states following the 2004 and 2007 accessions. Germany and Austria still apply restrictions to citizens from the 2004 accession countries (A8), and will do so for the maximum allowable period (to 2011), while Romanians and Bulgarians also face temporary restrictions on free movement. In a political logic which reveals how far free movement has been significantly about supranationally regulated labour migration rather than about citizenship rights, these restrictions were imposed to protect labour markets and social protection systems against free movement of workers (Kvist, 2004).

Second, as Geddes (2008, pp 42-9) points out, there are several, if limited, ways in which legally resident TCNs might be able to access the supranationalised right of free movement: for example by being a dependant of an EU member state citizen, or by being a citizen of a third country which has generated a special admission agreement. Third, the social, economic and political rights do not always accrue to EU citizens working in a second member state and can be rather limited if they are one of a small number of 'posted workers' (for further discussion, see Carmel and Paul, 2009).

Fourth, and importantly from the perspective of this book, the apparently fundamentally different legal treatment of different kinds of migration which puts intra-EU migration outside migration law and into the realm of internal market governance co-exists with sometimes exclusionary and discriminatory practices at local level. As demonstrated by Woolfson (2007), and by Wilkinson and Craig in Chapter Ten (this volume), in some circumstances, the distinction between EU citizen migrants and TCNs, in conditions and terms of employment (including employment in informal labour markets), is not always as clear-cut as the free movement/migration distinction would imply. In addition, examples of the return of Romanian Roma to Romania following arson attacks in Belfast (BBC, June 2009), or the state deportation of Romanian Roma from Milan, provide indicators of a contentious policy environment, where feelings of fear and prejudice apply to migrants unsystematically, and where distinctions between EU and non-EU migrants exist legally and matter politically, but do not always provide protection from practices of social segregation and exclusion.

That this ambiguity has been considered problematic – in need of making coherent – was reflected in a pair of directives introduced in 2003 and 2004, on the rights of long-term resident TCNs, and the right to free movement by EU citizens respectively. Regarding TCNs moving to the EU, there were two directives, securing rights to family unification (Council of the European Union, 2003a), and of permanent residence, to some TCNs (Council of the European Union, 2003b). The latter directive deliberately attempts to proximate the rights of legally resident TCNs more closely to those of EU citizens, by securing their status as denizens, and generating minimum standard rights (notably the right to permanent residence after five years' legal stay, and the right, once permanently resident, to move to another member state). This right to stay is conditional on non-recourse to social assistance and employment records, and is also subject to conditions of public order and public security. Nonetheless, combined with the anti-discrimination directive, this has established a considerable rights-based orientation for legally resident TCNs.

In terms of the governance of free movement as a domain distinct from migration, the 2004 directive on rights to free movement was specifically intended to create a coherent, consistent policy from existing regulations and case law. It generated coherence by explicitly articulating the difference and the overlaps around the rights to free movement of EU citizens. Two elements remain salient: the right of the citizen and their family to move and reside in any other member state and the free movement of labour as a 'fundamental freedom of the internal market' (Council of the European Union, 2004, p 1). These are related but not the same, and as a result, the former remains conditional on non-recourse to social assistance, although consequent expulsion should not be automatic, and regarding the latter, the economically active have privileged rights of residence, access to social benefits, and, if employed, protection from expulsion (Council of the European Union, 2004, Articles 6, 7, 14). After five years' legal continuous residence in the second member state, residence becomes unconditional (Article

16), with expulsion only possible on 'serious grounds of public policy or public security', and if resident for 10 years, or if a child, only on 'imperative grounds of public security' (Article 28). With the 2003 and 2004 directives, permanent residents of the EU are permitted to become fully-fledged EU denizens – not able to access full political and citizenship rights, but clearly permitted to access rights, and to experience economic and social integration in markedly different terms to non-permanent residents, and in remarkably similar terms to EU citizens.

In the most recent legislative and programmatic developments, the 'free movement' versus 'migration' distinction nonetheless continues in law. The new Treaty on the Functioning of the EU (TFEU), ratified as part of the Lisbon Treaty in December 2009, deals with free movement in title IV, while migration is dealt with under title V, 'Freedom, Security and Justice'. Yet, under the same Treaty, the Charter on Fundamental Rights becomes part of Union law. As a result, mobility is, after all, moving into the domain of freedom, security and justice, not as part of migration policy, but as a fundamental right. The action plan set out by the European Commission to implement the five-year Stockholm Programme on 'Freedom, Security and Justice, 2010-14, makes mobility a priority as a 'core right', which 'needs to be rigorously enforced. Mobility should be enhanced by removing the barriers citizens still face' (CEC, 2010a, p 4). This appears to shift the question of free movement unambiguously out of the terrain of internal market governance, and at the same time, to mark the distinction between EU citizens and others. However, in the same action plan, TCNs are also seen as beneficiaries of the Charter (CEC, 2010a, pp 2, 6). This has the potential to substantially enhance the rights of permanent resident TCNs, and to further blur the distinction between these permanent residents and EU citizens. The remainder of this chapter reflects on how changing combinations of conditions have underpinned the construction of a governable terrain of *migration*.

'Managing migration': emerging agendas and changing architectures

Amsterdam to Lisbon: the persistence and changing place of security

It was the Treaty of Amsterdam, which came into force in 1999, via its inclusion under the heading of 'Justice and Home Affairs' in the Treaty (later 'Freedom, Security and Justice') which provided the first formal legislative role for the EU in migration policy, as opposed to the mobility policy. This was subsequent to the Dublin Convention on asylum law, and represented the consolidation of a politically informal, 'securitised' approach to border control and migration which had been emerging for some time (Guiraudon, 2000; Huysmans, 2006; Geddes, 2008). More recently, it has been argued that what is at stake is not security, but rather the idea of 'risk management' (Neal, 2009; van Munster, 2009), where the risks of public order, terrorism and cross-border crime are to be 'managed' in EU regulation. In both cases, the dominant view in the literature has been that

Amsterdam not only made migration policymaking part of EU governance, but did so in a way that privileged questions of border control, policing, expulsion and exclusion. The priorities and resources provided to common visa programmes, border control and policing activities gives credence to this perspective on the 'securitised' migration policy of the post-Amsterdam phase, especially that associated with the Tampere programme, which set out the agenda and policies for 1999-2004.

This period not only represented the zenith of Union activity in respect of security, but also its normalisation. In the period to the mid-2000s, in the production of numerous Commission reports and policy plans, the key policy and political task achieved was the introduction of 'efficient management of migration flows' as a legitimate part of EU migration governance, functionally distinct from the work of controlling, excluding and expelling undocumented ('illegal') migrants. Thus the Hague Programme (2004-09) and even the most recent Stockholm Programme, 2010-14 (Council of the European Union, 2009a), cannot be made sense of without some reference to the strong assumptions of securitised approaches to both asylum seeking and other, more explicitly 'undesirable', immigration. This applies notwithstanding the much stronger rights orientation of Stockholm (which itself emerged from the 2009 Lisbon Treaty). Bringing these two tendencies together is a large part of the work of assemblage which 'social integration' performs in migration governance.

Amsterdam was, in terms of institutional architecture for EU migration governance, a path-breaking moment, although a five-year transition period was established for moving to ordinary legislative procedures. Importantly for the evaluation of more recent developments, measures on legal immigration, even after the transition period, remained subject to unanimous agreement among member states. This of course made general lawmaking difficult, and between 2000-08 there were regular calls from the Council to the Commission to introduce draft directives regulating legal migration into the EU. But despite introducing several drafts of varying generality, hardly any were adopted by a Council hampered by the contentious domestic politics of migration and the difficulty in generating unanimous agreement (Luedtke, 2008). There were two significant exceptions directly concerned with the emergence of the 'managed migration' agenda, the first being the 2003 directive on long-term resident TCNs, and the other being the directive on the right to family reunification. There have been trenchant critiques of the family unification directive as being excessively restrictive in comparison to much existing member state legislation, and as having involved a marked reduction in the rights of refugees (Kostakopoulou, 2002; Uçarer, 2009), thus, despite its name, resting on security-based assumptions and approaches to migration governance. There have, however, been attempts to correct these problems and inconsistencies, and the question of rights to family unification seems to be priority for the Stockholm Programme (CEC, 2010a, p 6).

Furthermore, most recently, the TFEU makes an explicit legal commitment of the Union, under the area of 'Freedom, Security and Justice', to 'frame a common policy on asylum, immigration, external borders, accounting for solidarity between member states and fair to third country nationals' (Article 67[2]). This commitment is made more explicit in Article 79, which deals directly with immigration:

> The Union shall develop a common immigration policy aimed at ensuring, at all stages, the efficient management of migration flows, fair treatment of third-country nationals residing legally in member states, and the prevention of, and enhanced measures to combat, illegal immigration and trafficking in human beings. (Article 79[1])

The second part of the same Article states that according to the ordinary legislative procedure, the Union shall adopt measures to govern entry and residence, which will provide standard long-term visa and residence permits for individuals and families, define the rights of TCNs, and combat illegal immigration, unauthorised residence and trafficking. The choice of 'ordinary legislative procedure' is especially important because it (a) involves parliament in co-decision in migration governance, and (b) most importantly, it moves from requiring unanimity to qualified majority voting on legal immigration into the Union. Taken together, these two parts of Article 79 represent significant development in EU migration governance.

Ascendancy of managed migration: economism and utility

The agenda of 'managed migration' began to emerge in the EU in the wake of the adoption of the Lisbon Strategy in 2000, only a few months after the achievement of the apparently unassailable domination of securitised migration policymaking in Amsterdam. This was also when several member states developed policies to permit certain, especially high-skill, labour in-migration (notably the UK, Germany and Sweden), overturning restrictions on labour migration in place since the 1970s. 'Managed migration' assumes the necessary, and necessity of limiting, utilitarian contributions of migrants to economic growth through the efficient management of their entry and stay in a territory. It should do so by providing an incentive for (the right kind of) migrants to come to the EU, while assisting their ability to be subsumed into existing social structures via 'integration' measures, or, if less 'desirable', their return via very limited permits and 'circular migration' programmes.

Circular migration programmes – of which there are few in the EU, but which have been strongly promoted by the Commission – involve short, limited stays of migrant workers, usually to work in specific sectors, after which the migrant is required to leave, and must then wait a specified period before returning. The emphasis on circular migration for those migrants whose long-term residence is not desirable is often expressed as valuable for high-skilled migrants (see Chapter Five), but in effect, the benefits for EU member states arise from using circular migration for filling low-skilled labour market gaps. As a result, circular migration, promoted as a means to ensure that developing countries do not pay an excessive cost in the 'brain drain' of highly-skilled workers (for example, in IT or health sectors), and thus establishing the EU's appropriate liberal credentials (CEC, 2005d, 2007), seems more likely to be adopted in low-skill sectors and even seasonal work, where the loss of expertise and experience for the country of destination implied by circular migration is less severe than in high-skill sectors. The idea of circular migration is especially important in Southern Europe as a means of 'efficiently managing' migrants, by using circular migration schemes instead of using undocumented workers, who then stay and may be subject to regularisation programmes of migrant statuses when these are considered so problematic for other EU member states (OECD, 2009), and in practice can be opaque or even disadvantageous for migrants themselves (Sunderhaus, 2007; compare with Calavita, 2005; see also Chapter Six, this volume).

More concrete in terms of legal developments was the adoption in March 2009 of the European 'Blue Card' scheme (Council of the European Union, 2009b). This is an EU-wide work and residence permit, which not only regulates the rights of entry of high-skilled workers – it is designed to encourage them – with quotas for Blue Card entrants set by individual member states.[4] It also provides Blue Card holders with a privileged right of free movement in the internal market – the Card is valid for three years in the first instance, and after two years continuous employment, the holder is entitled to move to another member state to look for or to take up employment. For the first time this provides a Union-wide, Union-regulated, differentiated right of integration, and access to citizenship rights to workers on the basis of their economic value.

It is not just in relation to specific new schemes that the utilitarianism of the 'managed migration' agenda has manifested itself. Under pressure from France and Germany, the 2003 long-term residence directive included a labour market test, maintaining the focus of TCN rights as being directly associated with their utility and proven worth as workers (Groenendijk, 2007, p 443). In fact, this condition was the result of a Council compromise over originally even more virulent, labour market protectionist member state opposition to the directive, to the point where free movement rights of EU citizens could also be violated (see Luedtke, 2006, pp 435-6). In the new TFEU, part of the Article dealing with legal migration policies states that the substantial extension of EU policymaking rights in this field shall not 'affect the right of member states to determine overall numbers of admission to their member states' (Article 79[5]).

As Lavenex (2008) argues, this represents a victory for member states, but especially for Germany, for whom specific, labour market demand-driven migration policies are fundamental (see Chapter Seven, this volume; see also Menz, 2009). The result is substantial limits on the approximation of TCN and EU workers' free movement rights, to the detriment of the former (with the near exception of Blue Card holders). This tension is reflected in the Stockholm Programme, which requires a common migration policy for legal immigrants (Council of the European Union, 2009a), but where the Commission's action plan suggests this will comprise 'new and flexible frameworks for the admission of legal immigrants' enabling 'the Union to adapt to increasing mobility and to the needs of national labour markets, while respecting Member State competences in this area' (CEC, 2010a, p 6).

In addition, the importance of managing the utility of mobility and migration in European labour markets is given a new emphasis in the economic programme for the Union which replaces the Lisbon process (known as Europe 2020) (CEC, 2010a). As part of the 'flagship initiative' of policies in the 'Agenda for new skills and jobs', the third mentioned priority is 'to facilitate and promote intra-EU labour mobility ... and to promote a forward-looking and comprehensive labour migration policy which would respond in a flexible way to the priorities and needs of labour markets' (CEC, 2010b, p 17). The elision between labour mobility and labour migration policy in this 'Agenda' seems particularly salient, given the traditionally fundamental role played by the distinction between free movement ('mobility') regulations and migration policy in defining the limits and role of EU migration governance. It is also important given the enhanced role for the Commission in legal migration policy since the TFEU, and given the longstanding contestation between the Commission and some member states regarding the degree of integration of the rights of legally residing TCNs and EU citizens.

Linking utility and security via social integration

In this section we will see that the agenda of social integration of TCNs provides a way of linking and rendering coherent a terrain of migration governance which can promote the toleration of limited and specific legal immigration, and the control and exclusion of migrants (this is also clearly articulated in Article 79 of the TFEU). First, the integration of the economically useful TCNs into EU member state societies should enhance their economic and social utility. Second, the security imperative of integration policies is linked to questions of public order and socio-political integration. Effective integration can ameliorate anti-immigration public sentiment in this contentious arena, especially where public feeling and discourse appear to conflict with public economic rationales, requiring the management of one in pursuit of the other (see also the discussion on emotion and feelings in Chapter One).

This is not to say that there is not also a genuine interest in the social integration of migrants as vulnerable and excluded members of European societies. This concern has moved considerably up the political agenda in social inclusion and social protection in the last five years or so. For example, it used to be the case that in the OMC on social inclusion (later, social protection and social inclusion), migrants very often came at the end of a long list, effectively equivalising population groups in social need (for example, women, young people, people with disabilities, homeless people), or were barely considered at all (Council of the European Union, 2006). This indicated a lack of attention to the needs of migrants and migrants' specific relationships to labour markets and welfare provision in different member states.

However, a more expansive vision of integration was evident in the second half of the 2000s, in a twinned development, indicating a real attempt at creating coherence across policy domains, which gave greater priority to migrants' need for *integration as part of migration* policy, and also prioritised *migrants'* integration *in social inclusion policies*. Thus, in the Hague Programme on 'Freedom, Security and Justice' (policy programme for 2005-09), the integration of migrants moved for the first time beyond the question of supporting the victims of trafficking, to discussion of social integration in more substantial terms (CEC, 2003, 2004, 2005a, 2005b). Furthermore, in the same year, the Union established 'common basic principles' of integration. Although rather longer on the obligations than the rights of migrants, these principles also established the principle of access to education, and rights to free expression of religion. By the time the creation of a common immigration policy was gaining political ascendancy in the area of 'Freedom, Security and Justice', so was the issue of integration, complete with a budget for integration measures (see, for example, CEC, 2005c, p 12ff; Council of the European Union, 2007).

Two new developments represent significant consolidation and enhancement of these trends, and appear to embed the programme of integration as the key element around which migration governance is to cohere. First, since the 2009 Lisbon Treaty, countering social exclusion is now a legal responsibility of the Union, and the Charter of Fundamental Rights also has implications for the rights of legally resident TCNs. In consequence, the Europe 2020 social policy initiative 'European Platform against Poverty' singles out migrants as a special group, where the EU will 'develop a new agenda for [their] integration to enable them to take full advantage of their potential' (CEC, 2010b, p 18). Finally, from the more narrow view of social protection 'proper', the TFEU has a limited, but nonetheless significant statement on the role of the Union in supporting member states in establishing rights around employment conditions for legally residing TCNs (TFEU, Article 153). In even stronger terms, the recent action plan on the Stockholm Programme declares unambiguously that the Union has a responsibility to enable TCNs to 'benefit from the effective respect of the fundamental rights enshrined in the Charter of Fundamental Rights of the European Union' (CEC, 2010a, p 2).

However, the authentic agenda for the promotion of social integration is also always linked to facilitating migrants' utility, so that the justification of such 'rights' is not fundamental, but conditional on the economic contribution made: 'Robust defence of migrants' fundamental rights out of respect for our values of human dignity and solidarity will enable them to contribute fully to the European economy and society.... EU must strive for a uniform level of rights and obligations for legal immigrants comparable with that of European citizens. These rights, consolidated in an immigration code ... are essential to maximise the positive effects of legal immigration for the benefit of all stakeholders and will strengthen the Union's competitiveness' (CEC, 2010a, p 6). The integration agenda also meets utilitarian concerns regarding labour market mobility and labour market management, as we saw above with the ongoing attempts to integrate at least the free movement and labour market rights, if not the other rights of long-term resident TCNs. Coherence with the question of economic utility is also established in the valorisation of the integration, education and training for non-EU-citizen children in particular, which are subsequently to assist in securing the status and sustainability of welfare systems (see the discussion in Menz, 2006, especially pp 398-9).

In addition, the expression of interest in social integration should also not disguise the security-based origins of much of this policy. Thus 'security' is an element around which not just the control and exclusion of so-called 'illegal immigrants' but also the integration of legal immigrants can be partly assembled. The integration of migrants can be seen as addressing security concerns about public order, terrorism and larger questions of how to manage the cultural and social integration of immigrant communities, as well as anti-immigrant feeling among other publics (CEC, 2005c). The emergence of this agenda must be seen in the context not only of the Lisbon process, specific labour shortages and demography, but also in the context of terrorist bombs in Madrid and London, violent disturbances in England and France and the growing resurgence of far-right parties in the 2000s (see Boswell, 2007, on the non-securitised response to the bombings). It complements strategies pursued at national level (see, for example, Lawrence, 2006), where social integration binds together those to be integrated, and by default need not address those 'others' – the targets of securitised migration politics. A major part of the integration agenda concerns the education of non-EU citizen children which should, it is argued, not only enhance their future economic contribution (contributing to 'dynamic growth'; CEC, 2010a, p 6), but should also improve social tolerance of migration (and by implication, one assumes, of migrants) in conditions where legal migrant numbers need to increase for economic purposes (CEC, 2005c; see also OECD, 2009, p 71).

Vitally important for interpreting the place of EU migration governance in the production of differential inclusion is the impact of the separation of integration for the 'legal', 'high utility' migrants from the control of the 'illegal', supposedly unwanted. Despite the most recent statements on the rights and protection of migrants as vulnerable members of the EU, and despite the *de facto* utility of illegal employment in several national labour markets (see also Chapter Six, this volume), the social integration agenda does not address, and even disguises, the exploitation and the particular vulnerability of undocumented migrants, and of those legally resident migrants working illegally or in the informal economy. We know that it is precisely these migrants who are most in need of basic social inclusion and access to fundamental services (see Chapter Four). Yet they remain specifically excluded, as 'illegal migrants', from those able to access or legitimately claim a need or interest in social integration.

Conclusion

The emergence of EU migration governance around the three-fold distinction of utility, security and integration generates a coherent agenda, set of divisions and discursive and institutional conditions for the further construction of EU migration, which continues to cement the relationships established between free movement and migration, and between legal and illegal migration. It constructs, in effect, the governable terrain of migration – entrenching the 'management' of migration, from entry, residence, rights, integration and expulsion, where the former division between legality and illegality are joined in an integrated institutional, political and policy package at the heart of EU activities, assembled by the linking of these three elements. In consequence, at EU level, the differential integration of migrants is increasingly organised less around EU citizenship (although this remains significant), but rather around migrants' employment and their skill levels. This then affects the conditions under which employment history and long-term legal residence in the EU can be established by migrants.

This signals two political achievements. First, the valorisation of a particular self-image of the Union as socially integrative that disguises its exclusionary elements and constructs the Union as an imagined site of equality (between member states, citizens and legal residents). Second, it involves assembling EU migration governance around social integration to the point where this seems over-determined, as it simultaneously fulfils several contrasting goals from different policy fields. Thus social integration is expected to assist the contribution of migrants to economic growth, by providing an incentive for (the right kind of) migrants to come to the EU. At the same time, by assisting their ability to be subsumed into existing social structures, the agenda has the potential over time to displace contemporary problems of public order and social segregation. By permitting the integration, education and training for non-EU-citizen children, it seems to offer the possibility of securing the status and sustainability of welfare systems, and in conjunction with circular migration (for those migrants whose long-term residence is not desirable), it may provide for both high and low-skilled labour market gaps, without the ethical difficulties associated with encouraging the migration of high-skill workers from less developed countries. The social integration agenda offers an alternative strategy to regularisations, which in Southern Europe have been important mechanisms of 'migration management' but are considered problematic for other states, because social integration strategies and circular migration should resolve the problems of irregular migration and undocumented migrants in these countries.

Nonetheless, as argued at the beginning of this chapter, we should treat the EU as always inscribed within a configuration of national and local politics. EU migration governance involves the configuration and interaction of migration, free movement, social inclusion and labour market politics, broadly conceived, asserted as part of the polity and politics of the EU. But 'the EU' is always simultaneously co-produced and contested by national and local levels. The production of differential inclusion in practice is a result of simultaneous practical politics of national and local migration policymaking. That remains the subject of much of the remainder of this book.

Notes

[1] This chapter draws on some work originally presented as part of a jointly authored conference paper. An edited version of that paper, excluding this material, has been published elsewhere (Carmel and Paul, 2010). I am grateful to Regine Paul for her research assistance in preparing the conference paper and her permission to extract some of that paper here.

[2] For a first attempt at a detailed review exploring the contradictory dimensions of EU migration discourse, see Carmel and Paul (2010).

[3] Their view of the EU's polyarchy is too optimistic regarding the politically contested and hierarchical character of Union governance. Indeed I would go further even than Börzel's idea of the 'shadow of hierarchy' (2010), to talk of the heterarchy of EU governance. What both Sabel and Zeitlin, and Börzel draw attention to, is that both the Union and its policy and political outputs are subject to ongoing work of institutional and political construction among and between different policymaking levels.

[4] With appropriate documentation of qualifications, Blue Card permits are available to non-EU migrants with at least two-year employment contracts at a pay level at least three times the national minimum wage of the destination member state.

References

Baldaccini, A., Guild, E. and Toner, H. (2007) *Whose freedom, security and justice? EU immigration and asylum law and policy*, Oxford: Hart Publishing.

BBC news (2009) http://news.bbc.co.uk/1/hi/uk/8116063.stm, 24 June.

Bommes, M. and Geddes, A. (2000) *Immigration and welfare: Challenging the borders of the welfare state*, London: Routledge.

Börzel, T. (2010) 'European governance: negotiation and competition in the shadow of hierarchy', *Journal of Common Market Studies*, vol 48, no 2, pp 191-219.

Boswell, C. (2003) 'Migration and the externalities of European integration', *International Affairs*, vol 79, no 5, pp 1125-6.

Boswell, C. (2007) 'Migration control in Europe after 9/11: explaining the absence of securitization', *Journal of Common Market Studies*, vol 45, no 3, pp 589-610.

Boswell, C. (2009) 'Knowledge, legitimation and the politics of risk: the functions of research in public debates on migration', *Political Studies*, vol 57, no 1, pp 165-86.

Calavita, K. (2005) *Immigrants at the margins: Law, race, and exclusion in Southern Europe*, Cambridge: Cambridge University Press.

Carmel, E. and Harlock, J. (2008) 'Instituting the "third sector" as a governable terrain: partnership, procurement and performance in the UK', *Policy & Politics*, vol 36, no 2, pp 155-71.

Carmel, E. and Paul, R. (2009) *From stratification to bricolage: Politics, markets and migrant rights in the EU*, ECPR Biennial Conference, Potsdam, Germany.

Carmel, E. and Paul, R. (2010) 'The struggle for coherence in EU migration governance', *Rivista Politiche Sociale, Italian Journal of Social Policy*, no 1, pp 209-30.

CEC (Commission of the European Communities) (2003) *Communication on immigration, integration and employment*, COM (2003) 336 final, 3.6.2003.

CEC (2004) *Area of freedom, security and justice: Assessment of the Tampere programme and future orientations*, COM (2004) 401 final, 2.6.2004.

CEC (2005a) *Green Paper on an EU approach to managing economic migration*, COM (2004) 811 final, 11.1.2005.

CEC (2005b) *Policy plan on legal migration*, COM (2005) 669 final, 21.12.2005.

CEC (2005c) *A common agenda for integration. Framework for the integration of TCNs in the European Union*, COM (2005) 389 final, 1.9.2005.

CEC (2005d) *A strategy on the external dimension of the area of freedom, security and justice*, COM (2005) 491 final, 12.10.2005.

CEC (2007) *On circular migration and mobility partnerships between the European Union and third countries*, COM (2007) 248 final, 16.05.2007.

CEC (2010a) *Delivering an area of freedom, security and justice for Europe's citizens. Action plan implementing the Stockholm Programme*, COM (2010) 171 final, 20.4.2010.

CEC (2010b) *Europe 2020. A strategy for smart, sustainable, and inclusive growth*, COM (2010) 2020, 3.3.2010.

Council of the European Union (2003a) *Directive concerning the status of third-country nationals who are long-term residents*, 2003/109/EC.

Council of the European Union (2003b) *Directive on the right to family reunification*, 2003/86/EC.

Council of the European Union (2004) *Directive on the right of citizens of the Union and their family members to move and reside freely within the territory of the member states*, 2004/58/EC.

Council of the European Union (2006) *Objectives of the OMC for social protection and social inclusion*, March.

Council of the European Union (2007) *Council decision establishing the European Fund for the integration of third-country nationals for the period 2007 to 2013 as part of the general programme 'Solidarity and Management of Migration Flows'*, 2007/435/EC, 25.6.2007.

Council of the European Union (2009a) *The Stockholm Programme – An open and secure Europe serving and protecting the citizens*, 17024/09, 2.12.2009.

Council of the European Union (2009b) *Directive on the conditions of entry and residence of third-country nationals for the purposes of highly qualified employment*, 17426/08, 18.3.2009.

Esmark, A. (2007) 'Network management in the EU: the European Commission as network manager', in J. Torfing and M. Marcussen (eds) *Democratic network governance in Europe*, Basingstoke, Palgrave Macmillan, pp 252-72.

Faist, T. (1995) 'Boundaries of welfare states: immigrants and social rights on the national and supranational level', in R. Miles and D. Thraenhardt (eds) *Migration and European integration. The dynamics of inclusion and exclusion*, London: Pinter, pp 177-95.

Favell, A. (2008) 'The new face of East-West migration in Europe', *Journal of Ethnic and Migration Studies*, vol 34, no 5, pp 701-16.

Favell, A. and Hansen, R. (2002) 'Markets against politics: migration, EU enlargement and the idea of Europe', *Journal of Ethnic and Migration Studies*, vol 28, no 4, pp 581-601.

Geddes, A. (2008) *Immigration and European integration. Beyond Fortress Europe*, Manchester: Manchester University Press.

Groenendijk, K. (2007) 'The long-term residents directive, denizenship and integration', in A. Baldaccini, E. Guild and H. Toner (eds) *Whose freedom, security and justice? EU immigration and asylum law and policy*, Oxford: Hart Publishing, pp 429-50.

Guiraudon, V. (2000) 'European integration and migration policy: vertical policy-making as venue shopping', *Journal of Common Market Studies*, vol 38, no 2, pp 251-71.

Huysmans, J. (2006) *The politics of insecurity. Fear, migration and asylum in the EU*, London: Routledge.

Kostakopoulou, T. (2001) *Citizenship, identity and immigration in the European Union*, Manchester: Manchester University Press.

Kostakopoulou, T. (2002) 'Invisible citizens? Long term resident third country nationals in the European Union and their struggle for recognition', in R. Bellamy and A. Warleigh (eds) *Citizenship and governance in the European Union*, London: Continuum, pp 180-205.

Kvist, J. (2004) 'Does EU enlargement create a race to the bottom? Strategic interaction among EU member states in social policy', *Journal of European Social Policy*, vol 14, no 3, pp 301-18.

Lahav, G. and Guiraudon, V. (2006) 'Actors and venues in immigration control: closing the gap between political demands and policy outcomes', *West European Politics*, vol 29, no 2, pp 201-23.

Lavenex, S. (2001) 'Migration and the EU's new eastern border: between realism and liberalism', *Journal of European Public Policy*, vol 8, no 1, pp 24-42.

Lavenex, S. (2006) 'Shifting up and out: the foreign policy of European immigration control', *West European Politics*, vol 29, no 2, pp 329-50.

Lavenex, S. (2008) *Focus migration: European Union*, Focus migration papers, no 17, Hamburg: HWWI (www.focus-migration.de/European_Union.6003.0.html?&L=1).

Lavenex, S. and Uçarer, E.M. (eds) (2002) *Migration and the externalities of European integration*, Lanham, MD: Lexington Books.

Lawrence, J. (2006) 'Managing transnational Islam: Muslims and the state in Western Europe', in C. Parsons and T. Smeeding (eds) *Immigration and the transformation of Europe*, Cambridge: Cambridge University Press, pp 251–73.

Luedtke, A. (2006) 'The European Union dimension: supranational integration, free movement of persons and immigration politics', in C. Parsons and T. Smeeding (eds) *Immigration and the transformation of Europe*, Cambridge: Cambridge University Press, pp 419–41.

Luedtke, A. (2008) *Why a European Union immigration policy? A comparative study of national immigration politics and incentives for supranational delegation*, 49th Annual Convention, San Francisco.

Martiniello, M. (2006) 'Towards a proactive immigration policy?', in C. Parsons and T. Smeeding (eds) *Immigration and the transformation of Europe*, Cambridge: Cambridge University Press, pp 298–326.

McKee, K. (2009) 'Post–Foucauldian governmentality: what does it offer critical social policy analysis?', *Critical Social Policy*, vol 29, no 3, pp 465–86.

Menz, G.K. (2006) 'Useful Gastarbeiter, burdensome asylum seekers and the second wave of welfare retrenchment: exploring the nexus between migration and the welfare state', in C. Parsons and T. Smeeding (eds) *Immigration and the transformation of Europe*, Cambridge: Cambridge University Press, pp 393–418.

Menz, G.K. (2009) *The political economy of managed migration*, Oxford: Oxford University Press.

Morris, L. (2002) *Managing migration: Civic stratification and migrants' rights*, London: Routledge.

Neal, A.W. (2009) 'Securitization and risk at the EU border: the origins of Frontex', *Journal of Common Market Studies*, vol 47, no 2, pp 333–56.

Newman, J. and Clarke, J. (2009) *Publics, politics and power. Remaking the public in public services*, London: Sage Publications.

OECD (Organisation for Economic Co-operation and Development) (2009) *Workers crossing borders: A road map for managing labour migration (Part II of the International Migration Outlook 2009)*, Paris: OECD, pp 77–221.

Parsons, C. and Smeeding, T. (eds) (2006) *Immigration and the transformation of Europe*, Cambridge: Cambridge University Press.

Potemkina, O. (2005) 'A "friendly Schengen border" and illegal migration: the case of the EU and its direct neighbourhood', in J. DeBardeleben (ed) *Soft or hard borders?*, Aldershot: Ashgate, pp 165–82.

Sabel, C.F. and Zeitlin, J. (2010) 'Learning from difference. The new experimentalist architecture in the EU', in J. Zeitlin and C.F. Sabel (eds) *Experimentalist architecture in the European Union: Towards a new architecture*, Oxford: Oxford University Press, pp 1–28.

Schierup, C., Hansen, P. and Castles, S. (2006) *Migration, citizenship, and the European welfare state: A European dilemma*, Oxford: Oxford University Press.

Stone Sweet, A. and Sandholtz, W. (1998) 'Integration, supranational governance, and the institutionalisation of the European polity', in W. Sandholtz and A. Stone Sweet (eds) *European integration and supranational governance*, Oxford: Oxford University Press, pp 1-26.

Sunderhaus, S. (2007) 'Regularization programs for undocumented migrants', *Migration Letters*, vol 4, no 1, pp 65-76.

Uçarer, E.M. (2009) *Negotiating third country national rights in the European Union*, 11th Biennial International Conference of the European Union Studies Association, Marina del Rey, CA, USA.

van Munster, R. (2009) *Securitizing immigration. The politics of risk in the EU*, Basingstoke: Palgrave Macmillan.

Wallace, H., Pollack, M.A. and Young, A. (eds) (2010) *Policy-making in the European Union* (6th edn), Oxford: Oxford University Press.

Woolfson, C. (2007) 'Labour standards and migration in the New Europe: post-communist legacies and perspectives', *European Journal of Industrial Relations*, vol 13, no 2, pp 199-218.

FOUR

Human rights and the politics of migration in the European Union

Alfio Cerami

Introduction[1]

The politics of migration in the European Union (EU) is a topic that attracts increasingly scholarly attention, but is also subject to violent diatribes. The reasons are easy to understand; on the one hand, international migration produces a significant impact on the organisational and conceptual structures of European welfare systems, calling for a substantial redefinition of the main welfare functions, normative foundations, distributive priorities and key institutional features of existing national welfare arrangements, while on the other hand, and in a highly globalised environment, international migration also produces a significant impact on the governance structure of European member states, partially shifting the locus of authority from national to transnational institutions (see Chapter Three, this volume). Despite pragmatic considerations on the real possibility of EU member states to absorb a potentially increasing number of EU and non-EU migrant workers, the politics of migration in the EU also entails an international human rights dimension, often neglected by national and EU institutions. On the 60th anniversary of the United Nations (UN) Declaration of Human Rights (1948), a different, more inclusive and human rights-aware 'politics of migration' in the EU is needed. This 'new politics of migration' should look beyond the 'politics of regulation' as the current leading national and EU discourses seem to emphasise, but it should also involve a 'politics of integration' of non-EU citizens and the respect of their basic and inalienable human rights (such as the right to seek and find asylum).

As shown by the Berlusconi government's decision in May 2009 to refuse entry to Italian territorial waters of 227 'illegal' immigrants from Africa, sending them immediately back to Libya to inevitable further suffering (several other rejections have followed in the subsequent months) (BBC News, 2009; UNHCR, 2009a, 2009b; Amnesty International, 2010), the security dimension to migration policies chosen by the EU and its member states to ensure a 'manageable' and 'sustainable' migration within European borders raises several important ethical and moral questions. These questions concern the potential human rights violations that can be committed in the name of 'Fortress Europe'. In the 21st century, should the randomness of birth still dictate access to human rights, with citizens of the EU member states granted extended 'democratic benefits'[2] (see Offe, 2003), while many asylum–seeking, 'illegal' or 'undocumented' migrants are left to an unfortunate destiny? In other words, is it morally and ethically acceptable that a hierarchy of human rights beneficiaries is developed and legitimised both at national and EU level?

For the EU, these are far from irrelevant issues, since they call into question the human rights achievements of its institutions as well as those of its member states.[3] Yet, for EU institutions, international migration remains a particularly sensitive and difficult to manage problem. On the one hand, due to its multi–level governance (Hooghe and Marks, 2001), the EU finds itself in the position of constantly trying to accommodate the different interests and needs of its member states. On the other, due to its atypical political character, not corresponding to any of the systems that have emerged from the old Westphalian order,[4] the EU is also in the difficult position of defining itself by artificially removing, and then subsequently creating, new physical and conceptual boundaries (see also Bartolini, 2005; Ferrera, 2005). Europe's identity problem, as Favell (2005) has subtly defined it, is here not simply a problem of 'conceptual boundary drawing' (where does Europe really end?), but also, and perhaps even more importantly, a problem of inclusion and exclusion of citizens (who counts as Europeans?).

This chapter aims to address these issues, highlighting shortcomings, inconsistencies and more generally, human rights violations resulting from a still ambiguous 'politics of migration' in the EU. By adopting a human rights perspective, this chapter also highlights the presence of contradictory ideas, policies, programmes and philosophies, which, as the substantive content of the national and EU political discourses (see Schmidt, 2008), have influenced the communicative and coordinative actions of national and EU policymakers. As a result of an excessive attention given to security concerns (van Munster, 2009), the main argument put forward in this chapter is that a 'new politics of migration in the EU' has become a necessary and also a possible step: the EU can do much to ensure sustainable migration in full respect of human rights, launching, for example, new 'policy' venues (see Baumgartner and Jones, 1993; Guiraudon, 2000, 2003), where new ideas, interests and institutions based on universal moral respect and egalitarian reciprocity can be promoted. The aim of this chapter is, hence, not to provide a sterile critique of the shortcomings of EU policymaking, but rather, and perhaps more importantly, to highlight the prospects for future improvements.

In order to achieve this objective, this chapter proceeds as follows. The first section discusses the importance of discourses, ideas, interests, institutions and emotions in the process of EU migration policy formation. The second section then briefly introduces the citizenship dilemma that EU institutions face and, in particular, it describes the difficulties of how to make Europeans (in the sense of people with European identities) in the absence of traditional cultural, political and territorial boundaries. Finally, the third section offers some considerations on the human rights approach of the EU, proposing new ethical and moral discourses. In the conclusion, a normative critique of the existing dominant migration approach in the EU is conducted with the aim of increasing the prospects for a new, human rights–aware, migration politics.

Communicative action, discursive institutionalism and the formation of policy preferences

During the last three decades not only has the important role played by ideas and discourses in institutional and policy change been deeply explored, but also their interconnections with interests and institutions.[5] In this context, Schmidt (2008) provides a particularly comprehensive account of the drivers of institutional change, linking Habermas's *communicative action* arguments with new institutionalist explanations. She shows how ideas, as the substantive content of discourse, may be subdivided into three levels – policies, programmes and philosophies – and into two types – cognitive and normative. Policies, programmes and philosophies refer, respectively, to the policy solutions, to the specific agendas that underpin the policy solutions and to the paradigms that reflect the underlying assumptions and organising principles. For Schmidt (2008), cognitive ideas provide the guidelines and maps necessary to make policy action possible, while normative ideas refer to the values and norms that sustain and justify these. Discourse, by contrast, as the interactive process of conveying ideas, can materialise in two forms: the coordinative discourse, among policy actors, and the communicative discourse, between political actors and the public. According to Schmidt, ideas, interests and institutions are not separate and objective, but mutually constitutive and dynamic. They simultaneously structure and construct the internal preferences and actions of agents.[6]

Other important considerations that can help improve our understanding of institutional and policy change include the reflections of Pierre Bourdieu on 'policy field' (1981) and 'habitus' (1977), of Jon Elster on 'emotions' (1999, 2009) and 'rationality' (2008), of Paul Sabatier and Hank Smith Jenkins (1993) on 'epistemic communities and advocacy coalitions', and of Mark Granovetter (1985) and James March and Johan Olsen (1989) on 'social networks'. For Bourdieu (1981), a policy field is an institutional space where social and political actions take place. These are characterised by a specific *habitus* (Bourdieu, 1977), understood in terms of a set of acquired patterns of thoughts, behaviours and tastes which, subsequently, structure the perceptions and responses of agents to external challenges. Patterns of thoughts, behaviours and tastes do not emerge from an aseptic internalisation of externally induced social and institutional norms, but also have to do with the development of specific emotions. These structure and help the creation of a specified 'rationality' (Elster, 2008). As Jean de la Bruyère (2007, p 98) reminds us, 'nothing is easier for passion than to overcome reason, but its greatest triumph is to conquer a man's own interest' (quoted in Elster, 2008, p 2) and, of course, his or her pattern of behaviour. As emphasised by Elster (2008, 2009), emotions play a far from irrelevant role both in human as well as in institutional action. They influence and structure the dominant beliefs, preferences and opportunities of individuals that then lead to the preference for a determined (in our case migration) policy that institutional agents will be called to pursue. In a circular way, however, emotions also influence the actions of institutional entrepreneurs that will then go on to affect citizens' preferences (see also Chapter One, this volume). Especially in the case of migration policy, actions driven by feelings of fear, self-defence (or preventive attack), antipathy or other exclusionary and segregating sentiments towards migrants have contributed (and still contribute) to the preference for specific migration policy options, which, subsequently, arrive at the top of the political agenda. The places where preferences and a specific kind of (ir)rationality develop become, in this context, crucial, as are the interactions among the members of a particular policy community. As Sabatier and Jenkins (1993) have highlighted, in any institutionally driven process of preference formation, the role of epistemic communities and advocacy coalitions is important. The internal preferences of agents placed in key institutional environments shape future policy and institutional change through the production of new cognitive and normative ideas which underpin emergent communicative and coordinative discourses. As highlighted by Granovetter (1985) and March and Olsen (1989), economic, political and social action is entrenched in pre-existing socially driven interactions with, in Schmidt's terms, their specific communicative and coordinative discourses. To sum up, what counts in understanding institutional, policy and social change is not only the role that ideas and discourses may play, but also how institutions, strategic interests, emotions and social networks mediate and influence the formation of specific policy preferences.

The EU and the citizenship dilemma: how to 'make' Europeans

As in many other areas of EU policymaking, the establishment of a common European approach to migration has been a long and complex process of institutional and political bargaining, which has seen its core principles being developed and evolved in several intergovernmental conferences and meetings, and then being solidified in the major treaties regulating the functioning of the EU (see Bommes and Geddes, 2000; Guiraudon, 2000, 2003; Geddes, 2003, 2008). The first reference to the need for establishing a common approach to intra-European mobility was expressed in the Treaty of Rome (1957) which introduced the four key freedoms (free movement of capital, goods, services and workers) of the, at the time, European Community. Whereas the focus of the Treaty of Rome was almost solely centred on 'negative integration' (see Scharpf, 1999, 2009), that is to say, on the need to establish a European citizenship centred on economically based principles and rights, subsequent agreements and treaties have also included a security dimension. The Schengen Agreement (1985) and the Single European Act (1986) envisaged, for example, the removal of border controls so as to ensure the free movement of workers, but they also entailed special regulation for asylum-seeking, 'illegal' or 'undocumented' migrants. In the Dublin Convention (1990), the possibility of rejecting applications from asylum-seeking migrants was granted to the EU member states if the country where the migrants were coming from was addressed as 'safe'. The Treaty of Maastricht (1993) re-emphasised the security dimension of the EU migration politics, putting a primary focus on justice and home affairs through its three constituting pillars.[7] The Treaty of Maastricht clarified the issue of EU citizenship, expanding economic and social rights available for the citizens of the EU member states, but it implicitly created a hierarchy of human rights beneficiaries, excluding the majority of 'illegal' or 'undocumented' migrants access to full political, economic and social rights when not obtaining a 'legal immigrant' status in one of the EU member states (such as the right to political liberties, to a decent living standard, to social security, etc). Following this already established institutional and legislative pathway, the Amsterdam Treaty (1999) consolidated the security approach to migration regulating asylum (van Munster, 2009), immigration and external borders with the aim of creating a common European territorial and political space. Even in this case, special entitlements to the citizens of the EU member states were granted, subsequently excluding 'illegal' or 'undocumented' migrants from having access to full economic, political and social rights (see Bommes and Geddes, 2000; Geddes, 2003, 2008; Carmel and Paul, 2010).

As will be discussed in the course of this chapter, this lengthy and complex process of intergovernmental bargaining (see Guiraudon, 2000, 2003) has been characterised by an ambiguity of the EU discourse in which social construction of the 'illegal immigrant status' as well as the establishment of 'Fortress Europe' have been among the key elements for identity creation. During the years following the Treaty of Rome, substantially important rights have been granted to the citizens of the EU with the objective of creating a common European identity. This has included the free movement of workers, the portability of welfare rights and so on (see Chapter Three, this volume). Here, the exclusion of non-Europeans – even when they might have had the right as asylum seekers despite coming from a 'safe country' – has been the outcome of a contradictory exclusionary politics of migration, which, paradoxically, was functional for the construction of the European project. It clarified who belonged to the EU 'in' group and who belonged to the 'out' group. The first group primarily included citizens from the EU member states who, in this way, became a specific privileged category of workers and, subsequently, of human rights beneficiaries. The second group mainly involved citizens from non-EU member states, who were subjected to further restrictions, varying by individual member states, when entering the European continent (see Carmel and Paul, 2010).

As highlighted by Favell (2005), the dilemma that EU institutions have constantly faced has been a 'citizenship dilemma' or, in other words, the dilemma of how to 'make' Europeans in the absence of a clear political structure and territorial borders corresponding to the dictates of the old Westphalian order. Paraphrasing the famous sentence of Massimo D'Azeglio pronounced in the first parliament's meeting of the newly united Italian kingdom, once Europe was made, EU institutions and its member states still had to make Europeans, but also to decide who these Europeans really were. This process of identity building also implied, to cite Habermas (1989), a substantial transformation of the EU public sphere with new tasks and competencies that had constantly to be negotiated and acquired by EU institutions. This happened, however, in the absence of a clear 'politics of migration', where ethical and moral principles could openly be discussed and negotiated with the public, but were instead simply implemented through subsequent negotiations of policies with representatives of the EU member states and security officials. As will be argued, this 'policy without politics' strategy at the EU level followed by a 'politics without policy' strategy at national level, captured by Vivien Schmidt (2006) in her *Democracy in Europe*, has helped increase the 'democratic deficit' of the EU (see Follesdal and Hix, 2006), negatively affecting the lives of several million non-EU migrants. In fact, while it can be affirmed that, from a purely pragmatic perspective, and due to the 'negative integration' (Scharpf, 1999, 2009) approach of EU institutions, the EU has succeeded in building its citizenship prerogatives around the notion of an 'economic citizenship' which allowed extended human rights for most of the citizens of its member states (Everson, 1995; Wiesner, 2007); the human rights prerogatives for 'illegal' or 'undocumented' migrants have, necessarily, become a second order, if not even a third order, priority. This has occurred in spite of some positive results achieved by EU asylum laws to 'upgrade' domestic asylum laws in some member states (such as Estonia, Hungary, Latvia, Poland and Slovenia) (Thielemann and El-Enany, 2009).[8]

But how do we explain the security approach to migration chosen by EU institutions and its member states? How have national policymakers succeeded in exporting their concerns on national security at EU level? And why and how has it been possible, accepting that a partial shift from traditional security concerns is recently occurring (see Chapter Three, this volume), to find a new agreement among substantially different economic interests and needs emerging at EU level and among the member states of the EU? The following section addresses this issue.

New politics of migration of the EU: from 'venue shopping' to 'venue launching'

As described earlier, the EU approach to migration has, since its inception, favoured the conception of an 'economic citizenship' anchored to the single market. Ambiguously, the EU approach to migration has, on the one hand, been functional to the European project, creating simultaneously a widened and deepened Europe for EU citizens, while on the other, it subsequently resulted in the exclusion of many non-EU citizens from the single market (see the discussion on Schengen and 'Fortress Europe', Chapter Three). As shown by a recent study by Dehousse et al (2009), the market-oriented approach of the EU has not dramatically changed over time, with the legislative focus during the entire history of the EU integration project being on the creation of the single market and, in particular, in the areas of economic regulation, the harmonisation of the internal market and agricultural policy.

Using the concept of 'policy venue', Virginie Guiraudon (2000, 2003) has provided an extremely valuable explanation of the reasons behind the adoption of a particular migration policy approach. While the concept of 'policy venue', first developed by Baumgartner and Jones (1993, p.32), refers to 'institutional locations where authoritative decisions are made concerning a given issue', 'venue shopping' used by Guiraudon (2000, 2003), emphasises the actors' strategies, also taking into account the rule-bound context to which actors respond. She argues that actors seek new venues when they need to adapt to institutional constraints in a changing environment, but in order to do so, they must resort to new framing processes or policy images. Hence, according to Guiraudon, the importance for the policy process does not simply lie in institutional locations, but also in the human agency and associated interests, ideas and discourses that these actors promote (see also Schmidt, 2006, 2008). As a result, the key factors that help explain the final implementation of a specific policy option include not only the institutional locations (policy venues), but also agenda-setting procedures, leading ideas and discourses as well as the transnationalisation of national policymaking (see also Lavenex, 2006). Needless to say, the emotions of agents have played a crucial role here, since they have influenced dominant beliefs. Especially in the case of migration policies, these have corresponded to the defence and strengthening of EU citizens' rights in the hope of creating a larger and more secure Europe. It can therefore be affirmed that the possibilities of policy actors to buy ('shopping') a particular *policy instrument*[9] (such as border control measures or those aimed at preserving the already existing level of socio-economic security of EU citizens) have depended on the availability of this *policy instrument* in a particular arena, and also on the consensus that has been socially constructed among the actors.

This explanatory approach is helpful, in order to understand EU migration policies, for several reasons. It highlights the complex and multi-faceted role of EU policymaking institutions, as well as the associated interests, ideas, discourses and emotions. It also sheds light on the limits and perspectives of EU future innovative policies. These are linked to the consensus that can be found among a specific epistemic community and that, subsequently, influence the implementation of policies. In this context, Lavenex and Uçarer (2004) have provided an interesting discussion of the different types of Europeanisation of migration policies taking place at national level. These types of Europeanisation have varied, from fully voluntary to more constrained forms of adaptation, including a variety of modes such as unilateral emulation, adaptation by externality and policy transfer through conditionality (Lavenex and Uçarer, 2004, p 417). While for the cases of adaptation through unilateral emulation and externality the process of policy transfer is the consequence of adaptation started by a third party (although no formalised requirement exists), in the cases of policy transfer through conditionality (either when the changes fit domestic interests or occur under pressure), adaptation takes place due to the insistence of the EU, which plays the key role of policy entrepreneur (Lavenex and Uçarer, 2004, pp 420-1).

The reasons that push a country to adopt or reject a particular policy promoted by EU institutions can, therefore, be numerous. They can include, for example, the presence or absence of *institutional mis/fit* between the policy instrument promoted and the already existing institutional set-up of the implementing country (Börzel and Risse, 2003). Despite the presence of undeniable shortcomings and clear institutional difficulties, the EU has often succeeded in playing the important role of 'policy innovator'. In more than one case, the EU Commission, with the support of individual countries, has been able to propose and promote new policy ideas which other member states have been forced to accept in order to ensure the continuation of the European project (beneficial for all) (the 2004 enlargement of the EU is here the most emblematic example). Unfortunately, this important role as policy innovator has only to some extent involved migration policies. Due to the multi-level governance structure of the EU and to an ambiguous 'shadow of a hierarchy' between market and institutional priorities (Börzel, 2010), the Commission and the European Parliament have often been in the difficult position of not being able to 'create' autonomous and durable 'policy venues' or 'shopping venues' – that is, institutional locations where new policy ideas can be presented and sold. For the most part, each attempt at 'venue launching' has, in fact, been successful only when an agreement among all different views was found in intergovernmental conferences and meetings. The next and final section briefly highlights the difficulties of the EU approach to migration, while providing alternative arguments that can be promoted by EU institutions to launch new 'policy' and 'shopping' venues, so as to promote a different and more human rights-friendly approach to migration.

Some considerations on the human rights approach of the EU

As discussed above, one of the key features of the EU approach to migration has been its functionality in the construction of the European project. In the absence of clear territorial, political and cultural boundaries to delimit the frontiers of the EU, EU institutions and its member states have seen, in the virtual construction of a 'Fortress Europe', a way to resolve the institution's identity problem. This has included a simultaneous process of widening and deepening its borders through an active expansion of EU citizens' rights, but it has also resulted in a subsequent variable and uneven exclusion of asylum seekers, 'illegal' or 'undocumented' migrants from access to the single market. This simultaneous inclusive and exclusive boundary-building approach of the EU, accurately analysed by Bartolini (2005) in *Restructuring Europe*, has entailed, however, several negative connotations. Based on a Westphalian conception of the nation state, but applied to a supranational post-Westphalian entity with no stable historical, political, socio-economic and cultural borders, it has tended to produce inconsistencies and contradictions among the different areas of the political and public sphere. In the new globalised world, a different conceptual understanding of borders seems to be needed, with the locus of authority that necessarily has to include transnational environments, but also involving different peoples (*Völker*). This also implies the political, economic, cultural and social acceptance of political, economic, cultural and social diversities. In addition, the Westphalian conception of the modern state apparently assumed by EU institutions has been demonstrated to be obsolete also in terms of national solidarities, since the boundaries between national and transnational have been blurred by the emergence of new global risks (Heidenreich, 2006; Magnusson and Stråth, 2007).

Here, the issue at stake concerns how to harmonise different conceptions of national solidarities, which grant different types of economic, citizens' and welfare rights into a common European solidarity capable of accommodating different interests and needs. The EU, as a *sui generis* political entity – recall, for example, Jacques Delors' definition of the EU as an 'unidentified political object', Giandomenico Majone's (1994) *regulatory state*, Philippe Schmitter's (2000) 'condominio', John Ruggie's (1993) 'first truly postmodern political form', Jan Zielonka's (2006) 'neo-medieval empire', Fritz Scharpf's (2007) 'government of governments' or Vivien Schmidt's (2006) *regional state* (see also Graziano and Vink, 2007), to quote but a few – has based its legitimacy on forms of post-national or transnational solidarities that, in principle, transcended national borders, but that, in practice, have, for the largest part, been provided to a restricted circle of human rights beneficiaries, corresponding to the citizens of the EU member states residing in EU territory, even though some timid attempts to privilege some group of migrants, such as asylum seekers, have recently been conducted (see also the considerations in Geddes, 2008).

From a moral and ethical perspective, by artificially closing their borders to non-EU citizens, EU institutions have been confronted not only with a 'liberal paradox' according to which the logic of liberalism of openness promoted by all directorate-generals has corresponded to a political and legal logic of closure for asylum-seeking, 'illegal' or 'undocumented' migrants (Hollifield, 2004), but also to a 'human rights paradox', according to which one individual has received by birth the right to emigrate, as ratified in the 1948 UN Declaration of Human Rights, but not a right to immigrate which is at the discretion of the destination country (Dummett, 1992; Benhabib, 2004).

Benhabib's (2004, 2006) considerations on the ethical and moral dimension of new immigration politics/policies can be helpful here to improve the prospects for a future more inclusive and human rights-aware migration politics in the EU. As the author correctly reminds us, 'the right to hospitality' already discussed by Immanuel Kant ([1795] 1957) in 'Perpetual peace', is not a matter of philanthropy, but a matter of inalienable rights that all human beings possess. For Benhabib, in fact, new forms of post-national or transnational solidarity are not only necessary in the 21st century if the full benefits of globalisation want to be obtained (Benhabib et al, 2007; see also Beckert et al, 2004), but they also do not necessarily represent a threat to national identity.

The multi-faceted character of EU identities has already been emphasised by several scholars working on the different dimensions of EU citizenship and, in particular, by Medrano (2003), with his path-breaking study on the attitudes to European integration in Germany, Spain and in the UK and by Kastoryano (2007), with her investigation on 'transnational nationalism'. New forms of transnational citizenship (Bauböck, 1994), multiculturalism and immigration rights can, therefore, not only be envisaged at national and EU level, but are, despite the conceptual dilemmas of a double national and transnational citizenship identification (Duchesne, 2008), necessary for the continuation of the European project (Kastoryano, 2009).

As highlighted by Antoine Pécoud and Paul de Guchteneire (2007, pp 9-10), citizenship is a birthright that is difficult to justify (Carens, 1987, quoted in Pécoud and de Guchteneire, 2007, p 9), since it is impossible to justify priority given to some group to the detriment of the whole. Hence, continuing emphasis on restrictions to migration would not only contradict the spirit of liberalism and of globalisation, but would also contradict the basic assumptions of human rights which are inalienable and to be applied to all human beings regardless of their country of origin or residence. As argued elsewhere (Cerami, 2010), as no order among human rights can be conducted (it is impossible to state, for example, that the right to sufficient food comes before the right of not being sexually abused), so also no list of beneficiaries (whether country nationals or third-country nationals) can be made. Most importantly, in terms of human rights beneficiaries, concerns about citizenship conceptions based on *ius soli*, *ius sanguinis* or *ius domicili* seem to be partly unjustified here, since the basic and inalienable human rights that an individual possesses transcend national boundaries and cannot be applied to a single territory. To be clear, however, as Joseph Weiler has powerfully elucidated (2009, p 111):

> The real problem of the Community is the absence of a human rights policy [and politics] with everything this entails: A commissioner, a directorate general, a budget, and a horizontal action plan for making those rights already granted by the treaties and judicially protected by the various levels of European Courts effective. Much of the human rights story, and its abuse, takes place far from the august halls of courts. Most of those whose rights are violated have neither knowledge nor means to seek judicial vindication. The Union does not need more rights on its lists, or more lists of rights. What is mostly needed are programs and agencies to make rights real, not simply negative interdictions that courts can enforce.

If the EU, as a new transnational political entity, has to be sustained over time, new ethical and normative principles based on the full respect of extended human rights are urgently needed. The establishment of a new 'normative discourse' (Benhabib, 2004, 2006; see also Benhabib et al, 2007) based on new 'normative ideas' could be an important step here for further economic and social progress in the EU.[10] Universal moral respect and egalitarian reciprocity (Benhabib, 2004) could, in fact, easily replace the security or pragmatic discourses present in 'policy' and 'shopping' venues and intergovernmental conferences shift the debate from what is seen as a feasible solution in terms of a supposed pragmatic philanthropic hospitality (how many migrants can we accept each year in our territory?) to what is morally and ethically acceptable in terms of inalienable universal human rights (how many migrants are we ethically and morally justified to condemn to unavoidable further sufferings?). As highlighted by Bigo (1996), a different approach to migration could, in this case, become a crucial policy instrument for achieving EU future strategic and security objectives (see also Chebel d'Appollonia and Reich, 2008). The importance of economic and social remittances for security issues and international peace have been constantly reaffirmed in several studies (see, for instance, Faist, 2008), and, as Rodrik (2005) has powerfully demonstrated, free migration would reduce poverty world-wide and the associated conflicts and tensions, more than free trade or wrongly associated development aid strategies.

In this process of international modernisation and democratisation, the EU can do much. Immigrants' social rights depend not only on immigration regimes, but also on the welfare regime typology that a country has developed (Sainsbury, 2006; see also Geddes, 2008). Even though the impact of the EU on national welfare states has not been great, it is still in the position of contributing to its reform process by developing new policy priorities as well as by proposing changes in institutions and organisations that EU member states are called to implement (see Weiler, 2009; and the earlier discussion in this chapter). Shaping perceptions among the member states on international migration can also have important effects on the social construction of 'good' and 'bad' types of migration (thus reducing the development of hostile emotions towards immigrants). Here, it should not be forgotten that what is now understood as 'legal' and 'illegal' migrants has, at the end, been the product of a socially and discursively constructed reality promoted by security or excessively pragmatic officials, who are not rarely moved by an irrational emotional attachment to security or economic concerns. In fact, as van Munster (2009, p 30) has emphasised, 'being-without-documents is not illegal until it is discursively produced as such' with the subsequent 'illegalization of undocumentedness [that] has made it possible for undocumented immigration to be identified, categorized and managed as a dangerous population' (p 31). Lastly, since the reasons why people migrate are manifold (they include economic and political reasons, but also cultural and colonial linkages) (Castles and Miller, 2009; see also Chapters Five, Nine and Eleven, this volume), the EU, as a supranational entity, could also help move the debate on current migration rights beyond ambiguous considerations based on territorial belonging (either based on *ius soli*, *ius sanguinis* or *ius domicili*), to include elements of transnational solidarity (see Beckert et al, 2004).

Conclusion

This chapter has emphasised the importance of establishing a new migration politics in the EU based on new normative, moral and ethical principles, which fully take into account the changes in the globalised world. In contraposition to an approach where migration is based on an old Westphalian conception, this chapter has called the attention of EU institutions to the need to look beyond solely national solidarities and identities, launching new 'policy' and 'shopping' venues where new innovative communicative actions can take place. The results of this study demonstrate that 'venue launching' has become a crucial task, not only in finding a response to the democratic and human rights deficit that EU institutions are currently facing, but also, being functional to the European project, in resolving Europe's identity problem through the creation of new more inclusive transnational identities and solidarities. Paraphrasing Jürgen Habermas (1981), *new EU discourses based on new transnational normative, moral and ethical arguments* that emphasise universal moral respect and egalitarian reciprocity could not simply be envisaged in order to promote a different politics of migration, but also, to recall Bourdieu's (1981), new transnational 'policy fields' of social power, could be successfully put in place in order to ensure that no more human rights violations can be committed in the name of Europe, thereby fostering a different and more cosmopolitan conception of EU citizenship.

Notes

[1] I would like to thank Vivien Schmidt for extremely valuable discussions on the role of ideas and discourses in institutional change, Emma Carmel, and an anonymous reviewer for helpful comments on immigration policies in the EU.

[2] According to Claus Offe (2003), *democratic benefits* refer to all those benefits that facilitate the inclusion of citizens in society and that legitimise and stabilise the existence of a democracy. These *democratic benefits* include, for example, political liberties, and also having access to a sufficient income or to decent living standards.

[3] For a critical discussion of the human rights approach of the EU and its member states, see several assessments and press briefings of the UN Refugee Agency (UN High Commissioner for Refugees, UNHCR) available at www.unhcr.org/. In the specific context of African migration, see also Gebrewold (2007).

[4] The Westphalian order has been centred on the concept of nation-state sovereignty and, in particular, it has emphasised territoriality and domestic authority as natural elements for identity building. In the Westphalian order, nation-states as natural sources of citizenship therefore correspond to a group of people united by language and culture while sharing a similar territory.

[5] See, for instance, Habermas's (1981) *Theory of communicative action*. See also Campbell and Pedersen (2001), Hay (2006) and Schmidt (2006, 2008).

[6] For a more detailed description on the mechanisms of institutional change, see Cerami (2009, pp 37-41).

[7] The three constituting pillars of the Treaty of Maastricht are: (1) community; (2) common foreign and security policy; and (3) justice and home affairs.

[8] In certain cases, European cooperation on asylum has curtailed regulatory competition among member states and in doing so it has, to some extent, succeeded in halting the race to the bottom in protection standards in the EU (Thielemann and El-Enany, 2009). However, in terms of the real respect of human rights evidenced by member states' practices, the achievements of EU institutions remain limited.

[9] On the concept of *policy instrument*, see Lascoumes and Le Galès (2007).

[10] For an interesting discussion on progress, see Offe (2009).

References

Amnesty International (2010) *Amnesty International report 2010. The state of the world's human rights*, London: Amnesty International.

Bartolini, S. (2005) *Restructuring Europe. Centre formation, system building, and political structuring between the nation state and the European Union*, Oxford: Oxford University Press.

Bauböck, R. (1994) *Transnational citizenship: Membership and rights in international migration*, Aldershot: Edward Elgar.

Baumgartner, F. and Jones, B. (1993) *Agendas and instability in American politics*, Chicago, IL: Chicago University Press.

BBC News (2009) 'Italy turns rescued migrants back', Friday, 8 May (http://news.bbc.co.uk/2/hi/europe/8037803.stm).

Beckert, J., Eckert, J., Kohli, M. and Streeck, W. (eds) (2004) *Transnationale Solidarität: Chancen und Grenzen* [*Transnational solidarity: Chances and limits*], Frankfurt/New York: Campus.

Benhabib, S. (2004) *The rights of others: Aliens, residents, and citizens*, Cambridge: Cambridge University Press.

Benhabib, S. (2006) *Another cosmopolitanism*, Oxford: Oxford University Press.

Benhabib, S., Shapiro, I. and Petranović, D. (eds) (2007) *Identities, affiliations, and allegiances*, Cambridge: Cambridge University Press.

Bigo, D. (1996) *Polices en réseaux. L'expérience européenne* [*Policies in networks. The European experience*], Paris: Presses de Sciences Po.

Bommes, M. and Geddes, A. (eds) (2000) *Welfare and immigration: Challenging the borders of the welfare state*, London: Routledge.

Börzel, T. (2010) 'European governance: negotiation and competition in the shadow of hierarchy', *Journal of Common Market Studies*, vol 48, no 2, pp 191-219.

Börzel, T.A. and Risse, T. (2003) 'Conceptualising the domestic impact of Europe', in K. Featherstone and C.M. Radaelli (eds) *The politics of Europeanization*, Oxford: Oxford University Press, pp 55-78.

Bourdieu, P. (1977) *Outline of theory and practice*, Cambridge: Cambridge University Press.

Bourdieu, P. (1981) 'La représentation politique: éléments pour une théorie du champ politique' [Political representation: elements for a theory of the political field], *Actes de la Recherche en Sciences Sociales*, vol 36/37, pp 3-24.

Campbell, J.L. and Pedersen, O.K. (2001) 'Introduction', in J.L. Campbell and O.K. Pedersen (eds) *The rise of neoliberalism and institutional analysis*, Princeton, NJ: Princeton University Press, pp 1-25.

Carens, J.H. (1987) 'Aliens and citizens: the case for open borders', *The Review of Politics*, vol 44, no 2, pp 251-73.

Carmel, E. and Paul, R. (2010) 'The struggle for coherence in EU migration governance', *Rivista delle Politiche Sociali*, no 1, pp 209-30.

Castles, S. and Miller, M.J. (2009) *The age of migration. International population movements in the modern world* (4th edn), New York: Guilford Press.

Cerami, A. (2009) 'Mechanisms of institutional change in Central and Eastern European welfare state restructuring', in A. Cerami and P. Vanhuysse (eds) *Post-communist welfare pathways. Theorizing social policy transformations in Central and Eastern Europe*, Basingstoke: Palgrave Macmillan, pp 35-52.

Cerami, A. (2010) 'Human security in the Russian Federation', *Journal of Human Security*, vol 6, no 2, pp 7-27.

Chebel d'Appollonia, A. and Reich, S. (2008) *Immigration, integration and security: America and Europe in comparative perspective*, Pittsburgh, PA: University of Pittsburgh Press.

Dehousse, R., Deloche-Gaudez, F. and Jacquot, S. (eds) (2009) *Que fait l'Europe?*, [*What does Europe do?*] Paris: Sciences Po Les Presses.

de la Bruyère, J. (2007) *The characters*, Translated by Henry van Laun, Whitefish, MT: Kessinger Publishing.

Duchesne, S. (2008) 'Waiting for European identity…: preliminary thoughts about the identification process with Europe', *Perspectives on European Politics and Society*, vol 9, no 4, pp 397-410.

Dummett, A. (1992) 'The transnational migration of people seen from within a natural law tradition', in B. Barry and R.E. Goodin (eds) *Free movement: Ethical issues in the transnational migration of people and money*, New York and London: Harvester Wheatsheaf, pp 169-80.

Elster, J. (1999) *Alchemies of the mind*, Cambridge: Cambridge University Press.

Elster, J. (2008) *Reason and rationality*, Princeton: Princeton University Press.

Elster, J. (2009) 'Emotions', in P. Hedström &and P. Bearman (eds), *The Oxford handbook of analytical sociology*, Oxford: Oxford University Press, pp 51-71.

Everson, M. (1995) 'The legacy of the market citizen', in J. Shaw and G. More (eds) *The new legal dynamics of the European Union*, Oxford: Clarendon Press, pp 73-90.

Faist, T. (2008) 'Migrants as transnational development agents: an inquiry into the newest round of the migration–development nexus', *Population, Space and Place*, vol 14, no 1, pp 21-42.

Favell, A. (2005) 'Review article: Europe's identity problem', *West European Politics*, vol 28, no 5, pp 1109-16.

Ferrera, M. (2005) *The boundaries of welfare. European integration and the new spatial politics of social protection*, Oxford: Oxford University Press.

Follesdal, A. and Hix, S. (2006) 'Why there is a democratic deficit in the EU', *Journal of Common Market Studies*, vol 44, no 3, pp 533-62.

Gebrewold, B. (ed) (2007) *Africa and Fortress Europe. Threats and opportunities*, Aldershot: Ashgate.

Geddes, A. (2003) *The politics of migration and immigration in Europe*, London: Sage Publications.

Geddes, A. (2008) *Immigration and European integration. Beyond Fortress Europe?* (2nd edn), Manchester and New York: Manchester University Press.

Granovetter, M. (1985) 'Economic action and social structure: the problem of embeddedness', *American Journal of Sociology*, vol 91, no 3, pp 481-510.

Graziano, P. and Vink, M.P. (eds) (2007) *Europeanization: New research agendas*, Basingstoke: Palgrave Macmillan.

Guiraudon, V. (2000) 'European integration and migration policy: vertical policy-making as venue shopping', *Journal of Common Market Studies*, vol 38, no 2, pp 251-71.

Guiraudon, V. (2003) 'The constitution of a European immigration policy domain: a political sociology approach', *Journal of European Public Policy*, vol 10, no 2, pp 263-82.

Habermas, J. (1981) *The theory of communicative action. Volume one, Reason and the rationalization of society*, Boston, MA: Beacon Press.

Habermas, J. (1989) *The structural transformation of the public sphere*, Cambridge, MA: MIT Press.

Hay, C. (2006) 'Constructivist institutionalism', in R.A.W. Rhodes, S.A. Binder and B.A. Rockman (eds) *The Oxford handbook of political institutions*, Oxford: Oxford University Press, pp 56-74.

Heidenreich, M. (2006) 'Die Europäisierung sozialer Ungleichheiten zwischen nationaler Solidarität, europäischer Koordinierung und globalem Wettbewerb' [The Europeanisation of social inequalities between national solidarity, European coordination and global competition], in M. Heidenreich, *Die Europäisierung sozialer Ungleichheit. Zur transnationalen Klassen und Sozialstrukturanalyse*, [*The Europeanization of social inequality. On transnational classes and analysis of social structure*] Frankfurt am Main: Campus.

Hollifield, J.F. (2004) 'The emerging migration state', *International Migration Review*, vol 38, no 3, pp 885-912.

Hooghe, L. and Marks, G. (2001) *Multi-level governance and European integration*, Lanham, MD: Rowman and Littlefield.

Kant, I. ([1795] 1957) 'Perpetual peace. Translated by Lewis White Beck', in L. White Beck, *On history*, Indianapolis, IN and New York: Library of Liberal Arts.

Kastoryano, R. (2007) 'Transnational nationalism: redefining nation and territory', in S. Benhabib, I. Shapiro and D. Petranović (eds) *Identities, affiliations, and allegiances*, Cambridge: Cambridge University Press, pp 159-80.

Kastoryano, R. (2009) 'Introduction "multiculturalism": an identity for Europe?', in R. Kastoryano (ed) (translated by Susan Emmanuel) *An identity for Europe. The relevance of multiculturalism in EU construction*, Basingstoke: Palgrave Macmillan, pp 1-26.

Lascoumes, P. and Le Galès, P. (2007) 'Introduction: understanding public policy through its instruments – from the nature of instruments to the sociology of public policy instrumentation', *Governance: An International Journal of Policy, Administration, and Institutions*, vol 20, no 1, pp 1-21.

Lavenex, S. (2006) 'Shifting up and out: the foreign policy of the European immigration control', *West European Politics*, vol 29, no 2, pp 329-50.

Lavenex, S. and Uçarer, E.M. (2004) 'The external dimension of Europeanization. The case of immigration policies', *Cooperation and Conflict: Journal of the Nordic International Studies Association*, vol 39, no 4, pp 417-43.

Magnusson, L. and Stråth, B. (eds) (2007) *European solidarities. Tensions and contentions of a concept*, Brussels: P.I.E. Peter Lang.

Majone, G. (1994) 'The rise of the regulatory state in Europe', *West European Politics*, vol 17, no 3, pp 78-102.

March, J.G. and Olsen, J.P. (1989) *Rediscovering institutions: The organizational basis of politics*, New York: Free Press.

Medrano, J.D. (2003) *Framing Europe: Attitudes to European integration in Germany, Spain, and the United Kingdom*, Princeton, NJ: Princeton University Press.

Offe, C. (2003) *Demokratisierung der Demokratie. Diagnosen und Reformvorschläge* [*Democratisation of democracy. Diagnosis and suggestions for reforms*], Frankfurt/New York: Campus Verlag.

Offe, C. (2009) 'What, if anything, may we mean by "progressive" politics today?', Unpublished, Berlin: Hertie School of Governance.

Pécoud, A. and de Guchteneire, P. (eds) (2007) *Migration without borders. Essays on the free movement of people*, Oxford and New York: Berghahn Books.

Rodrik, D. (2005) 'Flexible globalizations', in M.M. Weinstein (ed) *Globalisation: What's new?*, New York: Council on Foreign Relations/Columbia University Press, pp 196-213.

Ruggie, J.G. (1993) 'Territoriality and beyond: problematizing modernity in international relations', *International Organization*, vol 47, no 1, pp 139-75.

Sabatier, P.A. and Smith Jenkins, H. (eds) (1993) *Policy change and learning: An advocacy coalition approach*, Boulder, CO: Westview Press.

Sainsbury, D. (2006) 'Immigrants' social rights in comparative perspective: welfare regimes, forms of immigration and immigration policy regimes', *Journal of European Social Policy*, vol 16, no 3, pp 229-44.

Scharpf, F.W. (1999) *Governing in Europe: Effective and democratic?*, Oxford: Oxford University Press.

Scharpf, F.W. (2007) *Reflections on multilevel legitimacy*, MPIfG Working Paper 07/3, Cologne: Max Planck Institut für Gesellschaftsforschung.

Scharpf, F.W. (2009) '*The double asymmetry of European integration or: why the EU cannot be a social market economy*', MPIfG Working Paper 09/12, Cologne: Max Planck Institut für Gesellschaftsforschung.

Schmidt, V.A. (2006) *Democracy in Europe. The EU and national polities*, Oxford: Oxford University Press.

Schmidt, V.A. (2008) 'Discursive institutionalism: the explanatory power of ideas and discourse', *Annual Review of Political Science*, vol 11, pp 303-26.

Schmitter, P.C. (2000) *How to democratize the European and why bother*, London: Roman & Littlefield.

Thielemann, E. and El-Enany, N. (2009) 'Beyond Fortress Europe: how European cooperation has strengthened refugee protection', Paper prepared for the European Union Studies Association's 11th Biennial International Conference, Marina Del Rey, Los Angeles, 23-25 April.

UNHCR (United Nations High Commissioner for Refugees) (2009a) 'Follow-up from UNHCR on Italy's push-backs', Briefing Notes, 12 May, Geneva: UNHCR (www.unhcr.org/4a0966936.html).

UNHCR (2009b) 'UNHCR interviews asylum seekers pushed back to Libya', Briefing Notes, 14 July, Geneva: UNHCR (www.unhcr.org/4a5c638b6.html).

van Munster, R. (2009) *Securitizing immigration. The politics of risk in the EU*, Basingstoke: Palgrave Macmillan.

Weiler, J.H.H. (2009) 'Human rights, constitutionalism, and integration: iconography and fetishism', in R. Kastoryano (ed) (translated by Susan Emmanuel) *An identity for Europe. The relevance of multiculturalism in EU construction*, Basingstoke: Palgrave Macmillan, pp 103-14.

Wiesner, C. (2007) *Bürgerschaft und Demokratie in der EU*, Berlin: LIT Verlag.

Zielonka, J. (2006) *Europe as Empire: The nature of the enlarged European Union*, Oxford: Oxford University Press.

FIVE

Labour migration and labour market integration: causes and challenges

Bent Greve

Introduction

> Differences in net economic advantages, chiefly differences in wages, are the main cause of migration. (Sir John Hicks, 1932, quoted in Borjas, 2000, p 3)

The quote by Sir John Hicks reflects the conventional wisdom of what is the main cause of migration, within and across borders. Even though there might be some truth in the statement, other factors also play an important role when it comes to understanding the complex patterns related to migration and human mobility. The context and theoretical starting point in Hicks' analysis is, in fact, based on traditional microeconomic theory, which emphasises the rational, utility-maximising individual (for a discussion, see, for instance, Borjas, 1994, 2000; Bonin et al, 2008; Krieger, 2008). This chapter interprets this approach and discusses other competing explanations. As will be shown, a critical view of the classical economy-driven explanations to migration can offer a much broader understanding of key migration patterns while providing insights into the factors that can facilitate or hinder migration, such as different institutional structures. One of the key arguments of this chapter is, in fact, that institutions and policies play an important role with regard to migration, even though they have been rather neglected elements in more classical rational choice-oriented economic approaches.

In order to substantiate this argument, this chapter first presents the classic push and pull factors related to legal and illegal migration. It also highlights their impact on sending and receiving countries as well as on different welfare states. By so doing, the chapter lays the foundation for a discussion about how different sectors of the labour market (agricultural, industrial, service, high/low skill) shape different forms of inclusion and exclusion of migrant workers. This seems to be particularly important if the context of different nationally embedded labour market traditions is to be considered. Important differences in labour integration also exist in terms of the gender segregation in the labour market and, more specifically, the degree of integration seems to depend on the different sectors in which men and women are working (such as construction and care). The chapter, hence, aims to address the question of the differential impact that national welfare and labour market policies may have on migration, directly or indirectly. It reviews legal labour migration as the archetypal migration by 'choice', which should fit most closely with rational choice theories, and examines the causes and the challenges it poses for societies of origin and destination. It queries the explanatory value of economic factors, such as differences in income or living standards, and challenges classical economic migration theory and labour market theory based on rational choice economic-maximising arguments. The case is made for the importance of several alternative factors that exert a substantial impact on labour migration, arguing that cultural and social factors can also play a determining role, influencing both the decisions of labour migrants and the main patterns of their migration.

Variations in migration and labour market integration

Despite increasing efforts by national and international institutions, figures and data on migration are often contrasting (compare, for example, data from the Organisation for Economic Co-operation and Development [OECD], International Labour Organization [ILO] and European Union [EU]). This creates several important analytical problems for assessing migration patterns, including reliability and comparability of the data (see also Marti and Rodenas, 2007; Chapter Two, this volume). As a result, this chapter sets out to highlight key *explanations* for a range of *types* of labour migration (see Figure 5.1), rather than empirically comparing them.

Migration, including its main drivers, cannot, in fact, be understood in simple terms, for example, taking into account only the mobility of an individual from, let's say, point A (the country of origin) to point B (the destination country). Migration is a complex and multi-dimensional process, and is therefore neither a single event nor a one-way moment of travel. Migrations vary according to different aspects and points in the life course, ranging, for example, from short-term to long-term migration, but also including significant return migratory flows. Migration can also take different forms due to the motivation for moving, whether due to conflicts, oppression and persecution, for family reunification or as job search related. Labour migration can be framed as the 'free' movement of *workers*, but it usually involves important regulatory constraints even at its most liberal, as in the case of the intra-EU mobility (see Chapter Three, this volume), as well as institutional factors which affect the decision and experience of migrants (discussed below as cross-border mobility). For most migrants, sectoral restrictions, including the attraction of workers with particular skills (for Germany, see Chapter Seven, this volume; for the UK, see Chapter Ten), or the *de facto* toleration of undocumented workers (for Italy, see Chapter Six, this volume), or even local level inclusion strategies (see Chapter Twelve, this volume) are all factors which play a significant role in shaping decisions to migrate to particular places; migrants' experience of their migration as well as migration's wider socio-economic impacts on countries of origin and destination.

Figure 5.1 brings together the different types and aspects related to migration with a special focus on labour market attachment. These different analytical approaches and levels will be used as a reference point in the analysis. It shows that it is not only economic (demand/supply) factors that need to be included in analyses, but also the ways in which the labour market is regulated, as well as the various reasons and characteristics of migrations, and how these aspects interact in the labour market. While Theodoros Papadopoulos discussed in Chapter Two the implication for migrants once in their country of destination, explanations of the drivers of migration indicate that these factors may also have affected patterns of migration in the first place. Combinations of types of migration with types of regulation and types of workers highlight, in this way, a large variety of migration patterns and relations, contributing to the explanation of why one single theoretical approach is not sufficient to explain migration in different labour markets.

This plethora of different types of migration also implies that scrutiny of causes and their impact can be very difficult, especially when trying to disentangle economic reasons for migration from other types of explanation. Different reasons for migrating or returning to the 'home country' are thus not necessarily captured by classical economic perspectives, but need to integrate several other cultural, social and individual motivations. Despite a plethora of other possible factors (such as psychological ones), the focus in this chapter will remain, however, on paid labour. This therefore excludes a focus on migration with the primary aim

Figure 5.1: Variations in migration and labour market intersection by characteristics

Types of migration
Work
Short term
Long term
Cross-border
Return
Free movement of workers within the EU
Other
Family reunification
Humanitarian
Education
Types of regulation
Market – demand and supply for labour
Institutional – easy access for certain wanted groups and barriers for others
Types of cause
Push – lack of job, civil war, low income
Pull – high income, welfare states, job, higher income, geographical distance, family already in country, language, culture
Types of workers
Unskilled
Skilled
Highly skilled, including intra-company migration

of family reunification, educational purposes or even illegal migration. For more information on these issues, see, for instance, the country studies in Part II of this volume, or Chapters Four and Eleven.

Explaining the relative impact of different factors on labour migration

As mentioned, migration rationales have been especially related to economic aspects, namely those related to the economic gains for individuals and the societies of destination or origin, related to movement of individuals from one country to another. The logic of orthodox economic analyses can be summarised as follows:

> … migration occurs when there is a good chance that the worker will recoup his human capital investment. As a result, migrants will tend to gravitate from low-income to high-income regions, and the larger the income differential between the regions or the cheaper it is to move, the greater the number of migrants. (Borjas, 2000, p 4)

Yet even on the basis of this kind of economistic reasoning, following assumptions of utility maximisation on behalf of migrants, there can be rather different and even contradictory logics that apply to how we can explain the causes and consequences of labour migration. These are addressed below in terms of the sending countries, receiving countries and migrants themselves, with particular attention paid in the latter to the non-economic framing of decisions to migrate.

Causes and consequences of leaving: countries of origin

As indicated in the quotation above, a lack of jobs, low living standards and poverty constitute persuasive factors in favour of moving from one country to another. These are, therefore, identified as the central push factors of migration, even though migrants may face a high risk of continuing to live in poverty or only being able to get the lowest paid jobs and living under poor housing conditions even in the new country of destination (Borjas, 1994). Another way of expressing this understanding of pull factors is that individuals will migrate if 'the expected utility of moving is higher than the expected utility of staying, net of migration cost' (Bonin et al, 2008, p 7). As a result of these considerations, unemployed individuals are characterised as having a higher willingness to move than employed individuals (Krieger, 2008). Such risks imply that individual utility and risk-aversion might be of central importance in explaining migration patterns between countries. Within this line of argumentation, we should expect differences in tax systems and welfare policies to play an important role (Tassinopoulos and Werner, 1999), as they would affect the 'expected utility' of migration for migrants, and for the countries of origin, where unemployed people migrate to other countries and send back remittances to families and communities at 'home' in the country of origin.

The economic argument is that individuals moving abroad reduce the pressure on the labour market and the welfare systems in the country of origin, while simultaneously contributing to its faster economic development through remittances sent back to their family members. It is this assumption that also supports or rationalises the state-led promotion of emigration from developing to developed countries (Yeates, 2009a). However, although the benefits of remittance were once widely promoted by the World Bank as an excellent source of funds for development, and substantial, non-aid contribution to developing countries' economies, they are no longer viewed so unproblematically even from the World Bank (see, for example, Munzele Maimbo and Ratha, 2006; for a more general critique of the migration and development 'nexus', see Raghuram, 2009). The criticisms centre round the highly localised benefits and the divisive role of remittances, which then promote uneven or inequitable development and do not necessarily compensate for the economic costs or social fragmentation and personal losses that result from large-scale emigration, nor compensate for the so-called 'brain drain', the loss of 'human capital' from countries of emigration; the promotion of and dependence on remittances can in some cases also have corrosive political effects (Kapur, 2006).

The potential for so-called 'brain-drain' is one of the best acknowledged problems for developing countries, to which we can also add the implied risk of a 'youth drain' (Krieger, 2008), that is to say, an excessive loss for a country of young and potentially productive cohorts, as young people are more likely to migrate than older cohorts (compare, for example, Eurostat, 2008). It is not surprising, however, that the young are more mobile than older people, as this is also, more generally, a classic mobility pattern within national labour markets (for an exception to this pattern, see Chapter Thirteen, this volume). This tendency might also be associated with the fact that the young have neither settled down yet, nor established their own family. The important role that personal and family-related decisions play, in this context, casts a further doubt on explanations that see the rational economic-maximising factor (such as the financial one) as the key element in the decision to migrate.

In terms of the consequences of these possible losses – of 'youth' and 'brains' – there is both 'human capital' loss (often of highly skilled workers) and also wastage of the social and public investment in the education and training of emigrants. The long-term consequences of high skill emigration for countries of origin is generally considered dependent on whether migration is short term or long term, and whether the individual continues to be employed. It is this consideration that offers part of the justification for the idea of promoting 'brain circulation', particularly in EU migration policymaking (see Chapter Three, this volume). The intention would be to create migration policies that encourage the permanent or periodic return of migrants so that the additional skills and experience they are assumed to derive from their migration experience could be shared with the country of origin. If highly skilled individuals migrate for a short period of time, then the return of increased knowledge and ability to perform better, as in the case of migrants from India (OECD, 2008), may make the migration beneficial.

However, the apparent benefits to countries of origin remain uncertain, especially as migrants often work in unrelated or lower-skill employment than their skill level than they would in sending countries; there are also few benefits for migrants, and many for the countries of destination, discussed below. The calculation of the economic impact and consequences, in this context, also becomes more difficult. It depends on the degree to which migrants in other countries are 'seen as investors, welfare providers, knowledge communities and technology harbingers to the home countries' (ILO, 2004, p 25).

Causes and consequences of arriving: countries of destination

Although it is often argued that migration can also depend on differences in welfare systems, no systematic data confirm this contention, and even in terms of the *logic* of the argument, it can be seen that contradictory logics might also affect migration patterns. So, a key argument against migration, based on the assumption of 'homo economicus', is that migration may produce a race to the bottom in terms of social protection and welfare. When there is insufficient labour or extensive welfare systems, migration could, for example, lead to social dumping, by reducing wage pressure on the labour markets while increasing unfair competition among workers and pressure on current welfare states.

However, given the current levels of migration, estimates about the impact of migration on wages indicate that this is in reality relatively low. An increase of one per cent in the share of immigrants in the labour force decreases wages by only 0.12 per cent (Longhi et al, 2005). To put it differently, while some very small negative effects of migration on wages (or on welfare states) can be observed, given the many other possible co-influencing factors (such as the structure of the economy, forms of market regulation, segmentation of labour markets and international competitiveness), the size of this negative influence seems to be rather insignificant. These considerations are also supported by several other studies as reviewed by the ILO (2004, p 32), which demonstrate that the impact of migration on the labour market is somewhat mixed. If these considerations are taken into account, another classical argument assuming a rather crude version of the utility-maximising individual, that high levels of taxes, especially income taxes, eventually drive people to migrate seems to have little empirical foundation.

Even assuming that economic motivations are at the forefront for labour migrants' decisions, in addition to consideration of taxes, broader costs (such as insurance, for example) and other types of transaction costs related to migration (housing, absence from the labour market in the country of origin) are, in reality, often taken into account as economic costs; it is the net economic impact which a rational individual will use. And none of these account for the other costs or expected advantages which must necessarily affect the decisions of individuals who are in fact socially embedded in families, social networks and who face cultural expectations and obligations which can affect patterns of migration.

The country of destination can benefit from the migration process, not only by filling niches in the labour market (the driver behind the currently dominant 'managed migration' agenda discussed in several contributions to this book), but in several cases it can also increase the production and productivity of firms. The issue about the increase in firm productivity is, however, highly controversial, since it depends on the level of qualification of workers and, in particular, on whether the skills of immigrants are fully recognised in the country of destination. Unfortunately, this is not often the case (Liebig, 2009).

Indeed, one of the risks attached to migration – for migrants, as well as for countries of destination – is also linked to the asymmetry in the use of already acquired human capital, mentioned in the discussion on brain circulation, above. The majority of migrants, in fact, lack those linguistic skills and the cultural capital that would allow them to get the most appropriate jobs related to their level of qualifications (Chaloff and Lemaitre, 2009). As already highlighted by Granovetter (1985), a further difficulty in finding a suitable job for migrant workers concerns the fact that several jobs still have to be found through participation in social networks. The limited 'social embeddedness' of migrants clearly limits this possibility.

Needless to say, a possible negative impact of migration on the labour market cannot be, in the long run, excluded *a priori*. This can include additional future burdens on the welfare state, especially with regard to income maintenance, healthcare and pension benefits. But given the usually young age profile of those migrating, a reduction of the possible negative effects of migration on existing welfare systems can be expected (Greve, 2007). When pressures on the labour market occur, these are, in contrast, more likely to involve possible burdens on the social welfare system caused by increasing levels of migrants' unemployment.

This situation begins to represent a serious problem for European societies, especially if the usually higher unemployment rates existing among the children and grandchildren of migrants are taken into account. The consequences of this negative situation depend, however, and to a large extent, on the specific institutional setting of national welfare systems, as well as to the extent to which the migrants or their families have contributed or not to financing the welfare system either through taxes or through social insurance contributions. One way of managing the potential negative effects are the 'brain circulation' policies promoted at EU level, which in practice turn out not only to offer uncertain benefits to countries of origin, but which also appear to offer considerably less uncertain benefits to countries of destination (see the discussion in Chapter Three, this volume).

The social costs of immigration can thereby become high if integration policies are inadequate, while the size of the costs and benefits associated with migration depend to a considerable degree on the extent to which labour markets and systems of social protection ensure and promote the integration of migrants (see

Chapter Two, this volume, and the case studies in Part II of this volume). Among the possible negative occurrences the receiving country may also witness important capital outflows, or at least, not accrue the full economic benefits of migrants' employment due to remittances. However, the benefits in terms of the profits accrued to the financial sector managing these flows, decreases in aid dependency and uneven patterns of remittances all complicate this picture (Munzele Maimbo and Ratha, 2006).

Beyond economic factors, migrant mobility can also be influenced by geographical proximity (Alvarez-Plata et al, 2003), and this indicates, at least within the EU, that distance is still an important element to take into account when investigating the patterns of migration. Yet despite the possibilities given by the free movement of workers in the EU,[1] migration of EU citizens is still of variable importance among member states, and this in spite of the fact that since 2000 many countries have witnessed the movement of construction and service workers (Eurostat, 2008; see Chapter Two, this volume), suggesting strong interaction effects between both economic push and pull factors (availability of jobs in particular sectors of the economy versus opportunities for employment in the home country), and other social and cultural issues, such as family, culture, language or previous experience of migration. Hence, the overall impact of migration on labour markets of countries of destination depends, to a large degree, on the type of labour migration, as well as on the time frame within which the examination of the impact is carried out.

Causes and consequences of labour migration: migrants and labour market segmentation

Different segments of the labour market might witness different problems in relation to migration. As migration is especially common either in the unskilled or in the highly skilled sectors of the economy, this necessarily has to become a central area of analysis. Migrants from the Eastern European member states to elsewhere in the Union countries have tended, so far, to be concentrated in low wage branches, such as construction and household work, filling, in this way, gaps in demand for labour, although at a low wage level (Alvarez-Plata et al, 2003). 'New' European migrants have often become placed in sectors of the economy strongly sensitive to business cycles (OECD, 2009), and this has, inevitably, corresponded to a higher risk of redundancy in times of economic crisis. As far as social patterns of migration are concerned, men continue to migrate more than women, the young more than older people, and unmarried more than married people. Interestingly, people who moved in the past might have a higher propensity to do so in the future (Bonin et al, 2008). Migrants also seem to be often over-represented in self-employment, and this can be either 'a blessing or a curse for migrant workers' (OECD, 2009, p 23) – a blessing, in helping them escape to involuntary unemployment or a curse, as those arriving without a job usually have a harder time finding a more profitable position (Chaloff and Lemaitre, 2009).

Specific problems for migrants tend therefore to be related to lower wages, higher unemployment rates and lack of integration in the labour market, especially the formal labour market. Reasons for this asymmetry between migrant and non-migrant patterns of employment can, in this context, be due to: (1) immigrants' lower productivity levels at the moment of arrival in the new country; (2) lower worker-to-job matching; (3) different reserve wages; (4) lower bargaining power; and (5) discrimination (Causa and Jean, 2007). In the first case, lower productivity on arrival can be explained by the absence of current knowledge of the new job culture or training requirements of the new country, but also by lower linguistic skills, as well as lack of recognition of skills and qualifications, at least among non-EU migrants (Chaloff and Lemaitre, 2009; Nerb et al, 2009). When qualifications are not recognised, several negative consequences in terms of job openings, earnings and risk of unemployment can emerge, thus constituting a severe barrier for being fully integrated in the labour market of the new country. The causes for the second pattern (lower worker-to-job matching) may depend, by contrast, on the fact that the wage gap between the wage in the home country and the one in the new country needs to be relatively high in order to attract workers.

In fact, migrants bear additional transaction costs when moving from one country to another. These include not only direct costs related to the new job *per se*, but also indirect costs associated with housing, family resettlement and so on. Since women migrate for different reasons, paradoxically also for bearing 'the responsibility for children', different 'reserve wages' for migrant workers are necessary so as to cover these additional expenses (McKay et al, 2009). The increasing number of women working in the domestic informal care sector, or in cleaning services in several European countries indicates, for example, a specific pattern of migration that is primarily based on women's low-paid employment with little or no social protection (Piper, 2009). This has consequences not only for the women themselves and their degree of integration and access to rights in the countries of destination, but also for the families and societies of the countries of origin (Yeates, 2009b).

The level of human capital can, in this context, have both a positive and negative impact on migration. All other things being equal, a higher level of human capital which cannot be used in the home country presumably increases the willingness to move, but also exposes migrants to new socio-economic risks, such as those associated with their integration in the new labour market. The worse match of migrants in the labour market can, lastly, also be another important factor attributable to discrimination, as is the presence of hiring queues or the absence of specific social networks in place when migrants search for employment (McGovern, 2007; see also Chapter Eleven, this volume).

Cross-border labour migration in the EU

Within the EU, increasing migration is an important cross-border phenomenon, although whether cross-border migration should be counted as migration or simply as commuting remains an open question (Tassinopoulos and Werner, 1999). Yet, cross-border migration can, as part of the free movement of labour, be seen as an important element of the European project, and, therefore, cross-border mobility should perhaps refer not only across borders of neighbouring countries (such as, between the Netherlands and Belgium), but also among more distant countries within the zone of the EU (for example, between Poland and the UK).

In more recent years and, in particular, after EU enlargement and the establishment of the Schengen Agreement, an increase in cross-border mobility *strictu sensu* can be observed, with the main drivers of this mobility being linked in particular to classical economic reasons (such as lack of jobs and income in the former Eastern European countries) (Galgóczi et al, 2009), even though cultural patterns, historical traditions and existing legislation play, perhaps, the determining role in deciding which country to move to. Still, however, mobility in Europe remains relatively low in comparison to the US, as the average between 2000 and 2005 was only one per cent per year against three per cent. The life mobility rate is only around four per cent within the EU, and the specific cross-border mobility as low as 0.2 per cent (Bonin et al, 2008). In 2006/07, cross-border mobility accounted for 780,000 people and primarily took place in the centre of Europe, even though migration between the Baltic and Nordic countries also increased (Nerb et al, 2009).

Several barriers to mobility still exist, however, especially when the question of cross-border mobility is examined. The main barriers found in a study on cross-border mobility between Sweden and Denmark concerned, for example, (1) breaking free from a secure position in the labour market (risk-aversion); (2) family; (3) language (despite the fact that the Swedish and Danish languages are similar); and (4) transport cost and time (Greve and Rydbjerg, 2003). Furthermore, the analysis highlighted uncertainty concerning taxation and social security-related issues that can limit decisions to move. Related incentives to migrate across the two borders depended, by contrast, on expectations of better economic conditions, such as a higher income, job security, career improvement and lower housing costs in the country of residence.[2]

Differences in culture also play a determining role as this might have implications not only about how work is conducted (see above), but also about integration and social relations present in the workplace in everyday life. Living in one country while working in another might, for example, prove a very different experience, as many colleagues discuss stories in the news or television programmes of the working country, not the country they are living in.

Labour migration, immigration and integration

Return migration is another important element in the analysis of labour mobility. In particular, the young may decide to return to the country of origin, especially to settle down and to establish a family, potentially resulting in 'brain circulation', resulting in potential positive benefits for the returning migrant and for their country of origin, although as discussed above, these benefits are by no means guaranteed or one-sided (see Chapter Three, this volume). For some, return to the country of origin can also take place as a result of changing evaluation of present circumstances in the country where they migrated. For example, they might have had higher expectations regarding their likely income, they might face persistent unemployment or they might witness a decrease in their overall wages and living standards (Jean et al, 2007).

Of course, some migrants also decide to settle in the countries of destination, as historical experience has shown that for many 'temporary migrants' this decision turned out to be a permanent one. Policies can, in fact, have an important impact on the degree of permanency that migration will have. Countries that are better able to integrate newcomers and to recognise their qualifications with more open labour markets will, presumably, not simply try to make people stay but also to integrate them in the new society, reducing social tensions while fully benefiting from the positive sides of migration. This can also involve important positive repercussions for the way children are integrated in the society and how they contribute to it (Liebig, 2009).

Those countries where migrant labour has been used to fill gaps in the labour market and who have a low level of welfare security are expected to have a higher rate of re-emigration, so that differences in labour market sectors also have an impact for migration. Given the ongoing restructuring of the economies in Europe towards the service and leisure economy, those employed in the more traditional industrial sectors will have a higher risk of being made redundant and therefore leaving. On the other hand, those who have taken up jobs in the service sectors may also have higher possibilities of obtaining a more permanent job as, given Europe's expected demographic development, there will be an increasing demand in this sector (Greve, 2007). In several countries, this also involves personal and welfare services that are expected to witness a high demand in the future. However, the impact of personal and life course trajectories should not be overlooked, as the experience of numerous so-called 'guestworker' programmes from the 1950s–1973/74 demonstrate (the German case is discussed in Chapter Seven, this volume).

In many areas, the structural development of the labour market can have an important impact on what is really needed and expected from workers in years to come. Despite the fact that more highly educated individuals are expected to have a higher chance of continuing to be active in the labour market, those who have higher education levels also have a higher propensity to return to their country of origin (OECD, 2008). A possible explanation for this rather surprising result is that, despite the higher chances of being integrated in the labour market of the new country, the new skills acquired can also be utilised with comparatively higher returns in the country of origin. As mentioned above, however, despite excessively rational economic-maximising considerations, cultural and individual reasons for return migration should not be forgotten.

All other things being equal, the recent economic crisis is likely to lead to a higher level of return migration, especially for those with a temporary residence or work permit. However, as Theodoros Papadopoulos discussed in Chapter Two, the pattern of migration is not, in practice, so easy to predict.

Can labour mobility be explained by economics?

Despite large variations in numbers of jobs, wages and attempts to remove barriers to move within Europe, migration has remained relatively low in the EU (Heinz and Ward-Warmedinger, 2006). This alone raises serious doubts about the real applicability of over-mechanicistic explanations based on economic theory that prove unable to offer a full account for the different varieties of migration and migration reasons. More nuanced versions of migration theory have, in fact, been developed in a large variety of disciplines, including economics, sociology, law, history and anthropology (Boswell, 2008; Brettel and Hollifield, 2008), even though there has still been little cross-disciplinary exchange. Despite the fact that pure rational choice economics has often been the main approach when discussing complex relations between migration and the labour market, the focus of this analysis has far too often concentrated on single explanatory factors related to willingness to migrate. The conventional way of understanding movement from point A to B for individuals and the possible consequences for societies has typically had its starting point in economic theory (Favell, 2008), but unfortunately, this has also often corresponded to its point of arrival.

As emphasised, economics alone is not able to explain complex patterns of migration and the mobility of individuals. This is for several reasons, but central is that utility and happiness are not only about money or expectations of increasing one's own economic standard (Wilkingson, 2008; Greve, 2010). Not only is the happiness of the individual crucial here, but so also is the overall quality of life, which can have a substantial impact on willingness to migrate (Krieger, 2008), and in which family relations and social ties play a determining role.

Mobility can sometimes also be explained in terms of the location, such as where migrants have already settled down, as elucidated in theories of migration systems (see Castles and Miller, 2009, pp 27-30). As discussed by Siniša Zrinščak (Chapter Eleven, this volume), existing networks and social contacts elucidate different types of migration from certain countries (even cities) to other countries (or cities), especially as already having an existing and functional social network on arrival gives a higher chance to the migrant of getting a job or being more integrated in the labour market or in society at large. Network theory might thus be necessary to illuminate the 'spatial, cultural and social dimensions' of migration (Piper, 2009, p 13).

Individuals who want to migrate must also take into account several other risk factors, of which only some can be interpreted in an economic perspective. This includes, for example, the often mentioned higher risk of unemployment. As demonstrated by Causa and Jean (2007), unemployment rates are generally higher among non-EU/non-English-speaking immigrants. Moreover, immigrants are not simply more likely to lag behind in relation to jobs, but also in relation to income and, as a result, to be at higher risk of seeing their position in their country of origin comparatively lowered. This might help in explaining why elites, but also skilled workers, often decide not to migrate despite possible higher income gains. As powerfully described by Clark et al (2008, p 135), 'the elite are at the top of the income distribution in the country where they live, but may well not be so if they emigrate'. From a sociological and psychological perspective, this can, perhaps, help to explain why some migrants become frequent visitors of their home country as they, when visiting, could provide unequivocal empirical evidence that, compared to others, they perform exceptionally well.

Social factors can also help here in explaining different patterns of migration, moving our knowledge beyond simplistic economic factors related to the 'heterogeneity' of individuals (Bonin et al, 2008, p 70). Close to several important co-influencing factors, such as prospects for housing, family and culture, the personal and psychological differences of individuals can also play a significant role, with some individuals more willing to move than others and not always for utility-oriented reasons, such as for love, to 'prove themselves' or more simply to 'explore the world'.

Conclusion

Migration is here to stay. However, if Europe converges economically, the motives to migrate will be different from the ones that have historically been seen as the main reasons to migrate (such as to find a job in another country or the ability to get a higher wage income). There are already significant signs of return migration at least from the old EU member states to the new member states (Galgóczi et al, 2009). The present economic and financial crisis with a higher level of unemployment will also reduce the options and use of migration as an important part of national and international labour market development. Given that insiders have a better position in the labour market, for the classical outsiders of the labour market, namely the migrants, the situation may become even more difficult in times of such crisis (Snower, 2002).

Migration inside Europe will be dependent on individuals getting a job they find more challenging, while at the same time making it possible to combine work and family life. Differentials in skill requirements may therefore be more important in the future, especially as part of the 'managed migration' agenda, than has been the case until now. This will be even more so if a substantial economic convergence takes place. One can question, of course, whether mobility within the EU should be characterised as migration simply because of historically drawn borders, or whether the Europeanisation and integration of the labour markets implicitly mean that national borders are, in reality, and to a much higher degree, irrelevant. A higher degree of integration of the labour market in Europe simultaneously increases and decreases the likelihood of migration. Integration makes mobility easier, but it also reduces the push factor to be mobile, according to a utility-maximising logic. Yet, as should be clear from this chapter, the dynamics – the causes and the challenges for migrants, their countries of origin and for the countries of destination – cannot be simply understood or evaluated by reference to a framework of economic rationality. Even in relation to labour migration, which should mostly closely conform to straightforward logics of utility maximisation, we find varying causes and implications of leaving, arriving and settlement. These range from the need to challenge assumptions about remittances, brain drain and brain 'circulation', to questions about the incentive effects of welfare and tax systems in countries of destination. Above all, it is clear that the logics and patterns of migration need to be understood in terms of contextual, situational and individual perspectives, and can only be explained when accounting for structural, institutional and policy interactions.

Notes

[1] Free movement of workers has been one of the cornerstones of the EU, even though for new member states there has been a waiting time before full rights have been acquired. The legal EU regulation of free movement, including the historical regulation of social security 1408/71, is outside the scope of this chapter; for an overview of the actual understanding of social security coordination and the new regulation 883/2004, see the special issue of the *European Journal of Social Security*, no 1-2, June, 2009.

[2] For a long time housing prices in Sweden have been comparatively lower than in Denmark, making it attractive to move to the Malmø area in Sweden and to live and continue to work in Copenhagen in Denmark. This can also be seen as an important peculiarity in cross-border migration where it is the housing market more than the labour market that seems to have an important impact on the mobility of individuals.

References

Alvarez-Plata, P., Brücker, H. and Siliverstovs, B. (2003) *Potential migration from Central and Eastern Europe into the EU-15 – An update*, Berlin: DIW.

Bonin, H., Eichhorst, W., Florman, C., Okkels Hansen, M., Skiöld, L., Stuhler, J., Tatsiramos, K., Thomasen, H. and Zimmermann, K.F. (2008) *Geographic mobility in the European Union: Optimising its economic and social benefits*, IZA Research Report No 19, Bonn: IZA.

Borjas, G. (1994) 'The economics of immigration', *Journal of Economic Literature*, vol 32, n0 4, pp 1667-717.

Borjas, G. (2000) 'Economics of migration', *International Encyclopedia of Social and Behavioral Sciences*, Section no 3.4, Article no 38.

Boswell, C. (2008) 'Combining economics and sociology in migration theory', *Journal of Ethnic and Migration Studies*, vol 34, no 4, pp 549-66.

Brettel, C. and Hollifield, J. (eds) (2008) *Migration theory: Talking across disciplines*, London: Routledge.

Castles, S. and Miller, M.J. (2009) *The age of migration. International population movements in the modern world* (4th edn), Basingstoke: Palgrave Macmillan.

Causa, O. and Jean, S. (2007) *Integration of immigrants in OECD countries. Do policies matter?*, OECD Economics Department Working Paper No 564, Paris: Organisation for Economic Co-operation and Development.

Chaloff, J. and Lemaitre, G. (2009) *Managing highly-skilled labour migration: A comparative analysis of migration policies and challenges in OECD countries*, OECD Social Employment and Migration Working Paper No 79, Paris: Organisation for Economic Co-operation and Development.

Clark, A.E., Frijters, P. and Shields, M.A. (2008) 'Relative income, happiness, and utility: an explanation of the Easterlin paradox and other puzzles', *Journal of Income Literature*, vol 46, no 1, pp 95-144.

Eurostat (2008) *Statistics in Focus no 98*, Luxembourg: Eurostat.

Favell, A. (2008) 'Rebooting migration theory', in C. Brettel and J. Hollifield (eds) *Migration theory: Talking across disciplines*, London: Routledge, pp 259-78.

Galgóczi, B., Leschke, J. and Watt, A. (2009) *Intra-EU labour migration: Flows, effects and policy responses*, Working Paper 2009.03, Brussels: ETUI.

Granovetter, M. (1985) 'Economic action and social structure: the problem of embeddedness', *American Journal of Sociology*, vol 91, no 3, pp 481-510.

Greve, B. (ed) (2007) *The future of the welfare state. European and global perspectives*, Aldershot: Ashgate.

Greve, B. (2010) *Et lykkeligt land? [A happy society?]*, Copenhagen: Nyt fra Samfundsvidenskaberne.

Greve, B. and Rydbjerg, M. (2003) *Cross-border commuting in the EU: Obstacles and barriers, Country report: The Øresund region*, Research Paper No 11/03, Roskilde: Department of Social Sciences, Roskilde University, Denmark.

Heinz, F. and Ward-Warmendinger, M.E. (2006) 'Cross-border labour mobility within an enlarged EU', European Central Bank Occasional Paper No. 52. Available at SSRN: http://ssrn.com/abstract=923371

ILO (International Labour Organization) (2004) *Towards a fair deal for migrant workers in the global economy*, Geneva: ILO.

Jean, S., Causa, O., Jimenez, M. and Wanner, I. (2007) *Migration in OECD countries: Labour market impact and integration issues*, OECD Economics Department Working Paper No 562, Paris: Organisation for Economic Co-operation and Development.

Kapur, D. (2006) 'Remittances: the new development mantra?', in S. Munzele Maimbo and D. Ratha (eds) *Remittances: Development impact and future prospects*, Washington, DC: World Bank, pp 331-60.

Krieger, H. (2008) 'Migration and mobility culture', in J. Alber, T. Fahey and C. Saraceno (eds) *Handbook of quality of life in the enlarged European Union*, London: Routledge, pp 355-84.

Liebig, T. (2009) *Jobs for immigrants: Labour market integration in Norway*, OECD Social Employment and Migration Working Paper No 94, Paris: Organisation for Economic Co-operation and Development.

Longhi, S., Nijkamp, P. and Poot, J. (2005) 'A meta-analytic assessment of the effect of immigration on wages', *Journal of Economic Surveys*, vol 19, no 3, pp 451-77.

Marti, M. and Rodenas, C. (2007) 'Migration estimation based on the labour force survey: an EU-15 perspective', *IMR*, vol 41, no 1, pp 101-26.

McGovern, P. (2007) 'Immigration, labour markets and employment relations: problems and prospects', *British Journal of Industrial Relations*, vol 45, no 2, pp 217-35.

McKay, S., Markova, E., Paraskevopoulou, A. and Wright, T. (2009) *The relationship between migration status and employment outcomes*, Undocumented Worker Transitions final report (www.undocumentedmigrants.eu).

Munzele Maimbo, S. and Ratha, D. (eds) (2006) *Remittances: Development impact and future prospects*, Washington, DC: World Bank.

Nerb, G., Hitzelsberger, F., Woidich, A., Pommer, S., Hemmer, S. and Heczko, P. (2009) *Scientific report on the mobility of cross-border workers within the EU-27/EEA/EFTA countries*, Munich: MKW Wirtschaftsforschung GmbH.

OECD (Organsiation for Economic Co-operation and Development (2008) *International Migration Outlook: SOPEMI 2008*, Paris: OECD.

OECD (2009) *International Migration Outlook: SOPEMI 2009*, Paris: OECD.

Piper, N. (2009) *Migration and social development. Organizational and political dimensions*, Social Policy and Development Paper No 39, Geneva: UNRISD.

Raghuram, P. (2009) 'Which migration, what development? Unsettling the edifice of migration and development', *Population, Space and Place*, vol 15, no 2, pp 103-17.

Snower, D. (2002) *The insider-outsider theory: A survey*, IZA Discussion Paper No 534, Bonn: IZA.

Tassinopoulos, A. and Werner, H. (1999) *To move or not to move – Migration of labour in the European Union*, IAB Labour Market Research Topics 35, Neurenberg: IAB.

Wilkingson, N. (2008) *An introduction to behavioural economics*, Basingstoke: Palgrave Macmillan.

Yeates, N. (2009a) 'Production for export: the role of the state in the development and operation of global care chains', *Population, Space and Place*, vol 15, no 2, pp 175–87.

Yeates, N. (2009b) *Globalising care economies and migrant workers: Explorations in global care chains*, Basingstoke: Palgrave.

Part II
Migration and social protection policies in
the EU: country studies

Towards a security-oriented migration policy model? Evidence from the Italian case

Tiziana Caponio and Paolo R. Graziano

Introduction[1]

The aim of this chapter is to provide an analysis of the evolution of migration policies in Italy, with a particular focus on the social protection offered to immigrants. With respect to most continental European countries, which experienced mass migration starting from the end of the Second World War, and to Finland and Eastern Europe, where migration is a completely new phenomenon, Italy (and Southern Europe more generally) can be considered as a 'quasi-new immigration country', since significant migration flows had already started in the second half of the 1970s. The first immigration law dates back to 1986, and since then an increasingly articulated set of norms and principles concerning both the regulation of new flows and the integration of regular residents has been adopted.

Over four million immigrants live in Italy today and most of them contribute – among other things – to the Italian welfare state system since they pay taxes and retirement contributions. According to Banca d'Italia data (2009, pp 62–8), the overall economic contribution of immigrants to gross domestic product (GDP) is slightly below 10 per cent. Furthermore, recent data (Caritas, 2008) shows that the employment rate for foreign immigrants is over 67.1 per cent, whereas the same rate is 58.1 per cent for Italians, and the participation rate is 73.2 per cent for non-Italians, whereas the same figure is 61.9 per cent for Italians, even though unemployment rates are more favourable to Italian citizens (5.9 per cent against 8.3 per cent for foreign citizens).

However, if we take a closer look at the companies where immigrants work, over 50 per cent of immigrants are employed in companies with fewer than 10 employees, whereas fewer than 17 per cent are employed in companies with more than 50 employees. The figures for Italian workers are quite different: almost 40 per cent are employed by companies with more than 50 employees, whereas about 28 per cent are employed in companies with fewer than 10 employees. Since Italian employment protection policies are mainly targeted at large companies (Jessoula et al, 2010), the low protection offered to workers of small-size companies has greater consequences on immigrants than on Italian workers. In other words, even for those 'privileged', that is, regular and working immigrants, access to social protection via their employment status is constantly at risk due to their specific working status. Clearly, the social protection opportunities for irregular migrants are even worse since they do not enjoy employment-related social benefits, creating sharply differentiated possibilities of integration for each migrant group.

Such a weak social position of immigrants in Italy can be regarded as a structural feature of the Italian immigration policy regime that the current centre-right government has indeed exacerbated but not created *ex-novo*. Since the first administrative regulations in the 1980s, a path was set following the principle of 'economic legitimation of immigration' (Finotelli, 2009, p 887), which looks at immigrants primarily as economic factors, with relatively little regard for social and humanitarian considerations. As we shall see, even attempts to deviate from this path, for example with the Turco–Napolitano Law (1998), have, in many respects, been poorly implemented.

This chapter is organised as follows. In the next section we provide relevant information on the changing nature of Italy, from an 'emigration' to an 'immigration' country, before presenting the development of Italian immigration – as well as immigrant – policies, and discuss their limited connection to social protection. The fourth section focuses on the 2009 Security Law and on the challenges that migration policy is currently facing. In the conclusion we attempt to make sense of the new Italian security-oriented migration policy model by suggesting some hypotheses of explanation.

From emigration to immigration: Italy as a quasi-new immigration country

Conventionally, the shift of Italy from an emigration to an immigration country dates back to 1975, when for the first time in Italian contemporary history the migration balance registered a positive turnout (Bonifazi, 2007). Yet, in the context of the economic recession of the time, such a change was not to be promptly acknowledged: in 1984, in a review article on immigration research in Italy, Rella and Vadalà (1984) devoted just two pages to foreign immigration, curiously stating that Italy was not destined to become 'a country of large-scale immigration' (p 151).

At the end of the decade, the inappropriateness of such a statement became increasingly evident: a growing body of social science literature started to deal with the Italian 'exceptional case'. The first studies carried out by demographers and sociologists emphasised the relevance of *push factors*, that is, world population imbalances, unemployment, social and economic inequalities, political turmoil and dictatorship (see contributions in: Cocchi, 1990; Delle Donne et al, 1993). Italy was regarded as an immigration country *malgré-soi*, also due to the restrictions introduced by other European countries after the 1973 oil crisis (Melotti, 1993), that re-directed migration flows towards less regulated Southern Europe as a second choice.

However, contrary to the conventional wisdom conveyed by these studies, foreign immigration flows towards Italy did not occur overnight, but appear to be strictly connected to the history of the country as well as to its dual model of economic development and familistic welfare state. First of all, it has to be considered that early foreign immigration flows towards Italy in the 1970s developed in the context of different *migratory systems*, that is, long established relations based on exchanges of goods, information flows and people (Castles and Miller, 2003). This is the case, for instance, of colonial relations with the Horn of Africa, which created a migratory system linking the main Italian cities, that is, Rome and Milan, in the first place, with Eritrea, Ethiopia and Somalia, through the families of Italian colonial officials coming back to their home country after the end of the Second World War with their domestic personnel. Similarly, Italian Catholic missions in countries such as Cape Verde and the Philippines actively promoted the arrival of women from these countries who were then employed as domestic workers by wealthy Italian families (Sciortino, 2004, p 118). Another important early migratory system was the one linking Sicily to Tunisia, which followed the return of Italian entrepreneurs because of Tunisian nationalisation policies in the 1960s, and which filled gaps in the fishing and agricultural sectors in Southern regions.

For migratory systems to enlarge and consolidate, favourable conditions have to be present in the country of arrival in terms of labour market opportunities and possibilities of entering the territory. As for the first point, the extremely segmented structure of the Italian labour market has to be considered. The development of the Fordist productive paradigm in the centre-north of the country provided new occupational opportunities for Southern regions' rural workers, but this did not imply the disappearance of informal and irregular employment in less productive economic sectors. On the contrary, the underground economy represented an important asset in the 1970s post-Fordist restructuring of the Italian economy (Reyneri, 2004). At the same time, the increasing female participation rate – especially from the middle class – triggered a new demand for domestic and care services which was satisfied by the hiring, often informally, of foreign women. The familistic welfare state, intended either as a variant of the conservative welfare regime accentuating its particularistic features (Sciortino, 2004), or as a specific, fourth model (Ferrera, 1996), and essentially centred on monetary transfers to family households, could reproduce itself without requiring either reforms aimed at expanding the range of public social services provided by the state, or changes in the gender division of labour within households (Schierup et al, 2006, p 171).

To sum up, foreign migration flows towards Italy developed in a context characterised by a latent, even though increasingly relevant, demand for low-skilled workers in the Italian segmented labour market, offering to foreigners non-qualified and often informal jobs in sectors such as domestic and personal care services, agriculture, retail and wholesale trade, hotels and catering and construction (Reyneri, 2008, p 113). These structural features of the Italian economy have been supported through the 1980s and 1990s by a contradictory legislation, combining a benevolent attitude towards illegal immigrants with scarce opportunities of integration. The phenomenon was implicitly conceived in terms of economic utility for the country. However, as we shall see below, such a functional or utilitarian consideration of immigration was made explicit only in 2002 by the Bossi–Fini Law (no. 189/2002), establishing what can be called a late, Mediterranean style of *guestworker* system. If, in the 'old' *guestworker* model, which characterised Germany and Switzerland during the Golden Age of welfare state development and economic expansion (1945–75), immigrants' recruitment was aimed at supporting production in the leading sectors of the national economy, in the late, Mediterranean version of the model the demand for immigrant workers is connected to specific peaks of productivity in the most low paid economic sectors of highly segmented labour markets. Furthermore, contrary to the classical German archetype described by the literature (but for a critical appraisal see Chapter Seven, this volume), participation in the labour market and inclusion in the welfare state no longer go hand in hand. On the contrary, the fragility of immigrants' legal status actually reduces any possibility of permanent settlement (Calavita, 2005).

Migration policies 'Italian style': what kind of social inclusion?

As stated above, a mismatch can be detected with respect to the relationship between the migration phenomenon in Italy and the development of migration policies. In fact, the arrival of the first immigrants in the mid-1960s occurred in an overall situation characterised by a lack of regulations on entry and admissions, and was dealt with in an extremely discretionry way. For example, in the mid-1960s a ministerial regulation (*circolare*) of the Italian Labour Ministry allowed work permits to those foreigners who were able to prove their entry before a specified date, which was then continuously postponed until 1981 (Colombo and Sciortino, 2004, p 52). In 1972 another *circolare* of the same Ministry restricted the legalisation of foreign domestic workers to those who held live-in contracts, thus protecting Italian workers from competition in the more convenient segment of hourly paid domestic work (Andall, 2000). It is only from the mid-1980s that Italian policies started to be structured in a more comprehensive fashion, tackling both immigration and integration issues through policies concerning the conditions of entry and admission to Italian territory on the one hand (immigration issues), and of access to citizenship rights and social services on the other (integration issues; see also Hammar, 1985). In what follows we will analyse Italian laws on immigration by considering both aspects, which will allow us to look at immigrants in their double relation with the welfare state (Sciortino, 2004), that is, both as providers and as beneficiaries of welfare services.

First phase (1986-97): a 'reluctant immigration country'

For the first time Law no. 943/1986 recognised full equality of rights between foreign and Italian workers, thus complying with the international obligations linked to the International Labour Organization (ILO) 1975 Convention (no. 143).[2] Four years later, in 1990, a second immigration law (Law no. 39/90) was adopted, and this time it was also a consequence of the murder of an African asylum seeker working irregularly tomato harvesting in the south of the country. Even though the offenders were a group of criminals who specialised in robbing the meagre salaries of the immigrant farmers, a hot debate on the failure of the previous law to prevent racism in Italy arose (Einaudi, 2007, p 141). Despite the media fanfare, the 1990 legislation did not constitute a radical change, but rather it showed a clear continuity with the previous one and with the administrative regulation through *circolari* described above. What were the main features of these first legislative steps?

First of all, as far as immigration policy is concerned, the two laws confirmed the protectionist bias towards the Italian workforce (Zincone, 2008, p 19): not only was priority in employment assigned to Italian and European Union (EU) citizens, but according to the 1986 Law, the contributory costs for non-EU workers was made 0.5 per cent higher in order to put aside resources for repatriation in case of dismissal. A complex system of inflows planning was introduced, based on a series of decrees issued by the Labour Ministry. However, these did not prove effective: not only were the decrees issued later than expected, but inflows were usually set at a very low threshold (Colombo and Sciortino, 2004, p 59).

Second, both laws introduced a generalised amnesty: the 1986 one led to the regularisation of 116,000 illegal immigrants, two thirds of whom were unemployed (Einaudi, 2007, p 131), while the 1990 amnesty was also opened to self-employed immigrants and asylum seekers, and allowed for the regularisation of 220,000 immigrants. The generosity of these amnesties, in terms of the categories of migrant allowed to apply, points out an implicit and pragmatic recognition of the crucial relevance of the informal economy in attracting immigrants to Italy. However, the 1990 Law also introduced new restrictions on entry conditions and expulsions, in order to meet the Schengen Agreement requirements, in part reflecting the securitising impact of EU migration policy.

As for integration policy, the 1986 Law did not provide any special budget, while the 1990 Law just allocated funds to regional authorities in order to establish first accommodation facilities to host the new regularised foreign workers. Despite the lack of national resources, throughout the 1990s some cities of the centre-north, such as Milan, Turin and Bologna, started to develop different kinds of programmes and practices of incorporation (Caponio, 2006, pp 78-85). Rather than a national integration model, a variety of local arrangements in immigrants' access to citizenship rights actually emerged, reflecting not only traditional gaps between Northern and Southern regions in terms of availability of social services and efficiency of the public administration, but also the varying degrees of decision-making power and institutionalisation of third sector organisations working in the field (Zincone, 1994; Caponio, 2006; see also Chapter Twelve, this volume). Whereas, for instance, the local administration in Turin could count on strong Catholic organisations also providing first shelter to illegal immigrants, in Bologna the weakness of these associations put the municipality under a greater pressure (Ponzo, 2008).

Hence, at the beginning of the 1990s, Italy can be characterised as a 'reluctant immigration country', borrowing the expression introduced by Martin (1994), whose policies combined limitations to foreign workers' active recruitment, tolerance towards illegal migrants with a lack of long-term opportunities for integration. The implicit assumption was that immigrants were to stay as long as the labour market requested their presence. This situation of 'subaltern integration' (Ambrosini, 2001) was also sanctioned by the 1992 citizenship reform: whereas the previous law set a five years' residence requirement for all foreigners in order to apply for naturalisation, the reform increased the period to 10 years for non-EU citizens.

Second phase (1997-2001): social integration first?

The Turco-Napolitano Law – named after the then Ministers of Social Affairs and Home Affairs of the first centre-left Prodi government and adopted in March 1998 – represented a paradigmatic shift. As far as immigration policy is concerned, the main purpose of the Turco-Napolitano Law was to combine the contrast of illegal immigration with increased opportunities of legal entry. A new quota system was introduced, with preferential quotas assigned to those countries that had accepted special agreements for the control of irregular flows and readmission of their citizens. Temporary detention centres were established to facilitate procedures of identification and repatriation of undocumented immigrants within a maximum of 30 days.

In the context of the annual quotas, immigrants could enter either on the basis of a contract or as job seekers, that is, thanks to the support of other regular immigrants, Italian citizens, non-governmental organisations (NGOs) or regional and local institutions, able to guarantee the immigrant's daily life costs for a maximum of one year.[3] This kind of permit represented a real novelty in the Italian context, allowing for a direct encounter between the foreign worker and the employer and acknowledging the importance of factors such as trust and personal knowledge for hiring decisions, which is particularly relevant in the domestic sector. As usual, the law was accompanied by another amnesty, although limited to undocumented workers, which allowed the regularisation of 215,000 immigrants.

But the real core of the new law is represented by the emphasis on immigrants' rights and access to the welfare state. Immigrant policies were centred around the concept of 'reasonable integration', implying both nationals' and immigrants' physical and psychological well-being on the one hand, and positive interaction between different groups on the other (see also Zincone, 2000). On the basis of these two principles, a number of policy measures aimed at fostering individual equality and at promoting intercultural relations were set in all the crucial spheres of immigrant social integration, that is, employment, health, education and professional training, housing and civic participation. A long-term residence permit was introduced in order to make more secure the legal status of those immigrants who had been legally living and working in Italy for over five years. Furthermore, in order to give effectiveness to the 'reasonable integration' model, a National Fund for Immigrant Policy was introduced and allocated to the regions on the basis of programmes agreed on with the municipalities. Moreover, consistent with the principle of protecting immigrants' physical and psychological well-being, undocumented foreigners were accorded basic rights of access to healthcare – not just to urgent care but also to preventive medicine – and education for their children.

However, pitfalls in the implementation of the law, and especially of its most innovative elements, cast doubts on the shared institutional intention of establishing a new Italian migration regime, more open towards legal entries and the settlement of immigrants in the country. As for immigration policy, quotas were set far below the estimated labour market needs (Colombo and Sciortino, 2003). This was particularly the case for quotas devoted to the sponsor system, set at just 15,000 residence permits per year which was regularly overcome in a few days (Reyneri, 2008, p 114). But what is more striking is the cumbersome implementation of the long-term residence permit or card. In 2000, an administrative regulation (Circolare no. 300/2000) subordinated the issuing of this document to minimum income requirements and to those holding a permanent work contract. Moreover, restrictions were also introduced to immigrants' access to social assistance (*assegno sociale*) and to special maternity allowances for single women and for mothers of a third child (or more), these latter limited to the holders of a permanent residence card. Notwithstanding these contradictions, the National Fund for Immigrant Policy did actually give a boost to regional integration policies, as pointed out by the annual reports of the Commission for Immigrants' Integration (Zincone, 2001). However, the federalist reform undertaken during these years, which came to an end during the centre-left government led by Giuliano Amato in May 2001, actually put the institutional system designed by the Turco-Napolitano Law on hold. There are currently no special national funds for integration policies, and regions receive only a general social policy budget. Recent studies show that not all the regions have continued to adopt specific immigrants' integration programmes after 2003 (Campomori and Caponio, 2009), when the federalist reform came into force. These programmes were only broadly sketched and left to the responsibility of local authorities, which followed them up in a very differentiated manner.

Third phase (2002-08): the late guestworker model

Against these inconsistencies of the 1998 Law, the reform approved in 2002 by the centre-right government, the so-called Bossi-Fini Law named after the two centre-right political ministers who undertook the initiative, clearly opted for what we call a *late guestworker* model. In this Mediterranean variant of Castles and Miller's (2003) German-style system, immigrants are channelled towards the most unstable positions of post-Fordist economic niches, characterised – also for the national workers – by flexible work contracts and few, if any, social protection rights.

According to the Bossi-Fini Law, admission depends on the availability of a job proposal and the residence permit is linked to the duration of the contract. In case of unemployment, only six months, instead of the previous period of one year, are allowed for further job search. Admissions continue to be based on annual quotas, but the jobseekers' permit has been eliminated. This has, in part, been substituted by a priority right to enter accorded to those migrants enrolled in the country of origin in specific training courses promoted by the provinces and/or the regions. The rationale is to allow the recruitment of immigrants in response to the specific needs of local labour markets. However, quotas assigned to this channel of entry have been very limited, and the regions have not taken advantage of this opportunity so far. In 2007, of a total 252,000 quotas, just 3,500 were linked to specific training courses (Colombo and Martini, 2007, p 80), but actually only Veneto applied for 330 foreign workers to be trained in different sectors such as tourism, care work and domestic services, healthcare, construction, agriculture and industry (see Caponio, 2007, pp 45-6).

Clearly, the link of the residence permit to the work contract, emphasised by the term 'stay contract' (*contratto di soggiorno*), satisfies the need for flexible labour while at the same time avoiding the social costs of immigrants' unemployment. However, this limitation of entry and stay requirements did not prevent the adoption of a new amnesty. This was at the centre of a hot political debate within the centre-right majority, with the Northern League strenuously opposing any regularisation (with the exception of domestic workers) against the Catholic parties, which finally succeeded in obtaining a general amnesty applying to all undocumented foreign workers and not just to those working in the personal care and domestic sectors (Colombo and Sciortino, 2003). Over 700,000 demands were presented, and over 650,000 accepted.

As for integration policies, the Bossi-Fini Law formally left untouched most provisions of the Turco-Napolitano Law. Yet the status of 'legal resident' has been made contingent on more frequent permit renewals, and restrictions have been introduced to family reunions with parents, while access to public housing has been limited to long-term residents or to those holding a two years' minimum stay permit. Immigrants as 'useful' workers are not supported in order to also become welfare consumers.

The late guestworker model presented so far could be regarded simply as the product of centre-right anti-immigrant policy provision. However, this is a questionable assumption if one considers the inaction of the second Prodi government elected in May 2006, that did not even reverse the most contested norms of the Bossi-Fini Law, and especially those regarding the link between stay and employment contract.

Consolidation of a link between migration and security

In 2008 the number of regular immigrants in Italy rose to 3,500,000, jumping from less than 1,500,000 individuals in 2000 (Caritas, 2008). Despite this increase and the ongoing debate regarding the need for new immigration policies, no new law has been passed until very recently, when Law no. 94/2009 was adopted (July 2009). It is explicitly devoted to security issues (in fact, it was labelled by the government and the press as *pacchetto sicurezza*, that is, a set of security measures), and it is intended to affect immigrants – especially irregular immigrants – in various ways. Here are the most important innovations introduced by Law no. 94/2009 divided into three policy sub-areas: irregular migration; access to the residence permit and to citizenship; and labour recruitment and admission.

First, the law introduces a new criminal offence which goes under the name of *reato d'ingresso e soggiorno irregolare* (entrance and irregular residence crime), which, in the first phases of the parliamentary debate concerning the law was supposed to be punished by imprisonment, whereas the law sets a fine of between €5,000 and €10,000 to be paid by the person convicted. In order to ensure effective expulsions, immigrants can be detained in temporary reception centres for up to 180 days (previously just a maximum of 60 days detention was allowed). If, however, at the end of this period expulsion cannot be executed, the police may issue an expulsion decree. Those who do not comply can be punished with imprisonment for up to a maximum of five years. Irregular immigrants are regarded as potential criminals, meaning that those who do not have a residence permit are more dangerous by definition. New opportunities have also been provided to the Italian police with the aim of stopping irregular immigrants even before they enter Italian land (the so-called *respingimenti*, or blockings). These have been severely criticised by both the EU and specialised United Nations (UN) agencies since they may significantly limit the recognition of asylum rights in the application of the international human rights charters (Pastore, 2009; see also Chapter Four, this volume).

If measures against illegal immigrants could be expected in a law on security issues, it is striking, however, to also find legislation concerning the status of regular immigrants. First of all, in order to apply for Italian nationality, an administrative fee of €200 has to be paid by the applicant. Moreover, restrictions on acquisition via marriage have been introduced. Italy has always represented an anomaly in Europe in this respect (Bauböck et al, 2006), allowing the acquisition of citizenship to foreigners married to an Italian citizen after six months of marriage. This favourable treatment, especially if compared to the 10 years required for naturalisation, has raised worries about 'convenience' marriages, and restrictions were already present in the centre-left government proposal (*Disegno di Legge Amato*, named after the then Home Affairs minister) presented it in 2006. The new law actually incorporates what was established by this proposal, requiring at least two years of residence in Italy, provided that no separation occurred at the moment that citizenship was formally granted.

Along with citizenship via marriage, the Security Law also introduces important innovations with respect to access to residence permits. Following similar policies undertaken since the late 1990s in most 'old' EU immigration countries such as France, Germany and the Netherlands (Michalowski, 2004; Joppke, 2007), all those who require a residence permit have to subscribe to an 'integration agreement' (*accordo di integrazione*). Similarly, the issuing of the long-term residence permit is subordinated to an Italian language test. However, the law does not provide specifications on the implementation of such measures, leaving space for discretional interpretation on the part of local police officers.

The Security Law also deals with issues of labour recruitment and admission, envisaging first, an Italian-style policy of incentives for high-skilled immigrants based on the simplification of the hiring procedures from abroad and on the possibility for foreign students who have obtained a Master's or PhD degree in Italy to apply for a one-year jobseeking permit (Article 11-bis). Although not involving active recruitment (evident in the UK, for example), such an opening bears comparison with EU and other member states' policies on high-skill migration (for the EU, see Chapter Three, this volume, and for Germany, see Chapter Seven). It is perhaps especially interesting if one considers that, due to the actual economic crises, the Berlusconi government has decided to cut off entry quotas for 2009, with the exception of 80,000 seasonal workers. Yet a new amnesty, this time limited to domestic helpers and caregivers, was approved in August 2009.

Hence, even in times of economic crisis, Italy does not seem to be able to do without new entries of low-skilled workers, especially in the domestic and care sector. The presence of immigrants in this segment of the labour market is so relevant that the relatively low number of applications presented at the closure of the amnesty (30 September 2009), 300,000 against the 500,000 estimated by the Home Office Ministry, has put into question the demanding requisites of the legalisation. Employers must demonstrate they have a minimum yearly income of €20,000, which is far above the income provided by social pension benefits, or that they are severely ill and not self-sufficient. Moreover, the employer was required to pay a considerable amount in order to fulfil their contributory obligations to the hired worker.

This restrictive regularisation and stopping new flows of permanent workers has to be considered in the context of an almost complete opening of Italy toward immigrants from new EU countries: the moratorium on Romanian immigrants' free access to the Italian labour market excludes all the low qualified sectors in which they are traditionally employed such as construction, tourism, personal care and domestic work. Since Romanians no longer need a residence and work permit to stay in the country, it is very likely that they will be employed 'off the books', thus contributing to the flourishing informal labour market which has always constituted a crucial asset for the Italian economy and informal welfare, as pointed out earlier. In theory, the 2009 amnesty was also directed at EU nationals and Italian citizens working irregularly in the domestic and personal care sector and who wished to register their contract. However, no data is available on the number of people who actually took advantage of such an opportunity. In the lack of any effort to contrast informal hiring, it is very unlikely that workers and – most of all – employers will opt for registering the contract. This is even more the case with Romanian immigrants, whose migratory projects are still very focused on return: losses in terms of pension rights and contributions are likely to be underestimated vis-à-vis the possibility of sending more money back home (see Cingolani, 2009).

To sum up, recent Italian migration policy seems to be oriented at becoming more selective and targeted, with differential integration (see Chapter One, this volume) dependent on the favouring of the high-skilled, and of specific categories of low-skilled workers such as domestic helpers and caregivers. Yet at the same time, integration policy does not set a clear path for social inclusion, but is constructed around employment, rather limiting the acquisition of the stay permit and of the long-term resident card. Access to citizenship through naturalisation continues to be extremely restrictive. In the Italian security-oriented migration policy model, immigrants as providers of social protection do not seem to be entitled to any protection for themselves. Those who cannot prove they have a job enabling access to a regular residence permit are simply treated as would-be criminals whose living conditions are made increasingly harsh. But what are the political and institutional reasons for such a policy development? Let us turn to the concluding section of this chapter, where we will try to answer this crucial question.

Conclusion

Scholarly literature has looked at Italy as a paradigmatic case of the Southern European migratory regime, together with Spain, Portugal and Greece (King et al, 2000; King and Ribas-Mateos, 2002). These countries share remarkable similarities in terms of timing of migratory flows and patterns of immigrants' insertion in the labour market. With respect to immigration policy, a key characteristic is usually identified as the absence of active recruitment or effective flows programming vis-à-vis some tolerance on irregularity and the periodical adoption of amnesties (Pastore, 2004). On the other hand, as far as integration policy is concerned, this is usually depicted as poorly developed (Baldwin-Edwards, 2002) and territorially fragmented (Caponio, 2010), reproducing the more general structural weakness of the welfare state in these countries.

In consequence, immigrants' access to social rights is extremely uncertain, not only for tolerated illegal immigrants, but also for those with regular residency. As emphasised in this chapter, just like in other less developed welfare state policies (such as reconciliation policies; see Graziano and Madama, 2009), integration policy in Italy is a consequence of both vertical and horizontal fragmentation, since not only is the acquisition of rights for immigrants very slow and therefore the 'types' of legal statuses quite variable (*horizontal fragmentation*; see also Sciortino, 2004), but there is also a complex distribution of competences among the various levels of governments which makes both working and social life quite difficult for immigrants in Italy (*vertical fragmentation*; see also Caponio and Colombo, 2005).

In contrast to this weak position of immigrants with respect to citizenship rights, their relevance is clear if we consider the current needs of the overall welfare system of Southern European countries and of Italy in particular. Faced with a rapidly ageing population, the contribution of immigrants to the sustainability of the pension system and to an increasing demand for care services is crucial. In fact, feminisation of flows is another common feature of the South Mediterranean migration regime (Bettio et al, 2006), and Italy is no exception.

In the Italian case, immigrants are praised insofar as they fill gaps in the less attractive sectors of the labour market, but far less as would-be citizens or welfare beneficiaries. This 'economy of otherness' (Calavita, 2005) that is, based on the work of people who are kept distant from full access to citizenship rights, does not seem very different from the idea of treating immigrants as so-called *guestworkers* along the lines of several countries' post-war immigration policies. Yet, if in the post-war Fordist economy foreign workers could at least aspire to enter the core productive sectors of the time and be admitted to the rights attached to the status of 'blue collar', this is not the case nowadays, especially in Southern Europe and in the domestic services, where forms of pre-Fordist work relations, such as informal hiring and personal subordination, prevail (although see Chapter Eleven, this volume; see also Chapters Seven and Eight, this volume, for evidence of such practices elsewhere).

As we have pointed out, this contradiction has lain behind immigration and integration policy in Italy since the first administrative regulations of the 1980s. The 1986 and 1990 Laws just allowed for mass regularisations that were followed neither by effective admission policies nor by adequate integration provisions. The 1998 Turco-Napolitano Law apparently changed this path by setting the basis of an Italian model of integration that intended to combine equality in access to social rights and openness towards intercultural dialogue. Yet the then centre-left government did not pursue consistent implementation, as pointed out by adopted legislation, constraining access to certain social provisions and the administrative directives which introduced limitations in the acquisition of the long-term resident card. The economic legitimisation of immigration clearly runs through Italian contradictory legislation, to be finally solved by the Bossi-Fini Law and the so-called *stay contract*, according to which any stay is allowed but only if based on a regular work contract.

Such a strong path-dependence of Italian policy (see Pierson, 2004; Streeck and Thelen, 2005) is also evident in the inaction of the second Prodi centre-left government as well as in the policy pursued by the currently in power centre-right Berlusconi IV government, which combines more selective – at least in its intentions – admission criteria, with new conditions for the acquisition of the stay permit and citizenship via marriage. In this context, the criminalisation campaign against illegal immigrants can be regarded as an attempt to re-frame the immigration issue in response to two main contingent pressures: the overall concern of the Italian electorate regarding security (Il Sole 24 Ore, 1/12/2009) and increasing parties' concern for specific security issues (*in primis*, the powerful regionalist party Lega Nord [Northern League] but also more generally at the heart of all the most important centre-left and centre-right political parties – see the various political programmes prepared for the 2008 Italian general elections) (see also the discussion in Chapter One, this volume, on feelings of threat and fear in shaping contentious politics of immigration). If and to what extent such a security turn marks a full paradigmatic change with respect to the generalised tolerance of irregular migration which has so far characterised the late, Mediterranean *guestworker* model, is still an open question. The openness towards new EU member states' citizens, in Italy essentially Romanians, seems to point out that irregular work, which is a feasible option if an immigrant does not have to renew their stay permit, is still very much tolerated if not fully, informally appreciated. As a matter of fact, the security measures hit clandestine, non-EU immigrants, whose conditions of exclusion and exploitation are likely to be exacerbated, while leaving untouched the underground economy, within which immigrants, ever more from new EU countries, continue to play a crucial role.

Notes

[1] A special thank-you to Ferruccio Pastore for his comments and suggestions.

[2] Italy strongly supported this Convention, which was regarded essentially as an instrument to protect its emigrants abroad (Colombo and Sciortino, 2004, p 54).

[3] The sponsor also guaranteed for the immigrant's return home in case of unsuccessful job search within the allowed one year.

References

Ambrosini, M. (2001) *La fatica di integrarsi. Immigrati e lavoro in Italia* [*The effort to integrate. Immigrants and work in Italy*], Bologna: Il Mulino.

Andall, J. (2000) *Gender, migration and domestic service. The politics of black women in Italy*, Aldershot: Ashgate.

Baldwin-Edwards, M. (2002) 'Semi-reluctant hosts. Southern Europe's ambivalent response to immigration', *Studi emigrazione/Migration Studies*, vol 39, no 145, pp 27–47.

Banca d'Italia (2009) *L'economia delle regioni italiane nell'anno 2008* [*The economy of the Italian regions in 2008*], Rome: Banca d'Italia.

Bauböck, R., Ersbøll, E., Groenendijk, K. and Waldrauch, H. (eds) (2006) *Acquisition and loss of nationality. Policies and trends in 15 European countries – vol 1: Comparative analyses*, Amsterdam: Amsterdam University Press.

Bettio, F., Simonazzi, A. and Villa, P. (2006) 'Changes in care regimes and female migration', *Journal of European Social Policy*, vol 16, no 3, pp 271-85.

Bonifazi, C. (2007) *L'immigrazione straniera in Italia* [Foreign immigration in Italy] (2nd edn), Bologna: Il Mulino.

Calavita, K. (2005) *Immigrants at the margins: Law, race, and exclusion in Southern Europe*, Cambridge: Cambridge University Press.

Campomori, F. and Caponio, T. (2009) 'Immigrazione' ['Immigration'], in S. Vassallo (ed) *Le regioni. Capitale sociale, equilibri politici e rendimento istituzionale* [Regions. Social capital, political balances and institutional performance], Research Report, Bologna: Istituto C. Cattaneo, pp 227-50.

Caponio, T. (2006) *Città e immigrazione. Discorso pubblico e politiche a Milano, Bologna e Napoli* [City and immigration. Public discourse and policies in Milan, Bologna and Naples], Bologna: Il Mulino.

Caponio, T. (2007) 'Il quadro normativo e le politiche locali' ['Relevant legislation and local policies'], in *Primo rapporto sugli immigrati in Italia* [First reports on immigrants in Italy], Rome: Ministero dell'Interno, pp 26-52.

Caponio, T. (2010) 'Grassroots multiculturalism in Italy: Milan, Bologna and Naples compared', in T. Caponio and M. Borkert (eds) *The local dimension of migration policymaking*, IMISCOE Report Series, Amsterdam: Amsterdam University Press.

Caponio, T. and Colombo, A. (2005) 'Introduzione' ['Introduction'], in T. Caponio and A. Colombo (eds) *Stranieri in Italia. Migrazioni global, integrazioni locali* [Foreigners in Italy. Global migrations, local integration], Bologna: Il Mulino, pp 7-19.

Caritas (2008) *Dossier statistico immigrazione 2008* [Statistical immigration dossier 2008], Rome: Caritas.

Castles, S. and Miller, M.J. (2003) *The age of migration. International population movements in the modern world* (3rd edn), Basingstoke: Macmillan.

Cingolani, P. (2009) *Romeni d'Italia. Migrazioni, vita quotidiana e legami transnazionali* [Romanians in Italy. Migration, family life and transnational ties], Bologna: Il Mulino.

Cocchi, G. (ed) (1990) *Stranieri in Italia. Caratteri e tendenze dell'immigrazione dai paesi extracomunitari* [Foreigners in Italy. Characters and trends of immigration from outside Europe], Bologna: Nuova Cappelli.

Colombo, A. and Martini, E. (2007) 'Il flusso legale di lavoratori dall'estero' ['The flow of legal foreign workers'], in *Primo rapporto sugli immigrati in Italia* [First report on immigrants in Italy], Rome: Ministero dell'Interno, pp 80-131.

Colombo, A. and Sciortino, G. (2003) 'The Bossi-Fini Law: explicit fanaticism, implicit moderation and poisoned fruits', in J. Blondel and P. Segatti (eds) *Italian politics 2003*, Oxford: Berg, pp 162-80.

Colombo, A. and Sciortino, G. (2004) *Gli immigrati in Italia* [Immigrants in Italy], Bologna: Il Mulino.

Delle Donne, M., Melotti, U. and Petilli, S. (eds) (1993) *Immigrazione in Europa: Solidarietà e conflitto* [Immigration in Europe: Solidarity and conflict], Roma: Cediss.

Einaudi, L. (2007) *Le politiche dell'immigrazione in Italia dall'Unità a oggi* [*Italian Migration policies from Italy's unification until today*], Roma–Bari: Laterza.

Ferrera, M. (1996) 'The southern model of welfare in social Europe', *Journal of European Social Policy*, vol 6, no 1, pp 17-37.

Finotelli, C. (2009) 'The North–South myth revised. A comparison of the Italian and German migration regimes', *West European Politics*, vol 32, no 5, pp 886-903.

Graziano, P. and Madama, I. (2009) 'Inside employment friendly welfare state reforms in Europe. Conciliation policies in Italy', Paper presented at the 3rd Annual RECWOWE Integration Week, Utrecht, 9-13 June.

Hammar, T. (1985) *European immigration policy. A comparative study*, Cambridge: Cambridge University Press.

Jessoula, M., Graziano, P.R. and Madama, I. (2010) '"Selective flexicurity" in segmented labour markets: the case of Italian "mid-siders"', *Journal of Social Policy*, vol 39, no 4, pp 561-83.

Joppke, C. (2007) 'Transformation of immigrant integration: civic integration and antidiscrimination in the Netherlands, France, and Germany', *World Politics*, vol 59, no 2, pp 243-73.

King, R. and Ribas-Mateos, N. (2002) 'Towards a diversity of migratory types and contexts in Southern Europe', *Studi emigrazione/Migration Studies*, no 145, pp 5-25.

King, R., Lazaridis, G. and Tsardanidis, C. (2000) *Eldorado or fortress? Immigration in Southern Europe*, Basingstoke: Macmillan.

Martin, P.L. (1994) 'Germany: reluctant land of immigration', in W.A. Cornelius, P.L. Martin and J.F. Hollifield (eds) *Controlling immigration. A global perspective*, Stanford, CA: Stanford University Press, pp 189-226.

Melotti, U. (1993) 'Migrazioni internazionali e integrazione sociale: il caso italiano e le esperienze europee' ['International migration and social integration: Italian and European experience'], in M. Delle Donne, U. Melotti and S. Petilli (eds) *Immigrazione in Europa: Solidarietà e conflitto* [*Immigration in Europe: Solidarity and conflict*], Roma: Cediss, pp 29-66.

Michalowski, I. (2004) 'Integration programmes for newcomers. A Dutch model for Europe?', *IMIS-Beiträge*, no 24, pp 163-75.

Pastore, F. (2004) 'Che fare di chi non dovrebbe essere qui? La gestione della presenza straniera irregolare in Europa tra strategie nazionali e misure comuni' ['What to do with those who should not be here? Managing illegal foreign presence in Europe between national strategies and common measures'], in M. Barbagli, A. Colombo and G. Sciortino (eds) *I sommersi e i sanati. Le regolarizzazioni degli immigrati in Italia* [*The drowned and the healed. Regularisation of immigrants in Italy*], Bologna: Il Mulino, pp 19-46.

Pastore, F. (2009) 'So strict, so open… A long-term perspective on Italian immigration policies', Paper commissioned by CentreForum, London (www. fieri.it/politica_migratoria_italiana_prospettiva_lungo_periodo.php).

Pierson, P. (2004) *Politics in time: History, institutions, and social analysis*, Princeton, NJ: Princeton University Press.

Ponzo, I. (2008) 'Quello che i comuni hanno in comune. Politiche locali di accoglienza per gli immigrati' ['What municipalities have in common. Local policies to accommodate immigrants'], *Polis*, vol 3, pp 451-82.

Rella, P. and Vadalà, T. (1984) 'Sociological literature on migration in Italy', *Current Sociology*, vol 32, pp 143-74.

Reyneri, E. (2004) 'Immigrants in a segmented and often undeclared labour market', *Journal of Modern Italian Studies*, vol 9, no 1, pp 71-93.

Reyneri, E. (2008) 'Italy', in E. Hönekopp and H. Mattila (eds) *Permanent or circular migration? Policy choices to address demographic decline and labour shortages in Europe*, Budapest: International Organization for Migration.

Schierup, C.-U., Hansen, I. and Castles, S. (2006) *Migration, citizenship and the European welfare state*, Oxford: Oxford University Press.

Sciortino, G. (2004) 'Immigration in a Mediterranean welfare state: the Italian experience in comparative perspective', *Journal of Comparative Policy Analysis*, vol 6, no 2, pp 111-29.

Streeck, W. and Thelen, K. (eds) (2005) *Beyond continuity. Institutional change in advanced political economies*, Oxford: Oxford University Press.

Zincone, G. (1994) *Uno schermo contro il razzismo* [*A shield against racism*], Rome: Donzelli.

Zincone, G. (ed) (2000) *Primo rapporto sull'integrazione degli immigrati in Italia* [*First report on the integration of immigrants in Italy*], Bologna: Il Mulino.

Zincone, G. (ed) (2001) *Secondo rapporto sull'integrazione degli immigrati in Italia* [*Second report on the integration of immigrants in Italy*], Bologna: Il Mulino.

Zincone, G. (2008) *Italian immigrants and immigration policymaking: Structures, actors and practices*, IMISCOE Working Paper, Amsterdam: International Migration, Integration and Social Cohesion (www.imiscoe.org).

SEVEN

Differential inclusion in Germany's conservative welfare state: policy legacies and structural constraints

Lutz C. Kaiser and Regine Paul

Introduction

The German welfare state and its emphasis on status maintenance seem to cement migrants' worse socio-economic position, and contribute to their exclusion. However, its contribution-based logic has also been the primary mode of initial welfare access for guestworkers (Bommes, 2000). This uneven impact of the welfare system interacts in complicated ways with education chances for the second and now third generation of immigrants, and with the formal integration mode of an ethnicity-centred migration model for ethnic German repatriates.

Scrutinising migrants' status in the German case, this chapter aims to develop arguments in the literature about the relative exclusion of migrants (Sainsbury, 2006) and the structural impact of welfare states on their social inclusion patterns (Morissens and Sainsbury, 2005; Schierup et al, 2006). It sets out to explain the system-specific modes of inclusion and their differential impact on migrants with the help of a policy legacy perspective. The second section contextualises the position of Germany's migrants today in a framework of historical policy legacies. This shows how statuses and rights of migrants have, until today, historically been derived from their entry as guestworker or ethnic German. In the subsequent section, the dominant domains of migrant inclusion are identified in this context, as are sources of intergenerational pathways of inclusion. We review empirical studies that have scrutinised migrants' social inclusion, labour market participation and links to educational attainment to illustrate and qualify the ways in which differential inclusion plays out in the German welfare state. This allows us to see how welfare inclusion logics have also affected traditional German ethnicity-based migrant inclusion. We finally pay a brief tribute to political participation as a cross-cutting rights regime. In sum, we identify and assess three main – yet not mutually exclusive – domains of inclusion: via the labour market in the case of the original 'guestworkers', via educational attainment and later employment prospects for second-generation German-born immigrants and via ethnicity-oriented 'management' of welfare biographies and political participation for ethnic German repatriates. We are also able to highlight some of the shortcomings and blind spots of the differential *social* inclusion arguments revised and qualified here, and to re-assess the mechanisms of inclusion the conservative-corporatist welfare regime (Esping-Andersen, 1990) opens and constrains for migrants.

Migration policy legacy in Germany: from guestworkers to immigrants

Migration policies in Germany – certainly up to 2005 – feature significant 'policy failures' and 'unintended consequences' of recruitment and settlement patterns (see also Rogers, 1985; Castles, 1986) that have contributed to a long-lasting negligence of the social integration aspect of migration and worker recruitment. As we argue later, the historical legacy has in the past led to what we might term 'chains of exclusion', where an inequitable education system, combined with a conservative welfare system and demand-driven migration policy, interacts to produce sustained inequalities, that is, differential inclusion (see Chapter One, this volume) between different (im)migrant groups due to the highly variable dominant domains of integration over generations. The negligence of explicit policies on integration, especially for so-called guestworkers, has only recently been addressed, while ethnic German repatriates have been institutionally supported much more and asylum seekers are excluded from most integration policies.

Policy vision of labour recruitment: failure of 'guestworker' rotation (1945-73)

From 1945 until the construction of the Berlin Wall and closure of the East–West German border in 1961, approximately 2.6 million Germans migrated from East to West Germany, satisfying a large part of the post-war labour demand. However, labour demand created by the so-called *Wirtschaftswunder* (economic miracle) of the 1950s led to difficulties for companies in filling difficult and dirty jobs in the heavy industries (Rogers, 1985), resulting in a policy of active recruitment of foreign workers (*Anwerbepolitik*) for the industrial and especially heavy industry sectors, such as coal mining and the steel industry, as well as in construction and hotel and catering. The first bilateral labour recruitment treaty between West Germany and Italy was signed in 1955 and further agreements signed with Greece and Spain in 1960. With increased labour shortages due to the border closure in 1961, additional recruitment treaties were subsequently arranged with Turkey (1961), Morocco (1963), Portugal (1964), Tunisia (1965) and Yugoslavia (1968). In 1969, Italian immigrant workers were the largest national group among the entire pool of immigrant workers, and in 1970 the peak of in-migration was reached, with almost one million new entrants. Despite the growing Italian community, by 1973 the largest single national group of foreign workers was Turkish, comprising approximately 605,000 immigrant workers and their family members.

Migrants were typically male, poorly educated blue collar workers, often from rural areas in their countries of origin, who were able and willing to manage heavy work duties often involving long working hours. Neither German language proficiency nor the promotion of further education and training for immigrant workers were considered necessary or appropriate. In common legislative language migrant workers were labelled '*Gastarbeiter*' ('guestworkers'), assumed and politically encouraged to remain in Germany in a two-year rotation system designed to prevent long-term settlement (the same approach was embraced in France, Switzerland and Sweden) (Rogers, 1985). Rotation was to be guaranteed by the limitation of work and residence permits (usually issued annually); the limitation of renewals only to cases in which employment continued; restrictions on family reunification and housing (the latter was mostly in the form of dormitories centrally distributed to workers); as well as exclusion from most political rights.

The power of the factual: settlement and the need for an integration policy (1973-78)

With the oil shock in 1973 and the accompanying recession and rising unemployment, the recruitment of migrant workers was stopped (so-called *Anwerbestopp*, or 'recruitment stop'), and immigration, especially from non-European Community (EC) member states, was officially banned in Germany along with most other European labour-importing countries. Some migrants did return to their countries of origin, and for the first time in the Federal Republic of Germany (FRG), from 1974 to 1977, net migration of foreigners was successively negative (see Figure 7.1). However, even though few migrants originally intended to stay permanently (Rogers, 1985, p 14), many did not return home: employment opportunities were often still worse in their countries of origin; migrants might not have reached the saving levels they had planned; while for others, *de facto* settlement meant home was no longer in the country of origin, despite the obstacles created in the receiving countries. (For reflections on contemporary implications of this experience for intra-European Union [EU] migration in the wake of the current economic crisis, see Chapter Two, this volume.)

However, neither the principle of rotation and non-settlement nor the 'halt' on new entries were ever fully implemented, giving the lie to the rhetoric of not being a country of immigration. Firstly, circularity of migration was never really implemented as rotation was not enforced, especially when workers continued to be employed. This was certainly due to the resistance of employers who appreciated trained and well performing migrant workers (Triadafilopoulos and Schönwälder, 2006). Secondly, European legislative frameworks for migrants created a significant, if gradual, expansion of rights (Hollifield, 2004; Joppke, 2005). For instance, by the late 1960s, provisions for family reunion were liberalised and social rights for guestworkers were extended, often following court rulings that reflected the 'liberal constraints' on migration control in democratic states.

The twin phenomenon of settlement and rights expansion meant that by 1973, there were approximately 2.6 million foreign workers already resident in Germany, many of whom were long-term residents. In 1968 the Ministry of

Labour had already found that 'more than 50 percent of male workers had been in Germany for more than 4 years and 41 percent were living with their spouses' (Triadafilopoulos and Schönwälder, 2006, p 10). As the official labour recruitment ban closed other channels of entry, family reunion continued in the later 1970s, throughout the 1980s and 1990s, to date.

Figure 7.1: Net migration in Germany, 1954–2007

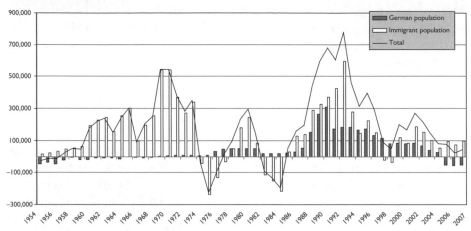

Source: Federal Statistical Office (2009)

However, the political rhetoric that Germany was 'not a country of immigration' meant that there was no pressure to accommodate the emerging needs of migrant workers nor to establish effective integration measures. There were some minor legislative changes – in 1978, for example, administrative regulations were reformed, enabling non-Germans to apply for a permanent residence permit (*unbefristete Aufenthaltserlaubnis*) after five years of stay, and for an even more secure settlement permit (*Aufenthaltsberechtigung*) after eight years. Also in 1978, the first government commission for the integration of immigrant workers and their families was convened, and a High Representative was established. In a memorandum from the head of the commission, comparatively progressive statements about the importance of integration were made (Kühn, 1979). However, policy reform would have required a paradigm change, and the acknowledgement of the permanence of immigration. This seemed politically out of reach, and, combined with party politics and a consensual decision-making process, often thwarted policy reform (see Green, 2004, for analysis of migration policy in the 'semi-sovereign' state). In practice, modes of differential integration have been established in the absence of formal integration policies. As the former 'guestworkers' were integrated via their employment in particular labour market sectors, the conservative welfare system, with its logic of contribution-based entitlement, meant that long-term residents, and especially those with rights of permanent settlement, also accrued social rights, including access to benefits such as unemployment and pensions

(Faist, 1998; Bommes, 2000). It is these former guestworkers who, integrated into the welfare system by virtue of their labour market participation, fit with Hammar's (1990) archetypical denizens – societal participants integrated via the domain of the labour market, accruing 'normal' social rights as a result, but without the political rights of citizenship, and often still at a disadvantage in terms of the conditions of their labour market participation (see below), and culturally and socially segregated (on the latter see Chapter Eleven, this volume). In addition, second-generation migrants' actual differential inclusion has, in practice, been structured by the interaction between the institutional architecture of a rigid education system and a conservative welfare state, as the third section of this chapter discusses in detail.

New immigrations in a changing world: towards restrictions and control (1980s and 1990s)

In the 1980s and 1990s German migration and (lack of formal) integration policy was challenged by the emergence of new immigrant populations, mainly comprising asylum seekers and ethnic German repatriates. In the 1970s and 1980s the inflow of asylum seekers and refugees was moderate and acceptance rates comparatively high (between 10 per cent and 30 per cent). The end of the Cold War, which saw German reunification and new border regimes at the new state's eastern edges, the collapse of the Soviet Union, civil wars in the Balkans and also the first Gulf Wars as well as changes in economic globalisation all had major implications for increased migration and changed migration patterns more generally (see Castles and Miller, 2009). In Germany, inflows from the former Yugoslavian and Soviet territories – both in the form of asylum seeking and ethnic German repatriation – were especially significant in the 1990s. The number of total registered asylum seekers peaked in 1992, with approximately 440,000 individuals. While about 1.34 million ethnic Germans immigrated between 1950 and 1986 (mostly from the territory of post-war Poland), another 1.05 million individuals mostly from ex-Soviet territories immigrated between 1986 and 1990, and almost 400,000 in 1990 alone (BAMF, 2009b; Hensen, 2009). The integration of this latter group was legally straightforward, as the German constitution automatically grants German citizenship to ethnic German repatriates, classifying Germany as an 'ethnic belonging' immigrant incorporation regime (compare Chapters Nine and Thirteen, this volume; see also Castles, 1995). Yet this combination of two new sources of immigration resulted in major social and political debate in the early to mid-1990s, with significant restrictive effects for both asylum seekers and potential repatriates. These debates were profoundly inflected with feelings of resentment, obligation, justice and contestations about what it means to belong and what it means to have a right to security (see also Chapter One, this volume, pp 8–11).[1]

The debate on asylum seeking became ever more focused on distinguishing legitimate and 'bogus' immigration, similarly associated with increases in asylum seeking in many European countries during this period (Sales, 2002; for Germany see Schönwälder, 1999). Hostility and political doubt also grew with regard to ethnic German immigrants whose integration might have been evaluated as a success story of German migration policy (Rock and Wolff, 2002). The advantageous treatment of ethnic German migrants – for example, access to German language courses, training, housing support, full welfare entitlements by acknowledging working biographies abroad (see also Bommes, 2000) and not least full political franchise – exposed the contrasting lack of support for other long-term resident migrants or even second-generation migrants born in Germany, and it also appears that the societal integration of ethnic Germans eventually turned out to be more difficult than expected, especially for the youngest generation (Brommler, 2006).

Policy change was introduced for both groups. The so-called asylum compromise between Christian and Social Democrats (which reconciled the constitutional tradition of protection with restrictive control objectives) introduced the 'safe third countries' principle in 1993, drastically limiting the legal possibilities for seeking asylum in the FRG. A blueprint of this policy was later uploaded into EU regulation via the asylum procedures directive (see also Menz, 2009). Administrative application and decision procedures were accelerated and a general work prohibition for asylum seekers during the initial 12 months of their stay in Germany was designed to prevent economically motivated entry. As a result, in the subsequent two decades the total numbers of asylum seekers dropped steadily, in recent years oscillating at around 20,000 per year with acceptance rates at about one per cent (BAMF, 2009a). As asylum procedures generally took several months and rejected applicants could often not be deported, staying in Germany as 'tolerated' residents (a status that does not guarantee any stable residence), the interdiction of employment and insecure legal status has formed a major obstacle to the economic and social integration of *de facto* (often even long-term) residents. Non-governmental organisations (NGOs) and trades unions have increasingly demanded a regulation of the legal residence status (*Bleiberecht*) of these migrants, including issues of work authorisation.

Ethnic Germans' right to enter Germany and to acquire citizenship was restricted by the Ethnic German Reception Law in 1990 (mainly raising the burden of proof of German ethnicity). A quota was established in 1993 limiting newcomers to approximately 200,000 per annum. To combat integration problems such as increasing unemployment among ethnic German migrants in the 1990s, proficiency in the German language was increasingly promoted in admission decisions (with almost half of all applicants failing the unofficial language test in the application interview) and language courses were offered (OECD, 2007b; Hensen, 2009).

'Managed migration': reappraisal of recruitment and integration policies since 2000

The new millennium saw two main – almost paradigmatic – changes in the German policy framework: the reappraisal of recruitment with the introduction and gradual expansion of exceptions to the 1973 ban, and a new focus on integration flanked by important changes in naturalisation practices. The first serious political debate about legal labour migration channels and reappraisal of active recruitment began in 2000,[2] when the introduction of a Green Card scheme for high-skilled workers made the question of whether Germany was a country of immigration redundant (Green, 2007; see also Menz, 2009). The declining dependency ratio in the social insurance system, structural and enduring labour shortages especially in skilled sectors necessary for economic competitiveness and increasing global competition for qualified personnel came to shape the public debate. In mid-2001, a government-established commission presented a report that focused on the demographic decline of the German working population and the importance of economy-driven migration management (BMI, 2001), echoing and shaping the EU's managed migration approach (see Chapter Three, this volume). The 2005 Act[3] eventually adopted did not include the most radical proposal, for a Canadian-style points-based system, but it represented a cautious liberalisation of labour migration rules.

A clear stratification of rights according to skill levels[4] structures the regulations in the Act, with liberalisation concerned mainly with 'high potentials' and later also migrant graduates educated in Germany. Skilled or unskilled newcomers can be assigned temporary residence permits (*Aufenthaltserlaubnis*) for employment under very specific and restrictive conditions and only with a concrete job offer. The permit is restricted to occupational sectors that the Labour Ministry issues, implying a demand-driven definition of shortages. Work authorisation is usually only granted after a labour market examination that establishes a need for non-German labour and the non-availability of domestic or EU workers.[5] Since 2005, high-skilled academics and researchers, in contrast, can be immediately granted a permanent settlement permit (*Niederlassungserlaubnis*), including the right to job search and free access to the labour market, but also immediate family reunion rights and labour market access for family members. In 2009, the Labour Migration Management Act (*Arbeitsmigrationssteuerungsgesetz*) was passed, aiming to increase the attractiveness of the German labour market for high-skilled migrants even further by granting secure residence status to foreign graduates from German universities (who are now allowed to stay on for job search), academics and the non-German high-skilled workforce. It seems that Germany has unambiguously entered the competition for the brightest minds that both the OECD and the EU Commission promote (Cerna, 2009).

The report of the 2001 Commission had emphasised the urgent necessity for policies to improve German language skills and integrate the migrant population in Germany, and these were reflected in the 2005 Act. Closely following the Dutch example, provisions such as a compulsory integration course including language classes and voluntary courses about German culture and the principles of the legal system have been established. In addition, from 1998 onwards naturalisation practices have introduced elements of a non–ethnicity-centred birthright approach into the formerly rather rigid German citizenship law. This reappraisal strongly reflected the Green Party's influence in government[6] and was intended to improve the integration and rights of long-term residents and German-born foreigners, to at least partially overcome the problematic mismatch between resident population and democratically enfranchised citizens (see Hammar, 1990).

Taken jointly, the emphasis on economic needs in a 'competition state' (Menz, 2009) and the eventual turn towards integration measures and more liberal citizenship policies created more rights for – mainly economically beneficial – resident workers, but at the same time also cemented a more restrictive stance on unwanted immigration, resonating with a 'managed migration' approach aimed at selecting and limiting flows on the basis of interlocking criteria.

Logics and modes of differential inclusion: welfare, migrant statuses and generations

We now turn to the modes of differential inclusion that migrants in Germany have experienced and discern some of the logics behind these. Social inclusion studies usually provide clear evidence for the relative exclusion of migrants in Western societies regarding their social rights and welfare access (see also Sainsbury, 2006). Yet, as Emma Carmel and Alfio Cerami argued in Chapter One (this volume), inclusion and exclusion patterns do not seem to be clear-cut but are in fact highly differentiated and depend on a number of features of the individual migrant as well as on structural factors in the country of destination. Analyses have shown, for instance, that structural specificities of welfare states impact on the extent and nature of the social inclusion of immigrants in different countries (Morissens and Sainsbury, 2005; Schierup et al, 2006).

By illustrating the main mechanisms of inclusion with statistical data, we are able to understand the interactions between a legal stratification of rights by status management, integration measures and targeting, labour market inclusion and economic performance and the consequent (highly variable) patterns of inclusion. Confirming and also qualifying previous studies, we show how differential inclusion is produced in a complex and interwoven function of migrants' legal status and their labour market performance, as different migrant groups have had a variety of pathways to integration primarily via different domains, for example via citizenship (ethnic Germans), the labour market (labour migrants) and education (second-generation immigrants).

A central role is ascribed to the logics of a conservative-corporatist welfare regime to which migrant workers gained gradual access through their employment and payment into German social security. Faist (1998) was one of the first to consider the role of different welfare state regimes in creating 'system–specific' paths of inclusion and exclusion for migrants. With its strong emphasis on insurance and status maintenance in a contribution-based system, the German conservative welfare state penalises long periods of unemployment or non-activity in the labour market, low-paid jobs and resulting low contribution records (see also Esping-Andersen, 1990). This mechanism, we argue, alongside other scholars, has especially disadvantaged second-generation native-born foreigners with lower educational attainment and insufficient job perspectives. There are also marked differentials among second generation migrants by country of origin, with Spanish and Polish migrants being treated similarly to Germans within one generation, and Turkish and Italian immigrants apparently faring poorly in terms of educational and labour market characteristics in the second generation (von Below, 2007). In contrast to this argument which is well recognised in the literature about the exclusionary logic of the conservative-corporatist welfare regime system, there is one migrant group, however, for whom this logic has been waived – ethnic German repatriates (Bommes, 2000). The interaction of the conservative welfare system with an ethnicity-based model of integration has created differential modes and indeed levels of inclusion for different groups of migrants in Germany, and is discussed in more detail in the next subsection (Marshall, 2000; Morris, 2003).

Demographics of the population with a migration background in Germany

Currently, approximately 12 per cent of the German population was born outside Germany. Including the children and grandchildren of people who moved to Germany as migrants, the proportion of individuals with a direct or indirect migration background amounts to about 19 per cent of the total German population (OECD, 2005). However, as shown in Table 7.1, the label 'migration background' covers various subpopulations of migrants.[7] About half of all individuals living in Germany with a migration background in a wider sense do not have German citizenship. Among them, are more than 11 per cent who did not experience migration themselves and were born in Germany. Comparing the population with a migration background with those who do not possess a migration background, striking differences in the average age and in the shares of the young and of the old cohort can be observed. The population with a migration background is considerably younger, although the implications of this are difficult to assess and rather depend on whether they are the result of the tendency of younger people to migrate and/or higher fertility rates among those with a migration background than those without.

The distinction between the subgroups is important especially with regard to pinpointing migration/integration policy planning. The acquisition of citizenship, as we saw above, has been distinguished by ethnicity, although this is beginning to change; there are substantial proportions of non-German citizens who were born in the country, with additional implications for political rights and integration. As discussed above, not only do migrants experience differential inclusion by the interacting logics of welfare, labour market and educational policies, but this is also affected by country of origin and cultural background.

Table 7.1: Population in Germany with and without a migration background, 2005

Population	With migration background		Without migration background	
	Million	%	Million	%
Total	14.8	100	67.1	100
Male	7.5	50.9	32.5	48.5
Female	7.3	49.1	34.6	51.5
German citizens	7.5	50.7	67.1	
with own migration experience	4.8	32.4	–	
without own migration experience	2.7	18.3	–	
Non-German citizens	7.3	49.3	–	
with own migration experience	5.6	37.8	–	
without own migration experience	1.7	11.5	–	
Average age	34.3 years		44.9 years	
share age <15	21.0%		11.6%	
share age >65	8.4%		22.5%	

Source: Federal Statistical Office (2009)

Labour market inclusion and educational performance

In Germany, with its contribution-based access to most welfare benefits, employment remains one of the most crucial factors for the successful integration of migrants, pointing to the more general function of labour markets as a social institution (Solow, 1990). Re-emphasising Faist's (1998) claim of 'system-specific' paths of inclusion, a recent cross-national comparison has highlighted how conservative welfare states interact with the labour market participation of migrants: the necessity of contribution for access to most benefits seems to incentivise active labour market participation to a greater extent than the more generous universal coverage of the Swedish welfare system (Koopmans, 2010). The labour market-oriented domain of inclusion is thus central for all migrants in Germany and has gradually created some social security for guestworkers in the past (Bommes, 2000). Indeed, reliance on post-government income among migrants is still lower today in Germany than in the Scandinavian welfare state of Denmark, for instance (Büchel and Frick, 2005).

Still, these reflections are by no means sufficient to conclude a perfect labour market and social inclusion of migrants in Germany. As in other OECD countries, migrants still suffer from unequal living conditions and education opportunities, with clear repercussions for their labour market participation (Lumpe, 2008). So despite the importance of labour market participation, the employment rate among the foreign-born working-age population in Germany is well below that of those born in Germany. The unemployment rate of foreign-born migrants significantly exceeds that of the German-born population (see Table 7.2; see also Algan et al, 2010). Most striking, however, is the employment gap of foreign-born women, who have an employment rate of approximately 46 per cent in contrast to 60 per cent for women born in Germany. Yet recent comparative research indicates that, firstly, Greek and Italian migrants of the first and second generation caught up to equal German non-migrants in terms of employment and, secondly, that the employment probability of second-generation women immigrants of all origins improves substantially as compared to the first generation (Algan et al, 2010).

Table 7.2: Employment and unemployment rate of German- and foreign-born population in Germany (15- to 64-year-olds, 2004)

	Employment rate		Unemployment rate		Ratio
	German-born	Foreign-born	German-born	Foreign-born	
Men	71.0	64.4	10.3	18.3	1.8
Women	60.5	46.4	9.6	15.2	1.6

Source: OECD (2007a)

These indications are supported by a comparative household panel study (Büchel and Frick, 2005) which found that in Germany, households with at least one foreign-born adult are considerably more reliant on non-market income such as public benefits and pensions than all-German-born households (and than comparable households in the UK, Spain or Austria, but less than in Denmark), even when controlling for various socio-economic measures. One negative consequence of this worse labour market position of migrants is endemic poverty. The poverty rates (calculated as 60 per cent of net equivalence income) of migrants significantly exceed those of Germans (see Figure 7.2): comparing the entire German national and migrant populations respectively, German citizens face a poverty risk of approximately 12 per cent as opposed to almost twice as high, at 28 per cent, for non-nationals in 2005. Even more marked is the difference for the population below 15 years of age, with a poverty rate of about 14 per cent without a migration background, compared to some 33 per cent for their counterparts with a migration background. This points to a problematic labour market inclusion of a second generation of migrants (see also Algan et al, 2010) that is closely related to socio-economic and especially education-related disadvantages of these young people in Germany, as the clarifications in the following section indicate (see Figure 7.3).

But let us first consider the specific situation of ethnic Germans, who are difficult to detect from statistics as their status of 'newcomers' is not generally accounted for, at least not for more than five years of initial stay (for problems of measurement, see also OECD, 2007b; Hensen, 2009). Until the 1990s the labour market integration of this migrant group seemed widely unproblematic as most

Figure 7.2: Poverty rates of the immigrant and the German population, 2005 (%)

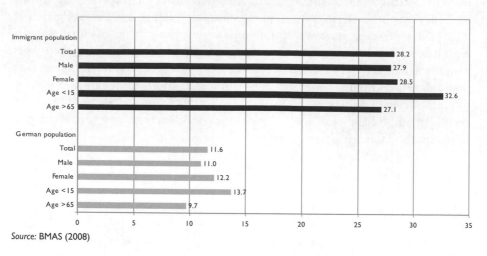

Source: BMAS (2008)

newcomers had sufficient German skills and qualifications to easily integrate, in economic terms (OECD, 2007b). Yet with the numeric increase of inflows in the early 1990s and the immigration of individuals and family members with insufficient German skills, unemployment figures for this group began to resemble the disadvantaged status of other migrant groups such as second-generation Turks (OECD, 2007b; see also Schmid, 2009). Specially targeted integration programmes have been initiated for language learning and eventually labour market inclusion of ethnic Germans. Falling unemployment rates among this group in the mid-2000s have been taken as a success of integration tools (see also Hensen, 2009). Adding to the generally more favourable position of ethnic Germans in the labour market, Bommes (2000) has also shown that the 'social construction of biographies' managed through welfare institutions helped ethnic Germans overcome their disadvantaged position as *de facto* migrants in some respects: they were 'treated as if they had spent their whole life in Germany; that is, as if they had accumulated biographically the chances of inclusion which made further social inclusions likely' (Bommes, 2000, p 101), which has helped ethnic German migrants fit into the logic of the conservative welfare system with 'mock' full contribution biographies. Some of these advantages in an ethnicity-based domain of inclusion have been withdrawn with the revision of the respective laws in the 1990s.

While differential inclusion patterns (via labour market contribution versus via status as a German national) seem to play out as regards foreign migrants versus ethnic German migrants, asylum seekers as another group to be distinguished certainly face the most exclusionary regime in terms of status and associated rights. Exclusion from labour market participation in the initial 12 months of residence and the often legally insecure status of so-called 'tolerated' migrants (who have not been granted refugee status but who cannot be expelled) makes them heavily dependent on benefits and adds to a perception of 'welfare scroungers' (see also Schönwälder, 1999; Sales, 2002). The seemingly uneven position of diverse migrant groups on the German labour market, their economic performance and social inclusion has led several scholars to the diagnosis of differential modes of inclusion (Marshall, 2000; Morris, 2002) shaped by institutionally manifested constraints. We find such a claim from Büchel and Frick (2005, p 206) confirmed in our brief illustrations: 'restrictions on access to the labour market and parts of the social security system that are related to citizenship or immigration status play an important role in limiting the economic performance of immigrants'.

Educational attainment and links to labour market participation

According to a common understanding, one main device to boost employability and social integration is education and training (Estevez-Abe et al, 2001). Skills, as the discussion of current tendencies in the previous section indicated, are also a central category for new admissions in 'managed migration'. This approach to employability and economic utility has several merits, but also substantial shortcomings. For newcomers it implies an easy and un-bureaucratic transmission and recognition of skills acquired abroad, which is not always the case in practice. For resident migrants, it implies the existence of non-discriminatory education systems that do not disadvantage pupils from comparatively poorer socio-economic backgrounds. Compared to other OECD countries, the German education system is often described as socially rigid, with its three-tier approach[8] and early categorisation of pupils into different paths at the ages of ten to twelve (Breen, 2004). Even though educational attainment of second-generation migrants in Germany seems to be better than that of their parents (Algan et al, 2010, migrants generally seem to have few chances to achieve a relatively high level of education that could guarantee good labour market performance and decent overall societal integration. The phenomenon of educational non-permeability often disproportionately affects families with a migration background, as Figure 7.3 indicates. This comparison of the educational and occupational attainment of the population with a migration background as opposed to the rest of the German population clearly highlights discrepancies. Interestingly, and despite the intergenerational improvement of educational levels, educational attainment gaps between immigrants and Germans also remain substantial for the second generation (Algan et al, 2010). Although the population with a migrant background constitutes approximately 19 per cent of the population in Germany, the share of migrants among those with no school leaving certification stands at an astonishingly high 60 per cent. The same pattern holds true with regard to the proportion of the population with no vocational training qualification. In this case, the disproportionate share of immigrants amounts to about 28 per cent.

When the educational performance of pupils of a second-generation migrant is compared with the performance of pupils with no migration background (as in the PISA-Study), clear differences in literacy – even more significant in Germany than in other OECD countries – can be observed between these two groups (see Table 7.3). This suggests that second-generation migrants seem to be heavily affected by the non-permeability of the education system and intergenerational immobility. Apparently many German-born foreigners do not obtain an adequate education and eventually struggle to find rewarding employment in adulthood. From a study of young Italian and Turk migrants of the second generation in Germany it seems that a strong 'intergenerational heredity' of educational attainment hampers young people's job chances and their social inclusion (von Below, 2007, p 213). While other studies have found that educational attainment substantially improves for the second generation of migrants, especially among males, this improvement does not seem to translate as significantly better employment prospects, which remain lower than that of Germans without a migration background (see also Algan et al, 2010). Some have hinted at other potential discriminatory factors at play (such as culture, attitudes and values etc; see von Below, 2007).

Figure 7.3: Educational and occupational attainment of the immigrant and the German population, 2005 (%)

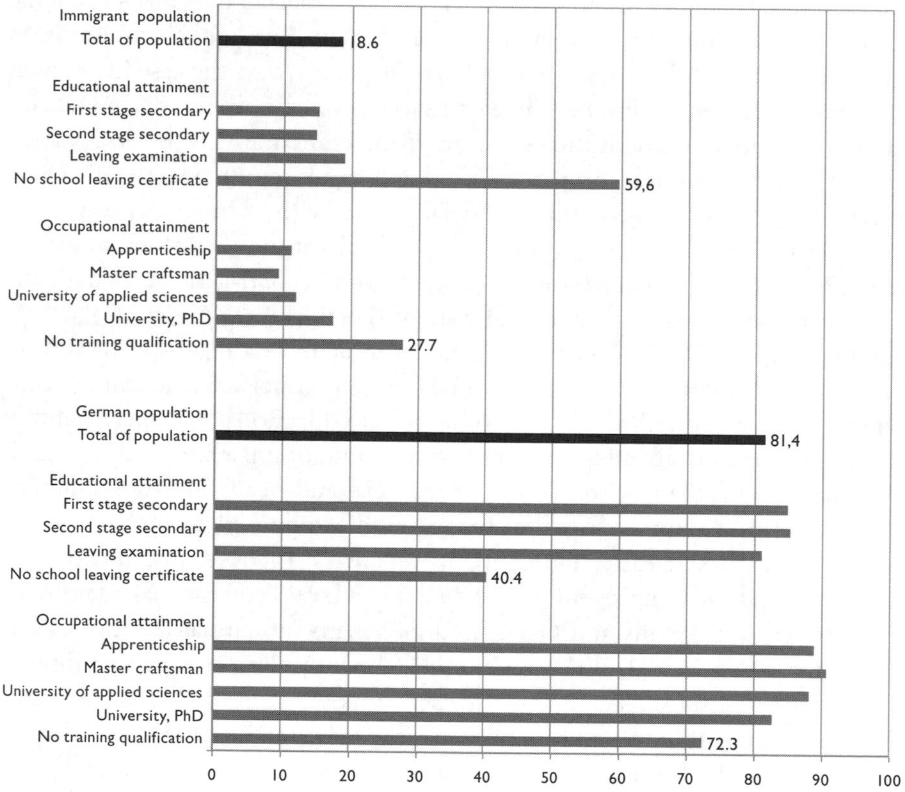

Source: BMAS (2008)

In sum, the rigid educational system combined with the partial intergenerational heredity of lower educational attainments and relatively worse job prospectives hampers migrants' (and also native-born second-generation migrants') labour market inclusion. As a function of conservative, status–maintaining welfare system logics, low labour market performance equals low levels of social inclusion. The conservative welfare system eventually cements something we could dub a chain of exclusion: social–educational–labour market and economic – and again social, over generations.

Table 7.3: Literacy point differences (reading skills) between second-generation migrant pupils and non-migration background pupils (15-year-olds)

GER	BEL	AUT	DNK	CHE	NLD	FRA	NZL	USA	SWE	CAN	AUS
96	84	73	57	53	50	48	22	22	20	9	4

Note: When interpreting differences in the PISA scores, a difference of at least 73 points on the PISA scale represents one proficiency level in reading literacy. A difference of one proficiency level can be considered as a comparatively large difference in student performance in substantive terms.

Source: PISA-Study (2003)

Political participation and civic integration

Contemporary research on different forms of political participation shows a clear bias of institutional opportunities and constraints against the participation of socially marginalised groups (Solt, 2008), and in the case of migrants, exclusion from political participation becomes even more severe. In Germany, with its exclusive definition of citizenship, non-EU migrants find themselves widely excluded from suffrage and political participation (Odmalm, 2005, 2009). Since the 1992 Maastricht Treaty, EU member state citizens are eligible to vote at local level, but that leaves major groups of residents (such as Turkish groups) without even these limited rights. Although Germany is by no means alone in this restrictive regulation within the EU (12 of the 27 member states do not permit non-EU nationals the right to vote; see Groenendijk, 2008), the comparatively important inflow of migrants and their settlement has significantly fed the pool of 'denizens' who are *de facto* permanent residents but who do not enjoy full political rights.

Unfortunately, the societal price of this political decision seems to be particularly high, as there is strong evidence that voting rights enhance a successful integration of migrants (Marcelo et al, 2003). In consequence, the lack of integration of minority ethnic groups into the political and societal culture of the country remains particularly pronounced in Germany, especially if compared to other European countries (for a review, see Koopmans and Duyvené de Wit, 2005). Even though some 'politically inclusive' initiatives at local government level have recently emerged, these are still not enough to provide for an overall and effective political participation (and not 'just' civic participation) (for a more extensive discussion, see Kaiser, 2009). As the challenges of integration and social protection that Germany currently faces are multiple (they imply economic, but also cultural and social factors), it seems to us that the question of political participation must be addressed alongside questions of economic and social integration. A lively and vigorous NGO sector with certain possibilities for civic participation, especially on a local and municipality level (Odmalm, 2009), which does exist for migrant groups, for example the big Turkish community, cannot substitute for formal political representation of *de facto* long-term and German-born residents. The restricted and somewhat arbitrary granted impact of civic organisations in the German corporatist polity (churches and trades unions are more systematically included in decision making than other interest groups; see Odmalm, 2009) cannot guarantee any political impact when it comes to arguing for the appropriate designation of resources to promote better education, better training, more integration measures and more social support to migrant and immigrant groups.

By contrast, ethnic Germans are by definition formally included in full political participation with their access to a German passport and citizenship. This differential treatment of long-term non-German residents as well as German-born non-nationals of second, and even third-generation migrants and some, ethnically defined migrants who are born abroad, has caused some debate and perceived inequalities. Irrespective of labour market performance and educational attainment, the guarantee of national citizenship and political rights in the ethnicity-oriented domain formally supports the relatively privileged mode of inclusion for this migrant group.

Conclusion

The interaction of policy legacies, migrant statuses and current migration and integration policies with different migrant groups' experiences in the labour market and the education system discussed in this chapter results in highly differential modes of inclusion. While there are no clearly determining consequences of the connection between status and rights, different migrant groups seem to encounter different logics of inclusion. We have identified three dominant domains of inclusion and discerned the logics and mechanisms behind these, illustrating that the different statuses ascribed to different migrants in Germany – which are echoed in their legal and welfare treatment – have significant consequences for migrants' rights and their experience of migration and/or immigration. First, in the ethnicity-oriented domain, ethnic belonging can grant privileged social rights, privileged rights to labour market integration, welfare access and political rights. In the case of ethnic German repatriates, therefore, the dominant domain whereby inclusion is achieved is that of ethnic citizenship. The second domain is labour market-oriented: integration is achieved and has to be earned by labour market participation and economic performance. The close links between contributions paid from wages and access to welfare rights in the conservative-corporatist regime can be a tool for gradual social integration, as in the case of guestworkers (Bommes, 2000), and it can even act as an incentive for employment more generally (Koopmans, 2010).

However, the links between intergenerationally significant socio-economic factors, educational attainment and labour market performance have indicated the significant drawbacks of the second inclusion domain. Structural disadvantages such as comparatively low educational attainment are often amplified for second and third generations in a rather rigid education system. By anchoring inclusion to labour market participation and performance, the conservative German welfare state can thus negatively influence the living conditions of immigrants over generations. This is where the third dominant domain of inclusion, skills orientation, acquires significance. Education and language training is, at least since the 2005 changes to migration law in Germany, increasingly understood as a key means to successful integration and as a tool to boost migrants' employability and labour market participation. This domain is especially important for immigrants born in Germany, but also for young ethnic Germans of lower educational levels who struggle to fully seize the paths of ethnic inclusion in the labour market.

The skill domain is of increasing importance in the recently established paradigm of 'managed migration' as it cuts across the ethnicity-based rights regime. In the competition for high skills, all foreign nationals with economically desired qualifications are now courted with a promise of stable status and rights (for example, *Niederlassunsgerlaubnis* [settlement permit]). At the same time, low-skilled newcomers of non-German nationality accrue rather unstable and highly conditional residence and social rights. But also, otherwise privileged ethnic Germans with full political rights find themselves excluded from the labour market and high levels of social inclusion if they lack an economically usable education level. The effects of a regulative focus on recruiting high-skilled migrants on the conservative-corporatist welfare regime logics and migrants' social inclusion are yet to be assessed.

Notes

[1] Some of these tensions were revealed in hostile criminal acts of far-right extremist groups including pogrom-like persecutions of foreign residents in Mölln and arson of an asylum seeker's home in Rostock in 1992, as well as the scandalised political response that followed.

[2] Due to massive labour shortages in the information technology (IT) sector (see Werner, 2001), the Green Card was initiated by Chancellor Schröder as an exception to the general recruitment stop. A quota limited entries to 10,000 IT specialists per year, or a maximum of 20,000 for additional demand (BMWA, 2000).

[3] An Act regulating the management and limitation of immigration, the residence and integration of EU citizens and foreigners.

[4] German law distinguishes between high potential (mainly university graduates or professionals with long-standing high-level job experience and high wages) skilled workers (corresponding to German vocational education of at least three years) and unskilled workers.

[5] For skilled migrants this includes language teachers, IT specialists (incorporating the old Green Card), blue collar workers and specialists, social workers, care workers and internationally exchanged employees of multinational companies (BMWA, 2004). In the case of unskilled workers, the list comprises seasonal workers, carneys (funfair workers), au pairs, housekeepers, entertainers and vocational trainees (BMWA, 2004). Unskilled labour recruitment is further restricted to authorisation via bilateral agreements.

[6] It was a key plank in the Green Party's 1998 election manifesto and became a prominent feature of the coalition agreement.

[7] This official data uses the 'narrow' definition of migrant background. It is a problematic proxy for 'migrant' as it includes all migrants (some of whom may be German), *and* all German-born foreigners, but does not include the German-born children of ethnic repatriates, nor the German-born children of non-national parents who are themselves naturalised (the 'wider definition'). On the significance of definitions and proxies for migrants, see Chapter Two, this volume. Despite these issues, this chapter adopts the crude shorthand 'immigrant' to refer to this definition of 'migration background', and 'German' to refer to the rest of the population, to avoid too much clumsy expression.

[8] Germany has a tripartite education system, which, although it varies from *Land* to *Land*, generally constructs pathways for children towards higher education or vocational training early on in school, and moving from one path to another is very difficult.

References

Algan, Y., Dustmann, C. and Glitz, A. (2010) 'The economic situation of first and second-generation immigrants in France, Germany and the United Kingdom', *Economic Journal*, vol 120, pp 4-27.

BAMF (Bundesamt für Migration und Flüchtlinge [Federal Office for Migration and Refugees]) (2009a) *Asyl in Zahlen 2008 [Figures for asylum 2008]*, Paderborn: BAMF.

BAMF (2009b) *Grunddaten der Zuwandererbevölkerung in Deutschland [Basic data for the immigrant population in Germany]*, Paderborn: BAMF.

BMAS (Bundesministerium für Arbeit und Soziales [Federal Ministry of Labour and Social Affairs]) (2008) *Lebenslagen in Deutschland. Dritter Armuts- und Reichtumsbericht der Bundesregierung [Life in Germany. Third poverty and wealth of the federal government]*, Berlin: BMAS.

BMI (Bundesministerium des Innern [Federal Ministry of the Interior]) (2001) *Structuring immigration – Fostering integration. Report by the Independent Commission on Migration to Germany*, Berlin: BMI.

BMWA (Bundesministerium für Wirtschaft und Arbeit [Federal Ministry of Economics and Labour]) (2000) *Verordnung über die Arbeitsgenehmigung für hoch qualifizierte ausländische Fachkräfte der Informations- und Kommunikationstechnologie (IT-ArGV)* [*Regulation on work permits for highly skilled foreign professionals in information and communication technology*], Bonn: Bundesgesetzblatt.

BMWA (2004) *Verordnung über die Zulassung von neueinreisenden Ausländern zur Ausübung einer Beschäftigung (Beschäftigungsverordnung, BeschV)* [*Regulation on the admission of foreigners for employment (Employment Regulation)*], Bonn: Bundesgesetzblatt.

Bommes, M. (2000) 'National welfare state, biography and migration. Labour migrants, ethnic Germans, and the re-ascription of welfare state membership', in M. Bommes and A. Geddes (eds) *Immigration and welfare. Challenging the border of the welfare state*, London: Routledge, pp 90-108.

Breen, R. (ed) (2004) *Social mobility in Europe*, Oxford: Oxford University Press.

Brommler, D. (2006) 'Neue Herausforderungen – neue Instrumente. Deutsche Aussiedlerpolitik am Scheideweg' ['New challenges – new tools. German ethnic politics at the crossroads'], in S. Ipsen-Peitzmeier and M. Kaiser (eds) *Zuhause Fremd. Russlanddeutsche zwischen Russland und Deutschland* [*Aliens at home. Russian Germans between Russia and Germany*] (transcript) Bielefeld: Bibliotheca eurasica pp 109-28.

Büchel, F. and R. Frick Joachim (2005) 'Immigrants' economic performance across Europe – does immigration policy matter?, *Population Research and Policy Review*, vol 24, no 2, pp 175-212.

Castles, S. (1986) 'The guest-worker in Western-Europe – an obituary', *International Migration Review*, vol 20, no 4, pp 761-78.

Castles, S. (1995)."How nation-states respond to immigration and ethnic diversity." New Community 21: 293-293.

Castles, S. and Miller, M.J. (2009) *The age of migration*, Basingstoke: Palgrave Macmillan.

Cerna, L. (2009) 'The varieties of high-skilled immigration policies: coalitions and policy outputs in advanced industrial countries', *Journal of European Public Policy*, vol 16, no 1, pp 144-61.

Esping-Andersen, G. (1990) *The three worlds of welfare capitalism*, Cambridge: Polity Press.

Estevez-Abe, M., Iversen, T. and Soskice, D. (2001) 'Social protection and the formation of skills: a reinterpretation of the welfare state', in P.A. Hall and D. Soskice (eds) *Varieties of capitalism. The institutional foundations of comparative advantage*, New York: Oxford University Press, pp 145-82.

Faist, T. (1998) 'Immigration, integration und Wohlfahrtsstaaten. Die Bundesrepublik Deutschland in vergleichender Perspektive' ['Immigration, integration and welfare states. The Federal Republic of Germany in comparative perspective'], in M. Bommes and J. Halfmann (eds) *Migration in nationalen Wohlfahrtsstaaten* [*Migration in national welfare states*], Osnabrück: Rasch, pp 147-70.

Federal Statistical Office (2009) *Bevölkerung und Erwerbstätigkeit* [*Population and employment*], Wiesbaden: Statistisches Bundesamt.

Green, S. (2004) *The politics of exclusion: Institutions and immigration policy in contemporary Germany*, Manchester: Manchester University Press.

Green, S. (2007) 'Zwischen Kontinuität und Wandel: Migrations- und Staatsangehörigkeitspolitik' ['Between continuity and change: immigration and nationality policy'], in M.G. Schmidt and R. Zohlnhöfer (eds) *Regieren in der Bundesrepublik Deutschland. Innen- und Aussenpolitik seit 1949* [*Governance in the Federal Republic of Germany. Domestic and foreign policy since 1949*], Wiesbaden: VS Verlag für Sozialwissenschaften, pp 113-34.

Groenendijk, K. (2008) *Local voting rights for non-nationals in Europe: What we know and what we need to learn*, Nijmegen: Migration Policy Institute.

Hammar, T. (1990) *Democracy and the nation-state: Aliens, denizens and citizens in a world of international migration*, Aldershot: Avebury.

Hensen, J. (2009) 'Zur Geschichte der Aussiedler- und Spätaussiedleraufnahme', ['History of ethnic German and late ethnic German admissions'] in C. Bergner and M. Weber (eds) *Aussiedler- und Minderheitenpolitik in Deutschland. Bilanz und Perspektiven*, [*Ethnic German and minority policy in Germany. Balance and perspectives*] Munich: Oldenbourg, pp 47-62.

Hollifield, J.F. (2004) 'The emerging migration state', *International Migration Review*, vol 38, no 3, pp 885-912.

Joppke, C. (2005) 'Exclusion in the liberal state: the case of immigration and citizenship policy', *European Journal of Social Theory*, vol 8, no 1, pp 43-61.

Kaiser, L.C. (2009) 'Diversity und interkulturelle Kompetenz in Kommunen' ['Diversity and intercultural competence in communities'], *Migration und Soziale Arbeit/Migration and Social Work*, no 3-4, pp 190-5.

Koopmans, R. (2010) 'Trade-offs between equality and difference: immigrant integration, multiculturalism and the welfare state in cross-national perspective', *Journal of Ethnic and Migration Studies*, vol 36, no 1, pp 1-26.

Koopmans, R. and Duyvené de Wit, T. (2005) 'The integration of ethnic minorities into political culture: the Netherlands, Great Britain and Germany compared', *Acta Politica*, vol 40, pp 50-73.

Kühn, H. (1979) *Kühn-Memorandum. Stand und Weiterentwicklung der Integration der ausländischen Arbeitnehmer und ihrer Familien in der Bundesrepublik Deutschland* [*Kühn memorandum*] [*Kuehn memorandum. State and development of the integration of foreign employees and their families in the Federal Republic of Germany*] Bonn: Bundesregierung.

Lumpe, C. (2008) 'The impact of immigration on the labour market. A survey', in H. Kolb and H. Egbert (eds) *Migrants and markets. Perspectives from economics and other social sciences*, Amsterdam: Amsterdam University Press, pp 20-45.

Marcelo, J., Vlasta, Z. and Hofinger, C. (2003) 'Voting rights support successful integration – a Vienna case study', in European Monitoring Centre on Racism and Xenophobia (ed) *Equal voices*, issue 12, Vienna: EUMC, pp 10-14.

Marshall, B. (2000) *The new Germany and migration in Europe*, Manchester: Manchester University Press.

Menz, G. (2009) *The political economy of managed migration: Nonstate actors, Europeanization, and the politics of designing migration policies*, Oxford: Oxford University Press.

Morissens, A. and Sainsbury, D. (2005) 'Migrants' social rights, ethnicity and welfare regimes', *Journal of Social Policy*, vol 34, no 4, pp 637-60.

Morris, L. (2002) *Managing migration: Civic stratification and migrants' rights*, London: Routledge.

Odmalm, P. (2005) *Migration policies and political participation: Inclusion or intrusion in Western Europe?*, Basingstoke: Palgrave Macmillan.

Odmalm, P. (2009) 'Turkish organizations in Europe: how national contexts provide different avenues for participation', *Turkish Studies*, vol 10, no 2, pp 149-63.

OECD (Organisation for Economic Co-operation and Development) (2005) *The labour market integration of immigrants in Germany*, Paris: OECD.

OECD (2007a) *International Migration Outlook: SOPEMI*, Paris: OECD.

OECD (2007b) *The labour market integration of immigrants in Germany*, Paris: OECD.

PISA-Study (Programme for International Student Assessment) (2003) *Learning for tomorrow's world – First results from PISA 2003*, Paris: OECD.

Rock, D. and Wolff, S. (ed) (2002) *Coming home to Germany? The integration of ethnic Germans from Central and Eastern Europe in the Federal Republic*, Oxford: Berghahn Books.

Rogers, R. (1985) *Guests come to stay: The effects of European labour migration on sending and receiving countries*, Boulder, CO and London: Westview.

Sainsbury, D. (2006) 'Immigrants' social rights in comparative perspective: welfare regimes, forms in immigration and immigration policy regimes', *Journal of European Social Policy*, vol 16, no 3, pp 229-44.

Sales, R. (2002) 'The deserving and the undeserving? Refugees, asylum seekers and welfare in Britain', *Critical Social Policy*, vol 22, no 3, pp 456-78.

Schierup, C.U., Hansen, P. and Castles, S. (2006) *Migration, citizenship, and the European welfare state: A European dilemma*, Oxford: Oxford University Press.

Schmid, A. (2009) 'Zur integration von Aussiedlern', [The integration of ethnic Germans] in C. Bergner and M. Weber (eds) *Aussiedler- und Minderheitenpolitik in Deutschland. Bilanz und Perspektiven [Ethnic German and minority policy in Germany. Balance and perspectives]* München: Oldenbourg: 67-78.

Schönwälder, K. (1999) '"Persons persecuted on political grounds shall enjoy the right of asylum – but not in our country": asylum policy and debates about refugees in the Federal Republic of Germany', in A. Bloch and C. Levy (eds) *Refugees, citizenship and social policy in Europe*, Basingstoke: Macmillan, pp 76-90.

Solow, R.M. (1990) *The labour market as a social institution*, Oxford: Oxford University Press.

Solt, F. (2008) 'Economic inequality and democratic political engagement', *American Journal of Political Science*, vol 52, pp 48-60.

Triadafilopoulos, T. and Schönwälder, K. (2006) 'How the Federal Republic became an immigration country. Norms, politics and the failure of West Germany's guestworker system', *German Politics and Society*, vol 24, no 3, pp 1-19.

von Below, S. (2007) 'What are the chances of young Turks and Italians for equal education and employment in Germany? The role of objective and subjective indicators', *Social Indicators Research*, vol 82, no 2, pp 209-31.

Werner, H. (2001) 'From temporary guests to permanent settlers? From the German "guestworker" programmes of the sixties to the current "green card" initiative for IT specialists', *ILO International Migration Papers*, vol 42, pp 1-25.

EIGHT

Welfare or work: migrants' selective integration in Finland

*Saara Koikkalainen, Timo Tammilehto, Olli Kangas, Marja Katisko,
Seppo Koskinen and Asko Suikkanen*

Introduction

All of the Nordic countries have historically been rather homogeneous in their national culture and population. In Finland, a country of 5.3 million inhabitants, the largest minority are Swedish-speaking Finns, who form about 5.4 per cent (290,000) of the population and enjoy extensive rights guaranteed, for example, by the fact that Swedish is the country's second official language. In addition, there is a small indigenous Sami population (9,000), and a Roma minority (10,000). The immigrant population was very small until the beginning of the 1990s with the arrival of the first larger groups, Ingrian return migrants from Russia and refugees from Somalia. During the labour migration period following the Second World War, Finland was still an emigration country. Because the differences in the standard of living were still great between Finland and its closest Scandinavian neighbour, a total of 530,000 Finns moved to Sweden to work in the booming economy in the 1960s and 1970s. Seventy-five per cent of all Finns who emigrated after the Second World War headed for Sweden, although an estimated half of them have since returned (Forsander, 2003, p 55; Korkiasaari and Söderling, 1998, pp 8-10).

The numbers of incoming migrants exceeded outgoing migrants for the first time as late as the beginning of the 1980s (Heikkilä and Järvinen, 2003, p 103). Since then the country has experienced a relatively fast process of internationalisation, including consistent annual increases in the numbers of migrants. In 2008 a total of 29,100 immigrants entered Finland, the highest number since the country's independence in 1917. Net immigration for the same year was 15,450, the highest number in the post-war period (Statistics Finland, 2009).

Increased movement from European Union (EU) countries, especially Estonia, partially explains the increase. According to the Organisation for Economic Co-operation and Development (OECD) *International Migration Outlook* (2008), 15,000 EU citizens entered Finland for work-related reasons, and another 14,000 were visa-exempt, largely berry pickers and seasonal workers in the market garden industry. Some 7,200 from non-EU countries were granted work-related residence permits in 2006, almost half of them Russians. As is evident in a comparison of the labour migration data and the long-term immigration numbers, many of the foreign workers are in Finland on a temporary basis. Yet work-related migration was only under 10 per cent of the total migration inflow. The most common reasons for migration were family-related immigration, including accompanying family (35.9 per cent) and free movers from elsewhere in the EU (38.7 per cent).

In 2008 Finland received 4,035 asylum seekers. In the past 10 years the numbers of favourable decisions, either the granting of asylum or a residence permit based on humanitarian reasons, have varied between 467 and 860 per year (Finnish Immigration Service, 2009). Living in Finland without official documents is difficult, and estimates on the numbers of illegal immigrants vary (see also Chapter Two, this volume). The Ministry of the Interior in charge of immigration matters has argued that the good standard of basic social security attracts asylum seekers to Finland. It has been suggested that asylum seekers deliberately destroy their passports to conceal previous applications in other EU states to avoid being labelled a 'Dublin case', subject to regulation under the Dublin Convention, thus facing deportation back to the original point of entry into EU territory. In response, the Ministry has proposed changing the law regarding the right to work while waiting for a decision on asylum applications. Immigrants who do not possess valid travel documentation would have to wait six months before being allowed to work in Finland whereas those with passports could work after three months.

In a way Finland still suffers from the so-called 'Somali shock', created by the sudden arrival of an ethnically distinct migrant group to a remote country in the midst of an economic recession in the early 1990s (Paananen, 2005b). The image of a group of young males from Afghanistan, Somalia or Iraq spending time playing football or sitting in a shopping mall cafeteria without any apparent need to work has been a strong motivator for voices criticising immigration. This discussion largely focuses on the level of social security and immigrants' possibilities of working for a living and provides concrete examples of the role and use of feeling and emotion in shaping immigration politics, discussed in Chapter One. As recent studies have shown, the labour market position of immigrants in Finland is vulnerable and unemployment continues to be a major barrier to integration (Forsander, 2003; Heikkilä, 2005; Pehkonen, 2006). Therefore access to the labour market, the right and responsibility to earn one's living, is central to the Finnish immigration debate.

This chapter looks at immigration to Finland from two different angles: from the point of view of the social security system and of labour market integration. The right to Finnish social security is dependent on the duration of stay and the prerequisites of the immigrant's residency. The principal rule is that a person migrating to Finland on a permanent basis is eligible for Finnish social security as a whole, although there are special regulations concerning earnings-related security. This chapter first gives a short overview on immigrant access to social security. Then the question of labour market integration is discussed based on recent research on immigrants in Finland.

The Finnish social security system

Historically speaking, Finland has been a latecomer in the field of social policy, particularly in social insurance, even though Finland developed a universal model of social protection earlier than most other European countries (Kangas and Palme, 2005). The leading idea for most benefits was based on 'people's insurance', protecting the whole citizenry. The universal model of social policy has offered a way of increasing solidarity between different layers of society and acted as an effective tool for nation building. However, a divide between 'rural' and 'urban' Finland conditioned the process of creating either a system with universal flat-rate benefits and basic security for everyone or a system with income-related benefits for the working population. This political dualism is still reflected in the income transfer system. All major 'basic security benefits' are administered by the National Social Insurance Institution (*Kela*), while all employment-related benefits, apart from sickness insurance, are administered jointly by the trades unions and employer organisations.

Those who intend to stay in Finland for longer than three months need a residence permit, with the exception of Nordic, EU and European Economic Area (EEA) citizens. A residence permit can be issued on the grounds of family ties, Finnish descent, return migration, studying, humanitarian reasons or employment. The first residence permit is always granted for a fixed term. The fixed-term permit can be either continuous (Type A, maximum duration four years at a time) or temporary (Type B, maximum duration one year at a time). The applicant must be able to support him or herself by working, or with a pension or some other form of regular income. In addition, an important criterion for the first permit is that the person will not require financial social assistance. Naturally this requirement is not applied to asylum seekers.

The legal status of immigrants moving to Finland or staying in Finland temporarily is significantly affected by whether Finland and the person's home country have a convention or an agreement on social security. For the intra-European migrants Regulation (EEC) No 1408/71 on the application of social security schemes corresponds to a multilateral social security convention (see Chapter Five, this volume, on the new regulation 883/2004). The Nordic countries have a mutual agreement on social security, which is more extensive than EU Regulation 1408/71, as it also covers students, pensioners and others outside the labour market.

The Finnish social security system is basically residency-based. Certain benefits are, however, employment-based, and the systems complement one another. Having Finnish citizenship or being liable to pay taxes in Finland do not, as such, entitle individuals to benefits. Three basic elements of the Finnish welfare state, each of which also bears some inherent risks for immigrants, are detailed below: close links to social risks, individuality, and residency-based benefits and services.

Close links to social risks

Social policy programmes are designed to respond to specific social risks, such as unemployment, old age or work disability, and not specifically to poverty or social exclusion. This has been a strength of the system, but concentrating on 'traditional' risks may cause problems as the system does not recognise potential 'new' risks. According to statistics, 43 per cent of the poor in Finland live alone but the status of 'living alone' is not a legitimate social risk that would entitle a person to benefits. When it comes to the social status of 'immigrants', there are only a few programmes specifically targeted at the immigrant population.

Individuality

Social insurance benefits and taxation are based solely on the individual's own work history, payments and income. This has been a clear advantage in abolishing disincentives for housewives or mothers to participate in the labour market. This model also comes close to what Yasemin Soysal (1994) calls personhood-based rights (in contrast to national rights), typical for post-national settings. However, there are also problems. First, some social benefits (such as housing allowance) are, for obvious reasons, linked to household income and some others (such as labour market subsidy for the unemployed), for not so obvious reasons, are dependent on household income. There is therefore a discrepancy between the individuality principle and household-based income testing. Second, the strong attachment to individuality is problematic for immigrant groups who have a wider understanding of the concept of family, as dependencies between adult generations are not recognised. For example, in the summer of 2009 the Finnish authorities decided to expel an elderly Egyptian woman, as in their interpretation grandmothers are not members of the core family, even though this particular grandmother's three sons and their families were legal residents in Finland.

Residency-based benefits and services

The first criterion for receiving benefits and services is residency, not employment. Thus, the coverage of social insurance is wider than in many other EU countries, which implies that immigrants may qualify for social benefits more easily than in other countries. In order to combat that 'problem' a number of changes have been made. Finland's membership in the EU gave impetus to some structural changes in the national social policy system to make qualifying for benefits harder for both incoming immigrants and emigrating residents. When joining the EEA in 1992 and the EU in 1995 a clearer demarcation was made between social insurance and non-contributory benefits. The former is governed by Regulation No 1408/71, which means that benefits are also payable to those who live abroad, whereas the latter are paid only in Finland.

Residency-based social security

Residency in Finland entitles individuals to basic social security. Hence the subjective scope of basic security benefits is extensive, but the financial level of the benefits is relatively low. Residency-based social security encompasses the rights to family allowances (child allowance, child homecare allowance), healthcare, sickness and parental benefits, national pensions (old age, disability and family pensions) as well as to the basic unemployment allowance and labour market subsidy. Moreover, the Finnish basic security also covers the right to subsidised child day care, old age services and the last-resort social assistance.

The right to residency-based social security is not tied to nationality, but is determined by the provisions of the Act on the Application of Residence-based Social Security Legislation (1573/1993). The legislation applies principally to those who reside permanently in Finland. If a person has bonds to two countries, the permanence of residency is assessed by examining, for example, the duration and reason of the residence, the place of residence of family members, school attendance of children and the type of employment and the location of the person's job. The intent to reside in Finland permanently can be proven by, for example, being a refugee or having a residence permit based on the need for protection, being a family member of a permanent resident or having an employment contract for at least two years.

Regulation No 1408/71 and international agreements on social security supersede the colliding national legislation. Social security benefits are divided into two different categories: first, those defined by the legislation of the country of employment, regardless of the country of residence, such as national pensions, child, mother and housing allowances. The second category refers to benefits that have features of both social security and social care and are paid only to those residing in Finland. These include, for example, pensioners' housing allowance, care allowance for children, certain services for people with disabilities and special support for immigrants.

Due to Regulation No 1408/71 the right to social security for employees/self-employed people moving from EU/EEA states is solely employment-based. They are subject to the social security legislation from the date of starting the employment or self-employment in Finland, provided that they are employed in the country for at least four uninterrupted months. Posted workers from EU/EEA states are an exception as they and their family members are subject to the legislation of the member state from which they are posted.

Those moving to Finland are subject to social benefits from the date of arrival to the country if their employment relationship starts immediately. The employment may consist of several work contracts if it is uninterrupted and fulfils certain requirements on working hours and earnings. Short-term employment lasting less than four months, such as seasonal agricultural work, does not entitle the worker to basic social security. Au pairs are not entitled to benefits either, as their earnings are usually below the minimum level required. The right to social security expires when employment finishes unless the person is considered a permanent resident in Finland on some other grounds. The social security of family members of workers moving to Finland is determined by whether they come from an EU/EEA state, another Nordic state or a country that has signed a social security agreement with Finland.

As the final form of social security, means-tested financial social assistance can be paid to all those who need support but are unable to make a living through paid work, self-employment or other benefits, such as healthcare benefit or the unemployment allowance. For humanitarian reasons this last-resort assistance can, in urgent cases, also be paid to foreigners who reside in the country temporarily.

Employment-based social security

In Finland employment-based social security consists of earnings-related pensions (old age and disability pensions and survivor's benefits), accident insurance and security against occupational accidents and illnesses as well as unemployment allowances.

Earnings-related pension security is regulated by different pension enactments. An immigrant gains a pension in accordance with Finnish pension legislation. Employment pension can be paid abroad while unemployment and part-time pensions are paid only to other EU/EEA countries. The private sector employee's right to, for example, the old age, part-time, rehabilitation and disability pension are regulated by the Employees Pensions Act 2006 (395/2006). The employer is obliged to pay for employee pension provision for work carried out in Finland, provided that the requirements on the age and the earnings of the employee are fulfilled. If Regulation 1408/71 or a social security agreement is applicable, the employer is liable to take out insurance for all of his/her employees. The employees also pay pension contributions. Immigrants working for a Finnish employer in Finland are also insured against occupational accidents and illness.

The general requirements for the earnings-related unemployment allowance are similar to those of residence-based unemployment security. Those who meet the general preconditions for unemployment security and the previous employment requirement (continuous insurance coverage of 43 weeks within the 28 immediately preceding months) are eligible for a flat-rate daily allowance, whereas members of an unemployment fund who have been insured for at least the 10 preceding months are entitled to a higher earnings-related daily allowance.

The Finnish social security system is rather complicated. As has been explained previously, not only is the nationality of the immigrant important, but the reasons for moving to the country and the intended length of stay also play a role in what particular benefits the individual is entitled to. Yet protagonists from the anti-immigration side of the multiculturalism debate often argue that the high level of social security, largely paid in cash, attracts refugees and asylum seekers to the North. In fact, Annika Forsander (2004a) argues that the dilemma of a Nordic welfare state, built on the idea of broad residency-based welfare rights, is that immigration policy becomes the *de facto* mechanism for defining inclusion in and exclusion from the welfare state. Immigration policy is used to restrict the granting of social welfare rights by selecting who can enter the country and for what kinds of reasons (Forsander, 2004a, p 2).

EU/EEA nationals are in many respects in a more privileged position than non-EU migrants or asylum seekers. First, in matters regarding residency, a wider family model is accepted, provided that the elderly parent, for example, has health coverage and sufficient financial means to reside in Finland. Second, mobile workers can enter Finland without a residence permit to look for work freely, whereas those from outside the EU need to apply for a residence permit while still in their home country. After four years the EU labour migrant can be granted a permanent right of residence. This is possible for the non-EU migrant only if s/he has held a continuous residence permit (Type A) for four years, not a temporary permit (Type B). Third, access to individual benefits varies according to employee nationality. An Estonian migrant labourer working in Finland is entitled to, for example, child allowance payable for children who continue to live in Tallinn, whereas his/her Russian colleague in a similar situation is not.

Studies have shown that dependency on welfare benefits is higher with immigrants than with Finns. In their study, Hytti and Paananen found that there was an attempt to integrate a large share of the immigrants who came to Finland in the 1990s to the work-oriented society through social security or active labour market policies. They conclude that in Finland integration into the labour market is held to be a basic right almost akin to citizenship (Hytti and Paananen, 2003, pp 81, 89). The next three sections examine the positioning of immigrants in the Finnish labour market.

Immigrants in the Finnish labour market: integration through work?

In her study on the vulnerability of immigrants in Finnish labour markets, Elli Heikkilä (2005) concludes that there is a strong association between nationality and unemployment. In 1999, the unemployment rate of migrants varied between 15 per cent and 17 per cent of the US and British migrants to 78 per cent, 76 per cent and 75 per cent of migrants originating from Bosnia-Herzegovina, Iraq and Somalia respectively. The unemployment rate of immigrants has on average been three times higher than that of the population as a whole. Even though the overall unemployment rate of migrants decreased from over 50 per cent in 1994 to just below 30 per cent in 2004, immigrants were still three times as likely to be unemployed than Finns (Heikkilä, 2005, pp 490-1; see also Heikkilä and Jaakkola, 2000). The differences between immigrant groups can also be observed in the field of social security. Helka Hytti and Seppo Paananen (2003) noted that the benefit recipiency rate of working-age Westerners from EU/EEA states, Iceland, Norway, Switzerland, North America, Australia and New Zealand, was only 13 per cent compared with a recipiency rate of 62 per cent among the refugee population, originating from countries such as Iraq, Somalia, former Yugoslavia and Vietnam (Hytti and Paananen, 2003, pp 79, 81).

Comparative analysis on immigrant labour market participation in various countries shows an interesting phenomenon: looking at different indicators, such as duration of unemployment and youth unemployment, the foreign nationals living in the Nordic countries are in a worse position when compared with other OECD countries. The differences between the labour market positions of nationals and non-nationals are greater and the relative share of unemployed foreign citizens is the highest in the Nordic countries Sweden, Finland and Denmark. In comparison, Southern European countries like Spain and Greece and settler societies such as Canada, the US and Australia seem better able to integrate immigrants to their labour markets (Forsander, 2004b; see also the discussion in Chapter Two, this volume).

Annika Forsander (2004b) argues that the reasons for this difference lie in the distinct nature of the Nordic labour markets. One barrier to labour market entry is the high cost of labour: as employer costs and minimum wage levels are high, there are few unskilled jobs available in the industrial sector. The high cost of labour also hinders the growth of labour-intensive service sector enterprises that could incorporate workers with lower education levels or poor language skills. And the high participation rates of women fill labour market gaps that might otherwise require foreign labour. The affordable municipal day care system facilitates women's work and also affects immigrants in another way. Private households are a major employer of immigrant women in the US and many other European countries. In addition, as immigrants are not part of the Finnish social networks that share information on job vacancies, they lose out on information on available jobs, as a remarkable number of them are filled through informal channels (see also Jaakkola, 2000).

In a situation where gaining access to work is difficult, immigrants become integrated with the welfare state through the benefits that they receive rather than the labour market itself. Forsander (2004b) argues that the more inclusive and universal the social benefits are and the more regulated the labour market is, the higher the threshold to the labour market. In the Nordic context integration through work is a difficult task, whereas countries with a liberalistic social model integrate immigrants better, as low social benefits, low taxes and a low minimum wage facilitate entry to at least certain parts of the labour market, such as the service sector (Forsander, 2004b).

In a study comparing migrants from the former Yugoslavia in Sweden and Austria a similar effect was observed. Recent immigrants in Sweden have an extremely low probability of labour force participation compared with Swedes, while those in Austria are involved in work to the same extent as Austrian nationals. The comparative study also revealed that the Yugoslav immigration in Austria is heavily employment-oriented and there is a demand for migrant workers in the low-status jobs in the industrial and service sectors. Finding employment is crucial, as in Austria long unemployment can lead to loss of a residence permit.

In the Nordic welfare state of Sweden, on the other hand, immigrants have a better chance of staying in the country even if they are not working, as they are entitled to social assistance, which provides very basic financial security (Kogan, 2002, pp 21-2).

In many cases transnational mobility leads to vulnerability in the labour market, as the loss of cultural capital, contacts, language and country-specific skills affect the individual's labour market position (see, for example, Nohl et al, 2006). It is often argued that the more distant the culture of a migrant, the more problems the immigrant faces in the destination country. Some researchers have even argued that there is a dual system of employment in the Finnish labour market, where those who succeed in finding work at the expected skills level mainly come from Western countries and have a higher, or more easily recognised, education, while those who cannot find work come from developing countries and/or have little education or work experience (Jaakkola, 2000; Heikkilä and Järvinen, 2003, p 112; Heikkilä, 2005). It has also been noted that foreign-born workers regularly receive smaller salaries than Finnish workers. There are signs of discrimination, but also of polarisation, of different categories of immigrants. In some categories, such as information technology (IT) or corporate management, the salaries of the foreign-born workers are higher than the average for the Finnish workers (Katainen, 2009).

The difference between immigrant groups can also be observed in the duration of unemployment and it is visible in evaluations made by the recruiters and employment agency workers, providing further evidence of the importance of emotion and feeling in shaping migrants' everyday experience of integration (see Chapter One, this volume). Migrants who, in the opinion of the recruiters share a cultural proximity to the Finnish culture, such as Ingrian Finns or Russians, are preferred to migrants coming from more distant places outside Europe. This fear of difference results in a hierarchisation of jobs based more on immigrant nationality than the education or competence of the job seeker. Immigrant labour market vulnerability is also visible in the temporariness of jobs: migrants are over-represented in the group that bears the highest risk of losing their jobs at the time of economic crisis (Forsander, 2003, pp 67-9; Heikkilä, 2005, pp 490, 494-5).

European experiences of working in Finland

Many of the studies related to immigrant experiences in Finland have focused on migrants who have been integrated into society more through the welfare system than the labour market. The experiences of the 'more privileged' migrants coming from Western or European countries have not received so much attention, perhaps because they do not generally require social services or integration assistance. In an online survey conducted during summer 2009 European migrants living in Finland were asked about their labour market experiences. The non-probability sample was small (*n*=51), but their answers to the open-ended questions did give some ideas about the positioning of Europeans living in Finland.[1]

Roughly half of the respondents were from old EU member countries (22) and half from new member countries (29), mainly from Latvia. Answering questions related to finding employment, a slight majority described more negative than positive experiences. The lack of language skills in Finnish was perceived to be the main barrier to employment. Discrimination was frequently mentioned: 'It was difficult [to find work], even though I was at the top of my profession before coming here. Then I experienced a three-year case of xenophobic discrimination, quite unbelievable then. [It] took me six years to find a permanent job' (male from the UK, 52 years old). Similarly the perceived closed nature of Finnish society was criticised: 'I find [it] difficult to find work there because of some lack of trust and openness of society regarding foreigners. Unless you are an IT specialist, finding work in Finland is a tough business' (female from Romania, 45 years old).

On the other hand, some transitions were smooth if the person in question was transferred to Finland by his/her own employer, for example: 'It was quite easy as I firstly took a foreign assignment to Finland with my present company and then moved to a local contract' (female from the UK, 40 years old). Several respondents also wrote that they did not really look for work but that work found them: 'I have been lucky, I did not really have to look for work as it was offered to me' (male from Hungary, 42 years old). Yet the vulnerability of the labour market position was visible, as he continued: 'But with funding my graduate studies has been problematic, and at one point I was unemployed for over a year'. Also, even though the first job was found with little difficulty, the same barriers had to be overcome when looking for a new job. Good language skills did not necessarily help, as this respondent who was fluent in Finnish analysed: 'Yes, moving to Finland was good opportunity for me. […] I have also searched for other job opportunities but in that I have not been successful and that is not easy to understand why it is so. As I am skilled, well educated and with experience in my thirties. With these assets there should be no problems with changing jobs, but it still is' (female from Latvia, 31 years old).

Many respondents commented that because of the language barrier and the 'closed' nature of the labour market the best option was to apply for jobs in some of the multinational companies that had a more flexible employment and language policy. This was also noted by Ödül Bozkurt (2006), who studied skilled migrants working in the Finnish IT and telecommunications sector. These migrants found settling in the office of a large multinational company easier than trying to integrate into a more national workplace, regardless of the other attributes of the work (Bozkurt, 2006, pp 238-40).

Yet the individual's position in the labour market depends on many other factors than mere nationality, as Tuomas Martikainen (2010) found in his study on Indian and Nepalese women, who had followed their husbands to Finland. Their position was quite different depending on whether their spouse worked in the IT or in the ethnic restaurant sector. The women whose husbands were working for companies such as Nokia were ready to follow their spouse's career to other foreign destinations, and they themselves were employed in similar international workplaces where English was the company language. The women in the ethnic restaurant sector were more interested in integration and educating their children in Finland. Access to work through family enterprises provided them with financial stability, but breaking free from this sector to pursue a different career was difficult. Also, Forsander (2003) notes that even though nationality is the most important factor explaining immigrant labour market integration, other factors, such as the educational background and the labour market value of that education, plays a role. Because of their insecure labour market position, she argues, many immigrants are trapped in the margins of Finnish society. To some extent this is a risk that the more educated immigrants also face when moving to Finland.

Unemployment and vulnerability

In 2007, the unemployment rate of foreigners living in Finland was 21 per cent compared with the general unemployment rate of six per cent. In addition, the labour market position of immigrant wage earners was more insecure than the position of their Finnish counterparts. Immigrants are often employed in non-standard work contracts, such as fixed-term or part-time contracts, with almost half of immigrant workers employed on fixed-term contracts (Forsander, 2007, p 328).

Short-term jobs may not grant the worker the right to a paid holiday, qualify him/her for higher income-related unemployment benefits or help towards gaining the right to apply for permanent residency. The immigrant worker may not get a prolongation for his/her residence permit if he/she is not paid during the intervals between employment contracts and is therefore not able to support him/herself. This is a threat mainly to non-EU workers, since EU citizens may reside in Finland as jobseekers for a reasonable time after losing their job, if they continue to look for and have a real chance of finding employment. During that time they are also entitled to social welfare benefits.

The economic situation, the working mechanisms of local labour markets and discrimination partly explain the high unemployment rate; however, the immigrant's own resources and language skills, education and work experience also matter. Education acquired in the country of origin does not necessarily transfer to the labour market of the country of destination, so the socio-economic status of migrants often decreases in the new home country (Nohl et al, 2006; Jaakkola and Reuter, 2007, p 338). Also, Finnish employers seem to value education received in Finland over experience gained abroad (Paananen, 2005a).

In a study of migrant practical nurses[2] working in the Finnish social and health care sector it was found that even in a sector employing many immigrants, the language barrier and 'closed' nature of the labour market were among the most important difficulties faced. Communities formed at work are important places for the creation of identities, social positions and relationships of power, as well as those of integration into the host society. Different meanings related to tasks, citizenship, ethnicity, age and gender are created in the everyday realities of the workplace. Different cultures embody maps of meaning that make the world understandable to those who share this understanding (see also Chapter Eleven, this volume). Facilitating immigrant access to Finnish society via work necessitates a deeper look into the formal and informal barriers of integration at the level of the workplace, especially in a field such as the healthcare sector, which may have to rely on an imported workforce in the decades to come.

Conclusion

The size of the foreign population living in Finland has traditionally been small and the country has only quite recently been faced with many of the questions related to integration and the positioning of migrants in society. Recent debates on the rights and responsibilities of immigrants have been influenced by the ongoing economic recession. Immigrants face a double dilemma: 'if you work, you take our jobs; if you do not work, you take advantage of our generous welfare system'.

Globalisation has changed production structures in a way that has decreased demand for the low-educated workforce in Europe: instead of workers moving, production itself has emigrated to countries with cheaper production costs (Castles and Miller, 1993; Kornø Rasmussen, 1997; Forsander, 2004a, p 3). As with the European continent as a whole, the migration routes leading to Finland have become diversified. Alongside refugees and asylum seekers and their families from developing countries, educated Westerners, Baltic labour migrants and the Ingrian Finnish return migrants are among the groups currently looking for a place in Finnish society.

However, all immigrants are not equal in regard to their right to social security or labour market access. For employees or self-employed people moving from EU/EEA states, permanent residency in Finland is not required and their right to social security is, in practice, employment-based. For immigrants from non-EU/EEA countries the requirement of residency in Finland can prove to be difficult to attain due to marginalisation in the labour market. On the other hand, not all EU migrants are 'privileged': in 2009 Bulgarians ranked third in the asylum seeker statistics right after Iraq and Somalia, even though as EU citizens their applications cannot be accepted (see the discussion on the varying domains through which migrants' differential inclusion is achieved in Chapter One, this volume). The suspected 'asylum tourism' is likely to change the procedures of providing asylum seekers with social assistance in cash during the waiting period, instead of providing them with food and housing, as is the case in many other European countries.[3]

Current global changes emphasise the importance of a well-functioning labour market to combat the worsening dependency ratio caused by an increase in the share of the economically inactive elderly population (EUPHIX, 2009). The OECD (2007, pp 96–115) has stated that the immigration policies of its member countries tend to follow a three-step procedure: attract, receive and integrate. In Finland the main focus has been on the first two phases while integration has proven more problematic. Current net immigration figures cannot ease the burden on the economical foundations of the welfare state, especially as the labour market capacities of foreign-born workers are not fully utilised. Large numbers of immigrants remain outside the labour force or participate in the labour market below their skill and education level (Salmenhaara, 2009).

As this chapter demonstrates there are both legislative and more profound structural and cultural reasons for this situation. The residency-based social security system providing a basic subsistence does not form a strong enough impetus for accepting any type of work, and on the other hand, the closed nature of the primarily national labour market does not provide easy access to jobs regardless of the efforts of the immigrants themselves. There are also signs of polarisation between different immigrant groups: an individual may end up in a certain labour market position more based on his/her national origin than individual talent or educational level. Improving the situation requires redirecting integration programmes in a way that facilitates immigrant participation in various on-the-job training activities, tailored education and training and which increases concrete interaction between the immigrant population, Finnish employers and society as a whole.

Notes

[1] The online survey was conducted in the summer of 2009 by Saara Koikkalainen as part of a larger study comparing the labour market experiences of transnationally mobile Europeans.

[2] Marja Katisko interviewed migrants from the Middle East (4), Africa (1), Asia (4), former Soviet Union (4) and the former Republic of Yugoslavia (1).

[3] For recent statistics on immigration and updated information on regulations, please visit the website of the Finnish Immigration Service at www.migri.fi

References

Bozkurt, Ö. (2006) 'Wired for work: highly skilled employment and global mobility in mobile telecommunications multinationals', in M.P. Smith and A. Favell, *The human face of global mobility: International highly skilled migration in Europe, North America and the Asia Pacific*, New Brunswick, NJ: Transaction, pp 211–46.

Castles, S. and Miller, M.J. (1993) *The age of migration. International population movements in the modern world*, Basingstoke: Macmillan.

EUPHIX (European Union Public Health Information System) (2009) *Population projections* (www.euphix.org/object_document/o5117n27112.html).

Finnish Immigration Service (2009) *Statistics on asylum and refugees* (www.migri.fi/netcomm/content.asp?article=3127&language=EN).

Forsander, A. (2003) 'Insiders or outsiders within? Immigrants in the Finnish labor market', in *Yearbook of population research in Finland 39*, Helsinki: Population Research Institute, pp 55-72.

Forsander, A. (2004a) 'Labour market integration in the Nordic welfare state – does work make you into a real Finn?', Paper presented at the 13th Nordic Migration Conference, The Academy of Migration Studies in Denmark (www.amid.dk/ocs/viewabstract.php?id=140&cf=1).

Forsander, A. (2004b) 'Social capital in the context of immigration and diversity: economic participation in the case of the Nordic welfare states', *Journal of International Migration and Integration (JIMI)*, vol 5, no 2, pp 207-27.

Forsander, A. (2007) 'Kotoutuminen sukupuolittuneille työmarkkinoille? Maahanmuuttajien työmarkkina-asema yli vuosikymmen Suomeen muuton jälkeen' ['Integration into a gendered labour market? Immigrant labour market position after a decade in Finland'], in T. Martikainen and M. Tiilikaine (eds) *Maahanmuuttajanaiset: Kotoutuminen, perhe ja työ [Immigrant women: Integration, family and work]*, Helsinki: Publications of the Population Research Institute D 46, pp 312-34.

Heikkilä, E. (2005) 'Mobile vulnerabilities: perspectives on the vulnerabilities of immigrants in the Finnish labour market', *Population, Space and Place 11*, pp 485-97.

Heikkilä, E. and Jaakkola, T. (2000) 'The economic status of immigrants in the Finnish labour market', *Nordia Geographical Publications*, vol 29, no 2, pp 59-75.

Heikkilä, E. and Järvinen, T. (2003) 'Migration and employment of immigrants in the Finnish local labor markets', in *Yearbook of population research in Finland 39*, Helsinki: Population Research Institute, pp 103-18.

Hytti, H. and Paananen, S. (2003) 'Foreign citizens in Finland as recipients of social security benefits', in *Yearbook of population research in Finland 39*, Helsinki: Population Research Institute, pp 79-90.

Jaakkola, M. and Reuter, A. (2007) 'Maahanmuuttajanaiset entisen Neuvostoliiton alueelta. Resurssit ja sijoittuminen työmarkkinoille ['Immigrant women from the former Soviet Union: resources and labour market positioning'], in T. Martikainen and M. Tiilikainen (eds) *Maahanmuuttajanaiset: Kotoutuminen, perhe ja työ [Immigrant women: Integration, family and work]*, Helsinki: Publications of the Population Research Institute D 46, pp 335-78.

Jaakkola, T. (2000) 'Maahanmuuttajat ja etniset vähemmistöt työhönotossa ja työelämässä' ['Immigrants and ethnic minorities in recruitment and working life'], in *Publication from the Labour Administration 218*, Helsinki: Ministry of Labour.

Kangas, O. and Palme, J. (2005) 'Coming late – catching up: the formation of a "Nordic model"', in O. Kangas and J. Palme (eds) *Social policy and economic development in the Nordic countries*, Houndmills: Palgrave Macmillan, pp 17-59.

Katainen, A. (2009) 'Ulkomaalainen saa huonompaa palkkaa useimmilla aloilla' ['Foreigners receive a worse salary in most fields'], *Tieto&Trendit 2/2009*, Helsinki: Statistics Finland (http://stat.fi/artikkelit/2009/art_2009-04-14_001.html?s=0).

Kogan, I. (2002) *Labour market inclusion of immigrants in Austria and Sweden: The significance of the period of migration and the effect of citizenship acquisition*, Working Paper 44, Mannheim: Mannheimer Zentrum fur Europäische Sozialforschung.

Korkiasaari, J. and Söderling, I. (1998) 'Finland: from a country of emigration into a country of immigration', in I. Söderling (ed) *A changing pattern of migration in Finland and its surroundings*, Helsinki: Publications of the Population Research Institute D 32, pp 7–28.

Kornø Rasmussen, H. (1997) *No entry. Immigration policy in Europe*, Series D 28, Copenhagen: Copenhagen Business School Press.

Martikainen, T. (2010) 'Perhe ja -avioliittomuuttajat lohkoutuneilla globaaleilla työmarkkinoilla: tapaustutkimus intialaisista ja nepalilaisista naisista Suomessa' ['Family and marriage migrants in segmented, global labour markets: a case study of Indian and Nepalese women in Finland'], in Vartia, Maarit (ed) *Työ ja ihminen: Monikulttuurisuus -teemanumero* [*Work and people: Multiculturalism theme issue*], Helsinki: Finnish Institute of Occupational Health.

Nohl, A.M., Schittenhelm, K., Schmidtke, O. and Weiss, A. (2006) 'Cultural capital during migration – a multi-level approach to the empirical analysis of labor market integration amongst highly skilled migrants', *Forum: Qualitative Social Research*, vol 7, no 3, article 14 (http://nbn-resolving.de/urn:nbn:de:0114–fqs0603143).

OECD (Organisation for Economic Co-operation and Development) (2007) *International Migration Outlook: SOPEMI 2007*, Paris: OECD.

OECD (2008) *International Migration Outlook: SOPEMI 2008*, Paris: OECD.

Paananen, S. (ed) (2005a) *Maahanmuuttajien elämää Suomessa* [*Life of immigrants in Finland*], Helsinki: Statistics Finland.

Paananen, S. (2005b) 'Maahanmuuttajien elinolot Suomessa' ['Living conditions of immigrants in Finland'], *Yhteiskuntapolitiikka*, vol 70, no 4, pp 460–2.

Pehkonen, A. (2006) 'Immigrants' paths to employment in Finland', in *Finnish Yearbook of population research*, Helsinki: Population Research Institute, pp 113–28.

Salmenhaara, P. (2009) 'The long-term labour shortage. The economic impact of population transition and post-industrialism on the OECD countries: the Nordic case', in *Finnish yearbook of population research*, Helsinki: Population Research Institute, pp 123–36.

Soysal, Y. (1994) *Limits of citizenship. Migrants and postnational membership in Europe*, Chicago, IL: University of Chicago Press.

Statistics Finland (2009) *Migration 2008* (www.stat.fi/til/muutl/2008/muutl_2008_2009-05-20_en.pdf).

Legislation

Act on the Application of Residence-based Social Security Legislation (1573/1993) (www.finlex.fi/fi/laki/kaannokset/1993/en19931573.pdf)

Council Regulation (EC) No 859/2003 of 14 May 2003 extending the provisions of Regulation (EEC) No 1408/71 and Regulation (EEC) No 574/72 to nationals of third countries who are not already covered by those provisions solely on the grounds of their nationality

Employees Pensions Act (395/2006) (www.finlex.fi/fi/laki/kaannokset/2006/en20060395.pdf)

Employment Accidents Insurance Act (608/1948) (www.finlex.fi/fi/laki/kaannokset/1948/en19480608.pdf)

Government proposal 76/2004 on amending the Act on the Application of Residence-based Social Security Legislation

Health Insurance Act (1224/2004)

National Pensions Act (568/2007)

Non-discrimination Act (21/2004) (www.finlex.fi/fi/laki/kaannokset/2004/en20040021.pdf)

Regulation (EEC) No 1408/71 of the Council of 14 June 1971 on the application of social security schemes to employed persons, to self-employed persons and to the members of their families moving within the Community

Regulation (EEC) No 574/72 of the Council of 21 March 1972 fixing the procedure for implementing Regulation (EEC) No 1408/71 on the application of social security schemes to employed persons and their families moving within the Community

Social Assistance Act (1412/1997) (www.finlex.fi/fi/laki/kaannokset/1997/en19971412.pdf)

The Bilateral Treaties on social security between Finland and USA (3 June 1991), Canada (28 October 1986), Chile (7 March 1997), Israel (15 September 1997) and Australia (10 September 2008)

The Constitution of Finland (731/1999) (www.finlex.fi/fi/laki/kaannokset/1999/en19990731.pdf)

The Nordic Convention of 18 August 2003 on Social Security between Denmark, Finland, Iceland, Norway and Sweden (http://untreaty.un.org/unts/144078_158780/17/8/8228.pdf)

Unemployment Security Act (1290/2002)

NINE

Migration in Hungary: historical legacies and differential integration

Ioana Rusu

Introduction

This chapter provides a brief overview of the main migration trends in Hungary since the fall of the Berlin Wall. It has two main objectives. First, it examines the most significant characteristics of the integration of migrant communities and second, it investigates the policy implications following accession to the European Union (EU) in May 2004 and to the Schengen Area in January 2008. Despite the increasing salience of the topic, migration is a recent phenomenon in Hungary. Prior to the fall of the Iron Curtain in November 1989, Hungary was a 'closed' country, with limited migration flows caused by the state-controlled inward and outward migration policy. Following the fall of communism and the subsequent opening of borders, the country experienced considerable migration inflows from neighbouring countries. This was particularly due to its geographical location, which made Hungary both a transit as well as a destination country for regular and irregular migrants. Accession to the EU and, more recently, to the Schengen Area, has expanded the rights and possibilities of Hungarians to move outside their country of origin and to work in certain EU15[1] countries which did not impose restrictions. Only Germany and Austria continued to apply free movement restrictions in the period 2009-2011, and these must be lifted by mid 2011.

Despite a common communist heritage with other Central and Eastern European countries (CEECs), Hungary represents a unique case study in the area of migration (for an in-depth analysis on European migration integration regimes, see Chapter Two, this volume). Its particularity lies in the peculiar structure of migration. The majority of migrants are ethnic Hungarians, often from neighbouring nations. For instance, the Hungarian Ministry of Foreign Affairs[3] reports that more than 2.5 million ethnic Hungarians still live in neighbouring states and might, as a consequence, one day increase the country's immigration inflows. This unique situation is rooted in the country's history. As a result of the Treaty of Trianon (1920), following its defeat in the First World War, Hungary lost more than two thirds of its national territories and people, and, as a result, millions of Hungarian citizens found themselves living in bordering countries, practically overnight. As discussed later in the chapter, the large number of ethnic

Hungarians in neighbouring nations has had a direct impact on the country's migration policy, since several reforms have been attempted to find a solution to this problem.

In addition to old and, still partially unresolved, issues concerning the integration or assimilation of migrants in Hungary, EU accession has also played a crucial role in the country's current migration policy. Compliance with EU rules and regulations has not simply had a direct impact on the legislation of the country, but it has also affected Hungary's relationship with neighbouring states. As argued by Lavenex (2001, 2006), in fact, the implementation of strict border controls and restrictive visa requirements has had the effect of 'sealing [...] the eastern border' of the EU (Lavenex, 2001, p 30), and it has also reinforced the foreign policy and security approach of European migration policymaking (Lavenex, 2006).

This chapter proceeds as follows. The first section provides a brief theoretical discussion of the determinants of migration. It emphasises the importance of economic, historical, institutional and cultural motives to migration. The second section offers a detailed overview of migration in Hungary. It highlights its particular context and most recent trends. The third section then discusses the main characteristics of migration in Hungary. It elucidates the impact of 'diaspora'-oriented migration policymaking on the integration of migrants. The fourth and final section concludes by examining the influence of the EU on Hungary's policy formulation.

Theoretical context

Hungary's accession to the EU has had a direct impact on its migration flows. Following accession to the EU, Hungarians acquired the option to move and work in certain EU15 countries, such as the UK, Ireland or Sweden, where labour restrictions were immediately lifted, or thanks to bilateral agreements with Germany and Austria (IOM, 2006). In 2004, the year of accession to the EU, outflow levels increased by 35 per cent as compared to the previous year (OECD, 2009a; author's own calculations). From an economic perspective, this increase in outflows can mainly be explained by the disparities in wages between Hungary and EU15 countries. These acted as 'pull factors' in attracting Hungarian migrants to 'Old Europe'. Similarly, Hungary's relative economic prosperity attracted immigrants from neighbouring countries such as Romania, Serbia and the Ukraine, whose economic development lagged behind. 'Push factors', such as poverty, unemployment and low wages, clearly drive people to leave their countries of origin for new destinations in search of fortune (Castles and Miller, 1998; Geddes, 2003). Consequently, in 2004, Hungary experienced the highest inflow of foreign workers in its history, whose number increased by 38 per cent when compared to the previous year (OECD, 2009a; author's own calculations).

However, it would be simplistic to assume that individuals migrate either due to increasing opportunities or based on a rational comparison of the relative costs and benefits (Castles and Miller, 1998; Chiswick, 2000). Factors such as historical and cultural ties also explain migration movements (Castles and Miller, 1998, p 23). For instance, James Hollifield (2000) has argued that networks, the civil, political and social rights of immigrants in the society of residence and shifts in public opinion also play a major role in sustaining migration flows, regardless of economic cycles (Hollifield, 2000; see also Chapter Five, this volume). As a result, migratory movements can be explained by state relationships, historical ties established between sending and receiving countries and interactions between social networks developed by migrants (Castles and Miller, 1998). As highlighted by Siniša Zrinščak (Chapter Eleven, this volume), the interaction between state–society structures is very important and also applies to the case of Hungary, where the majority of the immigrants are of Hungarian descent.

The 2.5 million ethnic Hungarians living in adjacent states generate an 'ethnically determined migration' which has already taken place in several other countries such as Germany or Bulgaria after the fall of communism. For example, in the early 1990s, hundreds of thousands of ethnic Germans (*Aussiedlers*) left Romania, Poland and the Soviet Union to move back to Germany (UN Expert Group Meeting on International Migration and Development, 2005). As in the case of Germany, ethnic migration has direct consequences on immigrants' social rights and integration within the country of destination (Bommes and Geddes, 2000). Ethnic Hungarian descendants from neighbouring states can acquire naturalisation after one year of permanent residence, while other immigrant categories may be naturalised after eight years of continuous residence (Tóth, 2005). Therefore, non-ethnic migrants face more demanding integration requirements, such as language examination and 'constitutional' knowledge (Tóth, 2005). Such privileges are not particular to Hungary, but were also given to *Aussiedlers* in Germany (Sainsbury, 2006). Bommes and Geddes' study (2000) comparing the position of ethnic Germans with the position of labour migrants in the German welfare system is a notable example, showing how these 'ethnic privileges' place these migrants in a more 'advantageous position' (Sainsbury, 2006, p 236) vis-à-vis other immigrant categories but see Chapter Seven, this volume. Although a similar impact study has not yet been conducted for Hungary, a similar situation is likely to occur with clear direct consequences for the social inclusion of immigrants into society.

In addition to this, public attitudes to migration are also linked to 'notions of competition for resources and theories emphasising the importance of "symbolic" values and culture' (McLaren, 2008, p 5). According to this approach, migrants compete with the existing population for economic and social resources, such as jobs, housing and welfare benefits. As a consequence, economic downturn and rising unemployment increase competition for labour market access, social infrastructure and community cohesion (Dobson et al, 2009). In this context, migrants who are perceived to have different values and ways of life from the existing population are not simply seen as a threat to the labour market, but also as a symbolic threat to cultural unity. This factor should not be underestimated since it can have a more powerful impact than mere labour pressures (McLaren, 2003, 2008; Lahav, 2004). In light of this, ethnic migrants who are perceived as being 'part of the nation' or of the dominant culture (Bommes and Geddes, 2000, p 98) are not simply more likely to be accepted by the existing population, but also to be integrated into the country of destination with greater political legitimacy than third-country nationals (TCNs) who do not have historical and cultural ties with the existing population and its socio-historical 'national' identity (see the third section of this chapter for a more detailed analysis; compare also with Chapters One and Thirteen, this volume).

Hungary's accession to the EU and to the Schengen Area has also implied increasing adaptive efforts to the EU *acquis* on free movement, immigration and asylum as a condition for full membership (Geddes, 2003, p 173). Hungary's geographical location has made it a transit point for migration movements in and out of the EU. According to the International Organization for Migration (IOM), Hungary is also at the heart of several of the most common routes for trafficking (IOM, 2006). As a result, within the EU framework, Hungary, as well as other CEECs, are not simply countries of emigration but also act as important 'buffer zones' that absorb migration flows directed to other European states (Lavenex, 1999). As a new member state, Hungary took significant steps towards compliance and harmonisation with EU standards on border management, visa regimes, prevention of irregular migration, counter-trafficking and smuggling, re-integration of returning nationals, management of labour migration flows, promotion of regular migration and respect for human rights (Geddes, 2003; Lavenex and Uçarer, 2004; IOM, 2006). Hungary was also called to establish readmission agreements of irregular migrants with neighbouring states, giving migration a foreign policy dimension (Lavenex, 2006). This fits the 'security approach' that has characterised the EU migration policy frame in the last decades (Bigo, 1996; Guiraudon, 2000, 2003). Subsequently, Hungary's obligations for EU membership and its compliance with EU rules and regulations in the area of migration seem to have 'helped breathe new life into the term "fortress Europe"' (Geddes, 2003, p 175), by installing new borders further east. In light of this security approach, EU accession has also led Hungary to implement migration policies that did not necessarily 'fit' with its economic and demographic objectives, that were rather more foreign policy-related issues (see the fourth section of this chapter).

Hungarian migration specificities

This section outlines the specific context of migration in Hungary, with a focus on more recent migration trends. Overall, Hungary has maintained a relatively steady net migration rate for the past 50 years (see Figure 9.1). Historically, during the four decades of communist regime, Hungary, like most Central and Eastern European societies, was a 'closed' country, which experienced limited migration flows due to state-controlled inward and outward migration. As shown in Figure 9.1, outflows were almost non-existent except for 1956, when approximately 200,000 Hungarians left the country. This date corresponds to the failed Hungarian revolution, after which borders were sealed. Up to the fall of communism in 1989, another 200,000 Hungarians are estimated to have left the country. From 1949 to 1989, migration flows into Hungary were minimal, except for 'two politically motivated waves'. Asylum was first granted to Greek communists in the 1950s and later to Chilean communists in the 1970s. During the 1980s, students from the Council for Mutual Economic Assistance (Comecon) and Comecon-supported countries (such as Cuba, Vietnam and Mongolia) accounted for the majority of inflows (Hárs and Sik, 2008, pp 73-5; see also Juhász, 2003).

Figure 9.1: Hungary's net migration rate, 1955–2007 (per 1,000 inhabitants)

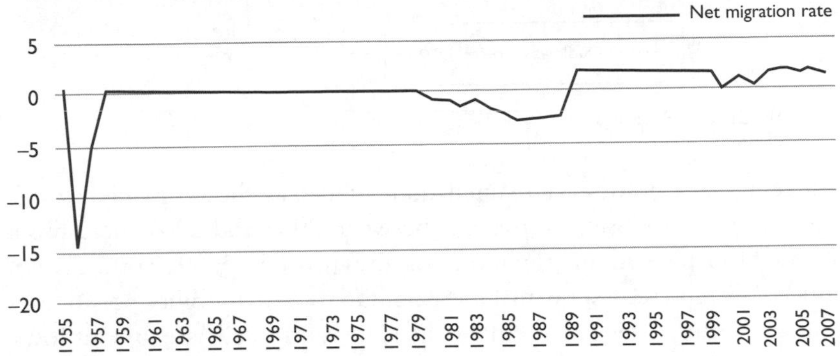

Source: OECD (2009a); author's calculations

In the 1990s, the migration situation of Hungary changed. Migration outflows from Hungary remained low in comparison to most other CEECs, but roughly equivalent to those of the Czech Republic (Wallace, 1998). Germany, Austria and the US represented the three main destinations for those who decided to leave Hungary to either permanently settle elsewhere or to temporarily work abroad. The social groups that emigrated the most were unemployed young men or students living in the West region of Hungary. The Roma population also showed a higher emigration potential than the non-Roma. The most important determinants to emigrate were 'knowledge of a foreign language' and 'previous migration experience' (Hárs and Sik, 2008, p 91). For inflows, the situation was different. Following the fall of communism, Hungary experienced considerable inflows from neighbouring countries, mainly Romania and the former Republic of Yugoslavia. While the majority of these migrants were ethnic Hungarians, some migrants from the former Republic of Yugoslavia were also asylum seekers fleeing war. Similarly, a considerable number of Chinese citizens entered the country during the same period because of the lack of visa obligations that existed between the two countries. As shown in Figure 9.2, this rise in inflows was followed by an important outflow as most of the migrants entering Hungary at that time either returned to their countries of origin or used Hungary as a transit point to Western Europe.

Figure 9.2: Migration inflows and outflows in Hungary, 1989–99 (000s)

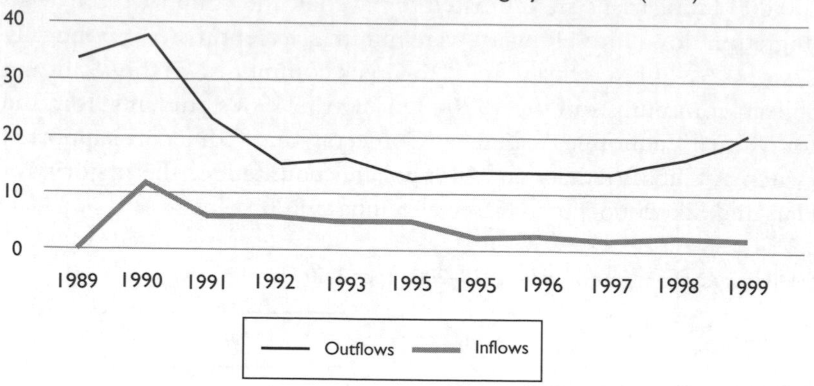

Source: OECD (2009a); author's calculations

In more recent years, outflows remained quite stable, as shown in Figure 9.3. Following Hungary's accession to the EU, between 2004 and 2007 there was a slight increase of 17 per cent in migration outflows (OECD, 2009a; author's own calculations). This represents a normal increase due to new mobility possibilities within the EU offered by enlargement. Despite this small rise in outflows, emigration continues to represent a limited phenomenon compared to other CEECs. A 2003 Labour Force Survey, carried out by the Hungarian Central Statistical Office (HCSO), showed that only four per cent of those aged 15-74 considered going abroad (Hárs et al, 2004, p 10). Among those, only 0.5 per cent expressed strong motivation to do so, and the majority of those who did migrate favoured Germany and Austria. The choice for these two destinations can be explained by the countries' historical ties with Hungary. The profile of migrants is similar to that for the transition years (1990–99), even though a significant number of highly skilled professionals, such as medical doctors, have been reported to go abroad (Hárs and Sik, 2008, p 97).

While outflows remained quite steady over time, inflows experienced a more 'turbulent' pattern. At the beginning of the last decade, the number of registered foreign migrants dropped. This is mainly due to a new classification of migrant categories effective from January 2001 (IOM, 2006). Afterwards, Hungary experienced a consistent increase in inflows, with a peak in the year following EU accession. Similarly to the situation in the 1990s, most foreigners continue to come from neighbouring countries. Romanians represent the largest foreign group, accounting for approximately 50 per cent of the foreign population since the beginning of the decade. The other major groups of foreigners are represented by Serbs, Ukrainians and Chinese. Similarly, the number of asylum seekers in Hungary rose during that same period. Their number increased by 112 per cent from 2004 to 2007 (OECD, 2009a; author's own calculations). In 2007, the main nationalities of applicants were Serbian, Vietnamese, Chinese and Iraqi. This rise in applications can be explained by anticipation of the new 'Asylum Act' effective from January 2008, which aligned Hungarian legislation with EU regulations implementing restrictive measures to combat misuse of asylum (OECD, 2009b). Shortly after the increase of inflows after accession to the EU, a considerable drop (24 per cent) in inflows can be noticed from 2005 to 2006 (see Figure 9.3). This can mainly be explained by the legislative compliance of Hungary as a new EU member state. As a new member and in view of its accession to the Schengen Area, Hungary implemented a strict visa regime and border management policy. An illustration of this direct effect on inflows is the substantial decrease of Romanian citizens entering the country: between 2004 and 2006 their number was reduced by half (OECD, 2008, p 278).

Figure 9.3: Migration inflows and outflows in Hungary, 2000–07 (000s)

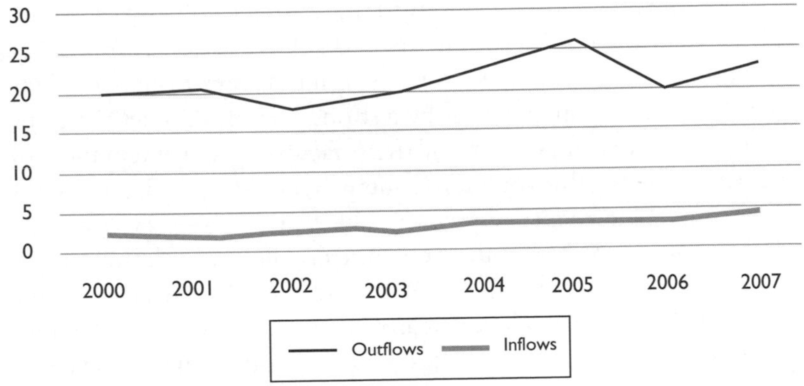

Source: OECD (2009a); author's calculations

Discussion

As mentioned, immigration in Hungary is a recent phenomenon and remains a secondary issue on the political agenda. The number of foreign citizens represents, in fact, less than two per cent of the total population. Although the majority of migrants entering the country represent ethnic Hungarian minorities living in adjacent nations, non-Hungarian migrants are also present. The two largest non-ethnic Hungarian immigrant categories are Chinese and African (mainly from West Africa) (Olomoofe, 2001; Gödri and Tóth, 2004; OECD, 2008). However, Hungary is facing challenges comparable to other European member states with a longer tradition of immigration. These challenges include demographic concerns due to an ageing and declining population, labour market shortages and integration of immigrants. With regard to the latter, as emphasised by Reitz (2006), determinants such as human capital in terms of education, professional experience, knowledge of the country's language, origins in terms of nationality, 'race', ethnic background, involvement in social and political life and immigrant status (labour migrant, asylum seeker, family reunification) have a direct impact on immigrants' integration into society. This section therefore discusses the integration of immigrants into the social, economic and political context of Hungarian society by studying the level of integration of the different migrant communities and by addressing the government's priorities in terms of migrant integration.

In terms of migrant labour market integration, in 2002, the Tárki Social Research Institute conducted a survey on 'The living conditions of immigrants migrating to Hungary' in order to identify the main factors that attracted migrants to Hungary and to measure the perception of personal integration of the migrants. The study involved interviews with 1,015 immigrants aged 18 and above. It should be noted that the majority of the interviewees were ethnic Hungarians from neighbouring countries. The study found a correlation between the ethnic background of migrants and their integration into the labour market. Ethnic Hungarians enjoyed not only a higher rate of employment than other TCNs, but were also more likely to find work within the mainstream economy. This finding can be explained by their knowledge of the language (according to several linguists, one of the most complex languages in Europe), by their common cultural background, by their family ties with the existing population or by a strong relationship network (for a detailed discussion on the importance of these factors in the integration of migrants, see Chapter Eleven, this volume). Contrarily, non-Hungarian migrants experienced higher unemployment and were most likely to become self-employed (Gödri and Tóth, 2004, p 415). This is the case, for example, for both the African and Chinese communities. According to Olomoofe (2001), African migrants experienced difficulties finding employment and were reduced to illicit activities and employment or prostitution. Similarly, most Chinese migrants were not able to find employment, and as a result became more easily 'involved in entrepreneurial niches that rely on ethnic networks to succeed' (Nyíri, 2005, p 668). According to Doering and Piore (1971), powerful groups, such as firms, professional associations and unions, tend to divide the job market into protected (core sector) and unprotected (peripheral sector) employment. Subsequently, immigrants tend to be excluded from the core sector because firms continue to hire employees based on credentials and experience acquired in local and national institutions. As a result, immigrants excluded from the core sector industries such as healthcare, finance, tourism and the car industry turn towards self-employment. Similarly, Greve and Salaff (2005) have argued that when the mainstream economy denies migrants the chance to work, they start enclave businesses since they can rely on co-ethnic networks for help and legitimacy.

Interestingly, for migrants able to find employment within the mainstream labour market, migration produced an overall positive employment change, especially for those with higher education and for those with professional and managerial experience prior to migration. However, the high-skilled migrants had to accept lower status positions at the beginning of their career (Gödri and Tóth, 2004, p 418). This finding matches the 'immigrant occupation mobility model' developed by Chiswick et al (2005). These authors show how immigrant occupational mobility tends to correspond to a 'U-shaped curve', with a downgrading effect from the last occupation prior to migration to the first occupation in the country of destination. Immigrants tend, therefore, to fare worst in the early years of settlement, but due to their original human capital (language knowledge, professional skills, etc) associated with new human capital investments in the receiving country (language courses, professional equivalence, etc), the effect diminishes and the curve goes up again. The depth of the U-shaped curve depends on the transferability of the skills of the immigrant: the lower the transferability of skills, the deeper the decline in occupation status from the last job in the country of origin to the first job in the country of destination.

Language, education credentials, professional skills and status (for example, asylum seekers are not allowed to work until they are granted refugee status) represent major barriers to accessing the mainstream labour market. However, other factors such as the existing population's attitudes towards immigrants also play an important role. Using 2002/03 data collected on 21 countries (including Hungary) by means of the European Social Survey, Semyonov et al (2008, p 6) show that, in general, '[...] immigrants [...] are perceived not only as a threat to the social, political and economic order [but also] as a threat to the cultural homogeneity and the national identity of the state'. This finding corroborates the importance of social networks, as well as of historical and cultural ties. As a result, ethnic Hungarian migrants are more likely to be positively perceived by the existing population than other migrants, and this has a direct impact on their integration. This statement is further supported by the findings outlined by the Tárki survey which showed that ethnic Hungarian migrants more than others declared feeling a 'sense of belonging' and enjoying social relations with Hungarian nationals (Gödri and Tóth, 2004, p 420). In this context, Hungary offered them 'an opportunity to leave behind their minority status' (Sik, 2007, p 105). The picture is different with the Chinese and African migrants. For instance, Pál Nyíri (2005) analysed the media discourse with regards to the Chinese migrants during the 1990s and early 2000 and found that the negative image portrayed by the Hungarian media which emphasised 'crime, illegal migration, and customs crackdowns on counterfeit or smuggled goods' (Nyíri, 2005, p 663) tended to spill over in the beliefs and attitudes of the population toward these migrants. As argued by Sik (2007, p 105), the main integration difficulty for non–Hungarian migrants still remains 'intolerance and discrimination'. Africans also suffered from racism and negative stereotyping (Olomoofe, 2001). The situation for the African community was more difficult when compared to the Chinese migrants, primarily because the latter have developed better networks enabling them to learn about settlement procedures in Hungary which, in turn, have facilitated their everyday life (Sik, 2007, p 107). Larry Olomoofe's (2001) study on the integration of Africans in Budapest found, for instance, that their status could be compared to that of the Roma population with: '[...] the association of subalternity with conspicuous sexuality and petty crime [is] similar to the perception of Roma by the majority population [...]' (Olomoofe, 2001, p 8). Although not a migrant community, the Roma population experiences several prejudices and discrimination at all levels of their life cycle, from education and employment, to housing (Bernát, 2009). In

2009, numerous acts of violence directed against the Roma were, in fact, reported, including physical violence and destruction of property. This has led the EU to repeatedly raise concerns about the treatment of this minority ethnic group in CEECs prior to and after their accession to the EU (OSCE ODIHR, 2004). Overall, migrants in Hungary face innumerable difficulties finding employment and housing, and accessing education and healthcare services, in part due to the fact that information is often not readily available to migrant communities. For example, residence permits allow immigrants to access social rights such as education, social services, healthcare, social protection and pension benefits (Nyíri, 2005), but few take advantage of these rights due to lack of information.

However, in light of the findings mentioned above, ethnic Hungarian migrants seem to benefit from a 'special' status within Hungarian society. Privileges that ethnic Hungarian migrants enjoy can also be related to the political agenda. The dominant political topic with regards to immigrant integration into Hungarian society has, in fact, always been related to diaspora issues. In 2001, for example, the Status Law came into effect, providing ethnic Hungarians with 'legal and symbolic support' but without encouraging them to move back to Hungary (Kovács, 2005). The Law did not encounter significant success and the number of issued work permits remained very low. Even with this limited success, the status of Hungarians received once again significant public attention. In December 2004, six months after Hungary's accession to the EU, a referendum was held on whether or not Hungarian minorities living abroad should receive Hungarian citizenship, raising issues with regards to citizenship, national identity, ethnic nationalism and immigration policy. Christian Joppke (2003) has defined this type of reform as the 're-ethnicisation' of citizenship through which the state provides citizenship privileges to people who are considered 'ethnic or linguistic relatives' (Joppke, 2003). Similarly, Bauböck (2005) stated in an interview, 'in many countries of Central Eastern Europe, citizenship policies appear to be more strongly shaped by concerns about expatriates, diasporas, and ethnic kin minorities in neighboring countries than by immigration'. This point of view has also been shared by Sik (2007, p 104), who emphasises the fact that 'unlike the German or the Israeli cases, Hungary's diaspora policy developed as a policy of shaping national identity and not as an immigration policy'. Even though the dual citizenship proposal failed at the polls, it aroused tensions with neighbouring countries (such as Romania) that regarded it as an invasion of their sovereignty, and caused implications for the definition of a Hungarian migration policy.

EU accession, conditionality and policy formulation

Prior to its accession to the EU and to the Schengen Area, and now as a full member state, Hungary has made and still continues to make changes to its legislation to comply with European asylum and immigration policy. Prior to EU accession, several laws, such as the Act on Hungarian Citizenship (1993), the Act on Entry, Residence in and Immigration to Hungary (2001) (commonly known as the Alien Act) and the Status Law (2001) defined national immigration policy (Office of Immigration and Nationality, 2010[4]).Following EU accession, three new major laws were issued. The first established the right to permanent residence for EU and European Free Trade Association (EFTA) nationals and their family members after five years of residence. The second law regulated the visa and residence permit system for TCNs. The third, the new Asylum Act, came into effect in 2008, and implemented more restrictive asylum measures to combat asylum misuse (OECD, 2009b).

Security and border management compliance in the fight against irregular migration, visa harmonisation, signature of readmission agreements with TCN governments, restriction of asylum measures and cooperation with the EU Border Management Agency Frontex, became a key part of EU accession requirements, leading Hungary to adopt a more restrictive migration policy (IOM, 2006). This can be seen, for example, in the rise in numbers of asylum applications prior to the introduction of the new Asylum Act that made the procedures more difficult, as well as by the considerable drop in immigrant inflows that occurred between 2004 and 2006.

Migration and asylum still remain closely linked to a country's sovereignty. Labour migration, integration and admission of TCNs are still mainly formulated at the national level with very little interference from 'Europe'. Nevertheless, EU asylum and migration policies exert a significant influence on national policy formulation and implementation (Schmidt, 1999). Europeanisation cannot, in fact, be solely confined to the impact of European integration and governance on the member states of the EU as a simple top-down process (Schimmelfennig, 2009, p 5); it also includes and 'works sideways through emulation, mimicking and lesson-drawing' (Börzel and Risse, 2007, p 485). However, as the Treaty of Lisbon entered into force on 1 December 2009, this contemporary situation is likely to be altered as the Treaty '[...] confirms the EU commitment to the development of a common immigration policy' (Article 79[4] of the Treaty of Lisbon[5]). In addition, as argued by Lavenex (2009, p 4), its implementation will extend '[...] decision-making rules based on qualified majority voting and increase the involvement of Parliament by extending its co-decision powers to the other field that had hitherto been excluded: labour migration'.

These changes will also have repercussions in terms of immigrant integration policies. As argued by Joppke (2007, p 4), although immigrant integration is increasingly coming into the remit of European Union law, real integration policies are still formulated at national level. Currently, the EU can improve coordination between member states and enhance the exchange of information, but it cannot make regulations. In 2004, for instance, the Council of Ministers adopted a series of Common Basic Principles on Integration that aimed at harmonising the approach to integration among member states. The underlying Basic Principles expressed by the EU are: (1) integration as a dynamic, two-way process of mutual accommodation by all immigrants and residents of the member states; (2) integration must be conducted in respect for the basic values of the EU; (3)

employment must remain a key part of the integration process; (4) basic knowledge of language, history and institutions of the country of destination is addressed as indispensable to integration; and (5) access for immigrants to institutions, as well as to public and private goods and services, on a basis equal to national citizens and in a non-discriminatory way is a critical foundation for better integration (Council of the European Union, 2004, pp 19-21). Despite their generality, these principles have not yet been transposed into legal rules and regulations (Lavenex, 2009, p 5). A question that still has to be answered is whether the introduction of the Lisbon Treaty will exercise an indirect pressure for faster implementation (for a more detailed discussion, see Chapter Three, this volume).

Policy transfer dynamics may play a crucial role here. Drawing on Dolowitz and Marsh's (2000) conceptualisation of policy transfer based on 'copying', 'emulation', 'combinations' and 'inspiration', Sandra Lavenex and Emek Uçarer (2004) have outlined 'four different modes of policy transfer' that may occur as a result of the external effects of EU immigration policies. In the case of CEE member states, adaptation to EU rules is likely to have been the result of targeted policy transfer (or policy diffusion) with *conditionality* having played an extremely important role in the overall process of implementation (Lavenex and Uçarer, 2004, p 435; see also Schimmelfennig and Sedelmeier, 2004, 2005). Similar findings on the importance of conditionality have also been highlighted by Falkner and Treib's (2008) study on implementation and compliance styles of EU member states. The authors demonstrated how pre-accession requirements represented a major incentive in the transposition performance of EU regulations in the Czech Republic, Hungary, Slovakia and Slovenia.

Despite the importance of conditionality in EU policy formulation, a problem has emerged in terms of the transposition process that has often depended on the specific circumstances in each country (Falkner and Treib, 2008, p 298). Although CEECs were, on average, considerably better at transposing EU directives than the older EU15 member states, the picture changed when it came to the application and enforcement stage, where '[…] many of the legal provisions that entered the statute books in order to fulfil the EU's social policy *acquis* have […] largely remained *dead letters*' (Falkner and Treib, 2008, p 306; emphasis added). Overall, it is not misleading to conclude that the higher the compatibility between European policies and national objectives, the easier it is for a member state to comply with EU rules and regulations (Börzel and Risse, 2007). This is also likely to apply to immigrant integration policies, with policies directed to the integration of migrants in Hungary more successful when they have an existing institutional foundation on which to build, as portrayed by the case of the ethnic migrants elucidated above.

Conclusion

This chapter has presented the main migration trends in Hungary and analysed the most salient immigrant integration and policy implications following the country's membership of the EU and to the Schengen Area. As has been demonstrated, Hungary's accession to the EU has had and continues to have an effect on its migration policy. Hungary's progressive alignment with the EU *acquis* on free movement, immigration and asylum involved strengthening border management and prevention of irregular migration and labour movements, harmonisation of visa regimes and the establishment of readmission agreements with neighbouring states. The outcome of this was an overall more restrictive immigration policy. Furthermore, as argued by Lavenex (1999), along with other CEECs, Hungary fulfilled an additional role of 'buffer zone' to absorb migration flows directed at other European member states. As a result of this, Hungary's compliance with EU regulations has tended to reinforce 'Fortress Europe' by installing new border controls further east.

Another important feature that characterises Hungary's migration policy is the 'diaspora-related issues' that still predominate the migration debate. Ethnic Hungarians coming from adjacent countries represent over 80 per cent of the total immigrant population (OECD, 2008). State relationships, historical ties between neighbouring countries and Hungary, and pre-existing interactions between social networks developed by migrants over many years help explain this 'ethnically determined migration' situation. This has important repercussions for the country's migration discourse. In this context, the animated referendum in 2004 on whether to grant citizenship to Hungarian minorities living abroad represents a clear example of the relevance of diaspora-focused migration policy in national political discourse which might still be able to create significant political tensions with neighbouring countries (such as Romania). This also raises important questions with regards to citizenship, national identity and ethnic nationalism as well as discrimination against, and social integration of, non-ethnic Hungarians.

As argued in several contributions in this volume (see Chapter One, this volume, for a summary), the importance of economic integration is clearly necessary in the integration process, but it does not guarantee social integration. Government policies have, in fact, an important direct influence over social attitudes and predispositions of the existing population towards migrants, and over immigrants' sense of belonging in their new society. These policies can contribute to encouraging tolerance towards immigrants among the resident population, and to political and social participation among migrants. As Hungary will continue to receive migrants from different cultural horizons, seeking the right policy approach towards integration and diversity management will require finding a balance between policies designed to assimilate migrants into the dominant cultural community and those aimed at embracing and promoting ethnic diversity. Experience from EU member states with a longer immigration tradition shows that this is a long, difficult but still necessary process of societal transformation.

Notes

[1] *EU15 includes* Austria, Belgium, Germany, Denmark, Spain, Finland, France, the UK, Greece, Ireland, Italy, Luxembourg, the Netherlands, Portugal and Sweden.

[2] A8 countries include the Czech Republic, Estonia, Hungary, Latvia, Lithuania, Poland, Slovakia and Slovenia.

[3] Ministry of Foreign Affairs of the Republic of Hungary home page (www.mfa.gov.hu/kum/en/bal/).

[4] Office of Immigration and Nationality (http://www.bmbah.hu/a_bah_ismertetese.php).

[5] The Treaty of Lisbon is available at http://europa.eu

References

Bauböck, R. (2005) 'Western countries tend to follow a liberalizing trend towards citizenship policies', Interview with Rainer Bauböck (www.migrationonline.cz), last accessed 8.1.2010.

Bernát, A. (2009) 'Roma in Eastern Europe', in *Roma in Central and Eastern Europe*, Leibniz: Gesis Leibniz Institute for the Social Sciences, pp 12–17.

Bigo, D. (1996) *Polices en réseaux. L'expérience européenne*, [*Policies in networks. The European experience*], Paris: Presses de Sciences Po.

Bommes, M. and Geddes, A. (eds) (2000) *Welfare and immigration: Challenging the borders of the welfare state*, London: Routledge.

Börzel, T. and Risse, T. (2007) 'Europeanization: the domestic impact of European Union politics', in K. Joergensen, M. Pollack and B. Rosamond, *Handbook of European Union politics*, London: Sage Publications, pp 483-504.

Castles, S. and Miller, M. (1998) *The age of migration: International population movements in the modern world* (2nd edn), Basingstoke: Macmillan.

Chiswick, B.R. (2000) 'Are immigrants favorably self-selected? An economic analysis', in C.B. Brettell and J.F. Hollifield, *Migration theory. Talking across disciplines*, New York: Routledge, pp 61-76.

Chiswick, B.R., Lee, Y.L. and Miller, P.W. (2005) 'A longitudinal analysis of immigrant occupational mobility: a test of the immigrant assimilation hypothesis', *The International Migration Review*, vol 39, no 2, pp 332-53.

Council of the European Union (2004) Press release 14615/04 (Presse 321) (www.consilium.europa.eu/ueDocs/cms_Data/docs/pressData/en/jha/82745.pdf).

Dobson, J., Latham, A. and Salt, J. (2009) *On the move? Labour migration in times of recession. What can we learn from the past?*, Policy Network Paper, London: Policy Network (www.policy-network.net).

Doering, P.B. and Piore, M.J. (1971) *Internal labour markets and manpower analysis*, Lexington, MA: Heath.

Dolowitz, D. and Marsh, D. (2000) 'Learning from abroad: the role of policy transfer in contemporary policy-making', *Governance: An International Journal of Policy and Administration*, vol 13, no 1, pp 5-24.

Falkner, G. and Treib, O. (2008) 'Three worlds of compliance or four? The EU-15 compared to new member states', *Journal of Common Market Studies*, vol 46, no 2, pp 293-313.

Geddes, A. (2003) *The politics of migration and immigration in Europe*, London: Sage Publications.

Gödri, I. and Tóth, P.P. (2004) 'The social position of immigrants', in T. Kolosi, I.G. Tóth and G. Vukovich, *Social report 2004*, Budapest: Tarki Social Research Institute (www.tarki.hu).

Greve, A. and Salaff, J.W. (2005) 'Social network approach to understand the ethnic economy: a theoretical discourse', *GeoJournal*, vol 64, pp 7-16.

Guiraudon, V. (2000) 'European integration and migration policy: vertical policy-making as venue shopping', *Journal of Common Market Studies*, vol 38, no 2, pp 251-71.

Guiraudon, V. (2003) 'The constitution of a European immigration policy domain: a political sociology approach', *Journal of European Public Policy*, vol 10, no 2, pp 263-82.

Hárs, A. and Sik, E. (2008) *Hungary in permanent or circular migration? Policy choices to address demographic decline and labour shortages in Europe*, Vienna: International Organization for Migration, pp 73-103.

Hárs, A., Simonovits, B. and Sik, E. (2004) 'The labour market and migration: threat or opportunity? The likely migration of Hungarian labour to the European Union', in T. Kolosi, I.G. Tóth and G. Vukovich, *Social report 2004*, Budapest: Tarki Social Research Institute (www.tarki.hu).

Hollifield, J. (2000) 'The politics of international migration. How can we "bring the state back in"?', in C.B. Brettell and J.F. Hollifield, *Migration theory. Talking across disciplines*, New York: Routledge, pp 183-237.

IOM (International Organization for Migration) (2006) *Migration management in Central and South-Eastern Europe*, Vienna: IOM.

Joppke, C. (2003) 'Citizenship between de- and re- ethnicization', *European Journal of Sociology*, vol 44, no 3, pp 429-58.

Joppke, C. (2007) 'Immigrants and civic integration in Western Europe', in K. Banting, T. Courchene and F.L. Seidle (eds) *The art of the state III: Diversity, recognition and shared citizenship in Canada*, Montreal: Institute for Research on Public Policy, pp 1-30.

Juhász, J. (2003) *Hungary: Transit country between East and West*, Berlin: Migration Citizenship Education (www.migrationeducation.org).

Kovács, M.M. (2005) 'The politics of non-resident dual citizenship in Hungary', *Minority, Ethnicity and Society Review*, vol 8, no 1, pp 50-72.

Lahav, G. (2004) 'Public opinion towards immigration in the European Union: does it matter?', *Comparative Political Studies*, vol 37, no 10, pp 1151-83.

Lavenex, S. (1999) *Safe third countries. Extending the EU asylum and immigration policies to Central and Eastern Europe*, Budapest: CEU Press.

Lavenex, S. (2001) 'Migration and the EU's new Eastern border: between realism and liberalism', *Journal of European Public Policy*, vol 8, no 1, pp 24-32.

Lavenex, S. (2006) 'Shifting up and out: the foreign policy on European immigration control', *West European Politics*, vol 29, no 2, pp 329-50.

Lavenex, S. (2009) 'European Union, country profile no 17', Country Profiles and Policy Briefs, Focus Migration (www.focus-migration.de).

Lavenex, S. and Uçarer, E.M. (2004) 'The external dimension of Europeanization. The case of immigration policies', *Cooperation and Conflict: Journal of the Nordic International Studies Association*, vol 39, no 4, pp 417-43.

McLaren, L.M. (2003) 'Anti-immigrant prejudice in Europe: contact, threat perception, and preferences for the exclusion of migrants', *Social Forces*, vol 81, no 3, pp 909-36.

McLaren, L.M. (2008) *One of us? Understanding public perception of labour migration in Europe*, Policy Network Paper, London: Policy Network (www.policy-network. net).

Nyíri, P. (2005) 'Global modernisers or local subalterns? Parallel perceptions of Chinese transnationals in Hungary', *Journal of Ethnic and Migration Studies*, vol 31, no 4, pp 659-74.

OECD (Organisation for Economic Co-operation and Development) (2008) *Perspectives des migrations internationales* [*International migration outlook. Annual Report*], Paris: OECD.

OECD (2009a) *Stat Extracts. Country statistical profiles 2009*, Paris: OECD (http:// stats.oecd.org/viewhtml.aspx?queryname=18155&querytype=view&lang=en).

OECD (2009b) *SOPEMI Country Notes 2009*, Paris: OECD (www.oecd.org/pu blicationanddocuments/0,3395,en_33873108_33873438_1_1_1_1_1,00.html).

Olomoofe, L. (2001) 'Africans in Budapest: an emerging subculture?', in P. Nyíri, J. Tóth and M. Fullerton (eds) *Diasporas and politics*, Budapest: Centre for Migration and Refugee Studies, pp 303-11.

OSCE (Organization for Security and Co-operation in Europe) ODIHR (Office for Democratic Institutions and Human Rights) (2004) *Annual report 2004*, Vienna: ODIHR (www.osce.org).

Reitz, J. (2006) *Recent trends in the integration of immigrants in the Canadian labour market*, Human Resources and Social Development Canada (www.rhdsc.gc.ca/ eng/cs/sp/hrsd/prc/publications/research/SP-672-01-07/page00.shtml).

Sainsbury, D. (2006) 'Immigrants' social rights in comparative perspective: welfare regimes, forms of immigration and immigration policy regimes', *Journal of European Social Policy*, vol 16, no 3, pp 229-44.

Schimmelfennig, F. (2009) 'Europeanization beyond Europe', *Living Reviews in European Governance*, vol 4, no 3, pp 5-22.

Schimmelfennig, F. and Sedelmeier, U. (2004) 'Governance by conditionality: EU rule transfer to the candidate countries of Central and Eastern Europe', *Journal of European Public Policy*, vol 11, no 4, pp 661-79.

Schimmelfennig, F. and Sedelmeier, U. (2005) *The Europeanization of Central and Eastern Europe*, Cornell, NY: Cornell University Press.

Schmidt, V. (1999) *The EU and its member states: Institutional contrasts and their consequences*, MPifG Working Paper 99/7, Cologne: Max Planck Institute for the Study of Societies.

Semyonov, M., Raijman, R. and Gorodzeisky, A. (2008) 'Foreigners' impact on European societies: public views and perceptions in a cross-national comparative perspective', *International Journal of Comparative Sociology*, vol 49, no 1, pp 5-29.

Sik, E. (2007) 'Path dependent problems: quasi-diasporic migration politics', in A. Buonfino, L. Byrne, E. Collett, J. Cruddas, R. Cuperus, J. Dijsselbloem, F. Dubet, L. Einaudi, E. Hillebrand, J. Kronig, R. Pearson, E.Sik, and C. Rumi Ibanez, *Contemporary Hungary in rethinking immigration and integration: A new center left agenda*, Policy Network Papers, London: Policy Network (www.policy-network.net).

Tóth, J. (2005) *Hungary: A case of ethnic preference in citizenship law*, Prague: Multicultural Center Prague (www.migrationonline.cz).

UN (United Nations) Expert Group Meeting on International Migration and Development (2005) *International migration in Central and Eastern Europe – Current and future trends*, UN/POP/PD/2005/12, New York: UN Population Division.

Wallace, C. (1998) *Migration potential in Central and Eastern Europe*, IOM Technical Cooperation Centre for Europe and Central Asia (http://iom.ramdisk.net).

TEN

Wilful negligence: migration policy, migrants' work and the absence of social protection in the UK

Mick Wilkinson and Gary Craig

Introduction

In this chapter we explore important issues concerned with the social exclusion and social segregation of migrant workers in the UK. Our main argument is that social and employment protection for this group of workers is often inadequate and that the UK government has a moral obligation to address these deficits. We argue that the UK has one of the least regulated labour markets of all 'developed' economies, and that the government's open invitation to migrant workers to meet the needs of the 'flexible' economy has generated a large pool of exploitable, largely unprotected labour. Many migrant workers in the UK do so under levels of exploitation that would meet the international legal definition of 'forced labour'. The chapter first sets out the national context of migration policies in the UK, reflecting on the long history of immigration to this former imperial power, and the historical significance of questions of 'race', ethnicity and racial discrimination to the integration of, especially, immigrant workers of the post–war period, and later their families as well.

The main body of the chapter examines the situation of migrant workers in the UK, in order to understand the very real and changing effects of interacting migration policies, labour market conditions and welfare policies on migrant workers. While restrictive policies were introduced to deal with marked increases in the number of asylum seekers from the early 1990s, similarly to other European countries, it is in the area of labour migration that most recent and contemporary policymaking has focused, with the introduction of a range of work permits for different categories of worker (for different economic sectors and skills levels) in the early 2000s, the 'open door' policy to migrants from the 2004 EU accession countries, to once again more restrictive policies from 2007/08. In addition, there is also in the UK an estimated substantial population of migrants residing or working illegally. Drawing on findings from two recent studies in England, the chapter goes on to assess the implications of the high degree of informalisation and flexibilisation of the UK's labour markets, combined with the lack of regulatory capacity, even where regulation should apply, for migrants' segregation and exclusion. In doing so, the chapter draws on two studies: a local case study on the numbers and needs of migrant workers in the Humber subregion in Yorkshire (Adamson et al, 2008) and an evaluation of the performance of the Gangmasters Licensing Authority (GLA), the national government regulatory body for migrant workers (Wilkinson et al, 2010).

National context

The colonial and mercantilist history of the UK means that it experienced ongoing inward migration, including settlement, from many areas of the world dating from before the early modern period – a pattern reflected in the populations of the major ports and the capital even in the pre-industrial period. Migration and mobility have, then, been important and normalised features of the political and economic landscape of the UK, but directly shaped by its colonial history and particular characteristics of its political economy.

Changing policy contexts and legacies

The early 20th century saw the first immigration act (Aliens Act 1906), an attempt to curtail new inward migration from Central and Eastern Europe, but it was in the early post-Second World War era that large-scale migration to the UK was generated most of all by the British government's drive for labour, when recruiting officers were sent to the Caribbean and to South Asia to fill large-scale labour shortages (Craig, 2007b). Migration in this period was driven primarily by the need for reconstruction and economic growth. Since then, millions of migrants have come to Britain, both from these parts of the world but also from South East Asia and from former colonies, to work and for the purposes of family reunification. The present minority ethnic population of the UK is about 11 per cent (that is, roughly seven million people). Many of these, second and third generation members of the minority ethnic communities, were born in the UK (43 per cent, according to the latest census). The UK's immigration policies are thus strongly linked to its colonial history and historically much debate and policymaking around social integration of immigrants has been less concerned with their status as 'immigrants' *per se*, but rather more concerned with 'race relations', discrimination and, latterly, institutional racism (Craig, 2002).

Immigration control has been an increasing concern of UK national governments, reflected in the first restrictive post-war immigration legislation of 1962 and 1968, limiting immigration to those with certified labour market opportunities (that is, work vouchers), together with dependants and family members of those already settled. Following the 1973 oil crisis, the pattern has been of increasing controls on immigration as a whole, interrupted only for special reasons such as international refugee crises. For most years until the mid-1990s, the total numbers of those migrating *into* the UK – of whatever status, economic migrant, family member, refugee or asylum seeker – has been fewer than those migrating *out of* the UK. This balance has shifted markedly since 2004 although the long-term picture is now unclear because of uncertainty about the aspirations for residence or citizenship of many of the migrants arriving from the 2004 and 2007 European Union (EU) accession countries.

This has corresponded to three kinds of development in UK national immigration policy in the last 15 years, focused around the construction of the 'needs' of the economy, the exclusion of unwanted 'economic migrants' (often cast as 'bogus' asylum seekers) and the contentious politics of integration in relation to the settled population (for a detailed discussion, see Somerville, 2007). The first policy development has been to control and reduce the increased number of asylum seekers, from the 1990s onwards. Along with the Dublin Convention that constructed the EU-level system of regulation of migrants seeking asylum, the UK also attempted to restrict access to both the labour market and welfare system in order to reduce 'incentives' for asylum seekers to come to the UK, as many were viewed in public and political discourse as *de facto* 'economic migrants'. The consequence has been a radical containment of their rights, controversially in the 1990s, by refusing access to the labour market and also offering barely subsistence benefits via a voucher system (Sales, 2002, p 457). And more recently, but also controversially, by continuing the separation (not merely segregation) of asylum seekers through the incarceration of asylum seekers, including children, in 'detention and removal centres' while their applications are processed.[1]

The second policy development has been to develop new systems for selecting categories of migrant worker. This programme of 'managed migration' was initiated by the New Labour government in 1997, to actively encourage temporary migration in the interests of the UK economy. The result was a rather complicated system of work and residence permits – from high-skilled workers to seasonal agricultural workers. In an additional policy shift that re-organised this system of 'management', and enhanced its focus on economic utility, a points-based system was introduced in 2008. Thus migrants can apply in a category based on a five-tier classification: tier one for highly skilled workers, businesspeople and graduates of UK universities, who can come to, or stay in, the UK without a job (for up to two years initially, with the possibility of extending to five years); tier two for skilled workers who must, however, have an employment contract, and are issued with a Certificate of Employment by employers (for up to three years); tier three for low-skilled migrants, a category of permit which has not been implemented, making entry to the UK for low-skilled employment no longer possible; tier four for students; and tier five for temporary workers of various kinds, requiring employment contracts (maximum stay of between 12 and 24 months). No tier five permit can be extended. Evidence of ability to financially self-support is required both for the 'points-based migrant' and any family dependants permitted to stay with them (with higher financial limits for tier one). The key marker for each category is that of economic utility, most marked by the ongoing suspension of tier three, but also by the tiered time limits attached to maximum permission to stay, as well as strictly controlled possibilities of switching from one category of permit to another.[2]

The third policy development has concerned questions of citizenship, with the aim of restricting permanent settlement in the UK, based on notions of suitability in relation to migrants' willingness or ability to integrate into the existing society.[3] In 2002, a new condition for acquisition of citizenship was introduced, a language requirement and also the passing of a 'knowledge of life in the UK' test. A further condition, that of being of 'good character' during the qualifying residence period, was introduced in 2006. The most recent legislation extended this approach and introduced very significant changes to citizenship legislation, which have important implications for the changing landscape of UK immigration and integration policies.

The Borders, Immigration and Citizenship Act 2009 constructed a regime of 'earned citizenship', where citizenship was to be 'earned' not merely by law-abiding residence and knowledge of the UK, but possible behavioural tests as well, according to an underlying presumption of 'civic nationalism' where 'shared values' are constructed as a gateway to settlement (McGhee, 2009). The Act, due to be implemented in July 2011, extended the required period for acquisition of citizenship from five to eight years, and for family dependants of citizens, from three to five years. However, this would be reduced by two years if the potential citizen had engaged in 'active citizenship' (voluntary social services, unpaid public or charitable service). Finally, and also important for the context of this book, the 2009 legislation will introduce a new status of 'probationary citizen', whereby after five years' residence, immigrants would, following the language and life in the UK test, become 'probationary citizens'. Subsequently, such 'probationary citizens' would be able to apply for citizenship status, or they can choose to remain as permanent residents. Probationary citizenship status, unlike the current entitlement of indefinite leave to remain, would not permit migrants to claim non-contributory benefits, and thus directly and explicitly represents an attempt to restrict the degree and form of 'social integration' available to even long-term UK residents.

Racism, discrimination and differential inclusion

The experience of minority ethnic migrants to the UK has generally been one of continuing structural racism and discrimination (Craig, 1999, 2001, 2007b). Since their first settlement, research has indicated the difficulties that most minorities have had in accessing welfare, in sustaining a level and quality of life equivalent to that of the mainstream population, in receiving the full benefits of citizenship and in creating effective mechanisms for their voice to be heard in policy and political discourse. These difficulties have continued to the present day (Modood et al, 1998; Platt, 2002). Thus, for example, minorities are more likely to experience poverty than the mainstream population, to live in poor housing conditions, suffer from poor educational attainment and have difficulties in accessing appropriate health service provision (Ahmad and Atkin, 1996). This applies to second and third-generation immigrants, despite formal entitlement to rights, and often British citizenship (see the discussion in Young, 2002).

Given the association of post-war migration and settlement in the UK with post-colonialism, much of the national debate about integration has centred around racism and discrimination. Issues were brought to a head with the enactment of the Race Relations Amendment Act (RRAA) in 2000, which followed on from the racialised murder of a teenage boy, Stephen Lawrence, and the consequent critique of structural racism developed against London's Metropolitan Police and many public and private organisations. The Act outlawed racial discrimination and required public agencies to have systems in place for monitoring ethnicity in employment and service, and for promoting 'race' equality. There is substantial evidence to suggest that many public agencies are still failing in their duty to promote racial equality, thus implying inequity for long-standing, legally resident immigrants, many of them British citizens, and their children (Craig, 2007b).

In terms of the relationship between migration, immigration and differential inclusion of settled migrants, the political and policy debate has continued in the last decade in heightened circumstances. The disturbances in northern cities in 2001 have led to responses focused on the need to promote 'community cohesion' (Cantle, 2001; Flint and Robinson, 2009), and this provided a major part of the underlying political and discursive context to the changes in citizenship law discussed above, although the government asserted that this was not a racialised issue (see also the discussion in McGhee, 2009).[4] The ongoing context of securitisation has also shaped policymaking in both integration and in asylum, not just in relation to exceptional threat (for example, terrorism), but as the 'politics of unease', a more normalised 'more continuous and technocratic debate that sustains or challenges the introduction of policing technologies for governing' (im)migrants (Huysmans and Buonfino, 2008, p 785).

More than this, however, as the population of minorities in the UK has grown and become more diverse, especially since the early 2000s, the complexity of labour market differentiation, of the interacting factors of skin colour, gender, country of origin and migration status as well as the position of labour market integration, has resulted in what Vertovec (2007) calls 'super-diversity'. The experiences of society and of migrants is radically more complicated than in previous decades, and demands different approaches to integration, which are still, problematically, couched in terms of ethnic difference, given the 'whiteness' of the post-accession migrations (but not, for example, of asylum seekers) (but see McDowell, 2007). To add to this, the social and economic trajectories of differing settled minorities have also tended to diversify so that the experience of minorities now is much more characterised by difference than by homogeneity.

Migrant workers

Under the pre-2008 managed migration programme, from the late 1990s, the UK government expanded existing temporary worker schemes and added new programmes, focused on recruiting highly skilled workers for specific gaps in the labour market. There are estimated to be about 1.4 million registered foreign workers in the UK. The number of 'illegal'/irregular workers in the UK is estimated at between 300,000 and 800,000 (for Chinese workers, see Pai, 2008;[5] see also the discussion in Chapter Two, this volume). In 2004, the UK, Ireland and Sweden were the only three nations to open their borders to 'free-moving workers' from Accession 8 (A8) countries (Kvist, 2004). Official statistics show the annual number of work permits issued to foreign-born workers rose from 40,000 in the mid-1990s to over 200,000 in 2004 (Flynn, 2005). Since May 2004, with EU expansion, approximately one million East European migrants have registered to work in the UK, with most (about 60 per cent) coming from Poland.

The post-2004 migration provoked concerns about job displacement of the UK workforce (concerns which most research suggests are groundless), about the impact on wages and skills levels (which are more grounded; see Galozgci, 2009), the potential for exploitation of these workers and the impact on sending countries. This has led to the extension of the Worker Registration Scheme (WRS) in 2009 for a further two years, to 2011, and to the restrictions on entry for employment of citizens from Romania and Bulgaria, who are largely treated as third-country nationals (TCNs).[6] Yet arguments about both general labour gaps, referencing the implications of the ageing population (Green, 2007), and also particular shortages – formerly in medicine, but also in dentistry, and most recently in pharmacy and midwifery – express policy and economic imperatives reflected in an increasing dependence on migrant workers, especially in some sectors of the economy, including low-skill sectors (RSA, 2006; Ruhs, 2008). This demand for low-skill work cannot be met from within the UK workforce. With the closure of legitimate migration for non-EU nationals to undertake low-skill employment from 2008, this is expected and assumed in government policy to be taken up by migrants from elsewhere in the EU (that is, A8 citizens under the WRS). Such assumptions do not, of course, take account of the presence or use of the illegal employment of migrants, especially in low-skill occupations.

Conditions of work and social integration for migrant workers

However, there is another side to the coin. The system of employment rights in the UK was, until the points-based system, extremely complex, with a variety of visas and work permits for different categories of workers and countries of origin, creating up to 80 routes for residence and employment, and involving a range of different agencies responsible for different aspects of migrants' lives (Craig et al, 2003). Those complexities have been compounded by language barriers, and sometimes by disinformation deliberately generated by exploitative employers

(Anti-Slavery International, 2006). As a result, many legal migrant workers are unaware of their rights and find themselves highly vulnerable (McDowell et al, 2009, p 12).

A wide range of recent research (House of Commons, 2004; Citizens Advice, 2005; Audit Commission, 2006; CRC, 2006; EMDA, 2006) has shown that many migrant workers worked for low pay (£100-£199 per week, 20-30 per cent less – often substantially so – than their UK counterparts, and often below the statutory minimum wage), longer basic hours (60 hours per week and sometimes considerably more) than is normal for their occupation, have no sick pay, paid holiday or written contract covering hours, conditions, pay and dismissal procedures. Similarly to migrants elsewhere, many have skills and qualifications far superior to those required for their work (hoping they will get higher skilled work later on). Most are not in touch with trades unions, although some major unions are now beginning to translate material into relevant languages and to make contact with migrants at their places of work. Many are unaware of their rights, and live in poor to appalling conditions, often six or more of mixed sex to a room. Some are content to accept these conditions because the wages – while illegal in the UK – are superior to those they could obtain in their countries of origin, and because they regard their stay as temporary. However, many feel exploited, angry and are at risk because of their working and housing conditions (Spencer et al, 2007). These, of course, not only have impacts on the workers themselves but also have ongoing effects on the institutional form of labour markets themselves.

Many migrants access employment via labour suppliers, called 'gangmasters', of which UK enforcement agencies estimate there may be as many as 10,000,[7] operating across various industrial sectors. Main sectors for their employment include agriculture, food processing and packing, construction, catering, leisure, hotels, cleaning, textiles and social and health care (Adamson et al, 2008; WRS quarterly data). While in 1973 the government launched the Employment Agencies Act under which all labour providers had to register and comply with legal standards,[8] in 1994 the Conservative government introduced the Deregulation and Contracting-Out Act, through which the system of agency licensing was abolished and action against exploiters became primarily dependent on victims' complaints.

Following the consequent enormous growth in the number of gangmasters, reports began to surface of poor treatment of temporary workers. Policy and political concern was finally focused as a result of two incidents: first, the death by asphyxiation of 58 Chinese people in a lorry entering a British port in 2000, and then the drowning of 23 Chinese shellfish-pickers in 2004 in Morecambe Bay in North West England. These forced the government to respond. However, the measure finally taken, the establishment of the GLA in April 2005, was enacted only after concerted pressure from trades unions in alliance with voluntary organisations and church groups.

The government limited the GLA's remit to those supplying labour in three industrial sectors: agriculture and horticulture, forestry and shellfish gathering.

Other key industrial sectors, including construction, hotels and hospitality, the care sector and contract cleaning, all now highly dependent on migrant labour (see, for example, EMDA, 2006; Anderson, 2007; Adamson et al, 2008; Glossop and Shaheen, 2009; Wilkinson et al, 2010), are beyond the GLA's remit and remain so poorly regulated as to be effectively a free-for-all zone for exploitative employers. Our research demonstrates clearly how gangmasters seeking to avoid regulation simply divert migrant workers under their control away from agriculture and into unregulated sectors. There are roughly 10,000 gangmasters operating in the UK; the GLA, however, has fewer than 30 inspectors. This is clearly not a meaningful response to the widespread problem of temporary worker exploitation.

The arrival of migrant workers also led to increasing and different demands on welfare service provision. Both statutory and voluntary service providers have called on central government to increase the resources available to them in order to meet these new demands (ICoCo, 2007). They criticise the lack of available information on the numbers of arrivals, their employment status, health and welfare needs and their likely length of stay. Our studies reveal how these difficulties are manifest.

Case study evidence: policy and service issues for migrant workers

In order to access the experiences of migrant workers, especially those on the margins of legality, or irregular migrants, it is necessary to undertake more specific qualitative case studies. The case studies explored here took place in the Yorkshire and Humber region that we call Eastern England for simplicity. They were based primarily on a mixture of secondary analysis of previously published research together with qualitative interviews with people providing statutory or voluntary services for migrant workers, and with the testimonies of migrant workers themselves.

Numbers

Estimates vary, but there may be in the order of at least 90,000 migrant workers who have arrived recently in the Yorkshire and Humber region under various schemes. Migrant workers, with Polish nationality workers being the largest group, form a significant part of the regional economy: 85 per cent of employers have recently experienced recruitment difficulties, 38 per cent turning to migrant workers to fill vacancies (Yorkshire Futures, 2006), and many recruiting migrant workers on a permanent basis.

The majority of migrants in our studies were aged between late teens and early thirties, with substantially more males than females, but with the gender gap reducing more recently. In rural areas there appeared to be two distinct categories of migrants. One constituted the more settled migrants, settling in for the medium to long term, residing primarily in private rented houses and flats, usually of poor quality. The majority of these were again Polish, with some Russians and Portuguese (some present since before 2004). As a result of migrants' geographical mobility, precise numbers were difficult to obtain, but expectations are of a significant undercount in official figures in any one area (NLDC, 2005).

The other major category comprised groups working on Seasonal Agricultural Workers Scheme (SAWS) projects, usually students in their teens and early twenties. These groups lived largely on caravan sites of up to 100 caravans near the greenhouses where they worked. The numbers of those employed on SAWS as a whole was far smaller than those employed via the WRS (a UK total of 21,000 SAWS places were reserved for 2010) and, because their stay was strictly temporary, the impact both on them and on local services was marginal.

Employment

New community migrants clearly filled jobs within the region where employers had previously had difficulties recruiting, and our research suggests that many businesses and farms in the subregion now depended on migrant workers for their prosperity – even their survival. Ironically, the migrant workforce appeared to be largely a well-educated and skilled workforce, often better qualified than their settled counterparts, yet primarily located at the bottom of the labour market. There were a range of barriers to their 'scaling up' to better jobs, including language difficulties, non-recognition of qualifications, lack of awareness of employment rights, lack of support, racism and institutional barriers in the application process (Clark and Drinkwater, 2008; Glossop and Shaheen, 2009). Alongside this we found widespread and calculated exploitation by gangmasters and employment agencies (for a discussion on domestic workers, see Anderson, 2007).

Migrant workers were generally paid the minimum wage, some much less, but frequently wages were reduced by systematic illegal or unfair deductions. We came across exorbitant fees for processing passports, for transportation to work or for inadequate safety clothing. Some had excessively high tax and National Insurance deductions from their wages that, it later transpired, were never paid to the taxation authorities. Working conditions were often appalling, sometimes dangerous. Unsocial hours were the norm, 12 and 16-hour shifts common, usually without overtime payments. Workers were sometimes called to do double shifts at a moment's notice and it was commonplace for those refusing to do so to be threatened with redundancy and loss of accommodation. Respondents gave accounts of systematic underpayment, often of hundreds of pounds, for hours worked, of being paid for one shift instead of two without redress and of complaints being met with threats of violence. Many paid a non-returnable signing-on fee, of up to £1,000, to an agency in their home country. On arrival, some were then faced with an unexpected similarly sized further signing-on fee in the UK, which had to be repaid immediately. The gangmasters then ensured that they earned insufficient monies to clear those debts. So, for instance, migrants were deliberately laid off work for periods during which time they continued to live in gangmaster accommodation, accumulating further debts: which is essentially debt bondage.

Exploitation was more likely where migrants were isolated – in rural parts of the subregion migrants were particularly prone to this. As one respondent observed, "their gangmaster has said to their employers if they don't do what you want them to do, just take them for a ride up the road and drop them off…". Respondents argued that the failure to tackle the problem of employer exploitation was rooted primarily in the inadequacies of enforcement agencies and in the lack of resources attached to the key policing body, the GLA.

Particular precariousness of irregular migrants

There are also a possibly substantial number of *irregular* migrants (see IPPR, 2006); factoring down from national estimates, they may number between 10,000 and 20,000. Local police and other respondents in our case study were aware of illegal migrant workers such as non-registered Chinese workers and of Brazilians using Portuguese documents. The picture was further complicated by the numbers of asylum-seeking refugees remaining after having been refused leave to settle. These were, for the main part, destitute and technically unable to access services other than basic healthcare. Some respondents believed the majority of irregular migrants had become illegal through the malpractice of gangmasters and employment agencies who had either not explained the necessity of registering with the Home Office, or had taken their papers for registration (see also McDowell et al, 2008). Others had been trafficked into the country illegally.

We found several defining features characterising the experience of undocumented workers. They:

- illegally resided in the UK in constant fear of deportation;
- often experienced exploitation in terms of housing and other 'services' provided by gangmasters;
- had little or no access to information, including their (limited) rights;
- could not secure legitimate work and the minimum wage;
- were isolated, freedom of association being prevented or discouraged;
- had language difficulties, compounding isolation;
- could not access medical services or mental health support;
- feared threats of violence to themselves and to their families in their country of origin;
- experienced physical, sexual and verbal abuse, and intimidation;
- worked long, unsociable hours, in sometimes hazardous conditions, for little, and sometimes no, remuneration;[9]
- could not complain or turn to the authorities, including employment-related enforcement agencies, for fear of deportation;
- shied away from other forms of support such as trades unions and voluntary agencies.

These circumstances meet the International Labour Organization (ILO) criteria for forced labour (ILO, 2004). Trades union activists reported particularly distressing circumstances including sexual exploitation, severe mental distress, rape and the kidnap of children, but with no possibility of redress because the workers were unregistered, thus liable for deportation if they came to the authorities' attention. This demonstrates the particular vulnerability of foreign workers in what is officially characterised as a 'flexible' labour market (see also McDowell et al, 2009).

Housing

For all migrant workers, alongside typical lists of false deductions were charges for exorbitantly priced multi-occupancy accommodation also provided by the gangmaster/agency. It is standard practice that migrant workers cannot leave that accommodation without also losing their employment. It is, however, often unsafe, appallingly overcrowded, with inadequate amenities. In many areas, migrants are crammed, often eight per property, into small houses of multiple occupation (HMOs). In one small town, housing officers identified "… 400-500 HMOs which are all overcrowded, all lack means of escape and decent fire precautions, all with one toilet when there should be two or three, inadequate kitchen facilities". Proactive enforcement of housing regulations is hampered by limited resources, and by the reluctance of migrant workers to come forward either because they have a historical distrust of statutory representatives, or through fear of reprisals from their employment provider. 'Hot bedding'– a practice whereby as one work shift get out of bed, another shift climbs in – was common in several areas. Apart from the affront to human dignity, there are clearly wider public health considerations.

Health provision

At the time of our studies, there was no *strategic* work being undertaken to ascertain the health needs of migrant workers in the case study region. This reflects a general historical failing within the NHS to target and respond to the needs of migrants (Ahmad and Atkin, 1996; Craig, 2007b). No one could provide any meaningful figures on residence, age, gender, or how many might therefore present to primary healthcare facilities, and there seemed among our interviewees to be a presumption (against the requirement in the RRAA 2000) to just treat [migrants] as a member of our population, rather than acknowledging the specific issues that arose for migrants. Several health professionals claimed that, as migrant workers were generally young, they had few health needs. Research suggests that this approach is at best myopic, at worst negligent (NEPHO, 2008). An earlier study in the region established that there were mental health issues among migrant workers (Robinson and Reeve, 2005), referring to social isolation, homesickness and 'the diminished quality of life and resultant mental health problems' (Wilkinson et al, 2010, p 20) of Portuguese and Eastern European communities. In addition, migrants faced a number of cultural barriers in accessing these and other health services, exacerbated by a lack of translation and interpreting services and of simple information factsheets.

Education

The pressures on education services reflected the most obvious ways in which temporary and unpredictable migration patterns could be disruptive to local providers. The number of children from Eastern and Central Europe presenting at schools across the subregion has increased significantly over the last two to three years. In Hull, for instance, in that period, there was an estimated sudden inflow of around 800 school-aged children from migrant worker families. One primary school had rapidly become cosmopolitan, its 200 children incorporating 28 nationalities – an example of 'super-diversity' (Vertovec, 2007) well outside the metropolitan areas traditionally associated with high numbers of different migrant groups. This necessarily presents significant challenges to all welfare and public service providers who are responsible for service provision that is essential for integration, especially in the case of language acquisition for adults and children, and access to schooling for children. In a context of poor understanding of and preparation for both the volume and complexity of migration to a local area, such public service providers are likely to play a significant role in assisting or ameliorating the differential integration of migrants and their families locally (see also Caponio and Borkert, 2010).

Advice and information provision

Migrant workers require assistance in obtaining a range of bona fide documentation – work permits, driving licences and National Insurance numbers, especially as the latter can later entitle them to contributory benefits and is a condition of legal employment. They also seek help in completing employment application forms, advice on employment rights and on how to address employment and housing exploitation. As with the settled population, they need support to deal with physical ill health and emotional trauma, sometimes also in coping with racist attacks. They need assistance with everyday basics such as signing up for energy and water supplies, advice on legal rights and responsibilities and in relation to accessing local services. It was clear that many did not know their rights or where to turn to for advice. Some were reluctant to seek advice for fear of drawing attention to themselves. Long working hours and language difficulties were also barriers to access, while service providers often did not know what migrant workers required or what they were entitled to, with little understanding from them of the differing legal conditions and social needs of migrant groups.

Community cohesion and community tensions

The 'new communities' were generally considered by respondents to be primarily law-abiding, quiet, responsible, respectful, clean living and church going. They tended to socialise at home within their communities, and in restaurants. However, some local authority officers told of appreciable levels of hostility among the settled community. Respondents reported sporadic cases of primarily verbal abuse, but occasional violence, against migrants, although this was geographically uneven. One respondent with direct links into the Eastern European communities told of constant undercurrents of hostility, and incidents of verbal and physical abuse: "The attitude of the English people, you know, everywhere you can see it and you can feel it". "What are you doing here? You have come here to take our job…."This reflects a wider national phenomenon of an increase in xenophobic attitudes (Craig, 2010), which has distilled into political demands for 'British jobs for British workers', and a strong anti-immigrationist tone to all political debate, reflected also in the election of fascist British National Party (BNP) representatives for the European Parliament and local council in the wider region (as elsewhere in the UK).

Conclusion

After several decades of light-touch regulation, the Organisation for Economic Co-operation and Development (OECD) suggests that the UK has one of the least regulated labour markets of all developed economies.This has allowed widespread and largely unchecked exploitation and abuses by unscrupulous gangmasters and criminal gangs, and the growth of what is effectively modern slavery (Craig, 2010: forthcoming). Recent government initiatives around managing migration, such as the new points-based system for work and study introduced in the summer of 2008, and around British citizenship from 2011 will, if anything, make the position of migrant workers still more vulnerable.There is already evidence of additional disadvantage for workers in the catering and healthcare sectors (House of Commons, 2009; MRN, 2009b). Nor can this discrimination, vulnerability or precariousness necessarily only be conceived in relation to racial discrimination. In addition to the longstanding frame of reference in the UK which linked immigration, ethnicity and integration, we now have additional (not alternative) policy frames linking country of origin, migrant status and employment conditions, to distinguish and exclude the supposedly 'unwanted' from access to basic social and political rights, where their tolerated economic activity in the informal labour market, rather than being a path to integration, compounds their exclusion.

Rising unemployment and falling employment as a result of the UK's economic recession will inevitably have an impact on temporary and agency working, with evidence to suggest that for labour suppliers the market is becoming more competitive (GLA, 2008). It is likely that the most unscrupulous labour providers and users will seek to cushion themselves from this downturn by further exploiting vulnerable workers. Our case studies suggest that there is little in place, by way of employment standards enforcement machinery, to prevent that from happening. With the notable exception of the GLA, which has been reasonably effective albeit within its limited remit, the UK employment enforcement framework has failed temporary workers in general and migrant workers in particular. The flexibility of the UK's labour market has now placed it, in social and employment policy terms, alongside Southern European countries (Alcock and Craig, 2008).

Large numbers of undocumented workers are residing in the UK, forming a substantial part of the settled population in comparison with many other EU member states (see Chapter Two, this volume). Many have become undocumented and thus perhaps illegal through no fault of their own. They contribute substantially to the economy (Craig, 2007a), but are forced to live an 'underground' existence, vulnerable to exploitation, and effectively unprotected by any of the labour-related enforcement agencies. A recent opinion poll by the Strangers into Citizens[10] campaign found two thirds of the public supported a one-off regularisation programme, and the Migrants' Rights Network (MRN) has now produced an authoritative and extremely detailed argument for regularisation (MRN, 2009a).[11]

While it is fair to say that, like central government, many local service providers were simply not prepared for the scale of recent in-migration, it is equally true that there has been little subsequent proactive engagement to ascertain the scale and nature of the needs of new communities. The style of integration envisaged under the regime of 'earned citizenship' and 'probationary citizenship' introduced in the 2009 legislation also suggests that neither national nor local government is equipped, or perhaps even willing, to respond to the complexity and variability of circumstances produced by current UK in-migration. Locally, this is in part due to pressure on resources – clearly a critical factor, especially in the current context of profound budget cuts – but it is also due to an inherently discriminatory culture. In the absence of a political lead to the contrary it may take a long time for that culture to change (providing an interesting comparison with cities in France and Italy; see Chapter Twelve, this volume). Elected local authority members often appear unwilling to prioritise the needs of migrant workers, whether for electoral reasons (not wishing to be seen spending taxpayers' monies on 'outsiders') or simply through prejudice. Local government, members of parliament and activists have argued that enhanced resources are necessary to enable them to meet the challenges posed by the presence of migrant workers and their dependants; perhaps they should also focus on the opportunities they present.

Notes

[1] The need to have regard for children's welfare under the 2009 legislation may have implications for their treatment, including detention.

[2] The conservative-liberal coalition government announced in May 2010 that it will introduce 'a cap' on numbers of non-EU migrants; at the time of printing, further details of the policy had not been confirmed.

[3] That this idea rests on problematic assumptions about the monolithic character of what constitutes 'society' from the settled communities of the UK has been raised (see especially McGhee, 2009).

[4] Restrictions and conditions have been introduced despite rhetorical gestures to the economic contribution made by migrants; studies sponsored by the Home Office, the International Organization for Migration, the Institute for Public Policy Research and the Royal Society for Arts all argued a net annual benefit to the UK economy of around £2 billion to £3 billion.

[5] Estimates range between 310,000 to 800,000.

[6] SAWS is now only available to Bulgarian and Romanian citizens.

[7] It is illegal in the UK to operate as a labour supplier without a licence from the GLA. However, many do so: the term 'gangmaster' has thus become strongly associated with illegality.

[8] www.opsi.gov.uk/RevisedStatutes/Acts/ukpga/1973/cukpga_19730035_en_1

[9] We found workers paid £50 for a 70-hour week: about 15% of minimum wage levels.

[10] www.strangersintocitizens.org.uk/

[11] The conservative-liberal coalition has rejected this policy option, although it had been proposed by the liberals before the May 2010 General Election.

References

Adamson, S., Craig, G. and Wilkinson, M. (2008) *Migrant workers in the Humber sub-region: A report for the Humber Improvement Partnership*, Hull: Humber Improvement Partnership.

Ahmad, W. and Atkin, K. (1996) *'Race' and health*, Buckingham: Open University Press.

Alcock, P. and Craig, G. (eds) (2008) *International social policy* (2nd edn), Basingstoke: Palgrave Macmillan.

Anderson, B. (2007) 'A very private business. Exploring the demand for migrant domestic workers', *European Journal of Women's Studies*, vol 14, no 3, pp 247-64.

Anti-Slavery International (2006) *Trafficking for forced labour in Europe*, London: Anti-Slavery International.

Audit Commission (2006) *Migrant workers and local cohesion, Report on East Riding of Yorkshire*, London: Audit Commission.

Cantle, T. (2001) *Community cohesion*, London: Home Office.

Caponio, T. and Borkert, M. (2010) (eds) *The local dimension of migration policymaking*, Amsterdam: Amsterdam University Press.

Citizens Advice (2005) *Supporting migrant workers in rural areas*, London: Citizens Advice.

Clark, K. and Drinkwater, S. (2008) 'The labour-market performance of recent migrants', *Oxford Review of Economic Policy*, vol 24, no 3, pp 495-516.

Craig, G. (1999) '"Race", poverty and social security', in J. Ditch (ed) *An introduction to social security*, London: Routledge, pp 206-26.

Craig, G. (2001) *'Race' and welfare*, Hull: University of Hull.

Craig, G. (2002) 'Ethnicity, racism and the labour market', in J.-G. Andersen and P. Jensen (eds) *Citizenship, welfare and the labour market*, Bristol: The Policy Press, pp 149-82.

Craig, G. (2007a) 'They come over here ... and boost our economy', *Regional Review*, Summer.

Craig, G. (2007b) 'Cunning, unprincipled, loathsome: the racist tail wags the welfare dog', *Journal of Social Policy*, October, vol 36, pp 605-23.

Craig, G. (2010) 'Flexibility, xenophobia and exploitation: modern slavery in the UK', *Social Policy Review 22*, Bristol: The Policy Press, pp 173-98.

Craig, G., Dawson, A., Hutton, S., Roberts, N. and Wilkinson, M. (2003) *International migration: The information base*, London: Department of the Environment, Transport and the Regions.

CRC (Commission for Rural Communities) (2006) *Rural disadvantage*, London: CRC.

EMDA (East Midlands Development Agency) (2006) *The dynamics of migrant labour in South Lincolnshire*, Nottingham: EMDA.

Flint, J. and Robinson, D. (eds) (2009) *Community cohesion in crisis?*, Bristol: The Policy Press.

Flynn, D. (2005) 'New borders, new management: the dilemmas of modern migration policies', *Ethnic and Racial Studies*, vol 28, no 3, pp 463-90.

Galgóczi, B., Leschke, J. and Watt, A. (2009) *Intra-EU labour migration: Flows, effects and policy responses*, ETUI Working Paper 2009/03, Brussels: ETUI.

GLA (Gangmasters Licensing Authority) (2008) *2nd year annual review – Main report*, Nottingham: GLA.

Glossop, C. and Shaheen, F. (2009) *Accession to recession*, London: Centre for Cities.

Green, S. (2007) 'Divergent traditions, converging responses: immigration and integration policy in the UK and Germany', *German Politics*, vol 16, no 1, pp 95-115.

House of Commons (2004) *Gangmasters (follow-up report)*, HC455, London: The Stationery Office.

House of Commons (2009) *Managing migration: The points-based system*, Thirteenth Report of Session 2008-09, Volume 1, 1 August, Home Affairs Committee, HC 217-1, London, The Stationery Office.

Huysmans, J. and Buonfino, A. (2008) 'Politics of exception and unease: immigration, asylum and terrorism in parliamentary debates in the UK', *Political Studies*, vol 56, no 4, pp 766-88.

ICoCo (Institute of Community Cohesion) (2007) *Estimating the scale and impacts of migration at the local level*, London/Coventry: Local Government Association/ICoCo.

ILO (International Labour Organization) (2004) *Human trafficking and forced labour exploitation: Guidelines for legislators and law enforcement*, Geneva: ILO.

IPPR (Institute for Public Policy Research (2006) *Irregular migration in the UK*, London: IPPR.

Kvist, J. (2004) 'Does EU enlargement create a race to the bottom? Strategic interaction among EU member states in social policy', *Journal of European Social Policy*, vol 14, no 3, pp 301-18.

McDowell, L. (2007) 'Constructions of whiteness: Latvian women workers in post-war Britain', *Journal of Baltic Studies*, vol 38, issue 1, pp 85-107.

McDowell, L., Batnitzky, A. and Dyer, S. (2008) 'Internationalization and the spaces of temporary labour: the global assembly of a local workforce', *British Journal of Industrial Relations*, vol 46, no 4, pp 750-70.

McDowell, L., Batnitzky, A. and Dyer, S. (2009) 'Precarious work and economic migration: emerging immigrant divisions of labour in Greater London's service sector', *International Journal of Urban and Regional Research*, vol 33, no 1, pp 3-25.

McGhee, M. (2009) 'The paths to citizenship: a critical examination of immigration policy in Britain since 2001', *Patterns of Prejudice*, vol 43, no 1, pp 41-64.

Modood, T., Berthoud, R., Lakey, J., Nazroo, J., Smith, P., Virdee, S. and Beishon, S. (1998) *Ethnic minorities in Britain: Diversity and disadvantage – The Fourth National Survey of Ethnic Minorities*, London: Policy Studies Institute.

MRN (Migrants' Rights Network) (2009a) *Irregular migrants: The urgent need for a new approach*, London: MRN, May.

MRN (2009b) *Migrants' Rights News*, August (www.migrantsrights.org.uk/mrn_news.php).

NEPHO (North East Public Health Observatory) (2008) *New arrivals in North East England: Mapping migrant health and NHS delivery*, Stockton-on-Tees: NEPHO (http://www.dur.ac.uk/ne.pho/index.php?c=2922).

North Lincolnshire Council (2005) *New communities mapping project 2005*, Scunthorpe: North Lincolnshire Council.

Pai, H-H. (2008) *Chinese whispers*, Harmondsworth: Penguin.

Platt, L. (2002) *Parallel lives?*, London: Child Poverty Action Group.

Robinson, D. and Reeve, K. (2005) *Minority ethnic housing experiences in North Lincolnshire*, Sheffield: Centre for Regional Economic and Social Research, Sheffield Hallam University.

RSA (Royal Society for the Arts) (2006) *Migration: A welcome opportunity*, London: RSA.

Ruhs, M. (2008) 'Economic research and labour immigration policy', *Oxford Review of Economic Policy*, vol 24, no 3, pp 403-26.

Sales, R. (2002) 'The deserving and the undeserving? Refugees, asylum seekers and welfare in Britain', *Critical Social Policy*, vol 27, no 3, pp 456-78.

Somerville, W. (2007) *Immigration policy under New Labour*, Bristol: The Policy Press.

Spencer, S., Ruhs, M., Anderson, B. and Rogaly, B. (2007) *Migrants' lives beyond the workplace*, York: Joseph Rowntree Foundation.

Vertovec, S. (2007) 'Super-diversity and its implications', *Ethnic and Racial Studies*, vol 30, no 6, pp 1024-54.

Wilkinson, M., Craig, G. and Gaus, A. (2010) *Forced labour in the UK and the Gangmasters Licensing Authority*, Hull: University of Hull.

Yorkshire Futures (2006) *Progress in the region, 2006*, Leeds: Yorkshire Futures.

Young, J. (2002) 'To these wet and windy shores: recent immigration policy in the UK', *Punishment and Society*, vol 5, no 4, pp 449-62.

Part III
Social and migration policy nexus: critical issues

Local immigrant communities, welfare and culture: an integration/segregation dilemma

Siniša Zrinščak

Introduction[1]

The role of social networks in the life of immigrants has been a highly debated topic highlighting the importance of cultural and social capital, both for migration as well as for the social orientation and integration of immigrants in the countries of destination (Castles and Miller, 2009, pp 27-30). More recently, the concept of transnationalism has come to the attention of the international academic community, highlighting the global character of migration movements and of their social networks. In this context, transnationalism requires the development of new ways of studying the integration of immigrants (Faist, 2000; Kivisto, 2003; Castles and Miller, 2009). Not denying the important role of global migrant networks for the integration of immigrants, this chapter concentrates only on local immigrant communities and their role in the life of immigrants. Furthermore, its aim is not simply to emphasise the importance as well as the ambiguities of the role played by local immigrant communities, but also to build a bridge between the study of welfare rights of immigrants and a broader investigation of the impact of rising ethnic (and religious) diversity in contemporary welfare state development. Generally speaking, there are two ways of studying the social position of immigrants. The first is based on an approach that looks at differences of social or welfare status of immigrants in comparison to non-migrants, such as in the fields of unemployment, poverty or different benefit recipients (Hatton and Williamson, 2005; OECD, 2007; Castles and Miller, 2009; Koopmans, 2010). An extension of this approach concerns the question of the general social features that influence differences, and more specifically the impact of welfare state models. The most interesting point to note in this respect is the existence of intra-regime variations (see Morissens and Sainsbury, 2005; Banting and Kymlicka, 2006). The second approach is more focused on the issue of increasing diversity, multiculturalism and the welfare state. The crucial question here concerns the possible trade-off between diversity and solidarity (see, for example, Taylor-Gooby, 2005; Banting and Kymlicka, 2006). This is part of a more general discussion of how to deal with ethnic, religious and cultural differences in contemporary European societies, and the ways in which immigration and integration policies are formulated.

Based on a literature review on immigrants, the welfare state and multiculturalism, and on the findings of the comparative research project 'Welfare and Values in Europe: Transitions related to religion, minorities, and gender' (WAVE), this chapter investigates the significance of local immigrant social networks (family, ethnic and religious organisations), drawing attention to their indispensable role not only in the more general social orientation of immigrants, but also in articulating and realising their welfare needs. Such a role in social integration and orientation emphasises the importance of cultural elements (such as religion, language, symbols, food, clothing and so on) in promoting the welfare rights of immigrants. As a result, this chapter confirms that immigrant social networks can also play an important role in the study of the welfare state and immigrants. The question of the integration of immigrants represents not only a question of the relationship between diversity and solidarity, but of the possibility of welfare state models to capture the different needs of minority populations.

The chapter is divided into six parts. This introductory section is followed by a theoretical discussion relevant for the study of the integration strategies of local immigrant communities. The third section provides basic information about the WAVE research project which constituted an empirical base for the chapter. Empirical findings are elaborated in two further sections, one of which deals with the role of immigrant social networks, while the other one interprets empirical findings about the role of social networks in the light of welfare state models. The conclusion summarises the main findings of the chapter.

Theoretical insights

As underlined in the introduction to this chapter, a common approach in social policy is to explore how different welfare states deal with the welfare needs of immigrants, as unemployment rates or social exclusion tend, for example, to be higher among the minority population. Despite the existence of differences among countries (in Australia and in the USA, immigrants are, for instance, better integrated in the labour market), high unemployment and low activity rates are prominent almost everywhere, revealing the disadvantaged position of immigrants in respect of country nationals (Castles and Miller, 2009, p 243). The situation improves, however, among the second generation of immigrants, although with large variations within the ethnic groups and the destination countries taken into account (for example, for the case of Germany, see Chapter Seven, this volume). With respect to gender, women also often have a more disadvantaged position. Of particular interest here is rising labour market segmentation, as according to the Organisation for Economic Co-operation and Development (OECD), migrants are more likely to be employed in temporary jobs than non-migrants in almost all (although there are some exceptions) European immigration countries (Castles and Miller, 2009, p 235). Do differences among countries depend on specific welfare state characteristics or other social features? Morissens and Sainsbury (2005) have explored this issue in great detail, analysing the social rights of immigrants and minority ethnic groups in six countries corresponding to different welfare regimes, according to the well-known Esping-Andersen typology (1990): liberal (UK and US), conservative (France and Germany) and social democratic (Denmark and Sweden). The authors started from the assumption that better outcomes for immigrants in terms of their participation in social transfer programmes and maintenance of an acceptable living standard could be found in welfare states with high levels of de-commodification (social democratic welfare regime) in contrast to welfare regimes with moderate (conservative welfare regime) or particularly low levels of de-commodification (liberal welfare regime). Their analysis showed that on the basis of the data on poverty, both immigration status and being a member of a minority ethnic group were associated with higher poverty risk across these different welfare regimes. Of particular interest here were intra-regime variations, as, for example, 'Swedish poverty rates for migrants and ethnic minorities are the lowest, while Danish poverty rates are the highest for ethnic minority migrant households and second highest for all migrant households' (Morissens and Sainsbury, 2005, p 645), even though these two countries belong to the same social democratic welfare model. A similar, although slightly lower, difference can also be found between the US and the UK, as in the UK there were much lower poverty rates than in the US, and both countries belong to the same liberal welfare regime. In general, however, the analysis of the effects of social programmes shows that in the analysed countries, immigrants tend to perform worse than citizens. What is important to note from that analysis is the inadequacy of the welfare regime approach to capture the complex differences that exist in the social rights of immigrants in various countries (see the discussion on migrant integration regimes in Chapter Two, this volume).

Laparra (2008) has also underlined the differences existing in Germany and Sweden, which are not only connected with welfare models, but also with their migration policies. While in Germany access to welfare is connected with employment status, the Swedish migration policies, following an egalitarian logic typical of the Scandinavian welfare regimes (welfare more based on residence rather than on employment), have tended to treat citizens and immigrants more equally, even though since the 1990s the association between reforms of social and immigration policy (particularly increasing restrictions in asylum policy) has had a negative impact on the status of immigrants. The claim of a failure in the cultural integration of immigrants in Europe requires special attention that has to be found in intensified debates, tensions and a shift in migration policies from 'promotion of multiculturalism' to 'promotion of integration' (see Afonso, 2005; Carrera, 2006; Kremer, 2008). There is even an argument that multicultural policies in connection with generous welfare states have produced negative integration outcomes visible in a low level of labour market participation, a high level of segregation and higher criminal behaviour (Koopmans, 2010), although this analysis did not focus on other quality of life indicators. In general, a trend from multiculturalism back to assimilation can be observed, even though it should be kept in mind that the concept of assimilation has also changed over time (Brubaker, 2001). Still, based on an examination of a number of European Union (EU) countries (Denmark, the Netherlands, Germany, France and the UK, among others), Vertovec and Wessendorf (2009) also noted the backlash of multicultural discourse, claiming at the same time that the promotion of integration defined as a new policy goal does not, in fact, differ much from previous multicultural policies.

The rising diversity of European societies puts on the agenda the general question of a possible erosion of welfare state models, starting from the assumption that, based on the US experience, a trade-off between diversity and solidarity may exist (see Alber, 2006). Anti-immigrant voices expressed by (extreme) right-wing politicians have contributed, in this context, to the erosion of solidarity(ies) on which different welfare states have been built during their history (see the discussion on contentious migration politics in Chapter One, this volume). The results of recent studies on this topic have been far from unanimous, however. In a study on welfare states in Europe and the US, Taylor-Gooby (2005, p 669) concluded, for instance, 'that [cultural] diversity does have a negative impact on welfare spending, but one that is much weaker and less significant in the advanced welfare states outside the US'. The impact of the political left is much stronger in EU countries, which contributes to the preservation of the welfare state against the negative impact of growing diversity.

Similarly, Banting and Kymlicka (2004) concluded that no evidence could be found that the adoption of multicultural policies leads to the erosion of the welfare state. In this debate, it is particularly important to note that the creation and development of multicultural policies does not seem to respond to changes in the composition and number of immigrant groups. The countries differ, for instance, in the ways in which they formulate their approach to different types of minorities, but, more generally, it seems difficult to apply the US experience to other (EU) context(s). Relations between immigrants, multicultural policies and the welfare state are, in fact, much more complex (Banting, 2005). In order to fully capture this diversity, not only is it necessary to introduce ethnic heterogeneity or other characteristics as crucial explanatory variables in the comparative study of social spending, but it is also necessary to develop a more subtle conceptualisation of the links that exist between multicultural policies and the political and economic integration of immigrants (Banting and Kymlicka, 2006). The crucial question is what will happen in the future, as there is a possibility that growing ethnic diversity will generate ethnically defined cleavages, which will, in turn, provide an additional impetus for welfare state retrenchments (Myles and St-Arnaud, 2006, p 349). In contrast, the importance of multiculturalism for welfare state development has been most radically argued by Parekh (2006), although it is still an open question to what degree his theory on multiculturalism is analytical and/or normative. The crucial difference between Parekh and other modern liberal thinkers such as Kymlicka, Raz or Rawls, lies in his conceptualisation of human beings, which requires a deeper understanding and recognition of culture in the sense of 'respect for a community's right to its culture and for the content and character of that culture' (Parekh, 2006, p 176). This implies a further acknowledgment of collective rights that can be exercised individually, but also collectively. However, the acknowledgment of collective rights, and particularly collectively exercised rights, calls for a rather radical reorganisation of the ways in which societies deal with different ethnic, cultural and religious identities. There are, in fact, no clear guidelines of how to resolve the complex relations that have emerged between a historically inherited identity of majority and multiple minority identities. An unavoidable step in this direction is, probably, the full acknowledgment of collective rights, mainly built around different cultural traditions. To sum up, as Parekh argues, 'what I might call a multicultural perspective is composed of the creative interplay of these three complementary insights, namely the cultural embeddedness of human beings, the inescapability and desirability of cultural diversity and intercultural dialogue, and the internal plurality of each culture' (Parekh, 2006, p 338). As is shown in this chapter, despite all debates about the sustainability of multiculturalism in Europe, the multicultural approach developed by Parekh offers valuable insights into the empirical evidence gathered through the WAVE project and, in particular, those concerning the role of social networks in the life of local minorities.

The importance of cultural aspects in the life of minorities has, in fact, often been emphasised in the literature on immigrants. Modern migration network theory has highlighted how macro- and micro-structures facilitate migration movements, but also how the informal social networks (micro-structures) developed by the migrants themselves can be successful for coping with problems related to migration and new settlements (for an interesting discussion, see Castles and Miller, 2009, p 28). However, this chapter is not concerned with migration processes *per se*, but more with the life of immigrant communities in the countries of destination, including not only the first generation of migrants, but of their children and grandchildren. Schrover and Vermeulen (2005) focus on several important factors necessary to understand the role and the possibilities of migrant communities: the migration process, the opportunity structure in the society of residence and the characteristics of the immigrant community. In their paper the relevance of gender is highlighted (for example, women are carriers of ethnic identity but are absent from the power structure of immigrant organisations), as well as the relevance of state relations (for example, relations with the societies of origin and destination), politics (for example, the political structure of the society and attitude of governments toward immigrant organisations) and size (for example, the volume of the immigrant population, and its capacities).

WAVE research project

This chapter originates from the comparative European project WAVE, funded by the EU Under the Framework 6 research programme scheme.[2] The project analysed social changes in Europe, particularly those related to religion, minorities and gender, and examined these dimensions through the prism of welfare. It started from an assumption that values promoted at the societal level have to be present in the expression and provision of individual and group needs of the religious or minority ethnic population. Therefore, it paid special attention to values that could lead to cohesion or conflict within society (between and within groups, with a special focus on minority/majority relations). Finally, the gender aspects of the position of minorities were of particular interest.

The project included 12 European countries and the empirical part of the study entailed in-depth qualitative research in medium-sized towns of these countries.[3] Based on the 'mapping process', the research groups were chosen as a subject of the in-depth research: in the majority of cases, Muslim groups (obviously of different ethnic backgrounds) were chosen, but there were also other ethnic and religious minorities, such as Jews, Germans from the former Soviet Union, FSU (in Germany), Pentecostals, Roma, Polish (in England), Ukrainians (in Poland) and so on. In each case, members of the majority (churches, welfare organisations, professionals from the majority population) were included in the research. Additionally, each country study focused on different welfare issues that, according to the researchers, presented in the best way the research topics, ranging from care for older people, reproductive health, the school system and care for children, provision of welfare assistance and other care services. The research applied a range of qualitative methods: observations, interviews, focus groups, media content analyses and analyses of other collected materials. Besides the local case study reports, research teams in each country also produced 'national reports', based mainly on the literature review about the researched issues. As the local case studies could be very local, preventing any generalisation, the national overview served to illuminate the meanings of locally generated data. The same approach is also used in this chapter. As it is mainly based on readings of the research report for each country, the examples provided below come from the local case studies, while the more general observations come from the national reports as well as other available literature.

Immigrants and their social networks

Family

The importance of the family as the basic social unit for different immigrants was stressed in all WAVE research reports. The majority reaffirmed that the importance of family was stronger for immigrants and more visible than for country nationals. The role of the family in the life of individuals also constituted one of the biggest differences between immigrants and the local population. There are several possible reasons for this. Life insecurities in general and difficulties in integrating in society (such as unemployment, difficulties in obtaining social rights, poverty and so on) move individuals closer to their families (including their extended family), where they are able to find support and solutions. The family also provides advice and assistance in many difficult situations (such as in the case of dealing with administrative procedures), while helping to connect individuals with other social networks that are important for social integration. But the family is also an important factor in keeping contact with the country of origin, through helping family members abroad by sending them economic remittances. The family also plays a very important symbolic value as a carrier of cultural identity, preserving the identity of their family members, while maintaining their cultural (primarily ethnic and religious) identities.

However, the role of the family is not unambiguous. First of all, the family is not capable of doing all that is expected of it, and this contributes to various tensions among family members, mostly along gender and generational lines. In addition, an apparent contradiction arises from the expectation that the family nourishes separate identities and, at the same time, socialises and integrates its members into the society of the destination country. These two important tasks are in permanent tension and several strategies of how different families cope with this emerge. In many cases family members rely on the help of other minority ethnic and religious communities that perform the same (in a way, contradictory) tasks. The crucial question here is how a society, and in particular the welfare system, evaluates the role of family. Misunderstandings can arise from the universalistic logic of the welfare state, and its willingness to help families (including those from minority communities) based on certain presumptions of what a (majority) family is and what needs it has. That was shown in the case of the family centre in the relevant locality in Sweden (Pettersson and Edgardh, 2008) and in the municipality public care service for older people in the Germany case (Albert and Leis-Peters, 2008). In these cases, public authorities expected that the services would also have been used by minorities. This was not the case, however, as immigrant families do not usually use public help for issues defined as the primary task of the family. For instance, there is a widespread feeling among immigrants that they have to take care of their parents and if parents go to nursing homes that means that the family has failed. Furthermore, if the family fails in that respect, then there is nothing left of a separate identity, that is, immigrant families become similar to the families of their society of residence, 'abandoning' their parents. Another example is the promotion of active parenting among immigrant communities which does not correspond to a gender division of labour among immigrants (Sweden), or organising of events by public authorities that do not respect the different daily routines of different families (for the English case, see Middlemiss Lé Mon, 2008): if family members usually work during nights, then they have completely different time schedules than the majority, and night shifts are more present among immigrant and minority communities than among majority communities.

Cultural and religious differences are most visible in respect to gender. Family is, for the majority of immigrants, a domain of women, and it is generally expected that women would take care of family members and transmit specific cultural values to their children, although this is also a task carried out by men in ethnic and religious organisations. Although the general picture suggests the special place of women for immigrant families, there are some very important exceptions. First, the way in which women are treated and the position they have in the family varies greatly from country to country and from cultural origin to cultural origin, and in this respect it is, for example, not possible to compare a Muslim woman of Bosnian origin in Croatia with a Muslim woman of Turkish or Iranian origins in Norway (Angell and Briseid, 2008; Geiger et al, 2008), as they are culturally (and in some cases religiously) very different. Nonetheless, the crucial question is how to draw a line between cultural and religious specificities that have to be respected, and occurrences that are seen as completely inappropriate for the majority in countries of destination, such as the oppression of women inside the family. This research suggests that there are no definitive answers on this issue and that answers have to be found in the continuous exchange of opinions between different communities. There are also other cultural differences that play an important role. Researchers noted that Ingrian women were more active and more involved in social networks than Ingrian men in the Finnish case study (Juntunen and Yeung, 2008), and German women who came from the FSU were more open and had better communication skills than their husbands (Biendarra, 2008). These skills helped them in finding jobs and other contacts within society more generally, thus contributing to easier integration in comparison to men.

Ethnic and religious communities

Immigrant organisations usually take the form of ethnic and religious communities. In some cases they overlap, while in others they are quite distinct. Religious communities include both churches and church-related or religiously inspired organisations. Ethnic and religious communities, much like the family, perform dual tasks. They are carriers of separate identities, and they serve as social networks, helping immigrants to be integrated into the society. They provide information and help with different administrative procedures, but they are also able to offer welfare assistance or other kinds of welfare services. The most important tasks carried out by these communities are education in the mother tongue and in a particular religion, but also helping to acquire the necessary skills in the host language.

The way immigrant organisations operate depends on several factors,[4] but their effectiveness also largely depends on how a society sees them, and, to a lesser degree, on the general position of the churches and other non-governmental organisations (NGOs) in the welfare system. The WAVE project in that respect provided some interesting insights. The Nordic countries, in connection with their universalistic welfare state, do not seem to provide much room for NGOs in delivering services, and the role of churches is generally quite limited, both in public life and within the welfare system. Still, recent cuts in welfare programmes have opened some space for other non-state actors. This is most visible in the case of Finland, which already had a tradition of a strong church (the Lutheran Church of Finland) involvement in social work activities, working in cooperation with the municipality and other organisations. There is also space for other minority religious communities, since the Lutheran Church of Finland and other minority churches devote much of their resources to working with immigrants (Juntunen and Yeung, 2008). In Norway, there is no formal place for either the majority church or minority communities in the welfare system (Angell and Briseid, 2008). Indeed, some programmes, such as the after-school homework assistance programme offered by a minority organisation could, seen from outside, contribute to the segregation of minority children, provoking some interesting public debates. However, the specific character of some welfare activities could contribute to the establishment of formal relations between minority communities and public authorities. Furthermore, despite limited involvement in service provision, local case studies in all Nordic countries showed more intensive contacts with minority organisations than in other European countries as well as public discussion about how to take into account the specific needs of immigrants. The same is true for England with its long history of immigration, and established ethnic and religious communities. Recently, the government's intention has been to deepen official multicultural policy by including minority communities in decision-making processes and trying to reach them through additional services that became very visible in our research (Middlemiss Lé Mon, 2008).

The German welfare system, on the contrary, traditionally involves NGOs, and churches in particular, in providing services, although it is restricted to traditional churches and church-related organisations (Caritas and Diakonisches Werk). There are numerous ethnic and religious immigrant organisations which focus on the different needs of their members, mostly cultural, religious and educational. However, our research noticed substantial dissatisfaction among them (Albert and Leis-Peters, 2008; Biendarra, 2008). Although many wanted to become welfare providers, and not only recipients, there are only few examples of immigrant organisations providing welfare services. In addition, it seems that they complain about insufficient funding and unequal treatment from the majority and official organisations, which prevented them from becoming partners inside the welfare state architecture.[5]

In Italy the number of immigrant associations is increasing, but these organisations tend to be very small, usually divided, or very informal, so it is difficult to judge their real effectiveness. They have no formal relations with welfare providers. Church-related welfare organisations play the most prominent role in Italian welfare provision (Frisina and Cancellieri, 2008). In that respect, our research showed that the situation was very similar, or even worse, in Greece (Fokas, 2008). There were some immigrant organisations, most of them religious, cultural or ethnic, but they were faced with some basic organisational problems – they did not usually have a place to gather, and it was particularly hard to organise a place for worship for minority religions. Communication between minority and majority organisations was quite limited in Greece.

In Poland and Croatia the situation seemed to be similar, even though these two countries did not have similar welfare systems (Borowik et al, 2008; Geiger et al, 2008). In Poland there was much more space for the Catholic Church to deliver services, while in Croatia the welfare system was predominantly public, with a quite limited role of churches and other non-state actors. The important factor here is that both countries (in the localities investigated in this project, but according to national reports, to a great extent in the countries in general) have not yet faced significant immigrations from abroad, and, as a result, the issue seems to concern more traditional ethnic or national (simultaneously religious) minorities, with a history of contacts and relations, such as the Ukrainians in Poland and Bosnians in Croatia. In both cases, however, language does not represent a problem in communication between minorities and majorities, although some tensions occasionally emerge. Moreover, their ethnic and religious organisations were focusing on some of the social, cultural and obviously religious needs of their members, but these were usually not involved in welfare provision.

Welfare state models and immigrant social rights

Some of the contributions discussed in the first part of this chapter (see, for instance, Morissens and Sainsbury, 2005; Banting and Kymlicka, 2006; Myles and St-Arnaud, 2006) have highlighted the (in)adequacy of welfare state models in researching the rights of immigrants, as well as their general social position in the respective countries. The analysis of research reports inside the WAVE project suggests, however, that in investigating the position of immigrants, cultural factors and the social position of immigrant organisations are vital factors, and this has far too often been overlooked by existing literature on immigrants and welfare. On this basis, this section focuses on how integration issues are correlated with different welfare state models. In doing so, it stresses the importance of immigration policies and minority formation, including the different effects of different types of immigrant organisations (Castles and Miller, 2009, pp 245-76), but also the relevance of multicultural policies when researching the social rights of minorities.

Following the Esping-Andersen typology (1990, 1999), the Nordic countries included in this research can be found in a group of social democratic states and they share several similarities concerning the position of immigrants. The research demonstrated that in all three countries there are, for example, many organisations established just to fulfil immigrant needs, and that noticeable attention is paid to the integration activities of immigrants. According to the research reports the problem of rising illegal immigration was not visible in the local cases and this, in a way, helps solve the problem of the different access to social rights. Needless to say, several other aspects that concern the lives of immigrants and the roles of their organisations can cause public tension and discussions, but a higher degree of cultural sensitivity seems to be present. There are official initiatives attempting to accommodate different values in the school system and in other welfare provision agencies. Namely, the need for accommodation comes from the acknowledgment that schools and other public institutions are supposedly secular, but in reality, are mainly based on the Christian tradition, which can cause tensions and debates about equal rights in a multicultural society.

Interestingly, England shows some similarities with the Nordic countries. Taking into account a long history of immigration, multicultural policies have been developed based on the recognition of group rights rather than individual rights. Tensions and problems concerning how to accommodate ethnic and religious rights also exist, but there is an extensive cooperation between religious organisations and public authorities at the local level. The government has even developed guidelines for local authorities for cooperating with religious organisations (Middlemiss, 2008). Our research in that respect confirmed the involvement of immigrant organisations, and the importance of building contacts between health and social workers and minority groups. Therefore, the English case confirms that the recognition and involvement of immigrant organisations in community development and inside the welfare domain in a way facilitates the tension between ambiguous tasks they have to perform: a task of maintaining separate identities and serving as a mediating tool in the integration of their members into society.

Germany is a conservative welfare state based on employment and citizenship (Esping-Andersen, 1990, 1999), which contributes to a differentiated treatment among the country's minorities, depending on their official status. In line with this categorisation, our research noted that, compared to the Nordic countries and England, there is much more cultural misunderstanding between the majority and the minorities in the welfare field. Here, the results of the report highlighted the very limited involvement of minority organisations in delivering welfare, and limited communication and hospitality from the side of the majority resident population. However, important generational differences connected with the history of the presence of each minority in Germany can also be observed. Still, the issue of how to maintain one's cultural identity, how to accommodate the German way of life and how to include minority communities in policymaking and delivering welfare remains unresolved.

Italy and Greece have been labelled as South European or particularistic welfare models (see Ferrera, 1996; Katrougalos, 1996), although important differences between these two countries also exist. The WAVE research reported both similarities and differences. In both countries the issue of illegal immigrants and their social rights remains a pressing issue and, in both countries, the immigrant organisations are not involved in policymaking and delivery. Cultural misunderstandings are present in both countries, but to a larger extent in Greece than in Italy. Greece is also a special case when it comes to its immigration policy, due to the high costs for residence permits and delays in administrative procedures, which associate insecurity and bad communication with civil servants, all of which contribute to the creation of obstacles in addressing the welfare needs of migrant communities. Communication between the majority and the minority in terms of contacts and the social involvement of immigrants is most limited in Greece compared to all the researched countries. The research also noted that Greece is a country with a high level of prejudice against religious minorities that influences the position of immigrant organisations.

There is no agreement in the literature about the existence of a 'post-communist welfare state', and even more so concerning the meaning of this term (see, for instance, Cerami, 2006; Bohle and Greskovits, 2007; Stubbs and Zrinščak, 2009). Similarities and differences between Croatia and Poland exist, and these countries have not yet faced major immigrant flows. Although religiously different, the cultural and even linguistic similarities of the majority population and large minorities (such as Ukrainians in Poland and Bosnians in Croatia) have caused most tensions. Nevertheless, there are some worrying trends that could be more important if these countries are to face up to immigration in the future. The research noticed that the division between 'us' and 'them' is very much present, and as the range of social problems (unemployment, poverty) strikes all the population, there is no sensitivity (nor policy) that takes into account the positions and needs of the minority populations.

Conclusion

By observing public debates and even some empirical trends, one could easily conclude that both the welfare state and multiculturalism are in retreat. However, this chapter suggests a more complex picture, which is in fact in line with many other empirical and theoretical studies (Banting and Kymlicka, 2006; Vertovec and Wessendorf, 2009, and so on). Kivisto has underlined, for example, that multiculturalism – as social policy – ought to be viewed as a form of assimilation or incorporation strategy that requires embracement by newcomers of core societal values, while simultaneously valorising ethnic diversity (Kivisto, 2003, p 29). In a similar vein, Castles and Miller (2009, p 311) have also emphasised that wider social changes – such as multiple identities – also exist. Our analysis highlights the importance of immigrant organisations and in particular the cultural aspects of their existence in shaping concrete experiences of integration. Although the role of local organisations is not unambiguous, and can indeed contain negative aspects (social control, exclusion of some members, emphasis on difference and segregation), their role in social orientation is indispensable, and the everyday life of many individuals relies on that role. Another aspect is also important. Welfare needs (like educational, health and long-term care needs) are not abstract, but are rooted and expressed in particular social/cultural terms, shaped to a great extent through collective action and collective experience. Hence there is a need to speak about immigrants and their welfare rights through multicultural lenses.

In addition, financial pressures on the welfare state stress the importance of different stakeholder involvement, which also opens a space for immigrant organisations. The voice of immigrants heard in our research emphasises the need for an open dialogue about their position, and that dialogue includes their local organisations as well as cultural aspects of their existence. Otherwise the welfare needs of immigrants (and of minorities in general) are not understood and consequently not met. We do not predict, however, that the situation in Europe will necessarily go in this direction. Still, perhaps there is room to understand that the welfare state needs to be reformulated along cultural lines, to facilitate the inclusion of immigrant communities inside the welfare state architecture.

Notes

[1] As this chapter is built on the empirical material deriving from the comparative research project, I am very grateful to all the researchers for their invaluable inputs. I particularly thank Effie Fokas, whose first draft of the comparative WAVE analysis served as a stimulus for this chapter, and the book's editors for their comprehensive comments on previous versions of this chapter. Thanks also to my Croatian colleagues, V. Baćak, S. Božić, M. Geiger, T. Puhovski and T. Vučković Juroš for comments and suggestions. Previous versions of this chapter were presented at the 6th Annual ESPAnet Conference: 'Cross-border Influence in Social Policy', Helsinki, 18-20 September 2008, and the 9th ESA Conference, Lisbon, 2-5 September 2009. Support for and funding from the Ministry of Science, Education and Sport of the Republic of Croatia 'Social cohesion indicators and development of the Croatian social model' is also acknowledged.

[2] More information about the project can be found at www.waveproject.org and in Fokas (2009).

[3] The countries included in the project were: Sweden, Norway, Finland, Latvia, England, Germany (one report was produced for Germany but two case studies were conducted in Germany, one in a town with a Catholic majority and one in a town with a Protestant majority), France, Poland, Croatia, Italy, Romania and Greece. However, as the work on the comparative analysis for this chapter started in early 2008, when research reports were not available for all countries included, this chapter analyses nine countries, thus excluding France, Latvia and Romania.

[4] There is not enough room here for more details, but big differences among immigrant organisations should not be forgotten, and in many of them, internal divisions are very much present.

[5] As underlined by Brubaker, critics have observed that the German system actually treats immigrants as passive clients of the charitable organisations, and also tends to reinforce and perpetuate a national origin distinction (Brubaker, 2001, p 537).

References

Afonso, A. (2005) 'When the export of social problems is no longer possible: immigration policies and unemployment in Switzerland', *Social Policy & Administration*, vol 39, no 6, pp 653-68.

Alber, J. (2006) 'The European social model and the United States', *European Union Politics*, vol 7, no 3, pp 393-419.

Albert, A.C. and Leis-Peters, A. (2008) *Germany. Reutlingen case study report* (www.waveproject.org).

Angell, O.H. and Briseid, K. (2008) *Norway. Drammen case study report* (www.waveproject.org).

Banting, K.G. (2005) 'The multicultural welfare state: international experience and North American narratives', *Social Policy & Administration*, vol 39, no 2, pp 98-115.

Banting, K.G. and Kymlicka, W. (2004) *Do multiculturalism policies erode the welfare state?*, Working Paper 33, Belfast: School of Policy Studies, Queens University Belfast.

Banting, K.G. and Kymlicka, W. (2006) 'Introduction: multiculturalism and the welfare state: setting the context', in K.G. Banting and W. Kymlicka (eds) *Multiculturalism and the welfare state. Recognition and redistribution in contemporary democracies*, Oxford: Oxford University Press, pp 1-45.

Biendarra, I. (2008) *Germany. Schweinfurt case study report* (www.waveproject.org).

Bohle, D. and Greskovits, B. (2007) 'Neoliberalism, embedded neoliberalism and neocorporatism: towards transnational capitalism in Central-Eastern Europe', *West European Politics*, vol 30, no 3, pp 443-66.

Borowik, I., Dyczewska, A. and Litak, E. (2008) *Poland. Przemyśl case study report* (www.waveproject.org).

Brubaker, R. (2001) 'The return of assimilation? Changing perspectives on immigration and its sequels in France, Germany, and the United States', *Ethnic and Racial Studies*, vol 24, no 4, pp 531-48.

Carrera, S. (2006) *A comparison of integration programmes in the EU. Trends and weaknesses*, Challenge Papers, no 1, March, Brussels: Centre for European Policy Studies (www.ceps.be).

Castles, S. and Miller, M.J. (2009) *The age of migration. International population movements in the modern world*, Basingstoke: Palgrave Macmillan.

Cerami, A. (2006) *Social policy in Central and Eastern Europe. The emergence of a new welfare regime*, Berlin: LIT Verlag.

Esping-Andersen, G. (1990) *The three worlds of welfare capitalism*, Cambridge: Polity Press.

Esping-Andersen, G. (1999) *The social foundations of postindustrial economies*, Oxford: Oxford University Press.

Faist, T. (2000) 'Transnationalization in international migration: implications for the study of citizenships and culture', *Ethnic and Racial Studies*, vol 23, no 2, pp 189-222.

Ferrera, M. (1996) 'Southern model of welfare in social Europe', *Journal of European Social Policy*, vol 6, no 1, pp 17-37.

Fokas, E. (2008) *Greece. Thiva case study report* (www.waveproject.org).

Fokas, E. (2009) *Welfare and values in Europe: A comparative cross-country analysis*, Report for the European Commission–funded Framework 6 project on 'Welfare and values in Europe: transitions related to religion, minorities and gender'.

Frisina, A. and Cancellier, A. (2008) *Italy. Padova case study report* (www.waveproject. org).

Geiger, M., Zrinščak, S. and Puhovski, T. (2008) *Croatia. Sisak case study report* (www.waveproject.org).

Hatton, T.J. and Williamson, J.G. (2005) *Global migration and the world economy*, Boston, MA: MIT Press.

Juntunen, E. and Yeung, B.A. (2008) *Finland. Lahti case study report* (www. waveproject.org).

Katrougalos, G.S. (1996) 'The South European welfare model: the Greek welfare state in search of an identity', *Journal of European Social Policy*, vol 6, no 1, pp 39-60.

Kivisto, P. (2003) 'Social spaces, transnational immigrant communities, and the politics of incorporation', Paper presented at the annual meeting of the American Sociological Association, Atlanta, GA (www.allacademic.com/meta/ p108188_index.html).

Koopmans, R. (2010) 'Trade-offs between equality and difference: immigrant integration, multiculturalism and the welfare state in cross-national perspective', *Journal of Ethnic and Migration Studies*, vol 36, no 1, pp 1-26.

Kremer, M. (2008) 'Meeting and mobility. Ethnic diversity in the Dutch welfare state', *Italian Journal of Social Policy*, no 1, pp 573-93.

Laparra, M. (2008) 'Southern Europe in the mirror of European traditional immigration countries', *Italian Journal of Social Policy*, no 1, pp 551-72.

Middlemiss, M. (2008) *England. Overview of the national situation* (www.waveproject. org).

Middlemiss Lé Mon, M. (2008) *England. Darlington case study report* (www. waveproject.org).

Morissens, A. and Sainsbury, D. (2005) 'Migrants' social rights, ethnicity and welfare regimes', *Journal of Social Policy*, vol 34, no 4, pp 637-60.

Myles, J. and St-Arnaud, S. (2006) 'Population diversity, multiculturalism, and the welfare state: should welfare state theory be revised?', in K.G. Banting and W. Kymlicka (eds) *Multiculturalism and the welfare state. Recognition and redistribution in contemporary democracies*, Oxford: Oxford University Press, pp 339-54.

OECD (Organisation for Economic Co-operation and Development) (2007) *International Migration Outlook: Annual report 2007*, Paris: OECD.

Parekh, B. (2006) *Rethinking multiculturalism. Cultural diversity and political theory*, Basingstoke: Palgrave Macmillan.

Pettersson, P. and Edgardh, N. (2008) *Sweden. Gävle case study report* (www. waveproject.org).

Schrover, M. and Vermeulen, F. (2005) 'Immigrant organisations', *Journal of Ethnic and Migration Studies*, vol 31, no 5, pp 823-32.

Stubbs, P. and Zrinščak, S. (2009) 'Croatian social policy: the legacies of war, state building and late Europeanization', *Social Policy & Administration*, vol 43, no 2, pp 121-35.

Taylor-Gooby, P. (2005) 'Is the future American? Or, can left politics preserve European welfare states from erosion through growing "racial" diversity?', *Journal of Social Policy*, vol 34, no 4, pp 661-72.

Vertovec, S. and Wessendorf, S. (2009) *Assessing the backlash against multiculturalism in Europe*, MMG Working Papers 09-04, Göttingen: Max Planck Institute for the Study of Religious and Ethnic Diversity (www.mmg.mpg.de).

TWELVE

Contentious opportunities: comparing metropolitan policymaking for immigrants in France and Italy

Manlio Cinalli and Alessandra El Hariri

Introduction

Immigration in France and Italy, whether referring to foreign workers, asylum seekers, undocumented migrants or reunification of family members, has stood out as a key object of political contention and policy intervention throughout the 2000s. In both countries, this has been a decade characterised by the political predominance of the right over the left.[1] Immigration has gained high salience, with major developments in terms of policy interventions and debates about enforcement of border controls, threats to national identity, human rights, international security and religious extremism among others. In this chapter, we aim to provide a detailed analysis of relevant policy processes in the two countries by focusing on the urban level. Our case studies are the cities of Paris, Lyon, Rome and Milan.

It is not only demographic reasons that make the inclusion of cities an important step in our research. The main point is that metropolitan policymaking often stands out as having some degree of autonomy in the field of immigration. For example, it may facilitate access of immigrants' associations to policymaking; it may create specific consultative structures to foster contact between local government and the migrant population. In so doing, metropolitan policymaking may alter the configuration of institutional provisions and policies that would otherwise be indistinguishable across a whole country, and have a profound effect on migrants' experiences of integration (see Chapter Eleven, this volume).

In particular, we aim to assess the extent to which actions of policymakers in our cities stand out as an autonomous force vis-à-vis the constraints of laws and institutional arrangements that are already in place, most often at the national level. Our analysis thus draws on a number of studies that, since the path-breaking work of Eisinger (1973), have emphasised the explanatory role of contextual environments and 'political opportunities' at the intersection of the urban and the national level of policymaking. We believe that the inclusion of the urban level is necessary to complement other approaches that have either tackled divergence and/or convergence of national models of citizenship (Ireland, 1994; Koopmans and Statham, 1999; Joppke, 2007) or have alternatively focused beyond the national level (Geddes, 2000; Guiraudon, 2001). Our main argument is that metropolitan politics is central to broader processes of multi-level governance in the field of immigration. That is, the latter needs to be understood within a theoretical framework that brings to the core of its analysis, territorial distinctions, different levels of government and variable configurations of power.

While keeping with the scholarly traditions of 'political opportunities', we question the idea of a straightforward relationship between top-down opportunities stemming from the policy domain and bottom-up contention originating from the public domain. We identify cities as crucial points of conflict and renegotiation, and evaluate the extent to which they can shape their own structure of political opportunities. Put simply, an immigrant's decision to settle within a precise city may represent a moment of key importance, since each city has specific characteristics in terms of access to its own processes of politics and policy, and hence, implications for the differential integration of resident immigrants (see Chapter One, this volume). Do cities generally align with, or can they indeed enter in opposition to, the more stable political provisions set by national governments? What are the main factors accounting for variations of policy actions and strategies at the urban level? To what extent do Lyon, Paris, Milan and Rome follow the restrictive decision making of national governments in the field of immigration? How do we account for variations across these four cities? And ultimately, do cities have a key role to play? Can they trust the force of their own policy interventions?

Theoretical background: the two strands of the political opportunities structure

While drawing on the scholarship of the 'political opportunities structure' (POS) (Tilly, 1978; Kriesi et al, 1995; Tarrow, 1998), we are aware that mobilisation in the public domain is not disconnected from (permanently in opposition to) elites, institutions and other actors in the policy domain (Fillieule, 2003; Cinalli, 2004; Hayes, 2005). Since policymakers and institutional actors may well play the double game of 'challengers' and 'insiders' at their convenience (Lolive, 1999; Della Porta and Andretta, 2002), the whole POS approach must be reshaped into a more dynamic model where the roles of challengers and insiders in political processes are detected in the concrete development of actors' interventions (Tilly and Tarrow, 2007). Accordingly, here we aim to evaluate the dynamic interactions that lie behind any particular form of political opportunities in the field of immigration, across different cities and different countries.

We disentangle the complex relationship between a stable strand of the political context – made of characteristics that can hardly be changed, for example, the degree of decentralisation – and a fluid strand of policy provisions in a given field, for example, the decision by a city authority to create immigrants' representative bodies. In so doing, we also answer the call of recent scholarship to analyse specific opportunities across policy and issue fields (Cinalli, 2004; Berclaz and Giugni, 2005; Koopmans et al, 2005). While it cannot establish whether politics determines policy, or vice versa (Lowi, 1972), our study evaluates how metropolitan policymaking fits with the broader institutional context, assessing the balance between the national state and its cities, the characteristics of variable political alignments between urban and national elites, as well as the space for direct intervention of local residents and citizenry.

In particular, the stable strand of the political structure is reconstructed here through analysis of national laws and institutions, whereas the fluid strand is evaluated through an appraisal of policy interventions at the urban level. The first strand is analysed along two standard dimensions of POS studies. First, the evaluation of the 'configuration of powers' refers to the level of state decentralisation; the distribution of power across institutions; the degree of electoral proportionality; and the shape of the party system. A stronger decentralisation at the national level, as well as at the sub-urban level of local districts, may well open opportunities for urban elites to intervene decisively within the field. In contrast, the predominance of legislative power over the executive, as well as a high degree of proportionality in the electoral system, will tend to constrain the initiative of urban power holders. Strong politicisation of issues of immigration and integration also call for a more detailed investigation of variable articulations of the right-left cleavage across the national and urban level.

The analysis of the second dimension, 'participation mechanisms', refers to crucial access points that allow for citizens' intervention. In this case, we refer to the existence of referendum arrangements; the provision of specific rights strengthening participation of individual citizens; and the availability of channels for the involvement of civil society organisations. All these 'mechanisms' provide a second layer of opportunities (and constraints) for urban elites, as they need to make the most of their closeness to the local citizenry without giving away privileged space for their own intervention.

Put simply, we use the POS concept here to account for variations in metropolitan policymaking. We systematically analyse policy interventions across cities, looking for their relationship with a number of stable features of the national political context. The main point is that political opportunities need to be analysed in their extensive articulations at the subnational level in order to capture relevant interactions going on across different levels of government and administration (Loughlin, 2007). This standpoint allows for intra-national comparison without losing the heuristic value of the political opportunities approach (Eisinger, 1973). Ultimately, by taking France and Italy together, we integrate the comparative and case study approach of other chapters of this book. The analysis of articulated mixtures of political characteristics and policy interventions across levels of governance offers detailed and textured insights into the institutional structuring and political dynamics of migrant integration in the four city cases.

Common contexts for a common challenge

Immigration provides a common challenge in France and Italy in spite of the significant differences in terms of 'types' of national legal conventions. In general we can say that a key distinction can be seen between types of immigrants who are more likely to enter France, and who are thus the object of its distinctive policies, and immigrants who are more likely to enter Italy. Thus, family reasons represent over 70 per cent of yearly admissions to France while in Italy the same type of immigration accounts for only 33 per cent of permits to stay.[2] Immigrant workers in France represent only about five per cent of admissions, while Italy has chosen to implement a selective immigration policy placing a significant emphasis on workers (see Chapter Six, this volume).

Republican France may stand out for its more inclusive stance vis-à-vis immigrants owing to its civic criteria for individual access to citizenship (Brubaker, 1992; Ireland, 1994). However, just as in Italy, France has generally taken a restrictive approach to new waves of immigration. Both countries have adapted to the type of immigration they are experiencing, placing specific policymaking under similarly restrictive national contexts. At the same time, it should be emphasised that different 'types' of immigrants are not often so clearly delineated, both in factual and legal terms, for example when a young person rejoins their parents to take a job in the country. In fact, labels referring to different categories of immigrants in France and Italy are often so comprehensive as to include a large and ill-defined number of common situations in both countries, including undocumented workers, overstayers, immigrants who have illegally trespassed frontiers, foreigners under threat of expulsion and even asylum seekers who have lost their case (de Wenden, 2002). 'Types' of immigrants also change in a way to match modifications of the legal framework (Ferré, 1997) as well as changing anti-immigrant rhetoric in the political discourse. The local politics of, and policies for, immigration have significant effects, then, on the experience of differential integration.

In France, the restrictive twist has been central to high politics from as early as the mid-1970s, just in the aftermath of the oil crisis, in a context of increasing unemployment and economic recession.[3] Since then, governments have favoured a stricter control of work migration and decreased tolerance for undocumented immigrants. Only high-qualified workers and workers with special qualifications in the economic sectors undergoing workforce shortages have been met with more open conditions. This trend has been reinforced throughout the last decade, owing to the growing necessity of a supplementary workforce in specific economic sectors. Recent policies have put emphasis on the idea of *immigration choisie*, referring to labour immigration that fits with French economic conveniences. Laws in 2003 and 2006 have also tightened conditions for entry and stay for types of immigrants that are most likely to enter France (Cinalli and Nasri, 2010). These laws have suppressed the full right to the residence permit for many categories of rejoining immigrants such as family members joining a residence permit holder, parents of national minors, spouses of nationals and foreigners living in France for over 10 years. Measures have been enforced against undocumented immigration, fraud and abuse of legal procedures. Furthermore, granting of permits has become dependent on fulfilment of the condition of 'republican integration'. Immigrants who are granted a first permit to stay have to sign a *contrat d'accueil et d'intégration* (welcome and integration contract), which demands compulsory attendance of 'civic training'. Applicants also need to go through interviews that assess their knowledge of the French language and their respect for Republican principles.

Italy has been characterised by similar restrictive reforms throughout the 2000s. Of course, many particular features of the Italian case may suggest low comparability with the French case. Not only was Italy a country of emigration until quite recently, it also never produced clear principles and policies in the field of immigration, preventing reception of more stable, organised and skilled migration flows. Yet these specificities have shaped a different ground within which similar policy interventions appear to have taken root. In 2002 the right-wing government introduced the Bossi-Fini Law (Law no 189/2002). This narrowed down immigrants' rights for entering and settling, facilitated recourse to deportation, made asylum regulation more restrictive and introduced crucial constraints for immigrants. The introduction of a working contract (*contratto di soggiorno*) made it more difficult to obtain a permit to stay. A further restrictive step was taken in 2009 with the introduction of the security package (Law 15 July 2009, no 94), which has modified criminal law (discussed in detail in Chapter Six, this volume), extending permanence within 'identification and expulsion centres' for undocumented immigrants and asylum seekers.

Similarities between the two countries can also be found in terms of political debate and politicisation of migration issues among political parties. In France, the right-wing government has started to move further right of the political spectrum, probably with the goal of closing any available political space for the extreme right of the *Front Nationale* (Tiberj, 2008). In public discourse the idea of undocumented immigration has been associated with that of crime, public danger and illegality. Or again, the effort at integrating 'good' regular migrants has been associated in the public debate with the struggle against 'bad' illegal migrants (Lessana, 1998), giving new force to an idea that can be traced as far back as 1974 (Blin, 2008, p 247). In the same way, Italian public discourse on immigration became gradually harsher following similar competition among political parties (Geddes, 2008). Overall the right-wing government has replaced the old style of bargaining between the political majority, opposition and civil society with a stronger and more unilateral intervention aimed at talking directly to public opinion (Zincone, 2006) (thereby enhancing the importance of emotion in shaping policy; see Chapter One, this volume).

Comparing cities: different answers under a common government

Moving from the national to the urban level, Table 12.1 shows that Lyon, Paris, Milan and Rome can be singled out for their crucial position in terms of extensive urbanisation and large presence of immigrants. Rome is the biggest city, with a global population of 2,718,768. Lyon is the smallest city, but it should be noted that it is placed at the core of a larger urban area, namely, Greater Lyon, where nearly 1,300,000 people live. More crucially, foreign populations are sizeable in all cases, with percentages varying between eight per cent in Rome and 14.5 per cent in Paris: this population is often concentrated in particular areas of the city.

Table 12.1: Population and administrative structures of Paris and Lyon, Rome and Milan

	Total population	Immigrants	Administrative districts	Administrative districts with larger presence of immigrants
Paris	2,125,246	Over 300,000 – nearly 14.5% of the global population	20 – with a directly elected council which elects an administrative district's mayor	18th and 20th
Rome	2,718,768	Over 200,000 – nearly 8% of the global population	19 – divided into 155 urban planning areas	1st (central area), 8th and 20th (suburb areas)
Lyon	445,274 (Greater Lyon has a population of 1.3 million)	Over 58,000 – nearly 13% of the global population	9 – they have a directly elected council which elects an administrative district's mayor	
Milan	1,299,633	Over 170,000 – nearly 13.5% of the global population	9 – each has a *consiglio di zona*, the decentralised structures of the municipal administration	Zone 2, Zone 9 and Zone 8

Sources: Paris and Lyon: INSEE 1999 census data; Rome and Milan: ISTAT data as at 31 December 2007

Hence, we can move on to evaluate the interactions taking place between the stable strand of the political structure, as provided by national laws and institutions, and its more fluid strand, made of the specific agency of policy elites and institutional actors at the urban level. Starting with the first dimension of configuration of powers, sub-local structures with real powers exist in Lyon and Milan, with powers in terms of budget management and implementation of basic services. They can advance proposals on certain key issues to the city council, for example, about urban planning. These sub-local institutions can also aim to promote citizens' participation through formal bodies, such as citizens' boards or the management of citizens' petitions and proposals. Electoral systems in the four cities are also comparable, since they are based on a predominantly majoritarian logic with a touch of proportionality.

Low variation is also noticeable in terms of the executive-legislative distribution of powers. Lyon and Paris are characterised by a predominance of the executive, but Milan and Rome have also seen the gradual strengthening of local government. As regards political alignment and opposition across the local and national level, leftist governments in Paris and Lyon are in opposition to their rightist national government, whereas rightist governments in Milan and Rome align politically with an equally rightist national government. As it has moved only recently to the right, Rome allows for the evaluation of changing relationships along the left–right axis across the national and the urban level. These variations can be easily grasped with a table portraying the four selected cities in their specific situations (see Table 12.2).

Table 12.2: Left-right cleavages across the national and the urban level in Paris, Lyon, Rome and Milan

	Right-wing local government	Left-wing local government
Right-wing national government	Rome (2008-09) Milan	Paris, Lyon Rome (2001-07)

Interesting variations are also noticeable along the second dimension of participation mechanisms. The local statute of Milan provides only for a type of consultative referendum that needs to be proposed by a certain number of citizens.[4] In contrast, in Rome, one finds both consultative and abrogative referendums, which can be proposed not only by a certain number of citizens but also by the city council;[5] the positive results of an abrogative referendum oblige the city council to make them effective through provision of law. In Paris and Lyon, decisional referenda have been instituted in 2003, following a revision of the French constitution. Yet they must be initiated by local authorities, and do not permit direct proposition by citizens. As regards other rights for the participation of individual citizens, French cities above 80,000 inhabitants like Paris and Lyon are obliged to create citizens' assemblies with a consultative role. While consultation processes are occasional in Italian cities,[6] Milan and Rome are provided with boards on specific issues that generally gather representatives of various organisations. Lastly, the situations of the four cities are similar in terms of the policy involvement of civil society organisations, as their involvement is usually optional and informal. Milan is the only exception, since an institutionalised consultation of civil society organisations takes place in the field of social policy through the role of a specific body made of relevant associations. We also found that *ad hoc* consultation boards can be set up on specific issues, such as disabilities.

Having assessed the more stable strand of the political context, we can now move to the analysis of its impact on metropolitan policy agency. Indeed, it is important to emphasise that our research shows that some crucial space is available for policy input at the urban level: Table 12.3 sums up our findings so as to emphasise key differences across cities.

Many local authorities agree that immigration and integration are the particular responsibility of national government. Yet French cities have also stood out as crucial partners in policies that are conducted under the responsibility of state actors and national public bodies, playing, for example, a relevant role alongside the ANAEM (*Agence Nationale d'Accueil des Etrangers et des Migrations*).[7] Policy interventions are predominantly conceived in socio-economic terms, often being combined with policies that target disadvantaged areas under the framework of the *Politique de la Ville*.[8] Most crucially, relevant variations in terms of local policy agency can be identified. In Paris, the metropolitan government has effectively broadened the scope of its interventions through the setting up of the *Contrat Urbain de Cohésion Sociale* (CUCS, 2007-09).[9] Policymaking has prioritised specific programmes that target immigrants facing integration difficulties so as to facilitate their access to public services and social aids. Lyon, however, has not shown the same effort to target immigrants; here, tough policymaking has focused on the fight against ethnic discrimination in employment and social housing.

Italian cities have also taken key policy responsibilities in the field of immigration. As in France, metropolitan elites in Rome and Milan have shown interesting variations in terms of their policy agency. In Milan, the metropolitan government has allocated key responsibilities to a specific social policy division.[10] While there has been no implementation of a special service dealing with immigration, two Foreigners' Offices were set up to offer a range of services. In Rome, policymakers have shown a somewhat different approach. As in Lyon, they have avoided centralised control. There has been no creation of a specific policy division: rather, two departments – namely the *Dipartimento delle Politiche Sociali* (Social Policy Department) and the *Dipartimento delle Politiche Scolastiche* (Education Department) – have played a crucial role in the field by tackling the issue transversally. In addition, there are no services that are based on nationality, although the need for more integrated interventions has led to the constitution of a dedicated office, namely, the *Delega alle Politiche della Multietnicità*. The shift of power to the right in 2008 has generated some changes, but these are far from being radical: the new metropolitan government dismissed the *Delega alle Politiche della Multietnicità* but left almost unchanged the type of available services. The new policy style, however, refers particularly to issues of emergency and security about undocumented immigrants and asylum seekers, suggesting sharper differentiation of integration services at this city level.

Relevant cross-city variations are especially noticeable in terms of the space which policymaking has opened for direct participation of immigrants. Overall, immigrants' involvement seems to be more articulated in France. Following the French Senate rejection of the law on non-EU citizens' right to vote in local elections, in 2001 the Paris local government set up the *Conseil de la Citoyenneté des Parisiens non Communautaires*, consisting of foreign citizens coming from non-EU countries. Headed by the mayor of Paris, the council does not have power

Table 12.3: Metropolitan policymaking on immigrant integration in Paris, Rome, Lyon and Milan

	Paris	Rome	Lyon	Milan
Establishment of specific departments	YES, there is a dedicated department (immigration and integration)	NO, there is no specific department devoted to immigration and integration	NO, there is no specific department devoted to immigration and integration	YES, there is a dedicated department (Social Policy Division)
Main fields of intervention	Labour market, social aids, citizenship rights, improvement of development building, urban redevelopment, education	There are no municipality services	Fight against discrimination. A special consultative body (GIPIV) was created in 2003 to advance proposals about social and labour market exclusion	Two Foreigners' Offices were set up and offer several services: information on immigrants' rights and duties and procedures, social and political assistance, assistance to women in difficulty, interpreters
Interventions through sub-urban administrations	Legal advice services: *Maison de justice et du droit, Relais d'accès au droit, Points d'accès au droit* (in the 18th, 19th and 20th *arrondissements*); services in immigrants' own languages: publications, interpreters, mediation centres, free French courses; support to special categories of foreign citizens: undocumented migrants, asylum seekers, women victims of violence	Services that are more likely to make immigrants more autonomous. Referring to undocumented migrants and asylum seekers the approach of the new administration is more based on emergency and security aspects. Some *Commissioni Consiliari Permanenti* on issues referring to integration and multicultural policies are set up	Access to public and private employment, vocational training, or prestigious higher education schools	No specific provisions
Establishment of immigrants' representative bodies	*Conseil de la Citoyenneté des Parisiens non Communautaires* (individual membership: 90 members who are foreign non-EU citizens); *Conseil des Résidents Etrangers d'Arrondissement* (in the 19th and 20th *arrondissements*)	23 additional foreign councillors (individual-based representation) in the city council; Immigrants' Municipal Consultative Body	*Conseil des Résidents Etrangers Lyonnais*, but the city council has no obligation to consult it	There are no immigrants' representative bodies
Citizenry involvement	Civil society organisations and/or associations can participate at the local level through the citizens councils	There is no institutionalised consultation of civil society organisations	Civil organisations are present in citizens councils. They also take part with local officials in permanent consultative bodies (for example, the Development Council).	There is an institutionalised consultation of civil society organisations through a specific body made of associations
Budget for immigration and integration	Nearly €10 million[a] are devoted to integration policies and fights against discrimination. That is, nearly 2.4% of the total budget devoted to the CUCS[b]	No specific budget	Information on budget devoted to immigrant integration policies are not available	Nearly 1.5% of the total budget is devoted to immigrant integration policies

Notes: [a] La politique d'intégration à Paris (www.paris.fr/portail/accueil/Portal.lut?page_id=7760&document_type_id=58&document_id=28645&portlet_id=17915).
[b] Contrat Urbain de Cohésion Social.

of voting, but has reflection and proposal tasks on every aspect related to life in Paris. Moreover, the mayors of the 19th and the 20th *arrondissements* have set up a *Conseil des Residents Etrangers d'Arrondissement* made up of foreign citizens coming from non-EU countries. Lyon has set up the same type of council, the *Conseil des Résidents Etrangers Lyonnais* in 2005 so as to improve channels for immigrants' participation with a view to building a 'residence citizenship'.[11] This council is a place of reflection and proposal, engaged in writing an activity report every year. No obligation, however, exists for the city council to consult with it.

In Italy, the 1998 law (Law no. 40/1998, the so-called 'Turco-Napolitano' Law) provided the opportunity for immigrants to be represented through the additional Foreign Councillor (*Consigliere Aggiunto*) in local councils, as well as the possibility for city councils to provide themselves with immigrants' consultative bodies (*Consulta Comunale per i cittadini stranieri e apolidi*). This type of body has been set up in Rome but not in Milan. In particular, foreign citizens elect the Immigrants' Municipal Consultative Body in Rome and it is characterised by a group-based type of representation, that is, representation intended to give voice to all the main ethnic and national groups to which migrants in Rome belong. This body takes part in the policy process, as it is consulted on local programmes about social integration, housing, public security and integration of immigrants in the labour market.

Conclusion

The main outcome of our study is that issues of immigration and the differential integration of migrants need to be studied by putting more emphasis on the characteristics of the political context within which migrants themselves settle. Conceptually, we have argued that aspects of the political context that affect mobilisation in the immigration field need to be sought not just in the stable strand of the institutionalised political system at the national level, but also in the more fluid strand made of interventions of policy elites at the urban level. That is, overall political opportunities are often based on institutional arrangements as well as by decisions that may be taken, and changed, by metropolitan policy elites in the field. We have here put policy actors' behaviour at the centre of our interest since their decisions indeed contribute in shaping the political context within which the political participation of different actors will then take place.

The main results of our investigation concern the assessment of policy decisions in the field of immigration along a number of cleavages, including left-right divisions, centre-periphery distinctions and the functional distinctions applicable across various levels of policymaking authority. For example, we have found that when metropolitan policymaking provides space for autonomous agency, a left-wing metropolitan government can engage in the provision of opportunities for immigrants. The case of Paris is a key example here, due to its extensive interventions in opening new access points for the political participation of immigrants. Yet the left-wing ideological axis is not necessarily decisive. Although left–wing governments are in place in both cities, Paris and Lyon have set up different approaches towards immigration and integration, with the Parisian government giving a higher priority to specific programmes directed towards immigrants who face particular difficulties, which focus on the main spheres of citizens' lives. Crucially, the treatment of Rome and Milan shows high salience of similar intra–national distinctions in terms of metropolitan policymaking: although characterised by a lower involvement of civil society organisations in the definition of local policies, Rome has set up representative bodies that, in contrast, are not present in Milan.

Not only did our study call for disentangling the role of political cleavages along the left-right axis from the specific impact of centre-periphery conflicts. It has also shown that metropolitan policymakers can gain awareness of the large available space for their agency, engaging in a relationship of dynamic interaction and renegotiation with more stable features of the national context. Intra–national differences in terms of policymaking provide striking evidence of the autonomy of local actors vis-à-vis the national level to pursue their goals. Take Paris once again. While restrictive measures have been implemented at the national level throughout the 2000s, local policymaking has decisively reduced their impact in the city; in fact, further affirmative actions have also been taken in terms of integration. In sum, political opportunities are often based on policy arrangements and decisions that may be taken, and changed, by policy actors at the local level.

Finally, we have shown that metropolitan policymaking matters. Too often the issue of immigration and integration are explained with very little or no reference to the macro–level of its own political environment. The decision to settle within a precise city stands out as a moment of key importance for immigrants, since each city has its own particular political borders in terms of access to its own processes of politics, policy and therefore, social and political integration. On the one hand, immigrants may be cautious about their final places of settlement: even when choosing to go where economic opportunities and family networks are strongest, the possibility could be seized to live within a context where policymaking is inclusive. On the other hand, metropolitan policymakers should be aware of the available space for their action so as to pursue more effectively decisions that will improve the political and social integration of immigrants, with overall benefits for the whole citizenry. Cities are, at least to some important extent, true rulers of the game. They can have a major say in the implementation of a national framework for the incorporation of migrants, but they can also renegotiate this latter framework to such an extent that they may end up providing distinctive mixtures of opportunities and constraints, unlikely to be repeated in other places.

Notes

[1] In Italy the right gained government in 2001, delivering almost immediately its first crucial 'reform' (the Bossi-Fini Law, no 189/2002). The ephemeral return of the left to power between 2006 and 2008 had no implications in terms of immigration policy. Back in government, the right engaged in further legislative restrictions. In France the

2000s opened with the *cohabitation* between a right-wing president and a left-wing prime minister. Yet 2002 marked the definitive defeat of the left, as it lost control of both the government and the majority in parliament.

[2] ISTAT, available online at http://demo.istat.it/altridati/permessi/index.html

[3] see also *Circulaires Marcellin-Fontanet*, 23 February and 15 September 1973.

[4] Clauses 11 and 12 of the Statute of Milan (www.comune.milano.it/portale/wps/portal/CDM?WCM_GLOBAL_CONTEXT=/wps/wcm/connect/contentlibrary/In+Comune/In+Comune/Normativa/).

[5] Clause 10 of the Statute of Rome (www.comuni-italiani.it/statuto/058/091/a10.html).

[6] Clauses 8 and 11 of the Statute of Rome and clauses 10 and 16 of the Statute of Milan.

[7] A state administrative institution dealing with the settling of foreign people.

[8] The *Politique de la Ville* aims at compensating the social and economic disadvantages of some specific districts in each city, by improving the daily life in these districts and preventing the risks of social exclusion. Additional means, in terms of budget and public staff, and differential procedures (for example, specific support to access to private or public employment) constitute the usual tools of such policies.

[9] Information is available online at http://sig.ville.gouv.fr/zone/CS1218

[10] As regards immigration policies, the social policy division is responsible for regular immigrants' integration and social insertion (www.comune.milano.it/).

[11] see also the mayor's speech of 20 April 2005 (www.lyon.fr/vdl/sections/fr/vie_democratique/democratie_de_proxim/le_conseil_des_resid).

References

Berclaz, J. and Giugni, M. (2005) 'Specifying the concept of political opportunity structures', in M. Kousis and C. Tilly (eds) *Economic and political contention in comparative perspective*, Boulder, CO: Paradigm Publishers, pp 15-32.

Blin, T. (2008) 'L'invention des sans-papiers. Récit d'une dramaturgie politique', ['The invention of sans-papiers. A play of a political dramaturgy'] *Cahiers Internationaux de Sociologie*, no 2, pp 241-61.

Brubaker, R. (1992) *Citizenship and nationhood in France and Germany*, Cambridge, MA: Harvard University Press.

Cinalli, M. (2004) *Horizontal networks vs vertical networks in multi-organisational alliances: A comparative study of the unemployment and asylum issue fields in Britain*, EurPolCom Working Paper 8/04, Leeds: University of Leeds.

Cinalli, M. and Nasri, F. (2010) 'Les acteurs du mouvement de soutien face à l'immigration illégale en France et en "Grande-Bretagne"' ['Pro-beneficiary movements and illegal immigration in France and the "UK"'], *Sociologie et Sociétés*, vol 42, no 2, pp 215-44.

Della Porta, D. and Andretta, M. (2002) 'Policy making and changing forms of environmental collective action: the case of the high-speed railway system in Tuscany', *Mobilization*, vol 7, pp 59-77.

Eisinger, P.K. (1973) 'The conditions of protest behavior in American cities', *American Political Science Review*, vol 67, pp 11-28.

Ferré, N. (1997) 'La production de l'irrégularité' ['The production of irregularity'], in D. Fassin, A. Morice and C. Quiminal (eds) *Les lois de l'inhospitalité, les politiques de l'immigration à l'épreuve des sans-papiers* [*Laws of inhospitality, immigration policies vis-à-vis the 'sans papiers'*] Paris: La Découverte, pp 47-64.

Fillieule, O. (2003) 'Local environmental politics in France: the case of the Louron Valley (1984-1996)', *French Politics*, vol 1, no 3, pp 305-30.

Geddes, A. (2000) *Immigration and European integration: Toward Fortress Europe?*, Manchester: Manchester University Press.

Geddes, A. (2008) 'Il rombo dei cannoni? Immigration and the centre-right in Italy 2001-6', *Journal of European Public Policy*, vol 15, no 3, pp 349-66.

Guiraudon, V. (2001) 'Weak weapons of the weak? Transnational mobilisation around migration in the European Union', in D. Imig and S. Tarrow (eds) *Contentious Europeans: Protest and politics in an emerging polity*, Lanham, MD: Rowman and Littlefield.

Hayes, G. (2005) *Environmental protest and the state in France*, Basingstoke: Palgrave.

Ireland, P. (1994) *The policy challenge of ethnic diversity*, Cambridge, MA: Harvard University Press.

Joppke, C. (2007) 'Beyond national models: civic integration policies for immigrants in Western Europe', *Western European Politics*, vol 30, no 1, pp 1-22.

Koopmans, R. and Statham, P. (1999) 'Challenging the liberal nation-state? Postnationalism, and the collective claims making of migrants and ethnic minorities in Britain and Germany', *American Journal of Sociology*, vol 105, pp 652-96.

Koopmans, R., Statham, P., Giugni, M. and Passy, F. (2005) *Contested citizenship: Immigration and cultural diversity in Europe*, Minneapolis, MN: University of Minnesota Press.

Kriesi, H., Koopmans, R., Duyvendak, J.W. and Giugni, M. (1995) *New social movements in Western Europe*, Minneapolis, MN: University of Minnesota Press.

Lessana, C. (1998) 'Loi Debré: La fabrique de l'immigré partie 1' ['Lessana Debré's Law: constructing the immigrant, part one'], *Cultures et Conflits*, no 29-30, pp 125-41.

Lolive, J. (1999) *Les contestations du TGV Méditerranée: projet, controverses et espace public*, [*Protests against the Mediterranean high speed train: project, controversies and the public space*] Paris: L'Harmattan.

Loughlin, J. (2007) *Subnational government. The French experience*, New York: Palgrave MacMillan.

Lowi, T.J. (1972) 'Four systems of policy, politics, and choice', *Public Administration Review*, vol 32, no 4, pp 298-310.

Tarrow, S. (1998) *Power in movement*, Cambridge: Cambridge University Press.

Tiberj, V. (2008) *La crispation hexagonale* [*The hexagonal contraction*], Paris: Plon.

Tilly, C. (1978) *From mobilization to revolution*, Reading, MA: Addison-Wesley.

Tilly, C. and Tarrow, S. (2007) *Contentious politics*, Boulder, CO: Paradigm Publishers.

de Wenden, C.W. (2002) 'Les sans papiers' ['The sans-papiers'], *Regards sur l'Actualité*, no 277, pp 43-53.

Zincone, G. (2006) 'The making of policies: immigration and immigrants in Italy', *Journal of Ethnic and Migration Studies*, vol 32, no 3, pp 347-75.

THIRTEEN

A categorical immigration policy: welfare, integration and the production of inequality[1]

John Gal and Jennifer Oser

Introduction

Welfare states have faced difficulties in integrating immigrants and in dealing successfully with issues of poverty and deprivation among members of this social group. In fact, this is the case even in those European welfare states that have the most generous welfare regimes. An alternative to the immigrant policies adopted in most welfare states is the categorical immigration policy that characterises the Israeli welfare state. This case is particularly interesting in that immigrants to Israel fare almost as well or better than veteran populations on a number of economic parameters. The goal of this chapter is to explore the contours of the unique immigration policy model adopted in Israel as a contribution to our understanding of the link between immigration and social policies in European welfare states.

Scholars have used a number of different comparative theoretical frameworks in order to examine the link between immigration and social policy. First, research regarding the impact of migration on the welfare state focused on aggregated welfare state contours (Freeman, 1986) as well as the fiscal implications of immigration due to the consumption of services and benefits by immigrants (Castranova et al, 2001; Borjas, 2002; Hanson et al, 2002; Coleman and Rowthorn, 2004; Nannestad, 2007). Second, a historical comparative approach aimed to learn from similarities and differences in immigration policies and immigrants' social rights in different countries over time (Ongley and Pearson, 1995; Freeman and Birrell, 2001; Fix, 2002; Castles and Miller, 2003). Third, the notion of regime (Esping-Andersen, 1990, 1999; Arts and Gelissen, 2002) has been employed to identify various immigration regimes regarding both the right to migrate (Baldwin-Edwards, 1991; Soysal, 1994) as well as immigrants' access to welfare state programmes (Dorr and Faist, 1997; Banting, 2000; Bambra, 2005; Hjerm, 2005; Morissens and Sainsbury, 2005; Sainsbury, 2006).

Building on this body of literature, the conceptual framework utilised here is an historical institutional analysis, an approach that has been a dominant force in the theoretical literature on social policy for well over a decade (Starke, 2006). Specifically, the interplay over time between two institutional levels is examined:

the right of immigrants to achieve legal residence and the additional conditions that determine access to social rights (Sainsbury, 2006). On the basis of this structure, we employ an institutional perspective to present a detailed study to explain the emergence and endurance of the categorical welfare system for immigrants in Israel. We then analyse the implications of this categorical system for immigrants as well as for other sectors in Israeli society. In conclusion we discuss the relevance of the Israeli case for European welfare states.

European welfare states and immigration

European welfare states are not immune from the challenges of the socio-economic integration of immigrants, even in those European welfare states that have comparatively generous welfare regimes. For example, in the classic social democratic regime of Sweden, which in comparative analysis demonstrates a more generous distributive approach towards immigrants than other major welfare states, immigrants fare more poorly than their native counterparts. Twice as many immigrants as native-born Swedes can be considered to be poor, and more than three times those who have been in the country less than 10 years. Almost half of the immigrant population can be classified as having poor material standards compared to less than one fifth of native-born Swedes (Hjerm, 2005). In addition, longitudinal research on immigrant poverty in Denmark and Sweden not only found that immigrants have higher poverty rates than natives in both countries, but also that this immigrant–native gap has clearly increased in both countries over time (Blume et al, 2007).

An analysis of 14 European countries found that immigrants have a higher risk of poverty compared to the native population throughout the European Union (EU). While some of the difference can be attributed to background characteristics of these two groups, the risk of poverty was still 6–15 per cent higher among immigrants even after controlling for individual differences and country-fixed effects (Lelkes, 2007). This poor socio-economic integration cannot be solely attributed to problems with labour market integration. A comparison of poverty levels of immigrants and citizens in diverse welfare states demonstrated that immigrants are less likely to enjoy a socially acceptable standard of living compared to their native counterparts, even when the market is the main source of income. This research also showed that transfers are less likely to lift immigrants out of poverty in general, and that when benefits are their main source of income they run a greater risk of poverty compared to native citizens (Morissens and Sainsbury, 2005). Research on the social income gap demonstrates that despite the comparable and often greater resources devoted to immigrants in terms of social supports, they do not fare as well as their native counterparts (Anastassova and Paligorova, 2006).

Despite the challenges inherent in these findings, Felix Buchel and Joachim Frick (2005) ask the provocative question 'does immigration policy matter?', and their answer is a resounding 'yes'. Their comparison of the economic performance of immigrants to the native population in a number of European countries controls for background characteristics and shows significant cross-country differences in the differential between immigrant and native-born income from employment and transfers. This suggests that country-specific institutional aspects regarding access to the labour market and the social security system influence the socio-economic integration of immigrants.

The Israeli case

The Israeli case is particularly interesting with regard to the challenges facing European immigration integration in that Israeli immigrants fare almost as well or better than veteran populations on a number of economic parameters. Although Israel is not a member of the EU, most observers agree that it has become similar to Western pluralist-liberal democracies in its social, economic and political characteristics (Levi-Faur et al, 1999). Israel's experience with absorbing large numbers of immigrants from diverse locations provides a useful example of the challenges increasingly facing European welfare states (Shuval, 1998; Geva-May, 2000). Figure 13.1 demonstrates the exceptionally high percentage of migrants in Israel compared to other welfare states, even in relation to the classic pro-immigrant countries like Australia, Canada and the US.

Figure 13.1: Migrants in selected countries, 2000 (% of population)

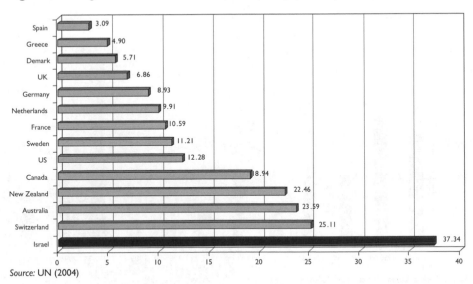

Source: UN (2004)

Yet it is not only the quantity of immigrants that makes Israel an interesting case for shedding light on migration processes in the 'New Europe'. In fact, Craig Parsons and Timothy Smeeding (2006) note that while Europe is over-represented as a host in international migration it is important to qualify the idea that the challenges facing Europe today regarding immigration are due to a simple rise in the number of immigrants. Reviewing research spanning the 19th century to the turn of this century they conclude that the significant increase of immigration to Europe in the late 1980s and early 1990s has since become moderated and cannot be considered to be part of a consistent upward trend. They conclude that this increase in migration to Europe is not unique in European history, such that there is no 'simple story of crisis-level inflows from a swelling sea of international migration' (Parsons and Smeeding, 2006, p 6). Rather, the most distinctive feature of recent migration to Europe is the ethnic diversity of the newcomers. The Israeli case offers insights regarding social policy tools for encouraging and supporting immigrants, while also sounding a cautionary note regarding the implications of preferential policies for certain populations on society at large.

Immigration policy in Israel

As a settler nation, immigration has been one of the defining characteristics of Israel since its founding in 1948. Established as a haven for Jews living outside the country, Israel has been engaged in absorbing Jewish immigrants for much of its short history. Israel has experienced a number of waves of immigration since the founding of the state, as demonstrated in the following figure (see Figure 13.2) of annual immigration.

Figure 13.2: Immigration to Israel, 1948–2004

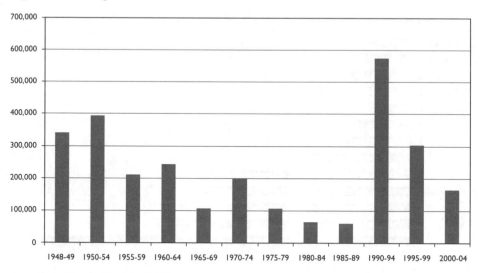

Source: Central Bureau of Statistics (2006)

The most recent wave of immigration occurred in the early 1990s, with 1,159,004 immigrants arriving in Israel between 1990 and 2001, comprising 16.5 per cent of the total population of the country (Central Bureau of Statistics, 2006). This wave was comprised primarily of immigrations from the former Soviet Union

(FSU) with a smaller population – approximately five per cent of the total – from Ethiopia (Sicron and Leshem, 1998). Alongside Jewish immigrants, since the early 1990s there has been an influx of overseas labour migrants, a major proportion of whom are undocumented (Amir, 2002; Raijman and Semyonov, 2004; Raijman, 2010). Following stringent state efforts to decrease the number of foreign workers which included major cuts in the number of authorisations for documented labour migrants, efforts to raise the labour costs entailed in their employment and an increase in expulsions of undocumented workers, it is estimated that they numbered 188,000 in 2004, 51 per cent of whom were undocumented (Rosenhek, 2000; Barzuri, 2005).

Immigration policy in Israel is based primarily on an ethnic implementation of the principle of *ius sanguinis* (the principle of descent), which in practice restricts the granting of citizenship to virtually only members of a specific ethnic group – in this case, for people of Jewish origin (Shuval, 1998; Joppke and Rosenhek, 2002; Friedberg and Kfir, 2005). This policy is a direct consequence of two early pieces of legislation adopted by the state. The Law of Return, enacted in 1950, is the centrepiece of Israeli immigration policy, and is grounded in the nationalist ideology of Zionism according to which Israel is a Jewish state that provides a haven and a homeland for the Jewish people. The Citizenship Law, enacted in 1952, is the major piece of legislation regulating Israeli citizenship. There is essentially nothing equivalent to the naturalisation process in the case of Jews because, as with other family-related perceptions of ethno-cultural membership, Israeli citizenship law views those eligible for return as already belonging to the constitutive community. They are considered, therefore, to automatically have a status equal to that of Israeli-born citizens (Klein, 1997; Shachar, 2000).

Israel has developed naturalisation requirements substantively similar to those of other welfare states for those who are ineligible for citizenship under the Law of Return. For example, Arabs and Jews born in the territory of Israel have the same right to acquire citizenship based on residence and birthplace. Yet Arabs who fled during the 1948 war and did not immediately return lost their citizenship. Many tried to return in the 1950s, but found it difficult to meet citizenship eligibility requirements. The Israeli government did not fully address this problem until 1980 when the government conferred citizenship retroactively on these Arab residents, thereby granting automatic citizenship to their children. While the formal naturalisation requirements are not more restrictive than those of other welfare states, they have historically been more discriminating in practice, and stand in stark contrast to the automatic and immediate conferral of citizenship that is granted to Jews (Klusmeyer, 2000; Shachar, 2000).

Additionally, there is an emphasis on republican perceptions of membership regarding the obligations citizens have toward the collective. Therefore, citizenship is not considered to be a passive bundle of rights, but rather an active practice epitomised by military service. Selective military recruitment policies and long-term benefits tacitly preserve structural inequalities among citizens, particularly between Jews and Arabs, leading to the creation of 'degrees of citizenship' (Shachar, 2000).

While clearly exclusionary, Israeli immigration policy is simultaneously very inclusive with regard to its definition of Jews as anyone who can successfully prove to have Jewish ancestry or to be an immediate family member of someone of Jewish ancestry. Due to cross-ethnic marriages in the Soviet Union, it is estimated that 25 per cent of the immigrants from the FSU are not Jewish (Central Bureau of Statistics, 2006, p 16). Thus, a significant proportion of the immigrants who have arrived in Israel in the last two decades have little connection to Judaism, and in the case of many immigrants from the FSU, are not Jewish at all (Lustick, 1999). In addition, the immigration policy is unconditional with regard to socio-demographic characteristics, thereby opening Israel's borders to Jewish immigrants regardless of age, income or physical condition. As a result of the fact that there are no limitations with regard to sources of economic support, the immigrant population has tended to include a large proportion of elderly immigrants as well as newcomers with very limited labour market skills or sources of capital, all of whom are eligible to migrate to Israel solely on the basis of their Jewish ancestry.

The categorical welfare state in Israel and immigrants

The social protection system in Israel is a relatively comprehensive system that was first established in the early 1950s, and was originally based on the British Beveridge model. The system was initially intended to be based primarily on social insurance principles such that the programmes would be universal and access would not be dependent on means testing. Old age and survivors' benefits were an early example of this type of benefit programme. In the years since, however, some means-tested programmes have also been introduced, such as Income Support, a selective social assistance programme adopted in 1980. However, the dominant form of benefit type incorporated in the system over time was that of categorical benefits.

Categorical benefits differ from the other two types of social security programmes in that they require neither an individual assessment of financial need nor a contribution record as a condition for eligibility. Right to benefit is determined primarily by the individual's belonging to a socially defined category. In more formal terms, these benefits can be defined as 'state-administered cash benefits paid to individuals who belong to socially-defined categories, regardless of their specific income status or prior contribution to a social insurance system' (Gal, 1998, p 77). While sometimes understood as universal or citizenship-based benefits, categorical benefits are not unconditional and, in fact, the conditions that determine eligibility for these benefits can be quite diverse and indeed stringent. Nevertheless, categorical benefits do tend to be less stigmatising than means-tested benefits and more accessible than the employment-dependent social insurance programme. As a result, take-up of benefits offered in programmes based on categorical principles will tend to be higher than those in programmes based on other principles.

Analysis of social spending shows that, in fact, categorical benefits dominate the Israeli system. This was true in the past (Gal, 2001) and remains the case today, despite a reduction in the proportion of social spending on this type of programme due primarily to a marked scaling back of the child benefit programme in the early 2000s. An analysis of the distribution of expenditure on social protection programmes by type in Israel reveals that categorical benefit programmes comprise 51.4 per cent of all spending, while only 37.7 per cent is devoted to social insurance programmes and 10.7 per cent to social assistance programmes (Gal, 2008).

Over time, the state has incorporated various programmes with provisions intended to deal with immigrants and their needs. Periodically it has also introduced specific programmes intended to deal with the unique needs of immigrants or difficulties in their access to existing programmes. The last major changes in the social protection system due to immigration were adopted in the wake of mass immigration from the FSU and elsewhere during the 1990s. On the whole, these changes have served to enhance immigrants' access to social support payments.

Israel's ethnic immigration policy, which offers formal integration into society to Jewish immigrants on arrival, has obvious implications for their ease of access to social rights. Since immigrants are eligible to receive citizenship or permanent resident status on arrival, in principle the conditions that determine their access to social protection programmes are identical to those of native citizens. However, because access to social insurance programmes requires a contributional labour market history and access to social assistance programmes generally requires a minimal period of residence, a number of statutory changes have been introduced to these programmes to ease immigrants' access, particularly for Income Support and Unemployment Insurance.

Yet it is the categorical emphasis of the social protection system in Israel that contributes most to the relative ease of access to social rights for immigrants. The implications of this categorical emphasis are that, for most contingencies, immigrants are neither required to have prior experience in the local labour market nor to undertake a means test in order to access benefits. Three levels of categorical benefits programmes can be identified: immigrant-specific benefit programmes, immigrant-oriented programmes and general categorical benefit programmes.

Regarding the first level, an example of an immigrant-specific programme is an old age benefit programme established specifically to deal with the needs of elderly immigrants who lack the contributory history required to access the standard universal old age benefit programme. This programme enables elderly immigrants lacking a minimal qualification period or a transferable pension from their country of origin to receive old age benefits equivalent to those offered to other citizens. The programme is nominally selective, but the high income ceiling of twice the average wage effectively makes this programme a universal benefit.

Another example is the absorption basket programme adopted in the beginning of the 1990s, which provides financial assistance to support immigrant households during their initial settlement period in Israel (Gal and Leshem, 2000). This is an unconditional cash benefit paid during the approximately six-month period during which the immigrant acquires basic Hebrew language skills, accompanied by a rental subsidy during this period and beyond.

The second level is comprised of categorical programmes initially developed for immigrants that can be accessed by native citizens. An example of this kind of benefit is the maternity benefit programme paid to mothers who give birth in hospitals, and is nominally intended to cover the initial expenses for newborn care. This programme was initially adopted in 1954 in order to motivate immigrant mothers living in transit camps to give birth in the safer environment of the hospital, but take-up of this benefit has since become universal. Another example is the Single Parent Family Law adopted in the early 1990s, which was advanced with the goal of meeting the needs of many single-parent families among the new immigrants from the FSU and Ethiopia (Ajzenstadt and Gal, 2001).

The third level includes categorical benefit programmes not adopted specifically for immigrants, but that are particularly accessible to members of this social group. This is the case for benefits such as child benefits and work injury insurance, both of which are neither means-tested nor dependent on any long-term labour market experience in Israel. The universal child benefits programme provides benefits for immigrant families with children under 18 immediately on arrival in the country. Work injury insurance is granted to individuals injured at work regardless of their length of residence and prior payment into the social security fund; hence, it is accessible to immigrants immediately on entry into the labour market.

The immigration–welfare state nexus and poverty among immigrants in Israel

This overview points to the development of an immigration–welfare state nexus in Israel that places great emphasis on categorical rather than means-tested or insurance-based benefits. This nexus has given immigrants access to social rights that is unique among welfare states. The findings of a secondary analysis of household expenditure surveys of the Israeli Census Bureau of Statistics indicate that immigrants' level of participation in the social protection system is slightly higher than that of native Israelis. In 2004, 81.8 per cent of post-1990 immigrant households received benefits of some sort from the social protection system, compared to 80.3 per cent of native Israeli households (Gal and Barzuri, 2007). The integration of immigrant households into the social protection system of the Israeli welfare state is also reflected in benefit take-up figures. Table 13.1, which is based on a secondary analysis of data from the 2004 Income Survey, shows that the take-up of old age benefits among immigrant men at the 'full' pension age (over 70), after which they are entitled to the universal old age benefit, is high and not much lower than that among native Israelis. Despite difficulties in

Table 13.1: Take-up of old age benefits among elderly men, 2004 (% of entire population)[a]

Population group	Current age (70-79)	Current age (80+)
Jews	93	92
Arabs	93	88
Post-1990 immigrants (aged <61 on arrival)	85	n.a
Post-1990 immigrants (aged >61 on arrival)	85	72

Note: [a] Thanks to Michael Shalev for his assistance in the analysis of this data.
Source: Analysis of Central Bureau of Statistic's 2004 Income Survey

comparing cross-national data, this take-up level appears to be particularly high compared to other welfare states (Nielsen, 2004).

Despite the economic downturn in Israel during the first half of this decade and the severe cuts in major social protection programmes, the combination of transfers and taxes during this period consistently lifted between 50-60 per cent of immigrant households above the poverty line. Figure 13.3 shows the proportion of poor households extracted from below the poverty line (defined as 50 per cent of the median household income) due to transfers and taxes. During this period, the positive impact of transfers and taxes on poor immigrant households has been greater than on the general population.

As a result, poverty levels among immigrants in Israel have tended to be lower or on a par with those of the general population. As can be seen in Figure 13.4,

Figure 13.3: The impact of taxes and transfers in Israel, 2001–07 (%)

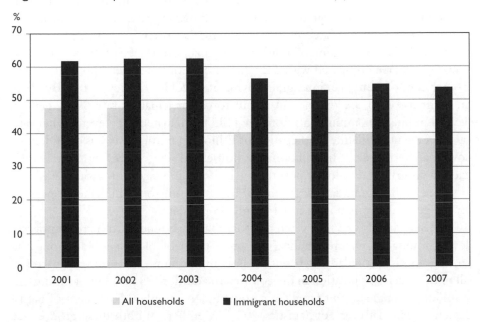

Source: National Insurance Institute (2007)

the proportion of immigrant households below the poverty line between 2001 and 2007 is lower than that of the general population.

Figure 13.4: Post-transfers and taxes poverty in Israel by categorical status (%)

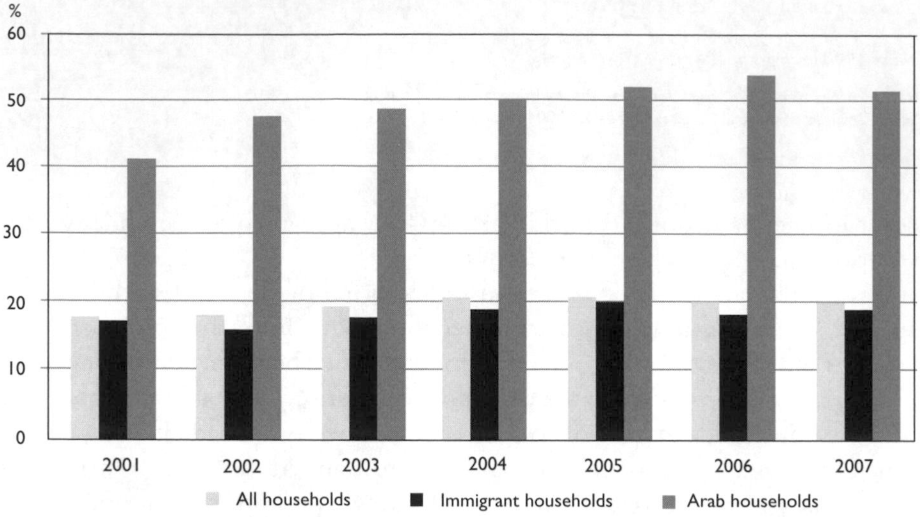

Source: National Insurance Institute (2007)

The relatively low poverty levels among immigrants in Israel are clearly not only the result of social protection programmes or high take-up rates of immigrants. The human capital of the immigrants, their socio-economic characteristics and their consequent success in integrating into the labour market are all contributing factors to these results, as indicated by the labour market participation of immigrants from the FSU and Ethiopia. Among immigrants from the FSU, 40 per cent had a college degree compared with only 27 per cent of the general population and 16 per cent of Ethiopian immigrants (King and Wolde-Tsadick, 2006). By 2003, in comparison to the 76 per cent labour force participation rate of the general Jewish population, immigrants from the FSU participated at an even higher rate, at 79 per cent, while the participation of Ethiopian immigrants was considerably lower, at 54 per cent. In addition, the household size of FSU immigrants has clearly contributed to lower poverty levels for members of this group. While 55 per cent of immigrant families with children have only one child, the proportion in the general population in Israel is only 35 per cent.

Yet there are also countervailing factors that have tended to increase poverty levels among Israeli immigrants. The proportion of older people among the immigrants is particularly high, with elderly immigrants constituting a quarter of all of the elderly population in the country. In addition, 25 per cent of immigrant families are single-parent families, in comparison to only 9.5 per cent of native Israelis (Central Bureau of Statistics, 2006). Members of both these groups face significant challenges in their efforts to attain financial security: elderly immigrants tend to lack income from occupational pensions and are often dependent on old age benefits, while single parents tend to work part time and lack additional sources of income other than social protection benefits. Thus, it would appear that as is the case in other welfare states (Buchel and Frick, 2005), the structuring of the social protection system and the ease of access to social rights contribute substantially to combating poverty among immigrants – and in the case of Israel, this contribution is a markedly positive one.

By contrast, the social welfare system is much less effective for other social groups that are not heavily supported. This is certainly the case for immigrant workers who come to Israel from elsewhere, who lack access to much of the social protection system and, as is the case in other European nations, have income levels that are significantly lower than those of other population groups (Bassok, 2007; see also Chapters Six and Twelve, this volume). The system is also less effective for Israel's Arab citizens. As can be seen in Figure 13.4, 40 to 50 per cent of Israeli Arab households remained in poverty after taxes and transfers during the first half of this decade (2001-04). Transfers and taxes lifted only 12 per cent of Arab households above the poverty line (National Insurance Institute, 2007). The limited effectiveness of the social welfare system in reducing the poverty rate among members of Israel's Arab citizens can clearly be linked to low market income, low labour market participation rates among Arab women and high fertility rates. Nevertheless, research indicates that the welfare state institutions' lack of effectiveness in extracting Israeli Arabs from poverty also reflects pro-immigrant social policy priorities and the structuring of the social welfare system (Lewin and Stier, 2002).

Explaining Israeli policy towards immigrants

How, then, can we explain the development of this generous categorical welfare system in Israel? The roots of both Israel's immigration policy and the treatment of immigrants by its social protection system can be linked to what Sammy Smooha (1990, 2002) has described as 'ethnic democracy'. This is a polity in which one of the state's ethnic groups has institutionalised dominance over state mechanisms. As an ethnic democracy, Israel offers formal citizenship rights to both Jews and Arabs, while members of the Jewish ethnic majority enjoy greater rewards from the state. This is particularly true for those, like immigrants, who are linked to supporting the Zionist goal of ensuring that Israel will remain a Jewish state (Peled, 1992; Shafir and Peled, 1998). This can be seen as a reflection of the institutionalised dominance of the majority ethnic group and its capacity to set policy and distribute resources in accordance with its desired goals.

The Law of Return, which provides the statutory framework for immigration policy, has been identified as one of the key components of Israel's ethnic democracy (Smooha, 2002). Despite the economic cost entailed in absorbing mass influxes of immigrants into the country, often during a very short time span, there has been no major debate in Israel regarding the justification or viability for this type of immigration policy. Critics of the Law of Return have failed to elicit any significant support for actual change in the law or in policy (Joppke and Rosenhek, 2002). Indeed, in a cross-national survey conducted in 2003, despite the extremely high levels of immigration to Israel during the 1990s and the financial costs that the absorption of these immigrants entailed, Israeli Jews were the least likely to say that the government spends too much money assisting immigrants, and were among the least likely to support reductions in the number of immigrants compared to citizens of other welfare states (International Social Survey Program, 2003).

The universalistic Beveridgean legacy of the Israeli social protection system and the country's adherence to formal equal rights for all of its citizens have generally prevented the introduction of any overt exclusionary elements within welfare state institutions. Particularly in recent years, the few attempts to introduce such exclusionary policies have been blocked by the political or judicial systems.[2] However, grafted onto the generally universal foundations of the Israeli welfare state, decision makers have sought to introduce programmes to address the specific needs of the members of certain social categories that have been identified by the state as more deserving than others. These programmes do not run counter to democratic principles and the notion of a universal welfare state by precluding the granting of services to all citizens; rather, they seek to offer additional services to members of specific groups. Since these programmes are intended for individuals identified as making a positive contribution to the common good, they are generally devoid of demeaning means tests or obstacles that may decrease take-up levels.

Immigrants (like military veterans, disabled soldiers, the families of fallen soldiers and victims of Nazi persecution) are one of the 'deserving' social categories identified by policymakers in Israel. They are perceived as contributing to the common good in that they play a crucial role in furthering the founding Zionist principle of the Israeli state – its serving as a homeland for the Jewish people. Moreover, this immigration to Israel contributes to a long-term demographic goal – the maintaining of a large Jewish majority (Rosenhek and Shalev, 2000).

While universalism is a defining characteristic of the Israeli social protection system, the existence of a relatively large number of non-means-tested categorical benefit programmes creates what can best be described as a 'categorical universalism' which benefits deserving social categories. An unusual immigration–welfare state nexus has thus been created in Israel due to the interface between an ethnic immigration policy and a social protection system based strongly on categorical benefits. The implications of this system are that it offers particularly good access to social rights for immigrants, while simultaneously exacerbating social gaps in Israeli society between the Jewish majority and the Arab minority.

Conclusion: categorical policies towards immigrants in a comparative perspective

An initial review of the socio-economic integration of immigrants to Europe may lead one to wonder if immigrant poverty is simply an intractable reality that cannot be fully ameliorated by social policy. The Israeli case demonstrates that immigrant poverty is not immutable. While the make-up of Israeli immigration includes some unusually well-off sectors, it also includes some unusually disadvantaged populations. The Israeli case shows the power of public policy in shaping welfare outcomes for immigrants.

It is noteworthy, however, that the price for achieving these positive results through catering to the needs of immigrants has been high. While 22 per cent of all social protection spending is devoted to immigrants, they comprise only 19.4 per cent of the population and contribute significantly less to social protection resources than the average citizen due to their relatively low income levels and the large proportion of non-working older people (Gal and Barzuri, 2007). Potentially even more problematic is the impact of these policies on social gaps in Israeli society. While the results of the structuring of this system and the efforts to enable immigrants' smoother integration into the labour market and society have been positive, the effectiveness of the social protection system among other social groups has been much more limited. This is the case for members of the Arab minority ethnic group in Israel. It is also true of overseas migrant workers.

Given the challenges facing the 'New Europe' regarding the immigration–welfare nexus, the Israeli case then provides both a note of optimism as well as caution. This case is cause for optimism in showing that immigrant poverty is not an intractable reality, and that welfare policy can greatly influence the socio-economic integration of immigrants. Yet the cautionary note is just as important given the diverse make-up of contemporary immigrants to Europe. Since welfare policies for immigrants inherently involve integrating a foreign population, they have great intrinsic potential to exacerbate existing ethnic tensions. They place a considerable financial burden on the state (in the short run at least) and entail the granting of preferential treatment to immigrants, inevitably at the expense of other groups in society. While the policies described in this chapter have proven viable in the case of Jewish immigrants to Israel due to the political inviolability of this type of migration, this clearly may not be so in other welfare states. Hence, policymakers must carefully weigh up the goals regarding immigration integration in light of the new ways in which recent immigration influences the make-up of European societies.

Notes

[1] Jennifer Oser's research for this chapter was conducted with the support of the Hoffman Leadership and Responsibility fellowship programme of the Hebrew University.

[2] See Rosenhek (1999) for a notable exception.

References

Ajzenstadt, M. and Gal, J. (2001) 'Appearances can be deceptive: gender in the Israeli welfare state', *Social Politics*, vol 8, pp 292-324.

Amir, S. (2002) 'Overseas foreign workers in Israel: policy aims and labor market outcomes', *International Migration Review*, vol 36, pp 41-58.

Anastassova, L. and Paligorova, T. (2006) *What is behind the native-immigrant social income gap?*, Luxembourg Income Study Working Paper 432, Luxembourg: LIS.

Arts, W.A. and Gelissen, J. (2002) 'Three worlds of welfare capitalism or more?', *Journal of European Social Policy*, vol 12, pp 137-58.

Baldwin-Edwards, M. (1991) 'Immigration after 1992', *Policy & Politics*, vol 19, pp 199-211.

Bambra, C. (2005) 'Cash versus services: "worlds of welfare" and the decommodification of cash benefits and health care services', *Journal of Social Policy*, vol 34, pp 195-213.

Banting, K.G. (2000) 'Looking in three directions: migration and the European welfare state in comparative perspective', in M. Bommes and A. Geddes (eds) *Immigration and welfare: Challenging the borders of the welfare state*, London: Routledge, pp 13-33.

Barzuri, R. (eds) (2005) *Undocumented foreign workers in Israel, 1999-2002*, Jerusalem: Ministry of Industry, Commerce and Labor [in Hebrew].

Bassok, M. (2007) 'Average salary in Israel NIS 7,922, foreign workers earn NIS 4,365', *Haaretz*, 9 October [in Hebrew].

Blume, K., Gustafsson, B., Pedersen, P.J. and Verner, M. (2007) 'At the lower end of the table: determinants of poverty among immigrants to Denmark and Sweden', *Journal of Ethnic and Migration Studies*, vol 33, pp 373-96.

Borjas, G.J. (2002) 'Welfare reform and immigrant participation in welfare programs', *The International Migration Review*, vol 36, pp 1093-123.

Buchel, F. and Frick, J.R. (2005) 'Immigrants' economic performance across Europe – does immigration policy matter?', *Population Research and Policy Review*, vol 24, pp 175-212.

Castles, S. and Miller, M.J. (eds) (2003) *The age of migration* (3rd edn), New York: Guilford Press.

Castranova, E.J., Kayser, H., Frick, J.R. and Wagner, G.G. (2001) 'Immigrants, natives and social assistance: comparable take-up under comparable conditions', *International Migration Review*, vol 35, pp 726-48.

Central Bureau of Statistics (2006) *Immigrants from the former Soviet Union*, Jerusalem: Central Bureau of Statistics [in Hebew].

Coleman, D. and Rowthorn, R. (2004) 'The economic effects of immigration into the United Kingdom', *Population and Development Review*, vol 30, pp 579-624.

Dorr, S. and Faist, T. (1997) 'Institutional conditions for the integration of immigrants in welfare states: a comparison of the literature on Germany, France, Great Britain, and the Netherlands', *European Journal of Political Research*, vol 31, pp 401-26.

Esping-Andersen, G. (1990) *The three worlds of welfare capitalism*, Princeton, NJ: Princeton University Press.

Esping-Andersen, G. (1999) *Social foundations of post-industrial economies*, Oxford: Oxford University Press.

Fix, M. (2002) 'Social rights and citizenship', in T.A. Aleinikoff and D. Klusmeyer (eds) *Citizenship policies for an age of migration*, Washington, DC: Brookings Institution Press, pp 62-78.

Freeman, G.P. (1986) 'Migration and the political economy of the welfare state', *Annals of the American Academy of Political and Social Sciences*, vol 486, pp 51-63.

Freeman, G.P. and Birrell, B. (2001) 'Divergent paths of immigration politics in the United States and Australia', *Population and Development Review*, vol 27, pp 525-51.

Friedberg, A. and Kfir, A. (2005) 'Policy-making and immigrant absorption', in D. Korn (ed) *Public policy in Israel: Perspectives and practices*, Lanham, MD: Lexington, pp 31-50.

Gal, J. (1998) 'Categorical benefits in welfare states: findings from Britain and Israel', *International Social Security Review*, vol 51, pp 73-102.

Gal, J. (2001) 'Values, categorical benefits, and categorical legacies in Israel', in A. Ben-Arieh and J. Gal (eds) *Into the promised land*, Westport, CT: Praeger, pp 115-36.

Gal, J. (2008) 'Immigration and the categorical welfare state in Israel', *Social Service Review*, vol 82, no 4, pp 639-61.

Gal, J. and Barzuri, R. (eds) (2007) *Immigration and welfare in Israel*, Jerusalem: Taub Center for Social Policy Studies in Israel [in Hebrew].

Gal, J. and Leshem, E. (2000) 'Examining changes in settlement policies for immigrants: the Israeli case', *Journal of Comparative Policy Analysis*, vol 2, pp 235-56.

Geva-May, I. (2000) 'On impacts of comparative policy analysis. Immigration to Israel: what other countries can learn', *International Migration*, vol 38, pp 3-45.

Hanson, G.H., Scheve, K., Slaughter, M.J. and Spilimbergo, A. (2002) 'Immigration and the U.S. economy: Labor-market impacts, illegal entry, and policy choices', in Boeri, T., G. Hanson and B. McCormick, B. (eds.) (2002) *Immigration policy and the welfare system*, Oxford: Oxford University Press.

Hjerm, M. (2005) 'Integration into the social democratic welfare state', *Social Indicators Research*, vol 70, pp 117-38.

International Social Survey Programme (2003) *National identity II* (www.gesis.org/en/data_service/issp/data/2003_National_Identity-II.htm).

Joppke, C. and Rosenhek, Z. (2002) 'Contesting ethnic immigration: Germany and Israel compared', *European Journal of Sociology*, vol 43, pp 301-35.

King, J. and Wolde-Tsadick, A. (eds) (2006) *Patterns of integration into employment of new immigrants aged 22-64*, Jerusalem: Myers-JDC-Brookdale Institute for Research on Immigrant Absorption [in Hebrew].

Klein, C. (1997) 'The right of return in Israel law', *Tel Aviv University Studies in Law*, vol 13, pp 53-61.

Klusmeyer, D. (2000) 'From migrants to citizens', in T.A. Aleinikoff and D. Klusmeyer (eds) *From migrants to citizens*, Washington, DC: Carnegie Endowment for International Peace, pp 1-24.

Lelkes, O. (eds) (2007) *Poverty among migrants in Europe*, Vienna: European Centre.

Levi-Faur, D., Sheffer, G. and Vogel, D. (1999) 'Change and continuity: a framework for comparative analysis', *Israel Affairs*, vol 5, pp 1-14.

Lewin, A.C. and Stier, H. (2002) 'Who benefits the most? The unequal allocation of transfers in the Israeli welfare state', *Social Science Quarterly*, vol 83, pp 488-503.

Lustick, I.S. (1999) 'Israel as a non-Arab state: the political implications of mass immigration of non-Jews', *Social Science Quarterly*, vol 83, pp 417-33.

Morissens, A. and Sainsbury, D. (2005) 'Migrants' social rights, ethnicity and welfare regimes', *Journal of Social Policy*, vol 34, pp 637-60.

Nannestad, P. (2007) 'Immigration and welfare states: a survey of 15 years of research', *European Journal of Political Economy*, vol 23, pp 512-32.

National Insurance Institute (2007) *Annual survey, 2006*, Jerusalem: National Insurance Institute [in Hebrew].

Nielsen, N. (2004) 'Social transfers to immigrants in Germany and Denmark', in T. Trances and K.F. Zimmermann (eds) *Migrants, work and the welfare state*, Odense: University Press of Southern Denmark, pp 245-84.

Ongley, P. and Pearson, D. (1995) 'Post-1945 international immigration: New Zealand, Australia and Canada compared', *International Migration Review*, vol 29, pp 765-93.

Parsons, C.A. and Smeeding, T.M. (eds) (2006) *Immigration and the transformation of Europe*, Cambridge: Cambridge University Press.

Peled, Y. (1992) 'Ethnic democracy and the legal construction of citizenships: Arab citizens of the Jewish state', *American Political Science Review*, vol 86, pp 432-43.

Raijman, R. (2010) 'Citizenship status, ethno-national origin and entitlement to rights: majority attitudes towards minorities and immigrants in Israel', *Journal of Ethnic and Migration Studies*, vol 36, no 1, pp 87-106.

Raijman, R. and Semyonov, M. (2004) 'Perceived threat and exclusionary attitudes towards foreign workers in Israel', *Ethnic and Racial Studies*, vol 27, pp 780-99.

Rosenhek, Z. (1999) 'The exclusionary logic of the welfare state: Palestinian citizens in the Israeli welfare state', *International Sociology*, vol 14, pp 195-215.

Rosenhek, Z. (2000) 'Migration regimes, intra-state conflicts, and the politics of exclusion and inclusion: migrant workers in the Israeli welfare state', *Social Problems*, vol 47, pp 49-67.

Rosenhek, Z. and Shalev, M. (2000) 'The contradictions of Palestinian citizenship in Israel: inclusion and exclusion in the Israeli welfare state', in N. Butenschon, U. Davis and M. Hassassian (eds) *Citizenship and the state in the Middle East: Approaches and applications*, Syracuse, NY: Syracuse University Press, 288-315.

Sainsbury, D. (2006) 'Immigrants' social rights in comparative perspective: welfare regimes, forms in immigration and immigration policy regimes', *Journal of European Social Policy*, vol 16, pp 229-44.

Shachar, A. (2000) 'Citizenship and membership in the Israeli polity', in T.A. Aleinikoff and D. Klusmeyer (eds) *From migrants to citizens*, Washington, DC: Carnegie Endowment for International Peace, pp 386-433.

Shafir, G. and Peled, Y. (1998) 'Citizenship and stratification in an ethnic democracy', *Ethnic and Racial Studies*, vol 21, pp 408-27.

Shuval, J.T. (1998) 'Migration to Israel: the mythology of "uniqueness"', *International Migration*, vol 36, pp 3-24.

Sicron, M. and Leshem, E. (eds) (1998) *A portrait of immigration: Processes of absorption of immigrants from the former Soviet Union, 1990-1995*, Jerusalem: Magnes [in Hebrew].

Smooha, S. (1990) 'Minority status in an ethnic democracy: the status of the Arab minority in Israel', *Ethnic and Racial Studies*, vol 13, pp 389-503.

Smooha, S. (2002) 'The model of ethnic democracy: Israel as a Jewish and democratic state', *Nations and Nationalism*, vol 8, pp 475-503.

Soysal,Y.N. (eds) (1994) *Limits of citizenship*, Chicago, IL: Chicago University Press.

Starke, P. (2006) 'The politics of welfare state retrenchment: a literature review', *Social Policy and Administration*, vol 40, pp 104-20.

UN (United Nations) (2004) *Trends in total migrant stock: The 2003 revision*, New York: Department of Economic and Social Affairs, Population Division.

FOURTEEN

Conclusions: what future for migration?

Emma Carmel, Alfio Cerami and Theodoros Papadopoulos

This book is concerned with the interaction of social and migration policies in specific political, economic and social contexts, which affect migrants' welfare, well-being and inclusion. In Chapter One its empirical and analytical terrain were outlined as centering on three elements: the analysis of combined and interacting *policy* fields, especially migration, integration and welfare and labour markets; the interaction of *polity* and *politics* in these policy fields across different levels of policymaking; and finally, the consequent implications of these dynamics for migrants' differential integration in European Union (EU) member state societies. In this final chapter, we review this terrain in the light of the book's contributions.

All the studies in this volume support the contention that contemporary migrants' dual relationship with the country of origin and country of destination, their 'transnationalism' – whether migration is temporary, circular, serial or permanent – is directly shaped by *policies*, *politics* and *polities* (institutions), over which most migrants have no control. States' and other institutions' practices matter in fundamental ways for migrants' experience of their migration, from entry, to residence, social entitlements, labour market access, income and well-being (see Crowley, 2001, 2005; Bigo and Guild, 2005; Hansen, 2009). The contributions in this volume have explored the dynamic interactions among these policy fields and the contentious politics that characterise them and their interaction. They have explored the ways in which these interactions played out across different levels of policymaking to structure and shape the conditions of possibility for policymaking. They have demonstrated how the stratification of rights between categories of migrant statuses is shaped by the main mode of integration (via, for example, ethnicity, nationality, family status, employment), applied to different migrant groups in different countries and historical contexts. They have also demonstrated how this could be cut across by the differentiated terms and conditions under which the mode of integration can be experienced (for example, privileged ethnicity, subject to different rights at different times; employment in the informal or formal labour market, in low or high-skill jobs, in a welfare system where social rights can be accrued). The rest of this chapter elaborates on the evidence presented in the contributions for the significance of interacting policies across institutional scales in shaping this differentiated integration. As mentioned in Chapter One, in some contributions, the interactions between historical legacies, discourses, political economy rationales and politicised emotion that shape possibilities for particular kinds of integration were more significant in one policy domain than another. Nonetheless, as noted in Chapter Two, the domains themselves are interrelated and have mutual effects. The differential integration of migrants across Europe and within member states is, therefore, the product of *politics*, *polity* and *policy* interacting across several domains, and with different dynamics and effects at different scales of governance. We conclude with some more general reflections on political and policy trajectories and challenges in the field of migration, migration policy and social protection.

Citizenship, ethnicity and country of origin

Despite Hammar's (1990) distinction between immigration policies (policies of border control, entry, exit) and immigrant policies (policies for integration), our contributions have demonstrated the intrinsic links between them. Several chapters have shown how immigrant policies, and especially national citizenship policies, have been significant in recursively shaping, and being shaped by, histories of immigration and modes of integration. It was in the field of ethnic and citizenship differentiation that our contributions drew attention to historical and policy legacies (Italy, Germany, Hungary and Israel) (North, 1990; Hall and Taylor, 1996; Pierson, 1996), but also cases where these have been overturned, or are changing (the UK, Germany). *Jus soli*, *ius sanguinis* or *jus domicili* are not simply concepts rooted in the political and institutional tradition of a country, but have their origins in the *cultural* and *emotional embeddedness* of immigration policies. Cultural factors are associated with the historical legacies of a country, its understanding of the immigrant status and its experience of immigration (van Oorschot et al, 2008). The most notable examples are those of Germany, Hungary or Israel, which provide evidence of differentially inclusive attitudes and policies that distinguish a privileged mode of integration for specified social categories (such as ethnic Germans, ethnic Hungarians or Jews). However, this also involves a differentiated exclusion strategy for other minorities, as in the case of the Turkish community in Germany, of the Chinese and African communities in Hungary or of the Arab community in Israel, and the number, scale and status of the differentiated subordinate or excluded groups both depends on and reproduces social, political and economic divisions (see Chapters Nine and Thirteen, this volume).

Cultural, religious and ethnic characteristics may play a prominent role, but more straightforward considerations about the willingness to accept and to live with different people can also become important elements of exclusion and segregation even when these perceived social incompatibilities do not necessarily represent a direct threat to the dominant culture, religion or ethnic composition of a country. As stated in Chapter One, attitudes towards the possible disruptive consequences of supposed negative *matching* (Stovel and Fountain, 2009) among those 'similar' (such as ethnic and resident Germans, Hungarians or Israelis) can also become an important factor in the exclusion and segregation of individuals, which do not stem from rational motivations (see Elster, 2008, 2009). Emotional attachment to the supposed good qualities of the homogenised insider group, 'us', 'the citizens', does not have simply a symbolic value for the members of the in-group, but also social boundaries which determine the beliefs about, as well as preferences and opportunities for, inclusion and integration for 'others'.

However, as the case of Germany and Israel shows, this is also not always straightforward: in the German case, not only were ethnic Germans not, at least for the first generation, able to access the same labour market opportunities as their non-migrant counterparts, despite their access to formal citizenship and other rights, but in addition, the changing political economy, changing levels and patterns in in-migration and the very presence of other immigrant groups in Germany made the degree of 'ethnic' distinction in policy no longer politically tenable by the early 21st century. In the case of Israel, in Chapter Thirteen John Gal and Jennifer Oser not only observe the success of the Israeli integration policies for immigrants, but note that ethnically and culturally distinct Ethiopian immigrants benefit much less; a pattern we can also see in other countries even where there is no formal or legal mode of integration which privileges some groups over others (see Chapter Ten, this volume).

In the British case, while historical patterns of migration and integration have been marked by institutionally normalised distinctions of 'race' and ethnicity, recent changes in patterns of migration, combined with increased diversity among settled communities, problematise these longstanding political categories of distinction. Here the contentious politics of migration – against the backdrop of heightened discourses of risk and security, combined with more local experience of concentrated social change produced by migration – have significantly, but by no means solely, resulted in changing the terms and conditions of naturalisation. These make citizenship something 'to be acquired' ('earned citizenship') rather than a state to be entered into. As such, the process of citizenship acquisition – of becoming 'entitled' to be British – becomes a marker of differential integration by insisting on a form of cultural and social and economic 'integration' prior to the acquisition of any social, economic or political rights. The exception here is to those rights granted by the EU's directive on long-term resident third-country nationals (TCNs). It is in such cases of the current or future construction of more restrictive policies at national level that one protective role for the EU can be seen.

Labour market and employment

There is evidence at national level, among all our case study contributions, of the promotion of common policies attempting to design selective labour migration policies, especially privileging high-skill selectivity, as part of the programme of managed migration. This is also reflected in one of the few EU direct 'successes' in the legal migration field, the creation of an EU-wide 'Blue Card' scheme for high-skill workers. In terms of integration into labour markets, our studies show that 'high-skill' workers may be granted privileges in terms of geographical and employment mobility, job search and residence, but may also still face discrimination and restrictions on their rights which are intended to limit or constrain the likelihood of their settling (see the examples from Germany and the UK). Nor are they exempt from the day-to-day discrimination more evidently displayed towards other groups (see the Finland example, also Chapter Eleven, this volume).

While the rhetoric of managed migration is usually deployed to legitimise specific forms of labour migration, it can also be a means to politically displace debate about the *de facto* utilitarian integration of irregular migrants in large sectors of some national economies (Bauder, 2006; Berggren et al, 2007; Anderson and Ruhs, 2010a). Asylum seekers might claim asylum in order to overcome their status as undocumented migrants; they might become irregular migrants by undertaking employment, either before their case is decided or following refusal. Similarly, legally working migrants might jeopardise their status by moving employers when not permitted to, or otherwise breaching their work or residence permits. In any case, although the 'unwanted' migrants of Europe are commonly bracketed under headings of ('bogus') asylum seekers and undocumented migrants, supposedly to be dealt with by securitised and restrictive policy measures, and often with little or no recourse to social welfare systems, these migrants are among the most vulnerable participants in the unregulated and informal labour markets of Europe (Anderson and Ruhs, 2010b). This combination of exclusion and vulnerability is almost impossible to overcome in the current institutional context, where at both *national* and *European* level the exclusion of such 'unwanted migrants' is assumed and politically nearly incontestable, while in practice, *local* authorities across Europe may face *de facto* demands given the social needs of these groups – for health and housing, for example. The exception among our contributions is the Finnish case (see Chapter Eight, this volume; see also Chapter Two for other Nordic countries), where access to welfare for migrants granted asylum means they are not forced to participate in the labour market, although this feature of the polity generates its own political and emotional feedback effects, as these migrants are criticised for not being in employment.

The economic situation of a country, the degree of regulation over labour market entry and how closely this is linked to migration policies overall (for example, specification of particular categories of workers) are, according to the contributions in this volume, significant factors affecting whether the main domain of integration is via the labour market, and under what terms this is achieved. In Chapter Six, Tiziana Caponio and Paolo Graziano emphasised the importance of highly fragmented labour markets which force new categories of migrant citizens to work in conditions of continuous uncertainty due to ever more restrictive legislation, combined with difficult labour and contractual conditions that often result in higher levels of working poor and, in some cases, also to something like forced labour (as in the case of Chinese or African illegal migrant communities). But, as demonstrated by Mick Wilkinson and Gary Craig (Chapter Ten, this volume), serious problems of social inclusion and integration may also emerge in arenas where labour market governance is essentially liberal. In this context governments play a key role in managing the inclusion and social integration capacity of labour markets (see Chapter Thirteen, this volume), and can do so in a variety of ways. In addition, they shape the dominance or otherwise of particular kinds of labour market participation which determine the terms and conditions under which migrants are integrated into the society of the destination country (for a detailed discussion, see Chapter Two, this volume). As the studies in this volume have highlighted, important exclusionary tendencies in markets may emerge (see, in particular, Chapters Nine and Eleven) and can reinforce other inequalities experienced by migrants, relating to the other domains, especially if distinctions and consequent inequalities are consistent across all levels of governance, from the EU to the local (for example, treatment of undocumented workers).

Leading EU and national discourses on this matter seem to emphasise the essential closure of the European continent, so as not to compromise the stability of the European project with its ambitious long-term economic and social objectives (Vobruba, 2007). Yet in reality, the goal of becoming 'the most dynamic knowledge-based economy in the world, capable of sustainable economic growth with more and better jobs and greater social cohesion' (European Council, 2000) involved the delineation of a range of roles for migrants in the EU's developmental project, exposing a radical contradiction between EU programmes of economic development and migrants' experiences in national labour markets, even before the economic crisis. Migrants to and within the Union fall among those to be included in the EU's project of economic development on a limited basis, even in part responsible for its success, as temporary workers, especially those with high skills and/or in the health field. And they number among those who are excluded – people entering, overstaying and working illegally in particular, representing an economic threat by not overtly contributing to the development of the new economy, and representing instead the low-skill economy which the Lisbon Agenda was expressly to have moved away from.

Such observations imply a different understanding of the European economic and social objectives as expressed by the Lisbon Strategy, which Emma Carmel argued (Chapter Three) are directly linked to the expression of Union concerns about 'managing migration' from the early 2000s. The importance of migration for the EU's economic and social vision could perhaps explain the ever-increasing policy attention granted to migration as a socio-economic issue in EU governance. This has resulted in its inclusion in the replacement to the Lisbon strategy, the so-called 'Europe 2020' agreed in March 2010, where the social interests of migrants and of immigrants seem to take considerably higher priority than previously. It can also be seen – more ambivalently here – in the creation of the new legal and governance framework within which EU migration is to be managed since the 2009 Lisbon Treaty came into force.

Welfare systems and social rights

Welfare institutions define the boundaries of inclusion and exclusion of citizens (Ferrera, 2005), among other things, through the ways in which their mode of access, benefit structure, management and financing of the welfare system are organised (Bonoli and Palier, 2001; Palier, 2010). As Taylor-Gooby (2009) argues, welfare systems are conceived of as sites of 'reciprocity, inclusion and trust'; they are important in collective identity, solidarity formation and claims making, but they are also simultaneously exclusionary and discriminating (Lister, 2003). Hemerijck (2010) has affirmed that the current nationally organised, nationally controlled European systems of social protection are simply not ready to deal with the emerging problem of migration (see also Kuhnle, 2000). In addition, both the structural organisation (polity) and the day-to-day implementation of policy in relation to welfare systems, especially as they apply to particular migrant groups, have a highly differentiating impact in practice. Analytical and research attention in this case is clearly warranted at local level: to local contexts and experiences of social need, social services provision and local politics (Caponio and Borkert, 2010; see also Chapters Ten, Eleven and Twelve, this volume).

In Continental welfare states, such as Germany and France, a Bismarckian model of social insurance remains the main characteristic, giving the priority of social policies to the maintenance of status differentials and active inclusion of existing professional categories. However, as Lutz Kaiser and Regine Paul show in Chapter Seven, while first-generation immigrants, including so-called guestworkers, appeared integrated via the labour market, which gave them access to social benefits as *denizens* (permanent residents with earned social rights, but no political rights), second and third generations of these settled communities are distinguished by country of origin in terms of how they have been able to access education, and in consequence, in how they are integrated into the labour market, which in turn has ongoing impacts on the continuing subordinate denizenship for some immigrant groups in particular (especially those of Turkish origin).

In Scandinavian welfare systems, by contrast, elements of universalism and egalitarianism play a bigger role. However, especially in terms of migration, extensive benefits are often translated to limited acceptance of beneficiaries primarily because of fear of welfare tourism (see Chapter Eight, this volume). Thus asylum – and subsequent family unification – become key mechanisms for entry, but as the mode of integration is via the social welfare system, and access to the labour market (and thus insurance-based benefits) very difficult, this involves *de facto* segregation and even exclusion from the non-migrant community. It is in these cases that social networks, informal welfare provision and cultural associations can be critical in enhancing well-being (see Chapter Eleven, this volume). In the UK, the liberal welfare regime is structured in relation to migration in ways that impose restrictions on access to the predominantly means-tested social assistance benefits. These restrictions have recently been enhanced and extended, and with the new citizenship law, this will harden ever further, so that not even high-skilled migrants are privileged above other migrants in relation to social benefits. In addition, as Mick Wilkinson and Gary Craig suggest in Chapter Ten, it is in service provision that many of the struggles and difficulties around welfare provision for migrants have arisen – from health services, to housing and education. This is all about local–national relations, and raises significant questions about the organisation of interest representation of migrants in areas that affect them directly (Chapter Twelve, this volume). The familistic Mediterranean welfare regime highlighted by Ferrera (1996) and discussed by Tiziana Caponio and Paolo Graziano in Chapter Six, includes, in this context, even more modest social protection for migrants than those systems of social protection discussed above. Historically the vulnerability of undocumented migrants has been addressed in some form by regularisation, but where the local level of politics, policy and polity have now become vital in shaping the possibilities for the integration of migrants in a nationally very hostile context.

Finally, in Central and Eastern Europe, the ongoing changes and developments in welfare systems result in more fluid 'regime' characteristics. Migration is not simply a very recent issue with not yet stabilised inflows and outflows of migrants (see Chapter Nine, this volume), but, being often framed in highly sensitive geo-political terms, it still includes several unresolved ethnic issues and is characterised by not having a common migration policy orientation (see Chapter Eleven), even though pressures for Europeanisation and harmonisation of policies are on the increase. Due to the communist heritage, in Central and Eastern Europe migration remains, in fact, very difficult to address. It implies a redefinition not simply of the past, but also of the present and future, opening up fragile political settlements and longstanding unresolved issues concerned with national composition, cultural and ethnic identity as well as geographical border extension.

Exclusion, risk and securitised differentiation

This book has focused primarily on migration and integration, and their relationship to the production of welfare and well-being. It is specifically not intended to focus on migration and criminal justice or international security issues, on which there is a substantial literature. However, questions of 'securitisation', particularly in the treatment of both asylum-seeking migrants and of irregular migrants (as the two politically least desired categories of migrant) have been consistently raised in the contributions. The classification and re-classification of migrant statuses in changing policy reforms in Germany, in the UK and in Italy, for example, link discursively, politically and institutionally to the exclusion, delegitimisation and control of some migrants, and to the subordinate relationship of particular migrant statuses to others. In many contributions, the discussion of migration and integration policies makes reference to issues of securitisation, the discourse and rhetoric of ontological threats and the symbolic and real exclusion of migrants on the grounds of 'security', or perhaps more appropriately, 'risk' (Neal, 2009; van Munster, 2009). These legitimise institutional arrangements that define threatening populations among a set of populations that need managing, organising (excluding and including) and integrating (in a strong normative sense) through policy. However, as discussed above, the treatment of asylum as one of security and exclusion is to miss a central relevant issue, that asylum seekers can often become immigrants – as refugees, or with other temporary, conditional or permanent permission to stay in the country of destination. In all these cases, they become subject to logics of integration, and this also plays a role in shaping migration and immigration debates, and in shaping the form and conditions of other migrants' integration.

The increasing intolerance towards members of the Muslim community in Europe and in the US following the terrorist attacks of September 11th 2001 is here an emblematic example (Nguyen, 2005; Wiegand, 2008; EUAFRA, 2009). This involves the increasing politicisation of cultural defence strategies put in place by an ever-larger section of the European population against an excessive multi-culturalisation of 'their' territory. These seem, in fact, to be linked not simply to objective economic, political and social threats, but, as discussed by Emma Carmel and Alfio Cerami in Chapter One, to sometimes profound emotional attachment to symbolic images, which can be constructed as intrinsic to a naturalised, de-historicised and homogenised 'national' culture. Attachments to nation are often profound – both in the construction of feelings of belonging and in constructing feelings about those who do, or 'should', not belong – which can then significantly influence preferences and possibilities for policymaking (Adida et al, 2010).

Despite substantial political rhetoric on the human rights achievements and integration capacity of European member states and EU institutions, there has only been uneven progress on achieving improvements in this area (for a recent review, see Parsons and Smeeding, 2006; Geddes, 2008; Fassmann et al, 2009; Favell and Recchi, 2009). 'Fortress Europe' is, for many poor and undocumented migrants, a harsh reality (Gebrewold, 2007); the 'liberal paradox' (economic openness and political/policy closure) (Hollifield, 2004) has direct consequences for individual migrants. In addition, however, we can also observe what Dummett (1992) and Benhabib (2004) refer to as a human rights paradox – that under the 1948 United Nations (UN) Declaration of Human Rights we have an individual right to emigrate from birth, yet there is no such corresponding right to immigrate (for a more in-depth discussion, see Chapter Four, this volume). In the face of the ongoing pervasiveness of politics of risk and security, and policies of control and exclusion at local, national and EU levels, the counter-tendencies – to social integration, to the recognition of basic rights of migrants – are likely to continue contributing to the differential integration of migrants overall, even if they are effective and significant for some migrants.

Migration, social protection and the challenges of integration

The relationship between migration, migration policies and social protection remains difficult to evaluate and is rarely put under serious theoretical and empirical scrutiny (exceptions include Clark et al, 2009; Düvell, 2009; Koopmans, 2010). Even when initial attempts to explore this issue have been conducted, the results are far from conclusive, often taking ambiguous positions on what the rights of immigrants in the destination country should really consist of (for a notable exception, see Pécoud and de Guchteneire, 2007). The contributions in this book have drawn attention to three cross-cutting interactions. First, our contributors have assessed the important interactions of *polity*, *politics* and *policy* in shaping the governance of migration in a range of policy domains. Second, the contributions have demonstrated the importance of addressing the interaction of politics, polity and policy *between* these domains, as it is this interaction between domains that structures the terms of migrants' integration. Finally, the volume as a whole has drawn attention to the interaction and layering of different levels of migration governance, and their implications for migrants' differential integration.

As highlighted by the contributions in this volume, the interaction between migration, migration policies and welfare has yet to provide consistent social protection for migrants in Europe, and the prospects for future improvements are rather uncertain. While migration is a topic at the top of the political agenda in many EU member states, and the subject of major changes in EU policymaking, the animated and emotional public debate at national and local level is often polarised and framed along an exclusionary axis, with clear preferences for the reinforcement of a so-called 'Fortress Europe' rather than the more positive, if often utilitarian, defence of the economic value of temporary migrants. In many countries, however, this debate between securitised exclusion and utilitarian selectivity is cut across by a more contrasting concern, expressing anxieties about the social, cultural and economic integration of existing immigrant and minority ethnic communities. This concern could result in more intensive efforts to generate social and political responsibilities for migrant integration, contrasting with simple exclusionary or utilitarian logics at a range of governance levels (see Chapters Three, Seven and Twelve, this volume).

The challenges of inclusion, integration and social protection that the current European welfare systems face are multiple, involve sometimes contrasting strategic interests and political forces, and cannot be resolved by simple incremental changes in migration policies, as many historical institutionalists might emphasise (see, for instance, Streeck and Thelen, 2005). To meet the challenges of integration would involve a change in the institutional structures (polities) that govern migration, including social protection, welfare more generally, labour markets and how they are jointly governed (see Chapters Two, Three and Five, this volume), as well as in the cultural and social understandings of 'feasible' migration and how it can be governed (see Chapters Four, Six, Seven, Nine, Eleven and Thirteen, this volume). Yet reform in this area, although difficult, should not be *prima facie* considered impossible. New more restrictive but also more tolerant ideas and discourses on a specific migration policy could materialise, influencing (or being influenced by) a change in emotions, beliefs, preferences and opportunities. As discussed in Chapter One, these changes in 'immigration *Weltanschauung*' (vision of the world) are structured by existing institutional practices and routines, but also simultaneously influence and structure the existing institutional set-up of a country, leading to new pathways of institutional change.

We conclude by saying that the above-mentioned challenges are not insurmountable. While not dismissing or under-estimating the continuing significance of labour market utility, cultural closure and securitised exclusion in shaping migration governance, especially at national level, a more open and socially inclusive understanding of migration and migrants' lives is not out of reach of politicians, policymakers or the population at large. It seems to us that there are major flaws in the EU's current approach to migration, but there are also, for example within the discourse of 'social integration', or in the experiences of local policymakers working with migrants, spaces for improving the living conditions of migrants and with it the democratic and economic achievements of EU member states. To reach such a position would require, however, a different interaction of *politics, polities* and *policies* across all levels in the EU. Without recognising the roles of the European and the local dimensions of migration governance, interacting with contentious politics and polities in member states, the likelihood is that the differential, uneven integration of migrants across the European social space will continue.

References

Adida, C., Laitin, D. and Valfort, M-A. (2010) 'Integration into Europe: identifying a Muslim effect', Paper presented at the Politics of Inequalities 3 Seminar, POLINE Network, Paris: Sciences Po, 17 March.

Anderson, B. and Ruhs, M. (eds) (2010a) *Who needs migrant workers? Labour shortages, immigration and public policy*, Oxford: Oxford University Press.

Anderson, B and Ruhs, M. (eds) (2010b) 'Researching illegality in labour migration: concepts, ethics and policy nexus, special issue, *Population, Space and Place*, vol 16, no 3, pp 175-252.

Bauder, H. (2006) *Labor Movement. How migration regulates labor markets*, New York: Oxford University Press.

Benhabib, S. (2004) *The rights of others: Aliens, residents, and citizens*, Cambridge: Cambridge University Press.

Berggren, E., Likič-Brborič, B., Toksöz, G. and Trimikliniotis, N. (eds) (2007) *Irregular migration, informal labour and community: A challenge for Europe*, Maastricht: Shaker Publishing.

Bigo, D. and Guild, E. (ed) (2005) *Controlling frontiers. Free movement into and within Europe*, Aldershot: Ashgate.

Bonoli, G. and Palier, B. (2001) 'How do welfare states change? Institutions and their impact on the politics of welfare state reform in Western Europe', in S. Leibfried (ed) *Welfare state futures*, Cambridge: Cambridge University Press, pp 37–56.

Caponio, T. and Borkert, M. (eds) (2010) *Local dimension of migration policymaking*, IMISCOE Reports, Amsterdam: Amsterdam University Press.

Clark, A., Sauger, N. and Senik, C. (2009) 'Welfare, well-being and immigration in Europe: evidence from the European Social Survey. Special Issue', *Social Indicators Research*, vol 91, no 3, pp 299–426.

Crowley, J. (2001) 'Differential free movement and the sociology of the "internal border"', in E. Guild and C. Harlow (ed) *Implementing Amsterdam*, Portland, OR: Hart Publishing, pp 13–34.

Crowley, J. (2005) 'Where does the state actually start? The contemporary governance of work and migration', in B. Didier and E. Guild (ed) *Controlling frontiers. Free movement into and within Europe*, Aldershot: Ashgate, pp 140–60.

Dummett, A. (1992) 'The transnational migration of people seen from within a natural law tradition', in B. Barry and R.E. Goodin (eds) *Free movement: Ethical issues in the transnational migration of people and money*, New York and London: Harvester Wheatsheaf.

Düvell, F. (2009) *Pathways into irregularity: The social construction of irregular migration*, Comparative Policy Brief, CLANDESTINO project, Athens: ELIAMEP.

Elster, J. (2008) *Reason and rationality*, Princeton: Princeton University Press.

Elster, J. (2009) 'Emotions', in P. Hedström and P. Bearman (eds) *The Oxford handbook of analytical sociology*, Oxford: Oxford University Press, pp 51–71.

EUAFRA (European Union Agency for Fundamental Rights) (2009) *Annual report*, Vienna: EUAFRA.

European Council (2000) 'Presidency conclusions', Lisbon European Council, 23 and 24 March (www.consilium.europa.eu/ueDocs/cms_Data/docs/pressData/en/ec/00100-r1.en0.htm).

Fassmann, H., Haller, M. and Lane, D. (eds) (2009) *Migration and mobility in Europe. Trends, patterns and control*, Cheltenham: Edward Elgar.

Favell, A. and Recchi, E. (eds) (2009) *Pioneers of European integration: Citizenship and mobility in the EU*, Cheltenham: Edward Elgar.

Ferrera, M. (1996) 'The Southern model of welfare in social Europe', *Journal of European Social Policy*, vol 6, no 1, pp 17–37.

Ferrera, M. (2005) *The boundaries of welfare. European integration and the new spatial politics of social protection*, Oxford: Oxford University Press.

Gebrewold, B. (ed) (2007) *Africa and Fortress Europe. Threats and opportunities*, Aldershot: Ashgate.

Geddes, A. (2008) *Immigration and European integration. Beyond Fortress Europe?* (2nd edn), Manchester and New York: Manchester University Press.

Hall, P.A. and Taylor, R.C.R. (1996) 'Political science and the three new institutionalisms', *Political Studies*, vol 44, no 5, pp 936–57.

Hammar, T. (1990) *Democracy and the nation state: Aliens, denizens and citizens in a world of international migration*, Aldershot: Gower.

Hansen, R. (2009) 'The poverty of postnationalism: citizenship, immigration, and the new Europe', *Theory and Society*, vol 38, no 1, pp 1-24.

Hemerijck, A.C. (2010) *In search of a new welfare state*, Oxford: Oxford University Press.

Hollifield, J.F. (2004) 'The emerging migration state', *International Migration Review*, vol 38, no 3, pp 885-912.

Koopmans, R. (2010) 'Trade-offs between equality and difference: immigrant integration, multiculturalism and the welfare state in cross-national perspective', *Journal of Ethnic and Migration Studies*, vol 36, no 1, pp 1-26.

Kuhnle, S. (ed) (2000) *The survival of the European welfare state*, London: Routledge.

Lister, R. (2003) *Citizenship: Feminist perspectives* (2nd edn), Basingstoke: Palgrave Macmillan.

Neal, A.W. (2009) 'Securitization and risk at the EU border: the origins of FRONTEX', *Journal of Common Market Studies*, vol 47, no 2, pp 333-56.

Nguyen, T. (2005) *We are all suspects now: Untold stories from immigrant communities after 9/11*, Boston, MA: Beacon Press.

North, D.C. (1990) *Institutions, institutional change, and economic performance*, Cambridge: Cambridge University Press.

Palier, B. (ed) (2010) *A long good-bye to Bismarck? The politics of welfare reforms in continental Europe*, Amsterdam: Amsterdam University Press.

Parsons, C.A. and Smeeding, T.M. (eds) (2006) *Immigration and the transformation of Europe*, Cambridge: Cambridge University Press.

Pécoud, A. and de Guchteneire, P. (eds) (2007) *Migration without borders. Essays on the free movement of people*, Oxford and New York: Berghahn Books.

Pierson, P. (1996) 'The path to European integration: a historical institutionalist analysis', *Comparative Political Studies*, vol 29, no 2, pp 123-63.

Stovel, K. and Fountain, C. (2009) 'Matching', in P. Hedström and P. Bearman (eds) *The Oxford handbook of analytical sociology*, Oxford: Oxford University Press, pp 365-90.

Streeck, W. and Thelen, K. (2005) 'Introduction: institutional change in advanced political economies', in W. Streeck and K. Thelen (eds) *Beyond continuity. Institutional change in advanced political economies*, Oxford: Oxford University Press.

Taylor-Gooby, P. (2009) *Re-framing social citizenship*, Oxford: Oxford University Press.

van Munster, R. (2009) *Securitizing immigration. The politics of risk in the EU*, Basingstoke: Palgrave Macmillan.

van Oorschot, W.J.H., Opielka, M. and Pfau-Effinger, B. (eds) (2008) *Culture and welfare state: Values and social policy in comparative perspective*, Cheltenham: Edward Elgar.

Vobruba, G. (2007) *Die Dynamic Europas* [*The dynamics of Europe*] (2nd edn), Wiesbaden: VS Verlag für Sozialwissenschaften.

Wiegand, I. (2008) *The protection of human rights and fundamental freedoms in the fight against terrorism: The case of the European Union after September 11, 2001,* Stuttgart: Ibidem Verlag.

Index

A

A8 migration 52, 159, 172, 182
asylum seekers 29, 32, 36, 71, 74, 75, 109, 122, 125, 126, 132, 144, 145, 148, 149, 154, 163, 164, 167, 177, 179, 181, 213, 216, 217, 220, 221, 248, 252
Amsterdam, Treaty 12, 54, 55, 56, 71

B

beliefs 9, 10, 70, 73, 167, 247, 254
Benhabib, Seyla 75, 77, 252
Bigo, Didier 77, 162, 245
Bismarckian welfare institutions 41, 250
Bommes, Michael 50, 70, 71, 121, 125, 126, 129, 130, 132, 136, 161, 162

C

Castles, Stephen 23, 77, 96, 107, 112, 122, 125, 154, 160, 161, 197, 198, 201, 206, 208, 227,
Central and Eastern Europe 23, 24, 27, 28, 32, 34, 42, 92, 94, 105, 159, 162, 168, 178, 187, 189, 251
circular migration 56, 57, 61
citizenship 26, 30, 31, 37, 38, 39, 40, 42, 43, 52, 54, 57, 61, 68, 70, 71, 72, 76, 78, 108, 109, 110, 113, 114, 115, 116, 117, 125, 126, 128, 129, 133, 135, 136, 145, 149, 153, 168, 171, 179, 180, 181, 189, 190, 207, 213, 216, 221, 222, 231, 232, 233, 237, 246, 247, 250
clandestines (*see* undocumented migrants) 117
contentious politics 2, 5, 7, 8, 14, 49, 53, 55, 58, 117, 179, 200, 213, 215, 217, 219, 221, 223, 245, 247, 254

D

decentralisation 214, 215, 218
  see also devolution
differential integration 1, 2, 6, 11, 12, 13, 36, 50, 52, 61, 115, 124, 159, 188, 214, 216, 222, 245, 246, 247, 252, 253
discourses 3, 5, 8, 9, 12, 36, 58, 67, 68, 69, 70, 71, 73, 77, 78, 167, 171, 179, 180, 200, 216, 217, 245, 247, 249, 251, 254,
discursive-institutionalism 3, 68, 69, 70, 72
  see also new-institutionalism
discrimination 7, 47, 53, 93, 151, 152, 153, 167, 171, 177, 178, 180, 181, 189, 220, 221, 248
Dublin Convention 54, 71, 144, 179

E

education 2, 6, 10, 13, 24, 34, 35, 37, 59, 60, 61, 87, 88, 89, 95, 111, 121, 122, 123, 125, 128, 129, 130, 131, 133, 134, 135, 136, 137, 138, 150, 151, 153, 155, 165, 166, 167, 168, 180, 188, 204, 205, 208, 220, 221, 250, 251
emotions 1, 2, 8, 9, 10, 11, 13, 14, 58, 68, 69, 70, 73, 77, 144, 151, 188, 217, 245, 246, 248, 252, 253, 254
Esping-Andersen, Gøsta 38, 122, 129, 199, 206, 207, 227
ethnic minorities/communities 10, 11, 13, 14, 42, 121, 122, 125, 126, 128, 129, 131, 132, 135, 136, 137, 144, 152, 153, 159, 161, 163, 165, 166, 167, 168, 171, 177, 178, 180, 181, 189, 197, 198, 199, 200, 201, 202, 203, 204, 205, 206, 207, 208, 220, 222, 230, 231, 232, 233, 237, 238, 239, 245, 246, 251, 253
European Union 1, 3, 4, 5, 10, 11, 12, 13, 14, 15-47, 49-66, 67-83, 86, 87, 89, 91, 92, 93, 94, 96, 97, 98, 109, 110, 113, 114, 115, 117, 123, 126, 127, 135, 137, 143, 144, 145, 146, 147, 148, 149, 152, 153, 154, 159, 160, 162, 164, 168, 169, 170, 179, 182, 200, 201, 220, 221, 222, 228, 229, 245, 247, 249, 252, 253, 254
  see also Europeanisation
Europeanisation 73, 98, 169
  see also European Union
exclusion *see* social exclusion

F

Finland 8, 9, 10, 11, 13, 26, 27, 29, 30, 31, 32, 33, 40, 47, 105, 143-58, 172, 204, 205, 209, 248
Fortress Europe 5, 67, 71, 72, 74, 171, 252, 253
France 9, 10, 14, 23, 26, 27, 29, 30, 31, 32, 33, 35, 40, 47, 57, 60, 114, 123, 190, 199, 200, 209, 213-26, 229, 250
free movement 3, 12, 28, 51, 52, 53, 54, 57, 58, 60, 61, 70, 71, 86, 87, 92, 94, 98, 159, 162, 171

G

Geddes, Andrew 5, 50, 52, 54, 70, 71, 75, 77, 160, 161, 162, 214, 217
Germany 7, 8, 9, 10, 11, 12, 13, 26, 27, 29, 30, 31, 32, 33, 35, 40, 47, 52, 56, 57, 76, 86, 108, 114, 121-42, 159, 160, 161, 63, 164, 172, 198, 199, 200, 202, 203, 207, 209, 229, 246, 247, 248, 250, 251

governance 1-20, 49-66, 67, 68, 74, 169, 214, 215, 248, 249, 253, 254
guest-workers 11, 121-42
Guiraudon, Virginie 4, 8, 34, 50, 54, 68, 70, 71, 73, 162, 214

H

high skill migration 114
historical-institutionalism 19, 253
   see new-institutionalism
historical legacies 4, 159, 245, 246
   see also path-dependency
Hollifield, James F. 75, 96, 123, 161, 252
human rights 2, 4, 10, 12, 67-83, 113, 162, 213, 252
Hungary 8, 9, 11, 13, 27, 28, 29, 30, 31, 33, 35, 40, 42, 47, 72, 152, 159-75, 246

I

ideas 68, 69, 70, 73, 74, 77, 78, 151, 254
'illegal' migration *see* irregular migration
immigrant communities 13, 14, 60, 97-212
inequality 23-47, 227
   see also poverty
informal labour market 3, 7, 53, 115, 189, 248
institutions 1, 2, 3, 4, 6, 11, 50, 51, 67, 68, 69, 70, 71, 72, 73, 74, 75, 77, 78, 79, 85, 86, 110, 132, 166, 170, 206, 214, 215, 218, 237, 238, 245, 250, 252
integration regimes 11, 12, 47, 159, 199
international organisations 162, 192
   see also EU
irrationality 8, 15, 69, 70, 98
irregular migration 13, 32, 34, 36, 37, 39, 41, 42, 61, 113, 117, 162, 169, 171
Israel 9, 14, 168, 227, 243, 246, 247
Italy 8, 9, 11, 12, 14, 23, 26, 27, 28, 29, 30, 31, 32, 33, 35, 40, 41, 47, 86, 105-20, 172, 190, 205, 207, 209, 213-26, 246, 251

K

Koopmans, Ruud 3, 5, 7, 41, 130, 135, 136, 197, 199, 213, 215, 253

L

labour, commodification of 34, 41, 199
labour market 1, 2, 3, 4, 5, 8, 11, 12, 13, 23, 28, 36, 37, 38, 39, 40, 41, 42, 43, 52, 56, 57, 58, 59, 60, 61, 85-101, 107, 108, 110, 111, 112, 114, 115, 116, 121, 124, 127, 128, 129, 130, 131, 132, 133, 135, 136, 137, 138, 144, 145, 146, 147, 149, 150, 151, 152, 153, 154, 155, 165, 166, 177, 178, 181, 182, 183, 185, 187, 189, 190, 198, 199, 221, 222, 228, 229, 232, 233, 234, 236, 237, 239, 245, 247, 248, 249, 250, 253, 254
labour migration 2, 12, 24, 27, 28, 51, 52, 56, 58, 85-100, 127, 143, 144, 162, 169, 177, 247

labour recruitment, stop of 24, 113, 114, 122, 124, 128
Lavenex, Sandra 3, 50, 51, 57, 73, 74, 160, 162, 169, 170, 171
Lisbon, Treaty 12, 54, 55, 59, 169, 249
local communities 3, 13, 14, 60, 88, 90, 153, 159, 163, 169, 178, 187, 189, 197-212, 246, 247, 248, 250, 253

M

Maastricht, Treaty 52-71, 79, 135
managed migration 5, 55, 56, 57, 91, 97, 127, 128, 133, 137, 179, 182, 247, 248,
mechanisms of institutional change 79
Menz, Georg 3, 5, 34, 39, 42, 50, 51, 57, 60, 126, 127, 128
migrant minorities 165, 168, 171, 190, 191, 198, 199, 200, 201, 202, 203, 206, 207, 208, 246
   see also ethnic minorities
migration governance 2, 3, 12, 34, 66, 253, 254
   see also governance
migration regimes 23-47, 39, 42, 77, 227
Miller, Mark J. 23, 77, 96, 107, 112, 125, 154, 160, 161, 197, 198, 201, 206, 208, 227

N

nationality 11, 13, 25, 34, 47, 113, 118, 137, 147, 148, 149, 151, 152, 153, 165, 169, 184, 220, 245
narratives 23, 25,
new EU member states 117, 159-75,
new-institutionalism 69
   see also historical-institutionalism, rational-choice institutionalism, sociological-institutionalism, discursive-institutionalism

O

opportunities 1, 5, 9, 10, 14, 28, 70, 92, 106, 107, 108, 110, 112, 113, 123, 130, 135, 160, 178, 190, 201, 213-26, 247, 254

P

path-dependency *see* new-institutionalism
   see also path-departure, path-creation
preferences 9, 10, 15, 69, 70, 247, 252, 253, 254
politics of migration 5, 12, 55, 67-83, 247
poverty 14, 59, 7, 88, 131, 132, 146, 160, 180, 197, 199, 202, 208, 227, 228, 234, 235, 236, 237, 239
   see also income inequality
pull factors 12, 85, 88, 92, 160
push factors 88, 98, 106, 160

R

racism 10, 109, 167, 178, 180, 181, 185,
rational-choice institutionalism 85, 86, 96
   see also new-institutionalism

regularisation 7, 26, 57, 61, 109, 110, 112, 114,
    116, 190, 251
risk management *see* securitisation
Rome, Treaty of 52, 70, 71

S

Sainsbury, Diane 5, 6, 39, 43, 77, 121, 128, 161,
    197, 199, 206, 227, 228
Schengen Agreement 70, 72, 94, 109, 159, 162,
    165, 168, 171
Schmidt, Vivien A. 3, 4, 68, 69, 70, 72, 73, 75,
    79
securitisation 5, 181, 251
segregation 1, 2, 6, 7, 10, 11, 13, 43, 53, 61, 85,
    177, 179, 197-212, 246, 250,
Single European Act 70
single market 52, 72, 73, 74
social insurance 91, 127, 145, 146, 232, 233,
    250,
social boundaries 6, 7, 9
social exclusion 59, 146, 177, 198,
social integration 11, 14, 36, 37, 49, 54, 55, 58,
    59, 60, 61, 110, 111, 122, 126, 133, 136,
    171, 178, 180, 182, 198, 203, 222, 223, 249,
    252, 254
social mechanisms 6, 8
    see also mechanisms of institutional change
social protection 1, 2, 4, 7, 11, 12, 13, 14, 42,
    52, 58, 59, 90, 91, 93, 105, 106, 112, 115,
    135, 145 168, 177, 232, 233, 234, 235, 236,
    237, 238, 239, 246, 250, 251, 253,
social networks 13, 14, 69, 70, 91, 93, 96, 150,
    161, 167, 171, 197, 198, 201, 202, 203, 204,
    250
sociological institutionalism
    see also new-institutionalism

U

undocumented migrants
unemployment 28, 91, 92, 93, 95, 97, 105, 106,
    112, 123, 124, 126, 129, 131, 132, 144, 146,
    147, 148, 149, 150, 151, 153, 160, 161, 166,
    189, 197, 198, 202, 208, 216, 233
United Kingdom 7, 8, 9, 11, 13, 15, 23, 26,
    27, 28, 29, 30, 31, 32, 33, 34, 40, 41, 47, 56,
    76, 86, 94, 114, 131, 152, 160, 177-94, 199,
    200, 202, 229, 246, 248, 250, 251
utility 12, 49-66, 85, 88, 90, 96, 97, 98, 108,
    133, 179, 254

W

welfare regimes 34, 38, 39, 41, 42, 77, 107,
    122, 128, 129, 137, 199, 227, 228, 250, 251

X

xenophobia 10
    see also racism